D0094238

WHEN STATES FAIL

WHEN STATES FAIL

CAUSES AND CONSEQUENCES

Robert I. Rotberg, Editor

PRINCETON UNIVERSITY PRESS   PRINCETON AND OXFORD

Published by Princeton University Press, 41 William Street,
Princeton, New Jersey 08540
In the United Kingdom: Princeton University Press, 3 Market Place,
Woodstock, Oxfordshire OX20 1SY

Library of Congress Cataloging-in-Publication Data
When states fail : causes and consequences / Robert I. Rotberg, editor.
p. cm.
Includes bibliographical references and index.
ISBN: 0-691-11671-7 (cl. : alk. paper) — ISBN: 0-691-11672-5 (pbk. : alk. paper)
1. Legitimacy of governments—Developing countries. 2. Developing countries—Politics and government. 3. World politics—1989– I. Rotberg, Robert I.

JF60.W46 2004
320'.01'1—dc21 2003041864

British Library Cataloging-in-Publication Data is available

This book has been composed in Galliard

Printed on acid-free paper. ∞

www.pupress.princeton.edu

Printed in the United States of America

10 9 8 7

ISBN-13: 978-0-691-11672-3

ISBN-10: 0-691-11672-5

Contents

Maps

Preface

THE HARVARD UNIVERSITY Failed States Project sought to learn how best to assess and to categorize the modern phenomenon of imploding nation-states. What were the distinguishing characteristics of state failure and state collapse in the post–Cold War world? Did state failure and collapse matter? If they did, how could state failure and collapse be prevented? How could the humpty dumpty of destroyed and fractured states, once disintegrated, be put back together?

Led by the World Peace Foundation and the WPF Program on Intrastate Conflict in the John F. Kennedy School of Government, Harvard University, the project enlisted the accomplished collaboration of more than forty gifted scholars and practitioners, nearly all of whom produced one or more (sometimes many more) versions of essays on the failed state problem or on examples of failed states. After a preliminary session at Wilton Park, in Great Britain, in 1999, the project convened three lengthy meetings at the Kennedy School from 2000 to 2001. The papers presented at those meetings, and the discussions about the topics and papers, eventually were transformed into the fourteen revised chapters in this book, and a complementary set of eleven revised country chapters in a companion volume: Robert I. Rotberg (ed.) *State Failure and State Weakness in a Time of Terror* (Washington, D.C., 2003).

The present volume includes an opening chapter that attempts to provide a classification and context for state failure. It is followed by two sets of chapters, the first on the nature and correlates of failure, the second on methods of preventing state failure and reconstructing those states that do fail.

The contributors to both volumes, the editor, and the Trustees of the World Peace Foundation all hope that these writings will focus deserved scholarly and policy attention upon and provide appropriate assistance to failed and collapsed states, to weak states in danger of becoming failed, and to those already failed states that are ready to be rebuilt. The inhabitants of the weak, failing, failed, and collapsed states will readily recognize themselves and their challenges in the chapters that follow.

In addition to the chapter contributors, all of whom labored hard and long to produce accessible and up-to-date path-breaking essays, the editor remains thoroughly grateful for Karin von Hippel's original stimulus, for the critical interventions of James Gow, Robert Orr, Richard Ullman, and Leonard Wantchekon, for Jean Mulot's helpful ideas, for the ability to discuss this topic before audiences convened by the Council on Foreign

Relations and the Indonesian Centre for Strategic and International Studies, for the steadfast editorial assistance of Deborah West, to Graham Allison and the Kennedy School's Belfer Center for Science and International Affairs for their unwavering support, and for the strong backing of the Trustees of the World Peace Foundation. Sylvia Coates prepared the index and Dimitri Karetnikov developed the maps.

—R. I. R.
14 July 2003

WHEN STATES FAIL

One

The Failure and Collapse of Nation-States

BREAKDOWN, PREVENTION, AND REPAIR

ROBERT I. ROTBERG

NATION-STATES FAIL when they are consumed by internal violence and cease delivering positive political goods to their inhabitants. Their governments lose credibility, and the continuing nature of the particular nation-state itself becomes questionable and illegitimate in the hearts and minds of its citizens.

The rise and fall of nation-states is not new, but in a modern era when national states constitute the building blocks of world order, the violent disintegration and palpable weakness of selected African, Asian, Oceanic, and Latin American states threaten the very foundation of that system. International organizations and big powers consequently find themselves sucked disconcertingly into a maelstrom of anomic internal conflict and messy humanitarian relief. Desirable international norms such as stability and predictability become difficult to achieve when so many of the globe's newer nation-states waver precariously between weakness and failure, with some truly failing, and a few even collapsing. In a time of terror awareness, moreover, appreciating the nature of and responding to the dynamics of nation-state failure motivate critical policy debates. How best to understand the nature of weak states, to strengthen those poised on the abyss of failure, and to restore the functionality of failed states, are among the urgent policy questions of the twenty-first century.

This book explores the nature of failure and collapse among developing world nation-states and examines how such faltering or destroyed states may be resuscitated.[1] It establishes clear criteria for distinguishing *collapse* and *failure* from generic weakness or apparent distress, and *collapse* from *failure*. The volume further analyzes the nature of state weakness, and it advances reasons why some weak states succumb to failure, or collapse, and why others in ostensibly more straitened circumstances remain weak and at risk without ever destructing. Characterizing failed states is thus an important and relevant endeavor, especially because the phenomenon of state failure is underresearched, with the literature hitherto marked by imprecise definitions and a paucity of sharply argued, instructive, and well-delineated cases. Further, understanding exactly why weak states slide toward failure will help policymakers to design methods of preventing failure and, in the cases of states that nevertheless fail (or collapse), to revive them and assist in the rebuilding of their nation-states.

States are much more varied in their capacity and capability than they once were. They are more numerous than they were a half century ago, and the range of their population sizes, physical endowments, wealth, productivity, delivery systems, ambitions, and attainments is much more extensive than ever before. In 1914, in the wake of the crumbling of the Ottoman and Austro-Hungarian empires, there were 55 recognized national polities. In 1919, there were 59 nations. In 1950, that number had reached 69. Ten years later, after the attainment of independence in much of Africa, 90 entities were nations. After many more African, Asian, and Oceanic territories had become independent, and after the implosion of the Soviet Union, the number of nations jumped to 191.[2] With East Timor's independence in 2002, that number became 192. With such explosive numbers, the inherent fragility of many of the new recruits (15 of Africa's 54 states are landlocked), and the inherent navigational perils of the post–Cold War economic and political terrain, the possibility of failure among a subset of the total remains ever present.

The Nature of Failure: Performance Criteria

Nation-states exist to provide a decentralized method of delivering political (public) goods to persons living within designated parameters (borders). Having inherited, assumed, or replaced the monarchs of yore, modern states focus and answer the concerns and demands of citizenries. They organize and channel the interests of their people, often but not exclusively in furtherance of national goals and values. They buffer or manipulate external forces and influences, champion the local or particular concerns of their adherents, and mediate between the constraints and challenges of the international arena and the dynamism of their own internal economic, political, and social realities.

States succeed or fail across all or some of these dimensions. But it is according to their performances—according to the levels of their effective delivery of the most crucial political goods—that strong states may be distinguished from weak ones, and weak states from failed or collapsed ones. Political goods are those intangible and hard to quantify claims that citizens once made on sovereigns and now make on states. They encompass indigenous expectations, conceivably obligations, inform the local political culture, and together give content to the social contract between ruler and ruled that is at the core of regime / government and citizenry interactions.[3]

There is a hierarchy of political goods. None is as critical as the supply of security, especially human security. Individuals alone, almost exclusively in special or particular circumstances, can attempt to make themselves secure. Or groups of individuals can band together to organize and purchase goods or services that maximize their sense of security. Traditionally, and usually, however, individuals and groups cannot easily or effectively substitute privately arranged security for the full spectrum of public-provided security. The state's prime function is to provide that political good of security—to prevent cross-border invasions and infiltrations, and any loss of territory; to eliminate domestic threats to or attacks upon the national order and social structure; to prevent crime and any related dangers to domestic human security; and to enable citizens to resolve their differences with the state and with their fellow inhabitants without recourse to arms or other forms of physical coercion.

The delivery of a range of other desirable political goods becomes possible when a reasonable measure of security has been sustained. Modern states (as successors to sovereigns) provide predictable, recognizable, systematized methods of adjudicating disputes and regulating both the norms and the prevailing mores of a particular society or polity. The essence of that political good usually implies codes and procedures that together comprise an enforceable body of law, security of property and inviolable contracts, an effective judicial system, and a set of norms that legitimate and validate the values embodied in a local version of the rule of law.

Another key political good enables citizens to participate freely, openly, and fully in politics and the political process. This good encompasses the essential freedoms: the right to participate in politics and compete for office; respect and support for national and regional political institutions, such as legislatures and courts; tolerance of dissent and difference; and fundamental civil and human rights.

Other political goods typically supplied by states and expected by their citizenries (although privatized forms are possible) include medical and health care (at varying levels and costs); schools and educational instruction (of various kinds and levels); roads, railways, harbors, and other physical infrastructures—the arteries of commerce; communications networks; a money and banking system, usually presided over by a central bank and lubricated by a nationally created currency; a beneficent fiscal and institutional context within which citizens can pursue personal entrepreneurial goals, and potentially prosper; space for the flowering of civil society; and methods of regulating the sharing of the environmental commons. Together, this bundle of political goods, roughly rank ordered, establishes a set of criteria according to which modern nation-states may be judged strong, weak, or failed.

Strong states obviously perform well across these categories and with respect to each, separately. Weak states show a mixed profile, fulfilling expectations in some areas and performing poorly in others. The more poorly weak states perform, criterion by criterion, the weaker they become and the more that weakness tends to edge toward failure, hence the subcategory of weakness that is termed "failing." Many failed states flunk each of the tests outlined earlier. But they need not flunk all of them to fail overall, particularly since satisfying the security good weighs very heavily, and high levels of internal violence are associated directly with failure and the propensity to fail. Yet, violence alone does not condition failure, and the absence of violence does not necessarily imply that the state in question is unfailed. It is necessary to judge the extent to which an entire failing or failed profile is less or more than its component parts.

Strong states unquestionably control their territories and deliver a full range and a high quality of political goods to their citizens. They perform well according to indicators like GDP per capita, the UNDP Human Development Index, Transparency International's Corruption Perception Index, and Freedom House's *Freedom of the World Report.* Strong states offer high levels of security from political and criminal violence, ensure political freedom and civil liberties, and create environments conducive to the growth of economic opportunity. The rule of law prevails. Judges are independent. Road networks are well maintained. Telephones work. Snail mail and e-mail both arrive quickly. Schools, universities, and students flourish. Hospitals and clinics serve patients effectively. And so on. Overall, strong states are places of enviable peace and order.

Weak states (broadly, states in crisis) include a broad continuum of states: they may be inherently weak because of geographical, physical, or fundamental economic constraints; or they may be basically strong, but temporarily or situationally weak because of internal antagonisms, management flaws, greed, despotism, or external attacks. Weak states typically harbor ethnic, religious, linguistic, or other intercommunal tensions that have not yet, or not yet thoroughly, become overtly violent. Urban crime rates tend to be high and increasing. In weak states, the ability to provide adequate amounts of other political goods is diminished or is diminishing. Physical infrastructural networks are deteriorated. Schools and hospitals show signs of neglect, particularly outside the main cities. GDP per capita and other critical economic indicators have fallen or are falling, sometimes dramatically; levels of venal corruption are embarrassingly high and escalating. Weak states usually honor rule of law precepts in the breach. They harass civil society. Weak states are often ruled by despots, elected or not.

There is a special category of weak state: the seemingly strong one, always an autocracy, which rigidly controls dissent and is secure but at the same time provides very few political goods.[4] In extreme cases, such as North Korea, the regime permits its people to starve. Cambodia under Pol Pot and Iraq under Saddam Hussein also qualify, as do contemporary Belarus, Turkmenistan, and Libya. Across recent times, the list of states that are fundamentally weak but appear strong is even more extensive.

Failed and Collapsed States

Failed states are tense, deeply conflicted, dangerous, and contested bitterly by warring factions. In most failed states, government troops battle armed revolts led by one or more rivals. Occasionally, the official authorities in a failed state face two or more insurgencies, varieties of civil unrest, different degrees of communal discontent, and a plethora of dissent directed at the state and at groups within the state.[5]

It is not the absolute intensity of violence that identifies a failed state. Rather, it is the enduring character of that violence (as in recent Angola, Burundi, and the Sudan), the consuming quality of that violence, which engulfs great swaths of states (as in Afghanistan, Burundi, Côte d'Ivoire, the Democratic Republic of the Congo—DRC—Liberia, and Sierra Leone), the fact that much of the violence is directed against the existing government or regime, and the inflamed character of the political or geographical demands for shared power or autonomy that rationalize or justify the violence in the minds of the main insurgents.

The civil wars that characterize failed states usually stem from or have roots in ethnic, religious, linguistic, or other intercommunal enmity. The fear of the other (and the consequent security dilemma) that drives so much ethnic conflict stimulates and fuels hostilities between regimes and subordinate and less-favored groups. Avarice also propels that antagonism, especially when greed is magnified by dreams of loot from discoveries of new, contested, pools of resource wealth such as petroleum deposits, diamond fields, other minerals, or fast-denuded forests.[6]

There is no failed state (broadly, a state in anarchy) without disharmonies between communities. Yet, the simple fact that many weak nation-states include haves and have-nots, and that some of the newer states contain a heterogeneous array of ethnic, religious, and linguistic interests, is more a contributor to, than a root cause of, nation-state failure. State failure cannot be ascribed primarily to the inability to build nations from a congeries of groups of diverse backgrounds.[7] Nor should it be ascribed baldly to the oppression of minorities by a majority, although such brutalities are often a major ingredient of the impulse toward failure.

In most failed states, regimes prey on their own constituents. Driven by ethnic or other intercommunal hostility, or by the governing elite's insecurities, they victimize their own citizens or some subset of the whole that is regarded as hostile. As in Mobutu Sese Seko's Zaire or the Taliban's Afghanistan, ruling cadres increasingly oppress, extort, and harass the majority of their own compatriots while privileging a more narrowly based party, clan, or sect. As in Zaire, Angola, Siaka Stevens' Sierra Leone, or pre–2001 Sudan, patrimonial rule depends on a patronage-based system of extraction from ordinary citizens. The typical *weak* state plunges toward failure when this kind of ruler-led oppression provokes a countervailing reaction on the part of resentful groups or newly emerged rebels.

In contrast to strong states, failed states cannot control their peripheral regions, especially those regions occupied by out-groups. They lose authority over large sections of territory. Often, the expression of official power is limited to a capital city and to one or more ethnically specific zones. Plausibly, the extent of a state's failure can be measured by the extent of its geographical expanse genuinely controlled (especially after dark) by the official government. How nominal or contested is the central government's sway over peripheral towns and rural roads and waterways? Who really expresses power up-country, or in districts distant from the capital?[8]

Citizens depend on states and central governments to secure their persons and free them from fear. Unable to establish an atmosphere of security nationwide, and often struggling to project power and official authority, the faltering state's failure becomes obvious even before, or as, rebel groups and other contenders arm themselves, threaten the residents of central cities, and overwhelm demoralized government contingents, as in Liberia, Nepal, and Sierra Leone.

Another indicator of state failure is the growth of criminal violence. As state authority weakens and fails, and as the state becomes criminal in its oppression of its citizens, so lawlessness becomes more apparent. Criminal gangs take over the streets of the cities. Arms and drugs trafficking become more common. Ordinary police forces become paralyzed. Anomic behaviors become the norm. For protection, citizens naturally turn to warlords and other strong figures who express or activate ethnic or clan solidarity, thus offering the possibility of security at a time when all else, including the state itself, is crumbling. High rates of urban crime, and the rise of criminal syndicates, testify to an underlying anarchy and desperation.

Failed states provide only limited quantities of other essential political goods. They more and more forfeit their role as the preferred suppliers of political goods to upstart warlords and other nonstate actors. A failed state is a polity that is no longer able or willing to perform the fundamental tasks of a nation-state in the modern world.

Failed states exhibit flawed institutions. That is, only the institution of the executive functions. If legislatures exist at all, they ratify decisions of the executives. Democratic debate is noticeably absent. The judiciary is derivative of the executive rather than being independent, and citizens know that they cannot rely on the court system for significant redress or remedy, especially against the state. The bureaucracy has long ago lost its sense of professional responsibility and exists solely to carry out the orders of the executive and, in petty ways, to oppress citizens. The military is possibly the only institution with any remaining integrity, but the armed forces of failed states are often highly politicized, devoid of the esprit that they once demonstrated.

Failed states are typified by deteriorating or destroyed infrastructures. Metaphorically, the more potholes (or main roads turned to rutted tracks), the more a state will exemplify failure. As rulers siphon funds from the state coffers, fewer capital resources remain for road crews, equipment, and raw materials. Maintaining road or rail access to distant districts becomes less and less of a priority. Even once-maintained basic navigational aids along arterial waterways (as in the DRC) fall into neglect. Where the state still controls such communications backbones as a land-line telephone system, that form of political and economic good betrays a lack of renewal, upkeep, investment, and bureaucratic endeavor. Less a metaphor than a daily reality is the index of failed connections, repeated dialings, and interminable waits for repairs and service. If private entrepreneurs have been permitted by the state monopoly to erect cell telephone towers and offer mobile telephone relays, such telephone service may already have made the monopoly obsolete. Even, or particularly, because there is no state to interfere, in a *collapsed* state privately provided cell telephone systems prevail over what might remain of the land-line network, as in Somalia.

When a state has failed or is in the process of failing, the effective educational and medical systems are privatized informally (with a resulting hodgepodge of shady schools and questionable health clinics in the cities), and public facilities become increasingly decrepit and neglected. Teachers, physicians, nurses, and orderlies are paid late or not at all, and absenteeism increases. Textbooks and medicines become scarce. X-ray machines break down and are not repaired. Reports to the relevant ministries are ignored. Citizens, especially rural parents, students, and patients, slowly realize that the state has abandoned them to their own devices and to the forces of nature. Sometimes, when a failed state is effectively split, as in the Sudan, essential services may be provided only to the favored half, but naturally not to the half in rebellion and engulfed in war. Most of the time the destroyed nation-state completely underperforms. Literacy rates fall, infant mortality rises, the AIDS epidemic overwhelms any health infrastructure that continues to exist, life expectancies plummet, and an already poor and battered citizenry becomes even poorer and more immiserated.

Failed states offer unparalleled economic opportunity—but only for a privileged few. Those clustered around the ruler or the ruling oligarchy grow richer while their less fortunate brethren starve. Immense profits are available from an awareness of regulatory advantages and currency speculation and arbitrage. But the privilege of making real money when everything else is deteriorating is confined to clients of the ruling elite or to especially favored external entrepreneurs. The nation-state's responsibility to maximize the well-being and personal prosperity of all of its citizens is conspicuously absent, if it ever existed.

Corruption flourishes, not only in failed states, but in them it often thrives on an unusually destructive scale. There is widespread petty or lubricating corruption as a matter of course, but escalating levels of venal corruption mark failed states: kickbacks on anything that can be put out to fake tender (medical supplies, textbooks, bridges, roads, and tourism concessions); unnecessarily wasteful construction projects arranged so as to maximize the rents that they generate; licenses for existing and nonexistent activities become more costly; and persistent and generalized extortion becomes the norm. In such situations, corrupt ruling elites mostly invest their gains overseas, not at home, making the economic failure of their states that much more acute. Or they dip directly into the coffers of the shrinking state to pay for external aggressions, lavish residences and palaces, extensive overseas travel, and privileges and perquisites that feed their greed. Military officers always benefit from these excessively corrupt regimes and slurp ravenously from the same illicit troughs as their civilian counterparts.[9]

An indicator of failure, but not a cause of failure, is declining real national and per capita levels of annual gross domestic product (GDP, or GNI, in the World Bank's latest compilations). The statistical underpinnings of most states in the developing world are shaky, but failed states—even, or particularly, failed states with vast natural resources—exhibit overall worsening GDP figures, slim year-to-year growth rates, and greater disparities of income between the wealthiest and poorest fifths of the population. High official state deficits (Zimbabwe's reached more than 30 percent of GDP in 2002) fund lavish security expenditures and the siphoning of cash by friendly elites. Inflation usually soars because rulers raid the central bank and also print money. From the resulting economic insecurity, often engineered by rulers so as to maximize their personal fortunes and their own political and economic power, there are many rents to be collected by entrepreneurs connected to the prevailing regime. Smuggling soars. When state failure becomes complete, the local currency falls out of favor and one or more international currencies takes its place. Money changers are everywhere, legal or not, and arbitrage becomes a steady pursuit.

Sometimes, especially if there are intervening climatic disasters, the economic chaos and generalized neglect that is endemic to failed states lead to regular food shortages and widespread hunger—indeed, even to episodes of starvation and to major efforts of international humanitarian relief. Natural calamities can overwhelm the resources even of nonfailed, but weak, states in the developing world. Yet when state competencies have consciously been sucked dry by unscrupulous rulers and their cronies, as in failed states, unforeseen natural disasters or manmade wars can drive ignored populations over the edge of endurance into starvation. Once such populations have lost their subsistence plots and their sources of income, they lose their homes and their already weak support networks and are forced into an endless cycle of migration and displacement. Failed states provide no safety nets, and the homeless and the destitute become fodder for anyone who can offer food and a cause.

A nation-state also fails when it loses legitimacy—when its forfeits the "mandate of heaven." Its nominal borders become irrelevant. Groups within the nominal borders seek autonomous control within one or more parts of the national territory or, sometimes, even across its international borders. Once the state's capacity to secure itself or to perform in an expected manner recedes, and once what little capacity remains is devoted almost exclusively to the fortunes of a few or to a favored ethnicity or community, then there is every reason to expect less and less loyalty to the state on the part of the excluded and disenfranchised. When the rulers are perceived to be working for themselves and their kin, and not the state, their legitimacy, and the state's legitimacy, plummets. The state increasingly comes to be perceived as being owned by an exclusive class or group, with all others pushed aside. The social contract that binds inhabitants to an overarching polity becomes breached. Various sets of citizens cease trusting the state. Citizens then naturally turn more and more to the kinds of sectional and community loyalties that are their main recourse in times of insecurity, and their main default source of economic opportunity. They transfer their allegiances to clan and group leaders, some of whom become warlords. These warlords or other local strongmen can derive support from external as well as indigenous supporters. In the wilder, more marginalized corners of failed states, terror can breed along with the prevailing anarchy that naturally accompanies state breakdown and failure.

A *collapsed* state is a rare and extreme version of a failed state. Political goods are obtained through private or ad hoc means. Security is equated with the rule of the strong. A collapsed state exhibits a vacuum of authority. It is a mere geographical expression, a black hole into which a failed polity has fallen. There is dark energy, but the forces of entropy have overwhelmed the radiance that hitherto provided some semblance of order and other vital political goods to the inhabitants (no longer the citizens) embraced by language or ethnic affinities or borders. When Somalia failed in the late 1980s, it soon collapsed. Bosnia, Lebanon, and Afghanistan collapsed more than a decade ago, and Nigeria and Sierra Leone collapsed in the 1990s. When those collapses occurred, substate actors took over, as they always do when the prime polity disappears. Those warlords, or substate actors, gained control over regions and subregions within what had been a nation-state, built up their own local security apparatuses and mechanisms, sanctioned markets and other trading arrangements, and even established an attenuated form of international relations. By definition illegitimate and unrecognized, warlords can assume the trappings of a new quasi-state, such as the internationally unrecognized Somaliland in the old north of Somalia. Despite the parceling out of the collapsed state into warlord fiefdoms, there still is a prevalence of disorder, anomic behavior, and the kinds of anarchic mentality and entrepreneurial endeavors—especially gun and drug trafficking—that are compatible with external networks of terror.

None of these designations is terminal. Lebanon, Nigeria, and Tajikistan recovered from collapse, and are now weak. Afghanistan and Sierra Leone graduated from collapse to failure. In 2003 Zimbabwe and Côte d'Ivoire were moving rapidly from strength toward catastrophic failure. Although a state like Haiti is termed endemically weak, most categorizations are snapshots. The quality of failed or collapsed is real, but need not be static. Failure is a fluid halting place, with movement back to weakness and forward into collapse always possible. Certainly, too, because failure and collapse are undesirable results for states, they are neither inevitable nor unavoidable. Whereas weak states fail much more easily than strong ones, that failure need not be preordained. Failure is preventable, particularly since human agency, rather than structural flaws or institutional insufficiencies, is almost invariably at the root of slides from weakness (or strength) toward failure and collapse.

Lebanon's experience is instructive. The inability of Lebanon's feuding sectoral leaders to adapt a 1943 power-sharing agreement to new political and social circumstances brought the divided state to its knees. During the nation's civil war of the mid-1970s, it collapsed. But once a cease-fire had been forged in 1990 and a new political compromise had been achieved through international mediation and the formal acceptance of Syria as a neighborhood hegemon, Lebanon could be revived as a functioning state, and slowly be reconstructed. Without guarantees of human security, and the cooperation of dueling leaders, which Syria compelled, any resuscitation of the post-collapse Lebanese state would have proven impossible.[10]

Contemporary State Failure, Collapse, and Weakness

This decade's failed states so far are Afghanistan, Angola, Burundi, the Democratic Republic of Congo (DRC), Liberia, Sierra Leone, and the Sudan.[11] These seven states exemplify the criteria of failure sketched out earlier. Somalia is the remaining collapsed state. Together they are the contemporary classical failed and collapsed states, but others were also once collapsed or failed, and additional modern nation-states now approach the brink of failure, some much more ominously than others. Another group of states drifts disastrously downward from weak to failing to failed. What is of particular interest is why and how states slip from weakness toward failure, or not. The list of weak states is long, but only a few of those weak and poorly governed states need necessarily edge into failure. Why? Even the categorization of a state as *failing*—Colombia and Indonesia, among others—need not doom it irretrievably to full failure. What does it take to drive a failing state over the edge into failure or collapse? Why did Somalia not stop at failure rather than collapsing?

These questions are answered in this opening chapter and, explicitly and implicitly, in nearly all of the remaining contributions to this volume. Of the failed and collapsed cases, not each fully fills all of the cells of the matrix of nation-state failure. However, to qualify for failure a state needs to demonstrate that it has met most of the explicit criteria. How truly minimal are the roads, the schools, and the hospitals and clinics? How far have GDP and other economic indicators fallen? How far beyond the capital does the ambit of the central government reach? Has the state lost legitimacy? Most important, because civil conflict is decisive for state failure, can the state in question still secure its borders and guarantee security to its citizens, urban and rural?[12]

Somalia, a nation-state of about nine million people with a strongly cohesive cultural history, a common language, a common religion, and a shared history of nationalism—failed, and then collapsed. How could that have happened? There are many possible explanations, but destructive leadership predominates. Similar but more conclusive than the experience elsewhere in Africa and Asia, the first elected, proto-democratic, postindependence civilian governments of Somalia proved to be "experimental, inefficient, corrupt, and incapable of creating any kind of national political culture."[13] General Mohammed Siad Barre, commander of the army, decided that the politicians were ruining the country, so he grabbed power in 1969, suspending the constitution, banning political parties, and promising an end to corruption.

Twenty years and many misadventures later, Siad Barre had succeeded in wrecking any semblance of national governmental legitimacy. Backed first by the Soviet Union and then by the United States, Siad Barre destroyed institutions of government and democracy, abused his citizens' human rights, channeled as many of the resources of the state as possible into his own and his subclan's hands, and at the end of the Cold War deprived everyone else of what was left of the spoils of Somali supreme rule. All of the major clans and subclans, other than Siad Barre's own, became alienated. His shock troops perpetrated one outrage after another against fellow Somalis. By the onset of civil war in 1991, the Somali state had long since failed. The civil war destroyed what was left, and Somalia collapsed onto itself.

In Afghanistan, Angola, the DRC, Liberia, and Sierra Leone, a series of fateful Somali-like decisions by rulers and ruling cadres eviscerated the capabilities of the state, separated each government from its subjects, created opposition movements and civil warfare, and ultimately ended the Potemkin-like pretense of international stature. Reno shows how President Stevens (1968–85) systematically reduced human security within Sierra Leone so as to maximize his own personal power, and how that rise in personal power permitted a quantum leap in his control over the country's rents and riches. Stevens "sold chances to profit from disorder to those who could pay for [it] through providing services."[14] He created a private military force to terrorize his own people and to aggrandize, especially in the diamond fields. As the official rule of law receded, the law of the jungle, presided over by Stevens, took its place. Institutions of government were broken or corrupted. The state became illegitimate, and a civil war over spoils, encouraged and assisted from outside, turned failure into a collapse. In 2002, after hideous atrocities, a brutal intervention by a West African peace enforcement contingent, much more war, and the arrival of British paratroopers and a large UN peacekeeping detachment, Sierra Leone recovered sufficiently to be considered failed rather than collapsed. That is, by late 2001, peace was largely restored and a government began to function, if only in limited ways. An election in 2002 capped the process of recovery back to mere failure.

Mobutu used analogous tactics in the patrimony of Zaire. As his people's self-proclaimed *guide*, or as the personalist embodiment of national leadership during the Cold War, he deployed the largesse of his American and other Western patrons to enhance his personal wealth, to heighten his stature over his countrymen, and to weave a tightly manipulated web of loyalties across the army and into all aspects of Zairese society. Every proper political and democratic institution was an obstacle to the edifice that he created. So was civil society, politics itself in the broad sense, and economic development. Letting the country's Belgian-built infrastructure rot, maintaining a colonial type of resource extraction (of copper, other metals, and diamonds), rebuffing the rise of a real bourgeoisie, and feeding his people puffery and false glories instead of real substance and per capita growth, he accentuated his own power, wealth, and importance. As with Stevens and Siad Barre, the modernizing state was the enemy. Mobutu had no sense of noblesse oblige. Lemarchand says that for Mobutu's state, patronage was the indispensable lubricant. Ultimately, however, "the lubricant ran out and the Mobutist machine was brought to a . . . standstill. . . . The inability of the Mobutist state to generate a volume of rewards consistent with its clientelistic ambitions is the key . . . [to] . . . its rapid loss of legitimacy."[15]

The warring divisions of the failed Sudanese state, north and south, reflect fundamental ethnic, religious, and linguistic differences; the consequences of Egyptian and British conquest and colonial administrative flaws and patterns; postindependence disparities and discriminations (the north dominating the south); and disagreements about who owns petroleum reserves located in the south. A weak state in the north, providing political goods at minimal levels for its mostly Muslim constituents, became the nucleus of a truly failed state when its long war with the south (from 1955 to 1972 and from 1983 through 2003) entered the equation. The Sudanese war has the dubious distinction of having inflicted the largest number of civilian casualties (over two million) in any intrastate war, coupled with the largest internally displaced and refugee population in the world (about four million). Slavery (north against south) flourishes, as well. Moreover, in the south, the central government's writ rarely runs. It provides no political goods to its southern citizens, bombs them, raids them, and regards black southerners as enemy. As a result, the Sudan has long been failed. Yet, northerners still regard their state as legitimate, even though the southern insurgents do not, and southerners have sought either secession or autonomy for decades. So long as oil revenues shore up the north, the Sudan is unlikely to collapse entirely.[16]

The paradigm of failure so well explored in the Somali, Sierra Leonean, Congolese, and Sudanese cases holds equally well, with similar but differently detailed material, in Afghanistan, Angola, Burundi, and Liberia. Indeed, Angola's killing fields and internally displaced circumstances were almost as intense and certainly as destructive as the Sudan's from 1975 to 2002. The wars in these four countries have been equally traumatic for ordinary combatants and hapless civilians unwittingly caught up in a vicious and interminable battle for resources and power between determined opponents. On the World Bank's Control of Corruption and Rule of Law indices, for example, Angola ranked very close to the bottom in 2000 / 2001. Burundi's majority-minority war has produced fewer deaths in recent decades, but it continues an enduring contest for primacy that antedates the modern nation-state itself. From birth economically weak and geographically limited, Burundi over the past ten years has found its capacity to perform fatally crippled by majority-backed insurgencies against autocratic minority-led governments. Burundi ranked very low on the rule of law indicator, counts a pitifully low GNI per capita for 2000 ($110), and its much abused citizens are estimated to have a life expectancy at birth of forty-two years, the lowest in our failed state sample except for Sierra Leone (thirty-nine years).[17] Liberia's recurring intrastate war renewed in 2003, with shadowy insurgents capturing a number of provincial towns and threatening Monrovia, the capital. President Charles Taylor had come to power in the same manner in the 1990s after his semiliterate predecessors had gutted the state from within.

Weakness and the Possibility of Failure

The terms "collapsed" and "failed" designate the consequences of a process of decay at the nation-state level. The capacity of those nation-states to perform positively for their citizens has atrophied. But, as the foregoing examples indicate, that atrophy is neither inevitable nor the result of happenstance. To fail a state is not that easy. Crossing from weakness into failure takes will as well as neglect. Thus, weak nation-states need not tip into failure. Nelson Kasfir's chapter in this volume indeed suggests that anarchy, security dilemmas, and predation all combine synergistically to tip a weak state into a failing or failed mode. At several stages, preventive or avoidance measures could arrest the downward movement, but once non-state actors have a cause and a following, and access to arms (as Michael Klare describes), halting the desperate spiral of failure is difficult. By this time, leaders and states engaged in self-destruction usually possess too little credibility and too few resources to restore trust and claw back from the brink of chaos. Many leaders hardly recognize or care (although Nicolas van de Walle is less negative in his chapter) about the depths of their national despair. Instead, they focus on the rents and advantages that are still to be had as the state succumbs and as warfare spreads.

There are several interesting cases that test the precision of the distinction between weakness and failure, and how and in what circumstances weak or even conflict-prone states survive.

Sri Lanka has been embroiled in a bitter and destructive civil war for twenty years. As much as 15 percent of its total land mass was, at times in the past decade, controlled by the rebel Liberation Tigers of Tamil Eelam (LTTE), a Tamil separatist insurgency. Additionally, the LTTE with relative impunity was able to assassinate prime ministers, bomb presidents, kill rival Tamils, and, in 2001, even destroy the nation's civil air terminal and main air force base. But, as unable as the Sinhala-dominated governments of the island were to put down the LTTE rebellion, so the nation-state remained merely weak, never close to tipping into failure. For 80 percent of Sri Lankans, the government always performed reasonably well. The roads were maintained, and schools and hospitals functioned, to some limited extent even in the war-torn north and east. The authority of successive governments extended securely to the Sinhala-speaking 80 percent of the country, and into the recaptured Tamil areas. Since the early 1990s, too, Sri Lanka has exhibited robust levels of economic growth. For these reasons, despite a consuming internal conflict founded on intense majority-minority discrimination and deprivation, and on pronounced ethnic and religious differences, Sri Lanka from the 1990s projected authority throughout much of the country, suffered no loss of legitimacy among Sinhala, and successfully escaped failure.

Indonesia is another case of weakness avoiding failure despite widespread insecurity. As the world's largest Muslim nation, its far-flung archipelago harbors separatist wars in Aceh in the west and Papua (formerly Irian Jaya) in the east, plus large pockets of Muslim-Christian conflict in Ambon and the Malukus, Muslim-Christian hostility in northern Sulawesi, and ethnic xenophobic outbursts in Kalimantan. Given all of these conflictual situations, none of which has become less bitter since the end of the Soeharto dictatorship, it would be easy to conclude that Indonesia is approaching failure. Yet, only the insurgents in Aceh and Papua want to secede and are battling the state. The several other battles take place within the state, not against it. They do not threaten the integrity and resources of the state in the way that the enduring, but low-level, war in Aceh does. In Aceh and Papua, the government retains the upper hand. Overall, most of Indonesia is still secure. In most of the country, the government projects power and authority. It manages to provide most other necessary political goods to most of Indonesia despite dangerous economic and other developments, including the growth of terroristic movements, in the post-Soeharto era.

What about Colombia? An otherwise well-endowed, prosperous, and ostensibly stable state controls only two-thirds of its territory, a clear hint of failure. Three private armies project their own power across large zones carved out of the very body of the state. The official defense and political establishment has renounced and lost authority in those zones to insurgent groups and drug traffickers. Moreover, Colombia is tense and disturbed, with bombings in Bogota, the capital, and in provincial cities. It boasts the second highest annual per capita murder rate in the world. Its politicians and businessmen routinely wear armored vests and travel with well-armed guards, a clear indication of the state's inability to ensure personal security. Even so, in much of Colombia, the state still delivers schooling and medical care, organizes a physical and communications infrastructure, provides economic opportunity, and remains legitimate. It also remains comparatively wealthy, with a per capita GNI of $2,020 in 2000.[18] Colombia is weak because of its multiple insurgencies, but is comparatively strong and well performing in the areas over which it maintains control. When and if the government of Colombia can reassert itself over the disputed zones and further reduce the power of drug traffickers, the state's reach will expand. Then this weak, endangered state will be able to move farther away from possible failure toward strength.

Zimbabwe is an example of a once unquestionably strong African state that has fallen rapidly through weakness to the very edge of the abyss of failure. All Zimbabwe lacks in order to join the ranks of failed states is a widespread internal insurgent movement directed at the government. But that could come, particularly if the political and economic deterioration of the country continues unchecked. In 2000 and 2001, GDP per capita slid backward by 10 percent a year. Inflation galloped from 30 to 116 percent and then to 275 percent in 2003. The local currency fell against the U. S. dollar from 38–1 in 2001 to 400–1 in the first half of 2002 and to 1700–1 in the second half. Foreign and domestic investment ceased. Unemployment rose to 80 percent in a country of 12 million. Health and educational services vanished. HIV infection rates climbed to 30 percent, with about 3000 Zimbabweans dying every week (2003). Respect for the rule of law was badly battered and then subverted. Political institutions ceased to function fully. Agents of the state preyed on its real and its supposed opponents, chilling free expression and shamelessly stealing a presidential election in 2002. The government's legitimacy vanished. Corruption, meanwhile, flourished, with the ruling elite pocketing their local and DRC war gains and letting most Zimbabweans go hungry. Real starvation appeared in mid-2002, despite food aid from abroad. All of this misery, and the tendency to fail, resulted (as it did earlier in the DRC and Sierra Leone) from the ruthless designs and vengeance of an omnipotent ruler.

Côte d'Ivoire slid rapidly in late 2002 from weakness to the edge of failure as two ethnically and religiously based rebel groups divided the once strong state into three segments. The intervention of 3000 French troops reduced the level of carnage and, in 2003, enabled a negotiated settlement to be crafted. But it conceded concurrent authority to northern Muslims, to the displeasure of the once dominant southern Christians. The northerners also gained physical control over key central and northern towns on the edge of the critical cocoa-growing areas of the south, and a key port was held by westerners. Presaging this sudden descent into near failure, with a national government being unable (since late 2002) to control its territory or perform the other routine tasks of a well-managed nation, was a decade of steady discrimination by southerners against northerners, the rigging or falsification of two presidential elections, and a government-sponsored pillorying and ousting of northerners. Whereas Côte d'Ivoire remained relatively prosperous throughout the 1990s, northerners perceived that they were steadily being denied access to that prosperity, and that southerners were more and more determined to keep exclusive control of the country's resources. Coups d'état, effective and attempted, and the exercise of military power, contributed to the state's growing lack of legitimacy in the north and west, and to the shift to insurgency in 2002. Weakness became near-failure rapidly. Côte d'Ivoire could easily join neighboring Liberia in full failure in 2003 or 2004.

Colombia, Côte d'Ivoire, Indonesia, Sri Lanka, and Zimbabwe are but five among a large number of early twenty-first-century nation-states at risk of failing. They each escape the category "failed," but only for the time being, and only if they each manage to arrest their descent toward economic and political failure, accommodate their insurgency or insurgencies, and strengthen their delivery of political goods to all, or almost all, of their citizens.

Tajikistan is a sixth state that harbors the possibility of failure, in this case of renewed failure. From 1992 to 1997, the government of Tajikistan projected power only in selected parts of the ramshackle nation; across vast areas, there was no government, war raged, and "the state lost its meaning."[19] Then Russia exerted itself in its former colony, claiming that its own security remained at risk because of lawlessness there. From 1999, Russia reinforced its major base in Tajikistan, and more and more became a force for stability against internal dissidence, as well as a buffer for the Tajik government against Taliban- or Uzbek-inspired adventurism. In this new century, despite its colonial heritage, Russia has become the guarantor of Tajikistan's integrity.

A number of other nation-states belong in the category of weak states that show a high potential to fail.[20] Nepal is a clear case since its Maoist insurgency began again roiling the mountains and plains of the monarchist country in 2002. Already hindered by geography and poverty, Nepal has never been a robust provider of political goods to its inhabitants. The palace massacre of 2001 undermined the legitimacy of the monarchy, and thus of the ruling government. With the flare-up of a determined rural rebellion in 2002, and Nepal's demonstrated inability to cope effectively, security of person and of regions became harder and harder to achieve, absent military assistance from India. Under these circumstances, Nepal can hardly project power or credibility. Failure becomes a distinct possibility in 2003 and 2004, despite a temporary cease-fire in 2003.

Likewise, the potential for open failure exists in those highly regimented states, such as Iran, North Korea, and Turkmenistan, which could implode as soon as a dictator or a dictatorial regime is toppled. Because such states are held together entirely by repression, and not by performance, an end to or an easing of repression could create destabilizing battles for succession, resulting anarchy, and the rapid rise of non-state actors. In nation-states made secure by punishment and secret intelligence networks, legitimacy is likely to vanish whenever the curtain of control lifts.

The Central African Republic (with a military coup in 2003), Kyrgyzstan, Kenya, and Nigeria all fit near Nepal on the continuum of first-variety weakness tending toward failure. Kyrgyzstan, with limited resources and arbitrary rule, has contended with a sharply contracted economy, poverty, and two forms of armed insurgency. Militant rivals for power remain, respect for human rights and democratic processes has slipped, and Kyrgyzstan's ability to emerge from inherited weakness is questionable, even with the building of a U.S. airbase and the arrival of free-spending Americans in 2002.

Kenya came in late 2002 to the end of twenty-five years of single-man rule. Although Kenya is intrinsically wealthy, its fortunes have been badly managed, corruption is rampant, and for 24 years a gang of ethnically specific thugs distorted the rule of law, limited the supply of political goods, battered civil society and human rights, and privileged a congeries of related ethnic minorities against larger and more central, but now marginalized, ethnicities. Battles royal for spoils in the post-Moi era could still lead to clashes between ethnic groups. A righting of scores could readily plunge Kenya into failure in 2003 or 2004.

Nigeria is a democracy under President Olusegun Obasanjo, but the historic rivalries between east and west, south and north, oil-states and non-oil provinces, Christian and Muslim communities, democrats and autocrats, and soldiers and citizens that have bedeviled Africa's most populous nation-state since independence in 1960 (and before) are still there, seething below a surface initially calmed or smoothed by the presence of Obasanjo.[21] Military dictators could reemerge, outright intercommunal conflict could readily reoccur, and the north-south divide could once again become an obstacle to strengthening a state already softened by economic confusion, continued corruption, and mismanagement. Nigeria also performs poorly as a giant state, and it provides political goods adequately at best across the vast mélange of poor and rich states that comprise its little-unified and very unglued whole. Intense competition in 2003 or 2004 could readily loosen the already tattered ties that keep Nigeria together.

Other weak states that contain the incubus of failure because of serious intercommunal antagonisms (the second variety), but have managed effectively, albeit possibly only for the moment, to come to terms with or to bridge their divisions, include Fiji, New Guinea, the Solomon Islands, the Philippines, Lebanon, Bolivia, Ecuador, Guatemala, Guyana, and Paraguay. Madagascar was also in that camp, but its highland-coast, light skin–dark skin, and Afromalagasy-Asiomalagasy compromises and accommodations came seriously unstuck in 2002, following a disputed presidential election. A strong state became a weak and sundered state almost overnight, as previously underclass highland Asiomalagasies saw an unprecedented opportunity to emphasize their own interests and oust an elected former dictator, and his dark-skinned Afromalagache associates, from power. Hostilities followed, and Madagascar quickly joined the ranks of developing world states in danger of failing.

Lebanon had disintegrated almost entirely before Syria's intervention enabled the geographical expression that Lebanon had always represented to become a state once again, and to begin to function internally and internationally. Syria gave a sense of governmental legitimacy to what had been a bombed-out shell of a polity. Lebanon today qualifies as weak, rather than failed, because its state has become credible, civil war is absent, and political goods are being provided in significant quantities and quality. Syria provides the security blanket, denies fractious warlords the freedom to aggrandize, and mandates that the usually antagonistic Muslim and Christian communities, and the battling groups within the Muslim community, cooperate. The fear of being attacked preemptively by rivals, or losing control of critical resources, is alleviated by Syria's imposed hegemony. In other words, Syria has reduced the salience of the traditional security dilemma, just as numerous UN blue helmets have done in Sierra Leone. Within that framework of supplied security, the Lebanese people's own traditional entrepreneurial spirit has transformed a failed state into a much stronger one.

A third variety of weak state includes the enduringly frail. Haiti, for example, has always been on the edge of failure, particularly during the nineteenth and twentieth centuries. But its entrenched weaknesses include no ethnic, religious, or other communal cleavages. There are no insurgent movements. Nor has Haiti experienced radical or rapid deflation in standards of living and national expectations, like Argentina in 2002 and Russia in the 1990s. Haiti has always been the poorest polity in the Western hemisphere.

Haiti's national capacity to provide political goods has steadily been compromised by autocratic and corrupt leadership, weak institutions, an intimidated civil society, high levels of crime, low GDP levels per capita—a per capita GNI of $510 in 2000, high rates of infant mortality, suspicion from or outright hostility by its neighbors, and many other deficiencies. Narcotics trafficking has been a serious problem since the 1980s. The Haitian government has been unable or unwilling to interdict smugglers in general and drugs transshippers in particular. Haiti, even under President Jean-Bertrand Aristide (1990–91, 1994–96, 2001–), has been gripped in a vise of weakness.[22] Yet, given very limited organized internal dissidence and almost no internal ethnic, religious, or linguistic cleavages within Haitian society—except a deep distrust by the majority of the upper classes, and of mulattos because of their historic class affiliations—the ingredients of major civil strife are absent. Failure demands communal differences capable of being transformed into consuming cross-group violence. Haiti thus seems condemned to remain weak, but without failing.

Examples of other nation-states that, given their geographical and physical legacy (and future peril in several cases because of global warming and cataclysmic climatic change), can be considered inherently weak include Burkina Faso, Chad, Ghana, Guinea, and Niger, in Africa; Georgia and Moldova in the former Soviet Union; and Cambodia, East Timor, and Laos in Asia.[23] Each has its own distinguishing features, and Georgia and Moldova battle their own so far successful separatist movements. Chad at one time harbored a vicious civil war, and Burkina Faso, Niger, Cambodia, and Laos are all ruled by autocrats unfriendly to civil society and to participatory governance. East Timor is a very new state, having been rescued and resuscitated by the United Nations after two bitter and unrewarding colonial interludes and a brutal final Indonesian spree of destruction and death. East Timor, even with UN help, has entered its full majority without a cadre of experienced professionals and bureaucrats, and without much in the way of physical resources. The willingness of these weak states to provide political goods in quantity and quality is severely limited at the best of times. Almost any external shock or internal emergency could push them over the brink.

Indicators of Failure

As the earlier parts of this chapter have suggested, the road to nation-state failure is littered with serious mistakes of omission and commission. Even in the modern states with inherited weaknesses, failure is not preordained. Impoverished, arbitrary, absent-minded creations predisposed to failure need not fail. Indeed, Botswana, dirt poor at independence, and a forlorn excuse for a state, created under determined and visionary leadership a nation-state strong enough to take full advantage of a subsequent, and much unexpected, resource bonanza. So did a sugar monoculture like Mauritius become transformed by determined visionary leadership into a thriving plural society based on manufacturing for export. In contrast, Malawi and Mali (two examples among many) remain weak and very poor (GNI per capita, \$170 and \$240, respectively, in 2000), albeit democratic, having both been unable in their different circumstances to overcome the arbitrary configuration of their borders, a mutual absence of easily exploitable resources, geographical hindrances, and decades of despotism. Climatic change could hit both Malawi and Mali particularly hard, too.

Nation-states are blessed or cursed by the discovery or absence of natural resources, like oil or diamonds, within received borders. But it is not the accidental quality of their borders that is the original flaw; it is what has been made of the challenges and opportunities of a given configuration that determines whether a state remains weak, strengthens, or slides toward failure and collapse. The colonial errors were many, especially the freeing of Africa south of the Sahara as forty-eight administrative territories instead of six or seven larger ones, and the abysmal failure to transfer the reins of authority much earlier and much more thoroughly to an *indigénat*. But it is not possible to predict this century's candidates for failure solely or even largely on the basis of colonial mistreatment. Van de Walle's chapter places much more causal weight on a series of poor economic choices, many of which were made by postcolonial leaders in their own personal interest.

Nor is it possible successfully to deploy the results of massive surveys of conflict and state collapse to predict failure. Esty et al. analyzed ethnic war leading to collapse, including twelve full collapses in forty years and 243 "partial" state failures, conflicts, and crises between 1955 and 1994, but only in states larger than .5 million.[24] They called state failure and collapse "new labels for a type of severe political crisis exemplified by events of the early 1990s in Somalia, Bosnia, Liberia, and Afghanistan. In these instances the institutions of the central state were so weakened that they could no longer maintain authority or political order beyond the capital city."[25]

Three strong indicators emerged from Esty et al.'s work (of seventy-five highly relevant variables): failure was likely when a nation-state favored a closed economic system—when openness to international trade was low or nonexistent; when infant mortality (a proxy measure for a society's quality of life) rates were high, that is, when the ratio of infant deaths per 1000 live births rose above the international median; and when a nation-state was undemocratic, for lack of democracy feeds on itself.[26] Esty et al. also concluded that decreasing and low GDP per capita levels were almost as strong an indicator of failure as infant mortality levels.

Unhappily, even though it is not implausible that high infant mortality rates are "associated with risk of state failure," rises in infant mortality, for practical predictive purposes, lag too far behind political and economic changes, which by themselves, are reasonable indicators of a propensity to fail. Likewise, as Esty et al. admit, infant mortality was a better indicator for democracies prone to failure than it was for less democratic cases—which, as this book has shown, are the more pressing category of states likely to fail. Closed economic systems, as in the extreme case of Burma after 1968, also predispose to failure; however, rapid falls in GDP per capita, purchasing power, domestic investment rates, and the like are surer and more readily apparent results and indicators of the possibility of failure. Esty et al. also report that trade openness works better for the less democratic regimes. As for the democracy indicator, Esty et al.'s findings are mostly tautological: A downward spiral of democracy obviously tends toward failure and, as they write, "partial democracies [especially in Africa] are indeed far more vulnerable to state failure-type crises than are either full democracies or autocracies."[27] The findings of this book dispute that very last point, but such a difference may arise because the Esty et al. definition of failure is much narrower (being confined to wars, adverse regime transitions, genocides, and politicides) than the one employed in this book. Furthermore, it is precisely because democratic states respond to popular discontent and accommodate dissident political challenges, while also maintaining normative and institutional inhibitions against massive human rights violations, that they fail to fail. Failing and failed states do not respond or accommodate effectively. That is what failure is about.

Three kinds of signals of impending failure—economic, political, and deaths in combat—provide clearer, more timely, and more actionable warnings. On the economic front, Lebanon in 1972–79, Nigeria in 1993–99, Indonesia in 1997–1999, and Zimbabwe in 2001–2002 each provide instances of how a rapid reduction in incomes and living standards indicated the possibility of failure early enough to be noted and for preventive measures to have been attempted. Donald Snodgrass's chapter contains the sorry data, and table 1.1 arrays the statistical depths of failure and collapse.

Once the downward spiral starts in earnest, only a concerted, determined effort can slow its momentum; corrupt autocrats and their equally corrupt associates usually have few incentives to arrest their state's slide since they themselves find clever ways to benefit from impoverishment and misery. As foreign and domestic investment dries up, jobs vanish, and per capita incomes fall, the mass of citizens in an imperiled state see their health, educational, and logistical entitlements melt away. Food and fuel shortages occur. Privation and hunger follow, especially if a climatic catastrophe intervenes. Thanks to foreign exchange scarcities, there is less and less of everything that matters. Meanwhile, in the typical failing state, ruling families and cadres arrogate to themselves increasing portions of the available pie. They systematically skim the state treasury, take advantage of official versus street costs of foreign exchange, partake of smuggling and the rents of smuggling, and gather what little is available into their own sticky palms. If it were possible reliably to calibrate the flow of illicit funds into overseas accounts, nation by nation, robust early warnings would be available. (David Carment's chapter arrays the many indicators that are plausible for early warning.) Absent detailed reports of such theft, the descriptors in this paragraph become very suggestive indicators that can be watched, in real time, and can forecast serious trouble, if not an end state of failure.

Politically, the available indicators are equally clear, if somewhat less quantifiably precise. A leader and his associates begin by subverting demo-

TABLE 1.1

Development Indicators for Weak, Failed, and Collapsed States

Country	*Human Development Index Rank (1999, out of 162)*[1]	*GNI per capita (US $)*[2]	*Illiteracy rate, adult male*	*Illiteracy rate, adult female*	*Mortality rate, under 5 (per 1,000 live births)*	*Life expectancy, at birth (years)*
Collapsed States						
Somalia	n.a.	n.a.	n.a.	n.a.	194.7	48.14
Failed States						
Afghanistan	n.a.	n.a.	n.a.	n.a.	279.4	42.96
Angola	146	290	n.a.	n.a.	207.8	46.58
Burundi	160	110	43.8	59.59	175.8	41.96
DRC	142	n.a.	26.9	49.79	162.53	45.75
Liberia	n.a.	n.a.	29.88	62.32	185.12	47.15
Sierra Leone	162	130	n.a.	n.a.	266.8	39.19
The Sudan	138	310	30.55	53.71	n.a.	56.17
Selected Weak States [3]						
Belarus	53	2870	0.26	0.56	13.85	68.11
Bolivia	104	990	7.99	20.72	79	62.56
Burkina Faso	159	210	66.07	85.92	205.8	44.22
Burma	118	n.a.	11.05	19.47	126.2	56.1
Cambodia	121	260	20.22	42.89	120.4	53.81
Chad	155	200	48.43	65.98	188.2	48.47
Columbia	62	2020	8.32	8.28	23.35	71.59
Côte d'Ivoire	144	600	45.5	61.37	180.24	45.82
Ecuador	84	1210	6.72	10.05	34.26	69.59
Fiji	67	1820	5.11	9.18	21.1	69.22
Georgia	76	630	n.a.	n.a.	20.82	73.03
Ghana	119	340	19.66	37.08	112.1	56.87
Guinea	150	450	n.a.	n.a.	161.36	46.31
Haiti	134	510	48.03	52.17	111.38	53.23
Indonesia	102	570	8.18	18	51.44	66.03

TABLE 1.1 (*cont.*)

Development Indicators for Weak, Failed, and Collapsed States

Country	*Human Development Index Rank (1999, out of 162)*[1]	*GNI per capita (US $)*[2]	*Illiteracy rate, adult male*	*Illiteracy rate, adult female*	*Mortality rate, under 5 (per 1,000 live births)*	*Life expectancy at birth (years)*
Iraq	n.a.	n.a.	34.4	54.13	121.3	61.06
Kenya	123	350	11.11	23.98	119.8	46.97
Krygyzstan	92	270	n.a.	n.a.	34.6	67.3
Laos	n.a.	290	35.88	66.78	n.a.	53.72
Lebanon	65	4010	7.86	19.65	29.96	70.4
Libya	59	n.a.	9.18	31.8	31.54	71.03
Malawi	151	170	25.54	53.49	193.04	38.8
Mali	153	240	51.09	65.6	217.6	42.27
Moldova	98	400	0.46	1.75	21.95	67.76
Mozambique	157	210	39.91	71.32	199.74	42.4
Nepal	129	240	40.44	76.03	104.7	58.86
Nigeria	136	260	27.58	44.27	153	46.83
North Korea	n.a.	n.a.	n.a.	n.a.	90	60.93
Papua New Guinea	122	700	29.43	43.22	74.66	58.59
Paraguay	80	1440	5.62	7.83	28.2	70.36
Philippines	70	1040	4.54	4.87	39.18	69.27
Soloman Islands	n.a.	620	n.a.	n.a.	26.72	68.57
Sri Lanka	81	850	5.58	11.01	17.86	73.14
Tajikstan	103	180	0.42	1.17	30.36	68.77
Zimbabwe	117	460	7.2	15.34	115.84	39.93

Source: This table was compiled by Carolynn Race, May 2002.

[1] United Nations Development Program, *Human Devlopment Indicators* (New York, NY), http://www.undp.org/hdr2001/back.pdf.

[2] This and all remaining indicators are from World Bank, *World Development Indicators 2002* (Washington, D.C.), http://www.worldbank.org/data/wdi2002. All data is from year 2000. GNI equals gross national income.

[3] No data available for East Timor.

cratic norms, greatly restricting participatory processes, and coercing a legislature and the bureaucracy into subservience. They end judicial independence, curtail the media, block civil society, and suborn the security forces. Political goods become scarce, or are supplied to the leading class only. The rulers demonstrate more and more contempt for their peoples, surround themselves with family, clan, or ethnic allies, and distance themselves from their subjects. The state becomes equated in the eyes of most citizens with the particular drives and desires of a leader and a smallish coterie. Many of these leaders grandly drive down their boulevards in motorcades, commandeer commercial aircraft for foreign excursions, and put their faces prominently on the local currency, on airports and ships, and on oversize photographs in public places.

Levels of violence provide a third indicator. If they rise precipitously because of skirmishes, hostilities, or outright civil war, the state can be considered crumbling. As national human security rates fall, the probability of failure rises. Not every civil conflict precipitates failure, but each offers a warning sign. Absolute or relative crime rates and civilian combat-death-counts above a certain number cannot prescribe failure. But they show that a society is deteriorating and that the glue that binds a new (or an old) state together is becoming fatally thin.

No single indicator provides certain evidence that a strong state is becoming weak or a weak state is heading pell-mell into failure. But a judicious assessment of the several available indicators discussed in this section, taken together, should provide both quantifiable and qualitative warnings. Then, avoidance maneuvers can occur and efforts at prevention can be mounted.

That said, research on failed states is insufficiently advanced for precise tipping points to be provided. It is not yet correct to suggest that if GDP falls by X amount in a single year, if rulers dismiss judges, torture reporters, or abuse the human rights of their subjects by X, if soldiers occupy the state house, or if civilian death rates rise more than X per year, that the state in question will tip for sure from weak to failing to failed. All we know is that the sum of those actions suggests that all is not well in the depths of Ruritania, that misery is spreading, and that the future of the state is in jeopardy.

The Hand of Man

State failure is largely man made, not accidental. Cultural clues are relevant, but insufficient to explain persistent leadership flaws. Likewise, institutional fragilities and structural flaws contribute to failure, as van de Walle's chapter suggests, but those deficiencies usually hark back to decisions or actions of men (rarely women). So it is that leadership errors across history have destroyed states for personal gain; in the contemporary era, leadership mistakes continue to erode fragile polities in Africa, the Americas, Asia, and Oceania that already operate on the cusp of failure. Mobutu's kleptocratic rule extracted the marrow of Zaire and left nothing for the mass of his national dependents. Much of the resource riches of that vast country ended up in his or his cronies' pockets; over four decades, hardly any wealth was devoted to uplifting the Congolese people, improving their welfare, building infrastructures, or even providing more than rudimentary amounts of human security. Mobutu's government performed only for Mobutu, not for Zaire.

Likewise, oil-rich Angola remains failed following three decades of war and, even within the large part of the country long fully controlled by the government of President Jose Eduardo dos Santos, it remains failed because he and his associates have consistently refused to deliver more than limited political goods to the bulk of their fellow countrymen. Ample oil wealth has been stolen or squandered, leaving the country with a notional GNI per capita of $240 in 2000.[28] President Stevens decapitated the Sierra Leonean state in order to strengthen his own power amid growing chaos. Sierra Leone, with its GNI per capita of $130 in 2000, has not yet recovered from Stevens's depredations. Nor has Liberia (GNI unavailable) been resuscitated in the aftermath of the slashing neglect and unabashed greed of Samuel Doe, Prince Johnson, and Charles Taylor. In Somalia (GNI also unavailable), Siad Barre arrogated more and more power and privilege to himself and his clan. Finally, there was none left for other pretenders to power and the rewards of power. The Somali state had been gutted, willfully, the abilities of the Somali government to provide political goods endlessly compromised, and the fall into failure and then into full collapse followed inexorably.

President Robert Gabriel Mugabe personally led Zimbabwe from strength to the precipice of failure, his high-handed and seriously corrupt rule having bled the resources of the state into his own pockets. He squandered foreign exchange, discouraged domestic and international investment, damaged local commerce, harassed the press, subverted the courts, and drove his country to the very edge of starvation.[29] (The GNI per capita of $480 is for 2000; generous estimates for 2002 suggest $200 as the appropriate figure.)

In Sri Lanka, Solomon and Sirimavo Bandaranaike, one after the other, drove the LTTE into reactive combat by abrogating minority rights and vitiating the implicit agreements on which the country had been created as Ceylon.[30] (The 2000 GNI per capita figure was $870.) In Afghanistan, Gulbuddin Hakmatyar and Burrhan ul-Din Rabani tried to prevent Afghans other than their own Pushtun and Tajik fellow nationals from sharing the perquisites of governance; their narrowly focused, self-enriching decisions enabled the Taliban to follow them in triumph in the 1990s and Afghanistan to descend into all-out terror.[31]

Wherever there has been state failure or collapse, human agency has engineered the slide from strength or weakness, and willfully presided over profound and destabilizing resource shifts from the state to the ruling few. As those resource transfers accelerated, and human rights abuses mounted, countervailing violence signified the extent to which states in question had broken fundamental social contracts and become hollow receptacles of personalist privilege, private rule, and national impoverishment. Inhabitants of failed states understand what it means for life to be poor, nasty, brutish, and short.[32]

The Context and Causes of Failure

There is a school of thought, represented in this volume in chapters by Christopher Clapham at the beginning and Jeffrey Herbst at the end, that suggests that state failure reflects misplaced forms of sovereignty. In certain areas of the world, the existence of states is a pretense, Clapham says, for want of anything else that the international system would recognize and accept. Full Westphalian sovereignty, to echo Krasner, should never have been accorded to fragile postcolonial entities with no history and experience of performing as or organizing a state.[33] A case can be made that state failure and collapse has been accelerated by the imposition of levels of state control upon indigenous societies unable to bear state-centered norms and such degrees of authority. At the very least, this viewpoint asserts, nation building before and after postcolonial independence was unworkable in every situation. Some nations were simply too inchoate and were destined to fail. Indeed, the modern state has worked best in the developing world where it inherited a preexisting traditional political culture of stateness. Those societies that best support effective statehood are those with precolonial echoes of state formation, Clapham argues. Places such as Somalia simply lacked the culture of or receptivity to the centrally directed state.

As ex-colonial territories became, *faut de mieux*, nation-states, so in many cases their weak social bases were compensated for by neopatrimonialism, the buying of clients, and a hierarchy of antidemocratic decisions that were difficult to sustain and ultimately led to state failure and collapse. Corruption, escalating levels of which are one of the indicators of state failure, accompanies neopatrimonialism and helps to bring states to failure. Bad governance is an inescapable corollary, and it has often preceded insurgencies within states. Indeed, Clapham and Herbst both suggest that state failure and collapse emanate not from artificial borders, colonial mistakes, colonial exploitation, or insufficient or misplaced tutelage, but from the automatic and premature assumption by former imperial administrative units of unsustainable state-like responsibilities. Together, but differently, they ask whether the polities that concern this book should ever have been considered states. Weakness may be inescapable in a category of recently minted twentieth- and twenty-first-century territories.

The remainder of this book takes the nation-state, whether appropriately or inappropriately so designated, as a given. Whatever their origins ontologically, states are the constituted repositories of power and authority within borders. They are the performers and suppliers of political goods recognized, strong or weak, by the international system. Some are weaker than others. Some are in danger of failing. Some have failed and collapsed. What separates the strong from the weak and the weak from the failed, and why? Those are the questions that motivate the analyses of the chapters in this book.

For Kasfir, failure equals domestic anarchy—an absence of controlling authority. Groups that once lived side by side and seemed to trust each other because they could depend on the state to protect them from harm or dangerous surprises, become motivated, as in the Côte d'Ivoire, by fear. Suspicion leading to hostility becomes a possibility as new antagonists arm defensively, or is it offensively? Individuals who looked to the state now look for protection to groups led by nonstate actors. This is an early tipping point—an indicator of coming failure. Such perilous situations strengthen the likelihood that the emerging classical security dilemma within the state will escalate into war, throwing several once-peaceful contenders into battles that each neither needed nor originally wanted.

Social grievances do not explain intrastate wars so effectively as does the security dilemma paradigm. But predation, which accompanies the satisfying of security claims, and interacts systematically with the claims of fear and potential preemption, is a parallel cause of the violence that tips a failing state into full failure. Preemptive strikes themselves often lead to predation. That is, when states are failing, the pull of material gain, when added to the push of fear, provide mutually reinforcing motives for attack that are stronger than just the one or the other factor. Once greed has claimed the behavioral goals of actors within failed states, however, peace becomes harder to achieve. Those who fear, and attack preemptively, want peace; those who are primarily predators thrive on war and the anarchic conditions of failed and collapsed states. Such a formulation contributes to an understanding of why Sierra Leone and the DRC both fell so far and so thoroughly.

Van de Walle's chapter puts less emphasis on predation and looting as causes for state failure, especially in Africa. In his analysis, how weak states respond to and handle their underlying economic frailties greatly affect their propensity to fail. Fiscal extraction, for example, is much more difficult and costly in big, empty countries and in inefficient or poorly led countries than it is in countries with sufficient governmental capacity. With low state revenues, government can obviously do less and provide fewer political goods. In failing states like Sierra Leone and Zaire in the 1980s, tax collections amounted to less than 10 percent of GDP. Yet van de Walle indicates that African governments typically employed far fewer workers per capita than European governments. However, those fewer workers nevertheless absorbed higher proportions of official expenditures, thus leaving little budgetary cash for the provision of public goods or the projection of governmental power and authority. Moreover, weak African governments, in contrast to those in Asia, systematically underinvested in the acquisition of human and physical capacity, boosted patronage over merit in their bureaucracies, and further undermined capacity to perform and protections against corruption and rent-seeking by politicians. Effectively marginalized civil services, in Africa more than Asia, also produced politically motivated and economically irrational policies. Economically driven crises, leading in many cases to failure, ineluctably followed.

Irrational economic decision-making limits state capacity. In contrast, weak states that follow sensible macroeconomic and fiscal rules become stronger over time. This virtuous cycle was found in Francophone West Africa, van de Walle reports, until postcolonial French constraints were loosened in the 1990s. In Anglophone and former Belgian and Italian Africa, by contrast, incautious and noncredible monetary and fiscal policies over the same period led to inflation, decreasing currency values, capital flight, declining foreign investment, a catastrophic decline in real civil service salaries, and losses of state legitimacy. As a consequence, rather than being motivated primarily by greed, leaders in those areas focused on expedient actions that could maintain themselves in power despite cascading economic disasters. States were hollowed out, their leaders seeking to swim but never to navigate, and to concentrate on themselves rather than on their responsibilities to the state and its citizens. Regarding motivation, van de Walle takes some issue with Reno, this chapter, and others: he says that state leaders do not willingly allow their states to fail; rather, they try to derive short-term advantage from every circumstance, and those actions lead their states downward into chaos.[34]

Van de Walle's chapter also examines two charges: that instability in Africa was accentuated by reduced aid-flows and that structural adjustment policies drove states to failure. He finds both charges false. The end of the Cold War resulted in no drop in aid. States, overall, were not forced to shrink and retrench. The scale of discretionary resources available to politicians did not decline. Public payrolls did not fall, with numbers of civil servants increasing over the period. Indeed, if structural adjustment contributed to failure it did so by allowing weak and badly performing regimes to gain (not lose) resources and thus stay in power. Conditionalities were mandated but never enforced, thus perpetuating poor policies and strengthening rent-seeking elites. Reform agendas were mostly honored in the breach, and structural adjustment thus comforted the status quo. As a result, the quality of African governance continued to decline and public infrastructures to fray.

State failure is always associated with intrastate violence, the rise of nonstate actors, an increased lethality of the weapons employed in offensive and defensive combat, a shady trade in small arms, and a reciprocal commerce in illegally mined and exported minerals, timber, narcotics, and women and children—indeed, in anything that will pay for the desired guns and ammunition. There is a tipping point, as Kasfir suggests, when nonstate leaders recruit followers and supply them with arms, the arms having been procured from smugglers, on a black market, or by theft or purchase from soldiers or official armories. Until this decisive moment, weak states may appear to be failing. But insurgent attacks, fueled by newly obtained arms or provoked by governmental errors or refusals to act (as in Côte d'Ivoire), plunge a failing state into a crisis from which it may—depending on the official response—never recover. Klare's chapter sets out the global character of the licit and illicit trade in small arms and light weapons and explains how both forms of commerce impinge on state failure. When an internal arms race has begun, time for peace is fast running out and failure is probable.

Unfortunately, small arms and light weapons are widely available and very affordable. Klare estimates that more than 550 million such instruments of death were in circulation in 2002. Existing international and regional efforts to limit the diffusion of weapons are still tentative. Since the ease of arming is one of the accelerators (if not a secondary cause) of state failure, preventing nation-states from failing in large part depends on making illicit arms transfers much more difficult and costly, on depleting surplus stocks, on bringing transparency even to the legal export of arms by governments, and on curbing the demand for arms by rebels. These are not new issues, as the many Afghan wars attest, but the failure and collapse of states and the misery that accompanies failure and collapse tie the small arms issue directly to explanations for failure.[35]

Revival, Resuscitation, and Reconstruction

Reducing the global incidence of state failure and collapse is essential to the peace of the world, to saving poor inhabitants of troubled territories from havoc and misery, and to combating terror. Prevention is always preferable and less costly than remediation. But worthy preventive efforts sometime fall short, and states stumble and truly fail. When that happens, and especially in the cases of states already failed and collapsed, the UN, international organizations, the major powers, regional hegemons, and coalitions of the willing all have a strategic and moral responsibility to intervene on behalf of beleaguered citizens and to reduce losses of life. Herbst goes farther and suggests a stage when the UN would "decertify" failing states, thus leading to a period of tutelage or, as Jens Meierhenrich's chapter suggests, "conservatorship." In such postconflict situations, there is a great need for conscientious, well-crafted nation building—for a systematic refurbishing of the political, economic, and social fabric of countries that have crumbled, that are failing to perform and provide political goods, and that have become threats to themselves and others. An atmosphere of security, a hint of good governance, and an inkling of prosperity all need to be provided, usually through outside assistance and outside support that reinforce positive initiatives on the ground.

The examples of Tajikistan and Lebanon suggest that failed states can be helped to recover. Even the seemingly hopeless cases, such as Somalia, are never beyond redemption. Likewise, the accomplishments of the UN transitional administrations in Cambodia and East Timor, as well as the NATO / UN interim administration in Kosovo, indicate that effective nation building is possible if there is sufficient political will and targeted and well-funded external aid.

In the last three cases an interim administration provided security, the key political good, and developed a rudimentary local police force, patiently trained local officials across bureaucratic departments, reintroduced legal codes and methods, and helped to rejuvenate and regularize the local economies. Eventually, the transitional governments registered voters and sponsored internationally supervised expressions of choice through the ballot box, thus permitting all three countries to emerge from their periods of tutelage. Home rule in Kosovo, and independence in Cambodia and East Timor, followed.

But in each of those instances, and in so many analogous situations, interim administrations have been anxious—very anxious—to "complete" their ostensible missions and leave. They preferred short-term fixes and quick reconstruction efforts to sustainable efforts of nation building requiring long-term commitments. Effective, enduring, resuscitation demands creating or restoring capacities for security, for governance, and for institution building. That sometimes takes a generation, or more. The uncomfortable but necessary lesson of the partially successful efforts to date is that the revival of failed and collapsed states will prove more lasting if the regional or international organization in command only very gradually, over a span of years, relinquishes authority to a new indigenous replacement. The rush to be off undercuts sustainability and often results in capacity building that is insufficient to shore up, much less repair, states that have lost their way.

The hierarchy of postconflict initiatives is explicitly or implicitly addressed in each of the chapters that follow. Their findings, and the logic of the failed state paradigm—where civil war and violence prevail—demonstrate that reconstructive endeavors depend entirely upon outbreaks of peace.

A lasting cease-fire must be achieved first, before any other improvements can be introduced. An interposing force or some other buffering method must be found to sustain the cease-fire, avoid skirmishes, and remove fears of opponents. Then it becomes imperative to disarm and demobilize combatants—a key procedure that was unfortunately omitted in Somalia in 1993.[36] In Mozambique, however, postconflict stability was greatly enhanced, and a smooth transition to the establishment of an effective government assured, by comprehensive demobilization, disarmament, and reintegration. Doing so included collecting and destroying weapons, even buried caches, offering former soldiers and their commanders the kinds of incentives that would induce them to comply and cooperate, and ensuring an atmosphere of fairness by the presence of international guarantors. Ex-fighters would and could go back to the land if conditions appeared conducive, materials and cash were provided, and the process of discovering and disposing of land mines became a national priority. Removing the land mines that were strewn across the landscapes of Afghanistan, Angola, East Timor, Mozambique, and Sierra Leone, and confiscating small arms, are continuing objectives of those who would strengthen the capacity for peace in these and other war-ravaged countries.

Before a peace process and accompanying demobilization can truly become a rebuilding endeavor, the transitional governing body must be able to deliver security throughout its domain. Roads must be made safe for travelers and commerce, if necessary by external peacekeepers. In Sierra Leone, only the arrival of British paratroopers and large numbers of UN blue helmets finally restored that failed state's sense of internal security in 2002. Only the intervention of the Syrian army in 1979 enabled Lebanon to begin to uncollapse itself. Only Australian and UN peacekeepers ended Indonesian atrocities in East Timor and created a foundation for efforts at nation building. Likewise in Afghanistan, a failed state with a terrible history of insecurity and low levels of law and order, a small contingent of international peacekeepers established a zone of human security in Kabul. But the countryside was left to the warlords, thus frustrating the interim government's ability to project power and restore good governance to the entire country. The U.S. reconstruction of Iraq depends upon strong security.

Afghanistan, Angola, Burundi, the DRC, Liberia, Sierra Leone, Somalia, and the Sudan remain the international community's greatest challenges. Without peace, nothing can be achieved. Without fundamental law and order, resuscitation and nation building are chimera. But once stability and confidence have been at least partially returned to these failed and collapsed states, transitional administrations and international agencies can together focus on three primary and parallel goals: jump-starting battered economies, re-introducing the rule of law, and rejuvenating civil society. The imperative economic initiatives (as Snodgrass indicates) include establishing fiscal and macroeconomic stability, controlling the money supply, paying civil servants and police officers, and putting people to work in new jobs.

Without those accomplishments, a new probity, and a coming sense of prosperity, the local economy will languish and continue to rely on dubious exports (opium, blood diamonds, and women and children). Absent a sense of positive change (Meierhenrich discusses how the state should be reformed in the minds of postconflict leaders and inhabitants), crucial foreign investment and trade, as well as aid from developed-world donors, will hardly flow in the required amounts.

An early necessity is an enforceable code of laws. The reintroduction of the rule of law can be done in stages, as human and physical capacity is rebuilt, but war-ravaged citizens will tentatively support reconstruction efforts only once they are certain that legal safeguards and legal redress will be available. A functioning court system should be among the first political institutions to be reborn. A renewed police force and corrections facilities are critical. Roads and telephone networks must be restored and refurbished. The central bank should be re-created. Teachers and health workers must be hired and their physical surroundings gradually rebuilt. Together, these and many other essential initiatives will reestablish a sense that a new government exists and has begun to work for, rather than against, the people.

Police personnel, judges, bureaucrats, and parliamentarians will have to be trained or retrained. Defense forces have to be reconfigured and their chiefs reoriented. Strong local leadership cannot be assumed but must be nurtured and strengthened. Once these advances start to succeed, it will then become important to convene a constituent assembly to write a new constitution and to anoint an indigenous government through well-prepared and well-supervised elections. Rushing forward into such a national contest is inadvisable before peace, law and order, and a capable administration are in place. Restoring the people's trust in the state provides an essential platform for the reconstruction of failed and collapsed states.

When states fail and collapse, the process of disintegration mutilates institutions and destroys the underlying understandings between the government and the governed. That is precisely why sustained state building requires time, massive capacity building, large sums from outside, debt relief, and appropriate measures of tutelage. Rich nations must promise not to abandon state rebuilding efforts before the tough work is finished—before a failed or collapsed state has functioned well for several years and has had its political, economic, and social health restored. The worst enemy of reconstruction is a premature exit by international organizations and donors, as in Haiti and Somalia.

The chapters that follow develop these themes at greater length. Nat Colletta et al. demonstrate that unless demobilization, disarmament, and reintegration occur at the end of hostilities, fighting will begin afresh, and a successful effort of reconstruction will prove impossible. In Sierra Leone, until 2001 the settlement of such questions was pursued imperfectly, and earlier ceasefires were never capable of being transformed into enduring platforms for peace. Moreover, when weapons were collected, they were neither stored securely nor destroyed. Unsurprisingly, those same guns were retrieved and used when the war resumed. In Somalia, the U.S. and UN relief force failed to attend fully to disarmament and demobilization, so reintegration was impossible, and what was left of the Somali state degenerated into warlordism and societal misery. Yet, in a number of other postconflict situations UN-administered disarmament and demobilization experiments proved successful: ex-combatants registered, surrendered weapons (sometimes for cash payments), saw that their weapons were made inoperative, received reintegration incentive packages, and trusted the procedures and the results. Further, where demobilization, disarmament, and reintegration were thorough, ex-combatants were quickly recruited into nascent police forces and retrained. Without strengthened police units, law and order in postconflict societies are almost impossible to sustain.

Colletta et al. advocate releasing ex-combatants from cantonment sites sooner rather than later so that they avoid becoming serious threats to security. In Uganda, the process was well managed. In particular, ex-combatants were sent on their way with monetized reinsertion packages—small cash grants, replenished regularly over a period of months. Doing so benefited the Ugandan rural economy and stimulated local economic responses—the classical multiplier effect.

The importance of restoring or creating social capital in postconflict societies is discussed in chapters by Daniel Posner and Jennifer Widner. But Colletta et al. also remind us that creating social cohesion around and through the ex-combatants is particularly critical, especially forging strong social relationships and trust across postwar fault lines. New governments do well to foster informal networks and voluntary associations of former soldiers. Existing community organizations can help to reintegrate former fighters and build social capital. In Cambodia, Buddhist village associations played such a role. In Guatemala, Mozambique, and Uganda, veterans' associations performed that function. Ultimately, Colletta et al.

say that all of the components of the full disarmament, demobilization, and reintegration package are critical to the security and performance of states recovering from extreme combat. It is the interplay of a community's physical and social capital and an ex-combatant's financial and human capital that determines the ease and success of posttraumatic social and economic reintegration.

Widner suggests that working with local officials to revive optimism and to ensure human security, enhance leadership capacity, and improve the delivery of basic services, are each fundamental components of effective postconflict reconstruction. Together, betterments in these areas produce trust between citizens and new governments. Because fostering attitudes conducive to investment, exchange, and compromise energize formerly war-torn countries, local and national efforts that bring such commitments to the fore are necessary but not sufficient. The role of women needs to be given special attention, too, for without restoring the trust and assisting in the revitalization of women and women's leadership in postconflict and posttraumatic situations (such as Afghanistan, the DRC, or Sierra Leone), less can be accomplished with speed and in a sustainable fashion.

Central to strengthening the commitment of citizens to their government is trust. Widner's survey data indicate that trust grows from reducing crime and strengthening the rule of law. Those actions ought to be priorities. So should strengthening government performance as it directly affects villagers, women, and townspeople—the provision of primary health care, road improvements, and clean water. Reducing income inequalities also seems to boost trust. Bureaucratic evenhandedness is good; the more fair the system, the better people feel. Accountability is essential. That means working to limit corruption, especially by making it easy for private parties to complain against officials. Further, if new governments can find ways at the community level to generate dense associational life—the life blood of social capital—the process of reconstruction will benefit, and leaders will be able to elicit positive degrees of cooperation from their followers.

But state failure almost always will have meant the atrophy or destruction of civil society, so renewing trust and rebuilding social capital will be difficult and slow even after basic public order and security have begun to be realized and disarmament and demobilization have been achieved. Nonstate actors with their predilection for looting the state are presumed to be hostile to associational activity; nevertheless, Posner's chapter indicates that under some circumstances state failure actually can energize associational activity. When a state disappears, as in Somalia, civil society can flower. Outsiders can help by approaching the problem counter-intuitively and supporting not associational groups per se but the communications infrastructure of civil society. In order to rebuild itself and then to assist in reviving a nation, the sinews of civil society need ease and transparency of communication. So donors could best help to resuscitate telephone and internet systems, patronize newspapers and other media, and strengthen road networks—the lifelines and lifeblood of civil society.

Restoring the Rule of Law

The survey data and the logic of the state failure process suggest that peace and security, disarmament and demobilization, and the reestablishment of confidence and trust need to be accompanied by a resumed or refashioned process of law. A postconflict police force cannot operate absent new national rules. Susan Rose-Ackerman's chapter provides a comprehensive examination of how the rule of law might best be restored in a postconflict setting. Unlike so many discussions of "the rule of law," she usefully breaks that broad concept down into its critical components. What becomes effective is the reintroduction of criminal law, property law, contract law, liability law, and constitutional law—that is, how the state's new relations with its postconflict citizens should best be organized and regulated. Further, she considers not just the formal rules, but also the ways in which those rules are embedded in an institutional and organizational nexus that values compliance.

Refashioning the criminal code provides a useful postconflict means of differentiating the old regime from the new as was done in South Africa. Instead of relying on criminal sanctions to punish dissent, a fresh legal code could specifically establish the freedom to assemble and sanction freedom of expression while decriminalizing libel and slander. Citizens in the resuscitated states should be free to criticize their leaders, subject to civil rather than criminal penalties. Similarly, the conduct of public officials could well be made more, rather than less, subject to oversight and criminal charges. Although settling scores with the former government is not a useful idea, per se, Rose-Ackerman favors the vigorous prosecution of corrupt officials from the old regime so as to set an instructive example for the new era. Meierhenrich argues that the recovery of truth by commissions and similar tribunals can assist postconflict states in their efforts at reconstruction.[37]

Even with a reoriented, modernized criminal code and new enforcement mechanisms (including the reorganization of the police and the corrections system), it will be impossible to jump-start the economy, and thus impossible to give citizens confidence enough to commit to their altered government, until the legal underpinnings of private economic activity are established. The power of the multiplier effect depends on a legal framework protective of commerce. That framework needs to be accessible, in a local (not a foreign) language, and modernized. (East Timor is experiencing a language dissonance.)[38] A new foreign investment code, and the enshrining of basic property rights in a constitution, as in Namibia, might grease the wheels of growth. Well-defined private property rights are essential. These should deal with the thorny issue of land tenure, and the conversion of privileges of usufruct into permanent rights to surveyed land, including easy transferability. Providing a healthy basis for democracy may depend, indeed, on reducing traditional forms of dependence by peasants upon big landowners. With regard to these and related questions, Rose-Ackerman argues that as beneficial as predictability and clarity of rules may be, rigidity is not helpful. In other countries, particularly regarding property questions, new regimes should carefully consider whether or not privileging the status quo will or will not prove helpful. In a similar manner, reforming preexisting contract law requires subtlety and an awareness of prevailing business norms. Resolving disputes in a fair but not overly rigid manner is important, and clear statutory rules can help to avoid disputes.

Finding legal mechanisms to hold public officials accountable is a critical aspect of postconflict reconstruction and social engineering. Specific limits on the arbitrary exercise of power by leaders and political institutions are helpful. One kind of innovation concerns rules that govern administrative procedures and that prescribe exactly how, and with what safeguards, rules must be developed and promulgated. Very helpful are truly independent organizations that can both monitor official behavior and sanction miscreants, and not merely report to a president or a parliament (as in Namibia). Anticorruption commissions have proven useful only in jurisdictions where leaders have supported their integrity and acted effectively on their findings.

Transparency is essential, so that even the posting of lists of basic citizen rights in public places and buildings is helpful. Indicating how and to whom citizens may complain is a further major advance. Antifraud hotlines and nontelephonic mechanisms are useful innovations that have been introduced into states in the developing world. A free media, encouraged to investigate and publicize the activities of the government in power, also assists the goals of accountability and transparency. A free media is greatly assisted, and citizens are empowered by legal codes that compel review and that make corruption and self-dealing harder to hide. In this last regard, especially in poor countries devastated by intrastate warfare, privately owned free-radio stations are usually more accessible to citizens than newspapers or television. They form a part of the chain of improved communication that can assist all facets of ongoing reconstruction efforts, particularly the revival of a civic consciousness at the village and town level. Failing and failed states (Zimbabwe is a recent example) censor television, ban and bomb private radio stations, attack the nongovernmental press, and generally suppress anything that smacks of accountability. Postconflict states build confidence by adopting a reverse strategy, the more strongly the better.

The rule of law need not be overly complex. Because citizens and judges in postconflict societies are unlikely to be well versed in inherited or reintroduced legal systems, there is value in simple laws that can be communicated directly to affected citizens. Procedural rules can be simplified so that magistrates without formal legal training might be able to be fair and inclusive, as well as efficient. Streamlining and simplification also make human resource capacity-building an easier endeavor, if no less urgent and puzzling. Moreover, if transparency and ease of understanding is built into legal systems from the onset of the revival of states, the trade-off between independence and accountability for judges becomes more manageable. Judicial integrity and independence are obviously critical in every state. Mechanisms must be installed to prevent the control of judgments by executives and legislatures. Equally, while still protecting the principle of judicial independence and impartiality, laws should enable citizens to act against judges who take bribes, act capriciously or improperly, or are impermissibly lazy.

Assured recourse to the law, a strong and fair criminal justice system, the ability to enforce contracts and property rights, and the availability of noncorrupt, efficient commercial dispute settlement mechanisms, gird efforts to revive destroyed and damaged economies. Already failing, failed, and collapsed states, especially those beset by intrastate war and those fitting this book's broader sample of weakness, will have experienced the loss of physical capital and human resource skills, and reductions in the utilization of capacity, declining investments in both human and physical capital, sundered infrastructures, and negative net investment. In states at risk of failure, inflation rises. GDP (now GNI) per capita recedes. Everyday life becomes less predictable as citizens more and more engage in opportunistic behavior. Crime rates rise. Thus peace and security and enforceable laws become essential precursors to nation-state restoration.

Jump-Starting the Economy

If sensible postconflict goals include economic growth and restoring prewar qualities of life and per capita consumption levels, then all of the disastrous downward shifts mentioned in the previous paragraph must be undone. To be sustained, regrowth needs to be based on investments in physical and human capital and not on resource stripping or foreign assistance. Snodgrass recommends a three-stage process of economic recovery:

financial stabilization, rehabilitation and reconstruction, and development. First, the postconflict administration should establish a macroeconomic environment conducive to growth, initially by reducing inflation to single digits, lowering government deficits, and managing monetary policy. External creditors should suspend debt repayments, most of which will anyway reflect borrowings by the discredited outgoing regime. Foreign trade rules should also be liberalized during this first phase. Second, after the ex-combatants are disarmed and demobilized and the security forces are retrained, the new government (and donors) should restore the national infrastructure, revitalize medical and educational service delivery systems, rebuild public institutions, and start training persons to play key roles—project appraisal, financial and economic policy making, and planning for all service areas—in the developmental phase. Third, the postconflict state should create a policy framework within which the private sector can contribute to growth and prosperity. A new legal approach will also be necessary, as Rose-Ackerman and Snodgrass both indicate. But so will a stripping away of regulations and practices that impede rapid growth. Economic diversification will be essential. Will the state continue to be interventionist, or to what extent will it stimulate and support market mechanisms? How will it work with international organizations and bilateral donors? Will it be able to modernize its tax and tariff regimes? Answers to those questions are urgently necessary before the revived state can hope to resuscitate its ruined economy.

Only once a transitional administration or a new government has secured the cities and the countryside and ensured human security, disarmed and demobilized, established legal norms, stabilized and reinvigorated the economy, reconstructed roads, and restored essential services such as schools and clinics, can or should its leaders and their opponents consider elections. That is the prescription. The reality is that elections sometimes must be used as war termination devices (as in Liberia). Or in some situations a quick election is essential if renewed warfare is the likely alternative. Agreeing to hold early (premature) elections, as in Bosnia, may also be essential to the forging of difficult peace agreements but not to the effective development of political institutions. Exit strategies may be predicated on holding timely elections (as in East Timor and Sierra Leone), whether or not the postconflict situations really are ready for or will be assisted by the holding of electoral contests before, say, the economy is strong or the contending parties have become reconciled. As Terrence Lyons's chapter indicates, the electoral record is mixed because each ballot-casting exercise serves multiple, contradictory goals. Elections are always essential to the launching of postconflict democracies, but they can also exacerbate competition, polarize already fractured societies, institutionalize existing imbalances of power, and retard as well as advance the transition from war and failure to resuscitation and good governance.

Voters go to the polls to ensure diverse outcomes—at earlier stages for security, at later stages, arguably, for potential performance and economic reward. Since a return to participatory politics is a key goal of postfailure reconstruction, consideration should be given as to how best to maximize popular participation through the ballot box. Lyons stresses the importance of demilitarizing politics and building strong political institutions before voters go to the polls; after the vote it may be too late. Demilitarization of politics includes the establishment of effective interim indigenous or international administrations, transforming previously contending military forces into political parties, and the formation of credible electoral oversight authorities. Postconflict elections are, after all, referenda on how best to sustain the peace as well as on how best, and under whose leadership, to revive dysfunctional countries.

What happens between a peace agreement and an election is just as, and possibly more, important than the terms of the agreement itself in determining a transition's success or failure. Institution building is critical, and bringing political institutions, norms, and national political debate to a level of functional maturity greatly improves the atmosphere of legitimacy within which elections can be held. Months rather than weeks of debate can boost confidence in the modalities of an election, and in electoral processes generally, or it can sour potential voters and reignite their fears. Timing always needs to be in critical balance. Lyons thoroughly explores the relevant sequencing considerations, and weighs the virtue of different electoral designs against the perceived needs of postfailure political leaders and parties.

He does not call, as Herbst and others might, for an internationally sponsored, neutral, world-wide elections commission to supervise or actually run elections in weak states. That new idea might substitute for outside electoral observers and could end controversy over the quality and probity of the elections held in post- or preconflict fractious states. Such a new institution could have prevented the stealing of the 2002 Zimbabwean presidential election, questions about the 2002 communal voting in Cambodia, the rigging of the 2002 Zambian elections, concerns about Nigeria's 2003 poll, and anxieties about many other events. Creating such a new organization, and staffing it, would prove yet another charge on the resources and manpower of the UN system, but once such a radical innovation became accepted, and became the electoral gold standard, many questions about the technical quality of elections, and their fairness, would recede.

Is the nation-state the only or the best unit for the organization of larger than city / town political units in the twenty-first century? Should the international community be able to withdraw recognition from failing or failed states? Should failing and failed states be capable of being sent temporarily for tutelage—an interim designation that served East Timor well from 1999 to 2002? Somalia still needs international assistance and administration; a period of UN-organized tutelage might help. Otherwise, says Herbst, the asymmetry of interests between predatory rulers and the forces of world order will continue to cause state failure to repeat itself. Indeed, without enforced tutelage or boundary adjustments (now anathema), failed states will continue to fracture into smaller and smaller pieces.

Herbst goes so far as to recommend that states that cease to exercise formal control over parts of their nominal territories should lose their sovereignty, that is, be decertified. They should also lose sovereign status if they fail to project authority or fail to provide basic services outside a capital or a few cities. If they are unable to perform, if they no longer supply political goods—in other words, if they are failing—they should be delisted. Membership in the UN General Assembly should not necessarily be forever. Decertification would be a powerful tool, recognizing a state's mortality or its propensity to fail. It could either be a way station on the road back to resuscitation, or a death warrant. Either way, it would put the residents of the decertified entity, its neighbors, and the international system on notice that something had to be done. A decertification process could also lead to the creation of new states, carved in many cases out of old. Secession would not be regarded as anathema, at least not in those cases where the receding state no longer broadcast power throughout its nominal boundaries. The Somalilands of the world would, under such a new dispensation, be candidates for recognition rather than dismay. Places of disorder, like Aceh in Indonesia, could conceivably qualify if they eventually met stringent criteria for power and performance.

The other contributors to this book generally disagree with Herbst's radical and despairing message. The organizing and central argument of *When States Fail: Causes and Consequences* is that repair and revival are possible outcomes. Indeed, given the international system's inertia, the predominant African and Asian norm against reconfiguring boundaries and refashioning states, and the major refocusing that would be required to follow Herbst's otherwise logical notions, preventing states from failing and reviving those that do fail remain the governing orders of the day.

In earlier, less interconnected eras, state weakness and failure could be isolated and kept distant from the developed world. Failure once held fewer implications for the peace and security of the world, and for the regions that surround weak and failing states. Now, however, as much as their citizens suffer, the failings of states also pose enormous dangers well beyond their own borders. Minimizing the possibilities of failure by strengthening the capacities of the nation-states of the developing world has thus become one of the critical all-consuming strategic and moral imperatives of our terrorized time. The chapters in this book demonstrate how and why states have failed and will fail, and how they can be revived and reconstructed.

Notes

1. This book and this opening chapter emerged from a five-year project of the World Peace Foundation and Harvard University's WPF Program on Intrastate Conflict, which addressed all aspects of state failure. More than forty collaborators, including all of the contributors to this volume, were involved in formulating the direction of the research and in reviewing the conclusions presented in this chapter and separately in Robert I. Rotberg (ed.), *State Failure and State Weakness in a Time of Terror* (Washington, D.C., 2003). That book contains case studies of Colombia, the Democratic Republic of the Congo, Fiji, Haiti, Indonesia, Lebanon, Sierra Leone, Somalia, Sri Lanka, the Sudan, and Tajikistan.

This chapter draws on concepts developed there and in my "The New Nature of Nation-State Failure," *Washington Quarterly*, XXV (2002), 85–96 and my "Failed States in a World of Terror," *Foreign Affairs*, LXXXI (2002), 127–40. With respect particularly to this chapter, I am very appreciative of the helpful and unstinting advice and ideas of Michael Ignatieff, Nelson Kasfir, and Susan Rose-Ackerman. Carolynn Race's research assistance was, as always, invaluable. Deborah West has managed much of the project and has helped successfully to shepherd and edit the many iterations of this book.

2. In Krasner's formulation, not all 192 are sovereign in the Westphalian sense. The compromises and ambiguities are endless. Stephen D. Krasner, *Sovereignty: Organized Hypocrisy* (Princeton, 1999), 8, 10, 20–25.

3. For political goods, see J. Roland Pennock, "Political Development, Political Systems, and Political Goods," *World Politics*, XVIII (1966), 420–26, 433.

4. See Erin Jenne, "Sri Lanka: A Fragmented State," in *State Failure and State Weakness*, 219–220.

5. For an instructive discussion of "insurgency"—"a technology of military conflict characterized by small, lightly-armed bands practicing guerrilla warfare from rural base areas"—see James D. Fearon and David D. Laitin, "Ethnicity, Insurgency, and Civil War," 7–12, unpublished paper presented at the 2001 APSA meeting.

6. Fearon and Laitin, 24, criticize the conclusions about greed driving civil war of Paul Collier and Anke Hoeffler, "On the Economic Causes of War," *Oxford Economic Papers*, L (1998), 563–73.

7. Fearon and Laitin, "Ethnicity," 3–6.

8. Some of these points were earlier made by I. William Zartman, "Introduction: Posing the Problem of State Collapse," in his edited volume, *Collapsed States: The Disintegration and Restoration of Legitimate Authority* (Boulder, 1995), 3. Zartman's overall definition: "Collapse means that the basic functions of the state are no longer performed, as analyzed in various theories of the state," (5). This

definition parallels what has been suggested here. The present book, however, parses "failed" and "collapsed," distinguishing them. It also details the "functions," suggesting which ones are critical.

The Failed States project at Purdue University defined failed states "by the patterns of governmental collapse within a nation which often bring demands (because of the refugees they foster, the human rights they abridge and their inability to forestall starvation and disease) which threaten the security of their surrounding states and region." The Purdue definition appears much less specific than the one employed herein. For the Failed States website at Purdue University, see www.ippu.purdue.edu/failed_states. Earlier, Gerald B. Helman and Steven R. Ratner ("Saving Failed States," *Foreign Policy*, LXXXIX [1992–93], 3) defined failed nation-states as entities "utterly incapable of sustaining" themselves as members of the international community. Civil strife, government breakdown, and economic privation are proximate causes of state failure. Their definition puts the onus on reputation rather than on performance.

9. In addition to Transparency International's Corruption Perception Index, and an elaborate Kennedy School of Government student quantitative measurement of outputs as proxies for Corruption, the World Bank Institute's 2001 Governance Indicators (http://www.worldbank.org/wbi/governance/pdf/2001kkzcharts.xls) evaluate the nation-states with which this book is primarily concerned according to their "control of corruption," as well as rule of law, government effectiveness, voice and accountability, and political stability. All of the failed or collapsed states rank at the bottom of the corruption measure, except for Sierra Leone. Those last data have an anomalous character. For the Kennedy School measurement, see Robert I. Rotberg, "Learning Through Projects: Solving for African Governance, Leadership, and Corruption," unpublished manuscript (Cambridge, Mass., July 2002).

10. Oren Barak, "Lebanon: Failure, Collapse, and Resuscitation," in *State Failure and State Weakness*, 318–26.

11. In 1995, Jennifer Widner suggested that the same states, plus Chad, Togo, and Congo-Brazzaville, had experienced "the collapse of political order" and authority had "disintegrated completely into civil war." Widner, "State and Statelessness in Late-Twentieth-Century Africa," *Daedalus*, CXXIV (1995), 136–37.

12. See the case material in Rotberg, *State Failure and State Weakness in a Time of Terror*.

13. Walter Clarke and Robert Gosende, "Somalia: Can a Collapsed State Reconstitute Itself," in *State Failure and State Weakness*, 133.

14. William Reno, "Sierra Leone: Warfare in a Post-State Society," in *State Failure and State Weakness*, 75.

15. René Lemarchand, "The Democratic Republic of the Congo: From Failure to Potential Reconstruction," in *State Failure and State Weakness*, 37.

16. Gérard Prunier and Rachel Gisselquist, "The Sudan: A Successfully Failed State," in *State Failure and State Weakness*, 103.

17. See table 1.1 for sources, as well as Daniel Kaufmann, Aart Kray, and Massimo Mastruzzi, "Governance Matters III: Governance Indicators for 1996–2002," World Bank Development Research Group (2003).

18. For a full set of development indicators for weak, failed, and collapsed states, table 1.1 to this chapter. All GNI figures are from 2000, and may be found in World Bank, *World Development Indicators 2002* (Washington, D.C., 2002).

19. Nasrin Dadmehr, "Tajikistan: Regionalism and Weakness," in *State Failure and State Weakness*, 245.

20. Since the list of weak states is long and the names on the list shift with some frequency, this chapter and the Harvard Failed States project have not compiled a full report on all of the states in the world that might be classified "weak". The states mentioned in these paragraphs represent the difficult and critical cases, as well as exemplars of the global range of weakness.

21. In 2002, Nigeria's parliament tried to impeach Obasanjo for acts of omission and commission.

22. Robert I. Rotberg, *Haiti's Turmoil: Politics and Policy Under Aristide and Clinton* (Cambridge, Mass., 2003).

23. A United States Institute of Peace Special Report—Timothy Docking, "Responding to War and State Collapse in West Africa" (21 January 2002)—calls Guinea a collapsed state.

24. Daniel C. Esty, Jack A. Goldstone, Ted Robert Gurr, Barbara Harff, Marc Levy, Geoffrey D. Dabelko, Pamela T. Surko, and Alan N. Unger, "State Failure Task Force Report: Phase II Findings," (31 July 1998). Earlier, most of the same authors produced "Working Papers: State Failure Task Force Report," (30 November 1995). The Esty et al. definition of failure in both versions of the report was much narrower than the definition used in this book, focusing on violence more than performance.

25. Daniel C. Esty et al. "The State Failure Project: Early Warning Research for U. S. Foreign Policy Planning," paper on the Failed States website, Purdue University, (West Lafayette, February 25–27, 1998). In the 1998 version of the Esty et al. "Report," 113 is the number of crises, not 243.

26. Fearon and Laitin, "Ethnicity, Insurgency," found no significant relationship between trade openness and civil peace.

27. Esty et al., "State Failure Task Force Report" (1998), 9.

28. U.S. Secretary of State Colin Powell told dos Santos in mid-2002 that it was time his government stopped stealing from the Angolan people. James Dao, "In West African Visits, Powell Seeks to Prime Oil Pumps," *New York Times* (5 September 2002).

29. See Robert I. Rotberg, "Africa's Mess, Mugabe's Mayhem," *Foreign Affairs*, LXXIX (2000), 47–61; Martin Meredith, *Our Votes, Our Guns: Robert Mugabe and the Tragedy of Zimbabwe* (New York, 2002).

30. Neil DeVotta, "Institutional Decay and Ethnic Conflict in Sri Lanka," unpublished manuscript (2002).

31. Barnett Rubin, "The Political Economy of War and Peace in Afghanistan," *World Development*, XXVIII (2000), 1789–1803.

32. With apologies to Thomas Hobbes, *The Leviathan* (London, 1651), 1, 13.

33. Krasner, *Sovereignty: Organized Hypocrisy*, 8, 10, 20–25.

34. Reno, "Sierra Leone," 77–78.

35. See also Michael Klare and Robert I. Rotberg, *The Scourge of Small Arms* (Cambridge, Mass., 1998).

36. Walter Clarke and Jeffrey Herbst (eds.) *Learning from Somalia: the Lessons of Armed Humanitarian Intervention* (Boulder, 1997), 242–44.

37. See also Robert I. Rotberg and Dennis Thompson (eds.) *Truth v. Justice: the Morality of Truth Commissions* (Princeton, 2000).

38. Ina Breuer, "The Experiences of Local Actors in Peace-building, Reconstruction and the Establishment of Rule of Law," unpublished manuscript (Singapore, 2002).

Figure 1.1 Collapsed, Failed, Failing, and Weak States, 2003. Region 1: The Americas. Credit: Dimitri Karetnikov.

Figure 1.2 Collapsed, Failed, Failing, and Weak States, 2003. Region 2: Africa. Credit: Dimitri Karetnikov.

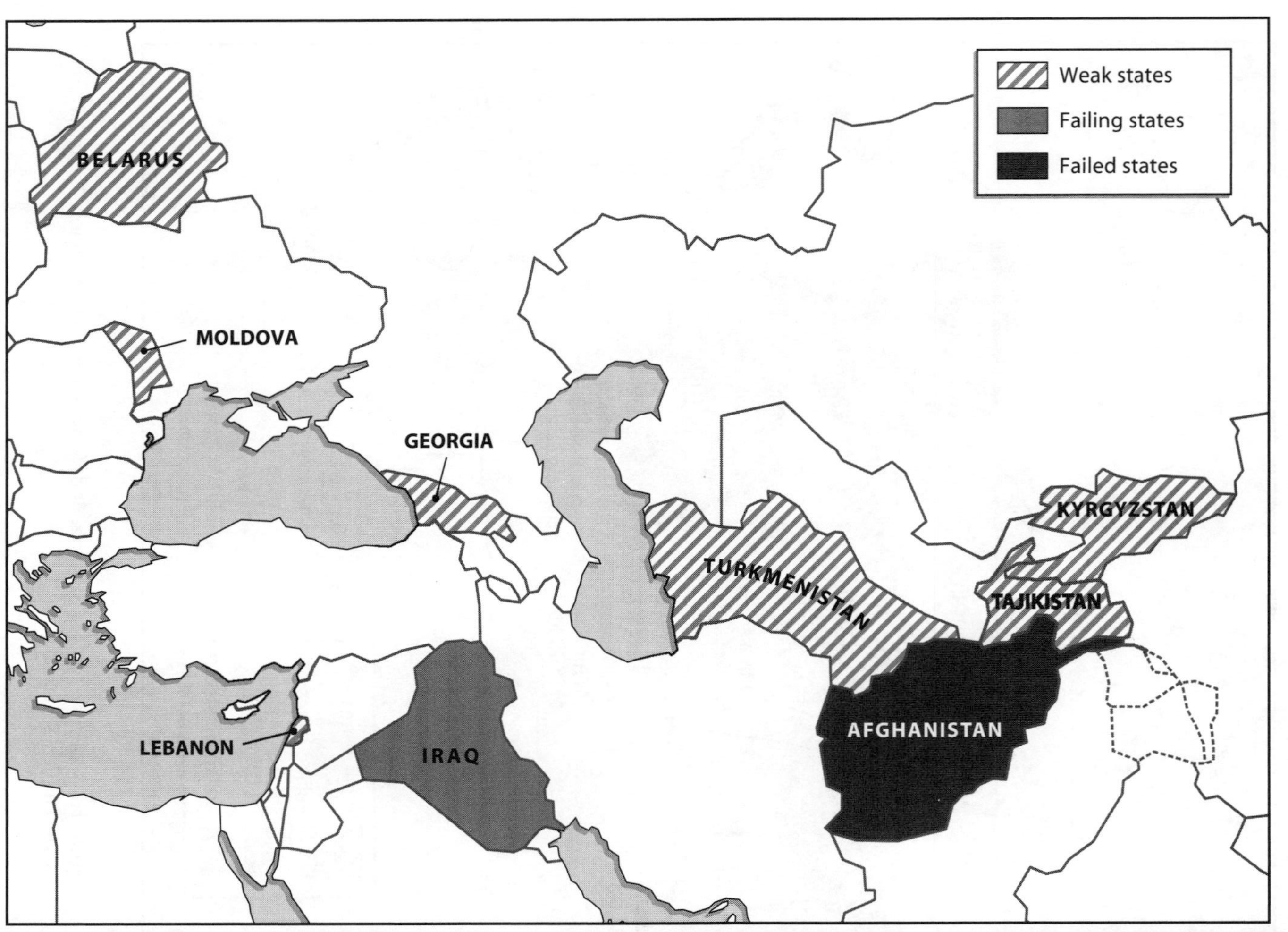
Weak states
Failing states
Failed states
BELARUS
MOLDOVA
GEORGIA
TURKMENISTAN
KYRGYZSTAN
TAJIKISTAN
LEBANON
IRAQ
AFGHANISTAN

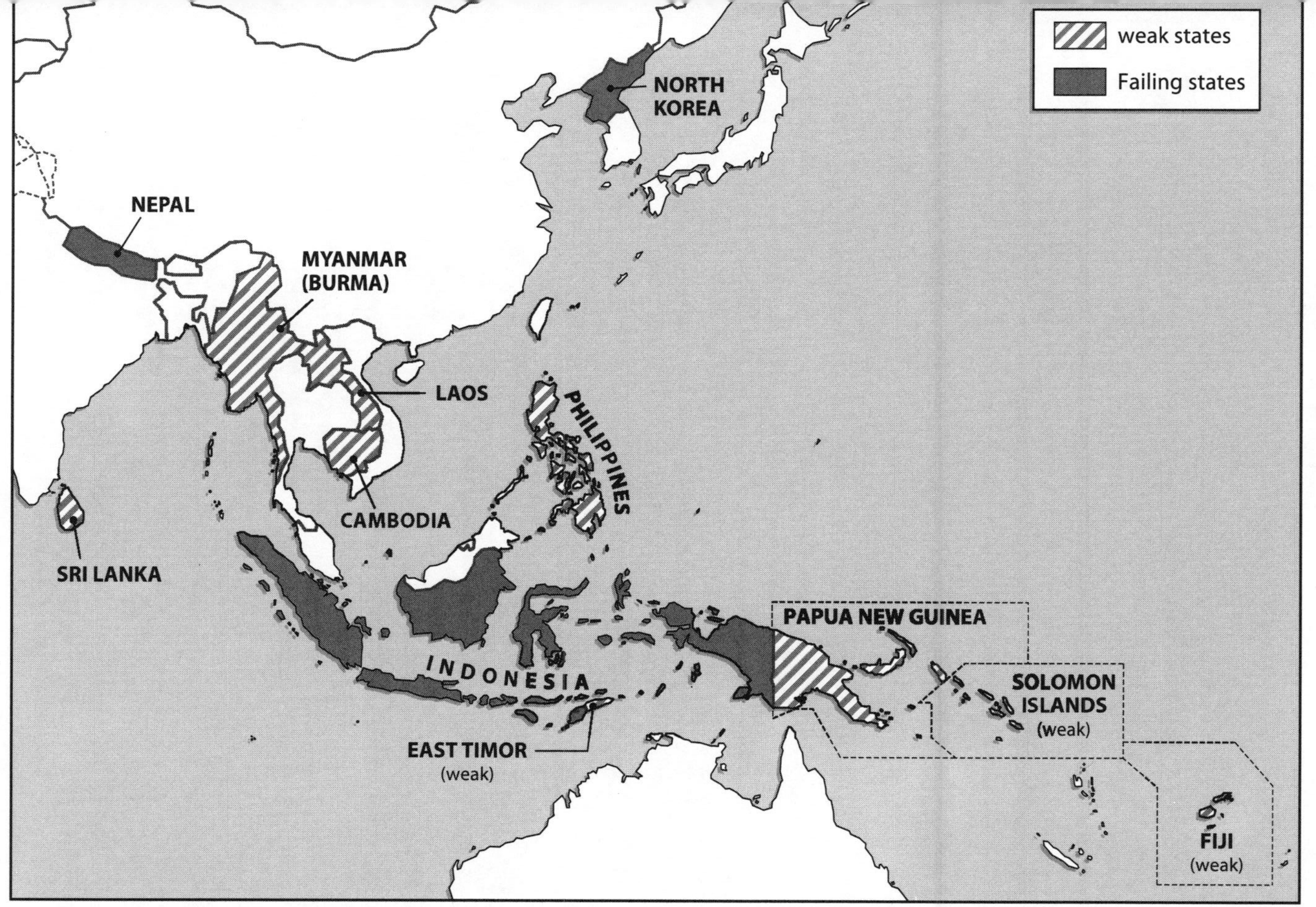

Figure 1.4 Collapsed, Failed, Failing, and Weak States, 2003. Region 4: Asia. Credit: Dimitri Karetnikov.

Part One

THE CAUSES AND PREVENTION OF FAILURE

Two

Domestic Anarchy, Security Dilemmas, and Violent Predation

CAUSES OF FAILURE

NELSON KASFIR

WHEN DO SECURITY dilemmas or predation explain the violence that accompanies state failure? Most accounts of civil breakdowns attribute violence to preexisting social grievances. But the dangers and opportunities that emerge in response to the breakdown of state institutions may also help to explain why violence threatens, erupts, or intensifies. When individuals, as well as the groups they join, see their rivals acquiring arms, they are likely to become increasingly suspicious of their intentions. Some of them may also take advantage of the failure of the state to enrich themselves by raiding their weaker neighbors. Their search for safety or material gain may make as important a contribution to violence as their adherence to long-standing cultural or ideological concerns. Nevertheless, it is a complicated task to determine whether security dilemmas or violent predation, or both, raise expectations of violence or actually provoke it. In this chapter, I develop five propositions that help to clarify whether security dilemmas or violent predation explain why individuals and groups resort to violence during as well as after state failure.

At the outset it is worth asking why social grievances often cannot provide adequate explanations for hostile threats and actions when state structures crumble. One of the characteristics of civil violence is the frequency and ferocity with which lifelong neighbors, friends, and even family members attack one another. People who had succeeded in living peacefully side by side suddenly find themselves caught up in deadly conflict. The social rules by which they had previously lived together no longer sustain their cooperation, nor provide them with guides for restoring peace. Since their cultural or ideological differences had not caused them to become enemies before, their responses to state breakdown, in some cases, may provide more relevant reasons for their hostilities.

Consider, for example, the puzzled and anguished reactions of some participants and victims involved in attacks in Bosnia, Liberia, and Somalia, cases that easily qualify as examples of state failure. Their surprise that violence has come from those with whom they had previously lived and worked provides an important clue that something new has disrupted their rules of cooperation. " 'They are the worst people in the world,' said one [Liberian] chief, speaking of the fighters, 'and they are our children.' "[1] "One [Somali] woman told of her shock: 'I knew this gunman. He stole the grass I was cutting to make soup. I grew up with him and knew who he was. That's what hurts.' "[2] "He told the story in a whispered mumble. They [Bosnian Muslims] were killed by Serbs who had been their friends, people who had helped harvest their fields the previous autumn, people with whom they shared adolescent adventures and secrets. . . . All of a sudden, seemingly without reason, they had turned into killers."[3] The gunmen also find these wars frightening. "But how can we come to town? We are afraid of each other because of the war. We are all Liberians but the war make[s] us to feel like that."[4]

Is there a pattern? Did these thieves and killers act because they belonged to groups implacably opposed to the groups to which their victims belonged? Or, did they act because they thought that their lives and the lives of their families depended on it? Alternatively, were they looking for loot, confident that the police would not, or could not, stop them? Or, were they manipulated by political entrepreneurs seeking material reward or career advancement? What causes the spiral of violence to increase following individuals' loss of confidence in the capacity of the state to protect them? Until close attention is paid to ethnographic accounts of each of these cases of civil violence, good answers to these questions will not be found. Nevertheless, these poignant observations suggest that more is probably going on than can be accounted for by the cultural or ideological cleavages that predate outbreaks of violence.

To gain more understanding of whether new motives that develop in response to state failure contribute substantially to understanding domestic violence, we need to look carefully at the assumptions underlying the application of security dilemmas and violent predation to incipient state failure and to its actual occurrence. State failure provides the limiting case for considering how individuals respond to the threat or occurrence of violence because they cannot turn to a neutral authority for help. In its most extreme form, state failure means the disappearance of both public authority and its supporting social norms. In other words, state failure creates domestic anarchy, which invariably involves the threat of violence, if not violence itself. Of course, individuals must cope with violence without public help in many states that do not fail completely, as well as in states that have not failed but that are embroiled in civil war. In the extreme case, however, the logic of the choices facing individuals will be easier to identify.

When state authority crumbles, individuals not only lose the protection normally supplied by public offices, but are also freed from institutional restraints. In response, they often seek safety, profit, or both. Their motives become more complex than when they could depend on the state. But, the occurrence of state failure is also a dynamic process in which individuals are likely to behave differently from each other due to variations in their resources, strategies for survival, and tolerance for risk. Others whose lives are intertwined with theirs will have to take these additional motives into account.

It seems highly unlikely that everyone will decide simultaneously to ignore state institutions. Individuals have different thresholds for yielding to either fear or greed. As more individuals fail to comply with or flout public authority, others become more likely to do the same. At some point, as the weight of quantitative individual decisions creates a qualitative change in state institutions, the force of public authority may simply vanish. Social scientists generally use a tipping model to explain this category of changes. The model can easily be extended to include the processes through which state failure typically occurs. Examining tipping behavior during the process of state failure can help identify when individual fears begin to create security dilemmas and when individual opportunities provoke violent predation.

Security dilemmas and violent predation are dissimilar processes, but the onset of state failure can trigger either or both. The first concerns the search for safety, while the other involves the attempt to acquire material gain. Both end up making everyone less safe. Both contribute significantly to cycles of violence and make it more difficult to restore the state or create a new one. The first is propelled by fear, the second by greed.

The security dilemma was developed in international relations to explain why states become antagonists locked into a cycle of continuing hostility when each of them prefers peaceful coexistence.[5] When the actions of a state seeking only to protect its members frighten a second state into arming itself for its own protection, and when this response causes the first state to redouble its efforts, the two have become opponents joined in a security dilemma. The efforts of each state to act rationally produce collective irrationality. Everyone's attempt to achieve peace increases tensions that could lead to war. Since the end of the Cold War, the security dilemma has been adapted from its applications in international relations to explain rivalries in domestic politics where the grip of state authority has become uncertain or has disappeared. In place of states as rivals, the concept is extended to explain the behavior of groups following the breakup of empires or the dissolution of states.[6]

The concept of predatory behavior, a notion common to both international relations and comparative politics, provides a competing explanation based entirely on greed.[7] It is a commonplace of history that states in their constant competition for power look enviously upon the resources of their neighbors and often loot or seize their territories.[8] Together, explanations based on security dilemmas and on threats of, or actual instances of, violent predation contribute to a more discriminating set of explanations of interstate hostility. However, it is not so easy to apply them, because the two concepts produce behaviors that is difficult to distinguish in practice. What appears to be predatory behavior to one state or group may look like protection from dangerous insecurity to another. Both can provoke the same preparations for potential hostilities. In addition, what starts out as either one can turn into the other.

Explanations based on greed have played so central a role in explaining domestic conflict that it would seem odd not to incorporate them in every investigation of state failure.[9] Yet Posen and the others cited earlier asked only whether security dilemmas were involved. Some more recent analyses of civil breakdown explicitly consider both.[10] They recognize that either or possibly both factors may explain preparations for hostile showdowns and subsequent violence. Even though it can be difficult for outsiders, and even for those engaged in domestic conflict, to tell who is seeking security and who is greedy, it would be a serious mistake to analyze one without looking for the presence of the other.

The central purpose of this chapter is to examine specific problems that must be overcome in order to use security dilemmas and violent predation effectively, either separately or in combination, to explain the pattern of violence when state failure is imminent or after it occurs. The following arguments prepare the way to understand when, why, and how security dilemmas and violent predation function when state authority breaks down:

- State failure must be understood to create domestic anarchy if it is to provide an appropriate analytic context for security dilemmas.
- The tipping model helps to explain why a security dilemma can trigger state failure.
- The notion of anarchy has the same effect after state breakdown as it does in interstate relations.
- Not all groups that emerge in failed states are the equivalent of states, making it more difficult to sustain the logic of the security dilemma, though not of violent predation.
- Security dilemmas in failed states differ conceptually from violent predation, but are difficult to distinguish in practice.

Conceptions of State Failure and Security Dilemmas

The literature on failed states includes various meanings for state failure. This is not surprising, as writers contemplating breakdowns in states as dissimilar as Haiti, Bosnia, Sierra Leone, or Somalia are often considering different problems, and many of their concerns have nothing to do with security dilemmas. They disagree over whether the point is to identify critical indicators that measure a state's political decline or the collapse of its authority; whether societal norms that survive the collapse of political authority can soften its impact; and whether state failure can take place slowly or must occur suddenly. Each of these positions identifies an important issue that results when states lose their capacities. But the kind of state failure that can produce a security dilemma has particular characteristics that exclude many analyses of domestic breakdown.

"State failure" is often used as the basis for discussing whether the international community should override claims of sovereignty by intervening in weak or virtually nonexistent states in response to human tragedies caused by their political decline. Failure, in this context, refers to critical indicators measuring whether the state is performing adequately or not—for example, whether its government no longer has effective control throughout the state's territory, or whether its military, police, and judicial systems function poorly.[11] State failure has also been applied more broadly to a "continuum" of decreasing governmental effectiveness that includes not only states in which central authority is entirely absent, but also states with merely a semblance of central authority, states that have ceded part of their territory to insurgent groups while effectively ruling the remainder, states with governments that have some power but are unable to meet most demands for public services, and states that rule despite the hostility of an ethnic majority.[12] The reason for making all of these distinctions is to design international interventions that are responsive to the specific characteristics of particular state failures.[13]

On the other hand, international intervention has been faulted for propping up regimes that would not otherwise survive. Military assistance, for example, may mask extreme state weakness by supporting the capacity for vigorous repression by venal governments that are utterly unable to manage society or direct change.[14] The problem of state failure for all three of these approaches is poor performance by the government. But lack of capacity is not the sort of state failure that is sufficient to produce a security dilemma. Only when poor performance causes individuals or groups to think that their potential rivals will not be restrained by state authority will the possibility of a security dilemma arise.

Thus, a collapse of state authority is necessary, not merely a steady decline in governmental performance or the support of its continued existence primarily through foreign assistance. Zartman takes this step by explicitly treating state failure as "the situation where the structure, authority (legitimate power), law, and political order have fallen apart."[15] But he does not go far enough. For him, state collapse is not necessarily bleak, since what results "is not necessarily anarchy," because "society carries on" and "politics and economics are localized."[16] In other words, sometimes society can take over when the state retreats.

He does not indicate how much social behavior can expand, but he suggests that societal activities may reduce the uncertainty caused by the withdrawal of state authority. Since it may result in a soft landing, he regards "state collapse as a long-term degenerative disease," rather than a sudden deflation of authority.[17] It is not surprising that Zartman does not address the formation of security dilemmas, since the presence of social norms and the slow decline of the state mean for him that anarchy does not exist. Instead, if the social norms that survive state collapse provide overarching rules that can either help groups assess each other's intentions, or reduce the necessity of forming groups for self-protection, security dilemmas are less likely to arise.

The creation of new states out of state failure may create the basis for a security dilemma, but not necessarily one in which *social groups* become the basis for an arms race. For example, while Posen treats "the collapse of imperial regimes . . . as a problem of 'emerging anarchy,' " his analysis in both of his case studies is ambiguous.[18] It is not clear in his account whether the protection of ethnic groups depends on how new states use their sovereignty or on how ethnic groups relate to each other. If the states of Serbia and Croatia or Russia and the Ukraine are the fundamental actors, then Posen has merely presented two garden-variety interstate security dilemmas. But even if, as he structures the argument, "proximate groups of people suddenly find themselves newly responsible for their own security," it is plain that these "groups" have the resource of internationally accepted state sovereignty available to create a security dilemma (Serbs and Croats) or to prevent one (Russians and Ukrainians).[19]

When the collapse of state authority is equated with domestic anarchy, conditions are ripe for security dilemmas. Groups that once lived together because they could depend on the state to protect them will suddenly become wary of one another.[20] Not only is state authority unavailing, but informal norms, ties of friendship, and obligations of neighbors are also cast aside.[21] As Yugoslavia fell apart, for example, " 'nationalists had to convince neighbors and friends that in reality they had been massacring each other since time immemorial.' "[22] Thus, a "strong" notion of state failure, one where there are no surviving ties to soften anarchy, provides the most appropriate setting in which to analyze security dilemmas.[23]

Tipping Points and Security Dilemmas in State Failures

Security dilemmas occur because large numbers of individuals in every society make decisions about their personal security that are contingent on their expectations about the decisions of others. The prospect of state failure as well as state failure itself (that is, the threat or realization of domestic anarchy) induces individuals to shift their commitments to obey authority from the state to smaller groups or organizations. But not all individuals at once. Some event, report, rumor or response by someone occurs, causing another individual to cross that threshold. The collective consequence of these individual decisions cannot be expressed simply as their cumulation. The pattern is both complex and reversible, because everyone does not make the decision at the same time or for the same reason. The argument does not work in the same way for violent predation. Even though anarchy also facilitates predation, it does not require the parties to engage in the same sort of mutual relationship as in security dilemmas.

The tipping model helps to elaborate the dynamic that causes a security dilemma in failing or failed states by exposing its internal relationships.[24] It asserts that for certain behaviors there are tipping points—critical masses—that will produce distinctive collective changes out of many incremental individual changes.[25] Its important characteristics are that individuals with different thresholds make conscious decisions involving membership in at least two groups, which lead to a chain reaction.[26] Threshold means "the number or proportion of others who must make one decision before a given actor does so."[27] The tipping model can accommodate situations in which some of the individuals make their decisions independently, while others act contingently.[28] In some cases, it may be possible to distinguish categories of individuals responding to fear, whose motives are always contingent on the decisions of others, from those acting out of greed, who may be responding independently or contingently.[29] Groups can be modeled in the same way as individuals, so long as it is reasonable to think of them as unitary actors. Where this assumption can be made, the interaction effects between greed and fear may contribute to a tipping explanation for a specific state failure.

Expectations about rivals or potential rivals can be as important as decisions or incidents in activating both security dilemmas and state failures. These expectations may be self-confirming when others evince attitudes or behavior that support the expectation. They may have no serious repercussions so long as the attitudes or behaviors that stimulate them occur infrequently or others believe they will be restrained by external institutions or internal group policing. But, as the tipping model implies, if the expected attitudes or behavior are perceived to be unrestrained or are repeated often, they may provoke a sudden collapse. The first individuals to flout state authority lead to the prospect of an ever-accelerating self-fulfilling prophecy. In addition, if the expected consequences are thought dire, the prospect of the worst case becomes much more likely. "If each of us believes that the other will attack without warning at the first opportunity, each of us may feel it necessary in self-defense to attack without warning at the first opportunity."[30] Thus, many security dilemmas that lead to state failure will begin before states fail.

However, not every expectation is self-confirming. "*Self-negating prophecies*," in which events that are anticipated to be horrific or inevitable cause actors to withhold confirming behavior, can reverse expectations.[31] Schelling also identifies "*self-correcting expectations*" when enough individuals alter their own behaviors so that an unpleasant outcome is avoided.[32] Individuals who do so are not necessarily sacrificing their own self-interest for the collective good. In calculating whether they are better off sticking with the state or joining a small group, they may feel that their chances for protection are better even within a weakened state than within a small group. In addition, they may think that the only group that they could join would attract attacks from more powerful rival groups. Thus, not all incipient security dilemmas necessarily lead to state failure. Nevertheless, tipping triggers state failures that are conducive to security dilemmas.

Anarchy and the Analogy between the International System and Failed States

Are failed states little international systems with similar security dilemmas and predatory motives? The central issue is whether anarchy means the same thing in both systems. From a neorealist perspective, David asserts that "once central authority collapses, a microcosm of the international system is replicated within the state."[33] Yet there are differences in the meaning of anarchy between the interstate and intrastate situations that would appear to make this analogy implausible. Anarchy is the essential condition for security dilemmas, but it works differently in the interstate system than it does in a failed state. It is a defining condition of the international system with which states must learn to live. But within the state, anarchy does not have a priori status, rather it emerges when the state fails and it disappears when state authority returns.[34] The solution for state failure is to eliminate anarchy by restoring the institutions of the former state, or by creating a new set of institutions in a new state.

Nevertheless, for security dilemmas the analogy between the two systems is not actually diminished by this difference, because the security dilemma does not depend on whether anarchy is inescapable or temporary. If people fear for their lives, they will seek to join and provide arms to groups or organizations that they hope will protect them, a process that can easily lead to an arms spiral. They will do so, even if they fervently hope that someone can put the state back together. Indeed, as Snyder and Jervis observe, "because individuals are more vulnerable than are states, the security dilemma is likely to be more severe in civil than in international anarchy."[35] Unrestrained predation would seem to lead to the same result. In fact, if the removal of institutional restraints is likely to be temporary, well-positioned individuals will be all the more emboldened to attempt a raid on members of an opposing group while they have the opportunity.

The similarity between international and local anarchy can be close or distant. In particular, the more suddenly and definitively the state fails, the more the ensuing domestic anarchy will resemble the anarchy of the interstate system. When state failure is sudden, leaders of emerging groups are less likely to have prepared interim arrangements. When state failure is definitive, no social norms will be able to buffer group relationships and, for better or worse, no new states will be able to employ sovereign authority. This strong version of state failure is an ideal type that mimics the "perfect" anarchy embodied in the interstate system. The situation in Somalia after Siad Barre fled Mogadiscio in January 1991 probably comes closer to this ideal type than any other case.[36] Of course, security dilemmas occur in cases of state failure that diverge from the conditions of this ideal type—as they also do within both weak and strong functioning states when internal war breaks out.[37] In general, however, the kind of anarchy induced by state failure is sufficient to precipitate a security dilemma.

Groups and States in Security Dilemmas

The first recourse to explanation of the violence following state failure is to the cultural beliefs or the cultural conflicts historically rooted in that society. "Ancient hatreds" or segmentary conflicts provide an immediate explanation for brutality among neighbors. The difficulty with this argument begins when the violence does not stop as it did in the past. If the rules of cultural reconciliation no longer function, it may be the case that culture cannot explain the violence by itself. Thus, it may be useful to turn to noncultural explanations, fear and greed, to find explanations that are more satisfying for the most unappetizing reason—they predict that under most circumstances violence is likely to start or continue. But the concepts of security dilemmas and violent predation do not dismiss the importance of culture out of hand. Instead, they make use of it to explain the operation of the groups necessary to their logic. Either the groups that provide security for their members after states fail become the magnets for increased insecurity, or they provide occasions for predation that sometimes result in further rounds of predation. However, to make either of these arguments work, the groups have to display specific characteristics, which are often overlooked by those who employ these explanations.

For security dilemmas to function in failed states as they do in international politics, groups must play a role equivalent to states. "Once central authority collapses," according to David, "domestic groups inside a country . . . behave much as states do in the international system."[38] However, there are two parts to the argument. It is not enough that public authority falls apart, there must also be units capable of providing protection. Unorganized individuals may be fearful, but they cannot create a security dilemma. Posen observes that "proximate groups of people suddenly find themselves newly responsible for their own security."[39] But the mere fact of their proximity does not determine whether they will organize, whether they will form one or many political units, or whether they will become sufficiently cohesive to act as if they were states. The case is different for predation. Individuals or bandit gangs who expect profit for themselves have a ready basis for collective action.

The differences between states and social groups go to the heart of the logic of security dilemmas. An underlying assumption of the security dilemma is that leaders have the capacity to commit their units to policies that their members cannot undermine. Otherwise, members of rival units would not have reason to fear them, because their lack of cohesion would greatly reduce the threat. States fulfill this criterion more effectively than most social groups. States are formal organizations with relatively clear determinants of membership and with leaders who usually have the legitimacy to make specific commitments, punish dissent, and make migration difficult. The security dilemma works because leaders or members of rival states usually expect citizens of a threatening state to acquiesce to their leader's policies rather than to oppose them or to flee, because of the costs involved. In addition, the rival state's leaders and citizens also know that even in the face of widespread dissent or large-scale migration, international acceptance of state sovereignty means that the leader of the threatening state may still be able to pose an effective threat. In other words, to a great extent the security dilemma can be effective among states because actors presume that the policies of state leaders do not necessarily depend on the wishes of their citizens.

The logic of the security dilemma among states works well because the units that respond to this logic tend to be impervious containers that can be committed by a relatively autonomous ruler. As a result, the construction of the unit in the security dilemma can be, and often is, taken for granted in interstate applications. But both "rulers" and "impervious containers" are implausible descriptions for most social groups. In general, social groups, particularly those that come to the fore in the absence of states, are informal collectivities whose membership may rapidly change and whose leaders often have little legitimacy and uncertain capacity to induce compliance among their followers.

The important point is that groups vary greatly in their internal signifying characteristics and in their levels of organization. Where boundaries are rigid and persist over time, as do the administrative boundaries separating states, and where leaders are selected on the basis of cultural or other legitimate rules, as is expected to happen in states, it seems likely that the character of the group will be more distinct and, therefore, that the analogy between groups and states will be stronger. In addition, where the inheritance of cultural categories or the dictates of a social situation create widespread agreement that each individual in a society can be assigned only one group identity, groups will more closely resemble the states of the international system.

Thus, determining whether groups can constitute a security dilemma involves inquiring into their internal characteristics in order to discover how much these characteristics shape the behavior of the individuals who join. The issue is complicated because the different theoretical approaches that have been developed to analyze ethnic groups also vary in their emphasis on inherited or primordial traits, as opposed to situation-based or constructed characteristics that cause individuals to choose particular identities.[40] Regardless of one's theoretical orientation, ethnic groups vary enormously in their reliance on inherited characteristics and the degree to which individuals are restricted to membership in only one group.[41] Ethnic groups, construed broadly, encompass all the different kinds of groups—cultural, religious, regional, and symbolic—that can serve as potential vessels for individuals coping with the absence of the state. Some groups, though far fewer than many journalists seem to think, have a deeply etched history of conflict, which, despite the repression of their confrontations for long periods, will give their members a ready basis for fearing members of other groups when common public institutions disappear. But there are also groups that have literally been invented by an accident of recent history—for example, the Nubians in Uganda, who wreaked great havoc during the regime of President Idi Amin.[42] In principle, invented groups should be expected to have weaker shared bonds and thus find it more difficult to achieve the organizational coherence needed to cause members of other groups to fear their joint action. Thus, some groups may better fit the requisites of the security dilemma than others.

Nevertheless, political uncertainties are intense and change with frightening speed in the wake of state failure. With changes in the political situation, individuals consider what options they have for joining ethnic groups. During a war, choosing sides often becomes a matter of life and death. Mixed parentage, lack of scarification, fluency in an appropriate language, and even physical characteristics are indicators that give some individuals ranges of choice. Thus, confronted by war, some individuals may successfully claim an identity because it gives them an opportunity to loot or hide. Alternatively, they may be forced by fear to assume an identity and become active in the corresponding group because others classify them so, even though they would be safer if they could only avoid being identified at all. When confronted by the *genocidaires*, some Rwandan children of mixed Hutu-Tutsi parents were luckier than others in the categories to which they were, often arbitrarily, assigned.

At the time of Thomas Quiwonkpa's and Samuel Doe's 1980 coups d'état in Liberia, being Gio or Krahn was politically irrelevant. But when the two coup leaders fell out, identity became one of several "major political cleavages at frightening speed."[43] Mobilization into armed factions in Somalia was based on clan or subclan membership, because that was how warlords recruited their followers. But there is a lively argument whether they abandoned the segmentary basis for resolving conflict among clans when they suppressed the roles of elders, who were the repositories of cultural rules.[44]

Competing political entrepreneurs create organizations that typically project a group identity. After Charles Taylor's National Patriotic Front of Liberia caused the Liberian state to collapse in 1990, other entrepreneurs formed their own armed factions, often recruiting on a cultural or a religious basis.[45] The factions that survived the infighting, often by happenstance, determined which ethnic cleavages became politically salient. Few of these organizations existed before the state failed. Furthermore, leaders sometimes initiated conflicts to solidify their hold on their soldiers. But the ethnic boundaries of their organizations turned out to be porous. As Ellis warns, "[I]n most circumstances this mobilization of ethnic identity was more rhetoric than reality, as every faction included substantial numbers of fighters of diverse ethnic origin."[46] A considerable degree of reification may be needed to give these often evanescent groups the illusion of solidity needed to support an explanation based on the operation of a security dilemma.

Distinguishing Security Dilemmas from Violent Predation

The difference between fear and greed in cases of domestic anarchy could not be more marked in theory, nor more difficult to disentangle in practice. The logic of security dilemmas contradicts the logic of predation. The first rests on the compatibility of goals that cannot be confirmed, while the latter rests on the incompatibility of goals that are all too easy to determine. Their structures also differ. The security dilemma requires a responsive relationship among two or more actors. Predation requires only the action of a single aggressor, plus, of course, an unwilling victim.

The point of the security dilemma is that all competitors prefer peace, but feel insecure about the intentions of their rivals. They would like to cooperate, because they share the same goal. If they could only be sure that their rivals agree, and will continue to agree in the future, they would neither prepare for hostilities nor engage in them. In this sense, they prefer the status quo: to live with other states or other groups that emerge after state failure, as they are presently constituted. So long as security is uppermost in their minds, they repress all thoughts of greed because such motives could initiate a security dilemma. If they are prudent, they will take into account the fears that they are likely to arouse not only among citizens of the state that they might have contemplated victimizing, but also among members of a third state who might fear that their state could be next. Uncertainty about the intentions of others is sufficient to cause actors to take provocative steps for their self-protection. But that is merely to identify motive—the desire of actors for security. The dilemma is not created until a group's rival makes a similar response. Because the response is provocative in its own right, it is likely to lead to a spiral effect. Both parties vainly seek what each only wanted the other to affirm in the first place.

The basis of predation, whether violent or not, is that competitors, who believe that they are secure, covet the possessions of others. They do not want to cooperate because they and their intended victims have incompatible preferences. They prepare for hostilities regardless of the intentions of their opponents. They wish to change the world from the way in which it is presently constituted. If we accept that some competitors can be secure, at least within a set of activities against a range of opponents, then they must possess a motive other than fear to explain their hostile acts or threats. A state that can expand its territory at the expense of another state without fearing for its security acts on the basis of greed. After Yugoslavia had fallen apart, ethnic cleansing within the territories of Serbia and Croatia could be carried out with impunity. "During the major episodes of looting, particularly the three battles of Monrovia in 1990, 1992 and

1996, people from all over Liberia and even from neighboring countries headed for Monrovia to join in the action and to get something of value if they could, before returning home."[47] In neither of these cases did soldiers or thugs act because they were worried about the safety of their states or ethnic groups. Acting on greedy motives is within the power of a single party. There is no dilemma for either the bully or the victim.

In any particular case, a full analysis has to include consideration of whether greed, fear, or both are present. In other words, more must be done than simply inspecting state failures to determine if a security dilemma has occurred. Assessing threats or violence on the basis of two motives is a more sophisticated strategy than assuming the presence or absence of only one. But the situation is likely to be more complicated. Pure cases of fear or greed are probably rare. One or more parties may have mixed motives. If so, both fear and greed are present. The problem then becomes one of determining which predominates—if it is possible to tell. Alternatively, parties to the same relationship may have singular, but different, motives. What is greed for one may be fear for the other. The dynamics in the relationship can turn either one into the other. What starts out as greed may become fear or vice versa. Consequently, it is often more useful to conceive of these confrontations as iterative and as reciprocal relationships among rivals rather than as single encounters.

The motives for accumulating weapons or initiating hostilities will be mixed in most cases—either each party will have a different motive, or one or more parties will have both security and predatory motives.[48] Parties will have different motives whenever one actor senses that another has developed an interest in predation. Any intended victim will feel more insecure knowing that a rival is eyeing its resources greedily. This expectation does not constitute a security dilemma, however, so long as the predator feels secure. Victims of predation or the threat of predation fear their rivals but are not locked into a reciprocal relationship with them.[49]

Actors in failed states are likely to have both security and predatory motives much of the time. Indeed, the first preference for any actor rarely accounts for its complete preference ordering. Even if it does, the actor's rivals cannot be sure. Motives of groups and individuals within groups in most failed states are likely to be mixed because control of the government provides both the most assured protection and the greatest promise of jobs and wealth. Even though state control may provide only a relative advantage and often not a decisive one, as in Chad in the 1970s, Uganda in the 1980s, and Liberia in the 1990s, no group will feel secure while state authority remains outside its grasp. In addition, control of the state gives its ruler the opportunity for patronage to buy off opponents. At the same time, control of the state provides wealth for the ruling circle, jobs for members of its group, and loot for its militia, opportunities unmatched in poor states at least by any other economic options. In other words, the same prize arouses—and satisfies—both fear and greed.

To make matters more complex, leaders may be greedy while their followers are fearful. Instabilities within groups generated by this combination help explain the willingness of both to incur the enormous costs of hostilities. In the volatile situations accompanying state failure, politicians fearful of losing the support of their followers may "gamble for resurrection" through ethnic outbidding and arming their followers to improve their chances of retaining leadership.[50] Whether the perceptions of followers are mistaken or not, their support of aggressive leaders is rational and may be driven entirely by security, since the consequences could be disastrous for them and their families. Nevertheless, many among them will probably also hope for personal profit. The task of analysis is made more difficult because fearful and greedy parties rarely want to admit their motives. It is rational for both of them to dissemble—either to protect themselves from attack or to surprise their adversaries or victims.

When both motives are clearly involved in threats and confrontations, it may be possible to determine which is more important. In cases of state failure, the problem will be to determine which actors ended up with more potent resources. In general, if the parties are approximately equal in strength, the likely outcome will be a security dilemma. If they are dramatically unequal, an attack by the stronger party will probably be predatory, while an attack by the weaker party is more likely to be based on security motives. It will be harder to establish that fear and greed are operating independently because they tend to interact. Snyder and Jervis provide an ingenious example in which "predatory and security motives are both present and can be treated as equal and independent": agreement by a third party to ally militarily with either of two parties attacked by the other.[51]

On the other hand, even where motives are not mixed, it may be extremely difficult for opponents to determine which motive is important to an actor. Motives are especially hard to distinguish when it is impossible to tell the difference between offensive and defensive capabilities. The logic of the security dilemma depends on the ability of a potential rival to distinguish defensive from offensive weapons as well as to assess whether the balance of capabilities favors one or the other.[52] The distinction between defensive and offensive military capabilities applies to predation in the same way. Since strong defenses in themselves pose no threat to rivals, they reduce both fear and greed. A strong offensive arsenal increases the possibilities for greed by an actor just as much as it motivates fear in his rivals. But the weapons available to groups acting in conditions of state failure are more restricted than those acquired by states. Groups suddenly finding it necessary to arm themselves, particularly when impoverished states fail, buy cheap weapons—small arms such as grenades, land mines, and, particularly, light machine guns.[53] These weapons are equally appropriate for defensive or offensive purposes. No other actor can tell whether these weapons are intended for protection or aggression and thus, if prudent, will presume hostile intentions and prepare for them.

When either a state or a group in a failed state becomes an aggressor, it takes risks. If the predator learns that the victim could harm it, what started out as predation will have been a serious miscalculation, risking the security of the aggressor.[54] If the victim can respond by forging alliances with other potential victims, together they may be able to turn the tables on the aggressor. Predation, in other words, may metamorphose into a full-fledged security dilemma.

On the other hand, the difficulty in making commitments that are perceived as credible may impel actors in security dilemmas to strike first to ensure their self-protection, and that could lead to predation. Any party that thinks it is likely to be worse off later will not want to settle if it believes it can protect itself better by attacking now.[55] No stronger rival, particularly one that will gain a majority position in running the state if an agreement is made, can give a credible guarantee that it will not abandon its commitment later and exploit its rival, since any edge that it gains in control over the state may later become a decisive advantage.[56] Nevertheless, however persuasive the security argument for attacking first is for the weaker party, the prospect of material gain or additional territory will make its initiative all the more promising. The weaker party would not attack if it believed that it had no chance to better its position through confrontation. So, the only relevant cases concern disadvantaged actors that are not decisively weaker than their rivals. Even if escape from a security dilemma is the main reason why an actor chooses to strike, who could ever say that greed was not an additional motive, the one that pushed it over the top? Furthermore, if one party to a security dilemma makes a serious miscalculation, another may find that it can hold the first one to ransom. Security dilemmas, therefore, can mutate into predation.[57]

These shifts of motive in either direction suggest that most analyses should be presented as dynamic rather than static. If security dilemmas spiral, they are dynamic, and they must be understood to consist of multiple encounters. Predation can spiral too. Either it may set off counterpredation, or as the "Munich analogy" suggests, the absence of a vigorous response may lead the stronger power to additional rounds of predation. On the other hand, often a single encounter will be adequate to frame an analysis of either a security dilemma or violent predation. If the analyst is interested only in establishing the conditions that might cause each side to fear the other or one actor to prey on another, it may be sufficient to frame the threat or onset of hostilities as a single encounter.

For example, when Posen constructs security dilemmas from the breakup of Yugoslavia and the former Soviet Union, he does not consider whether any group might have predation as its motive. Nor does he investigate how each group responded to protective measures taken by the other. Instead, he explains the historical disputes and military resources that would plausibly cause each group to fear the other.[58] Consequently, his analysis is static, focusing on the prospects for a single violent encounter, rather than on a spiral of fear—or the prospects for escalating predation. On the other hand, if the point of the analysis is to explain why violence and brutality expand over time, it will be necessary to investigate how actors become locked into reciprocal and iterative relationships with their rivals, relationships that may eventually involve both security and predation, even if only one motive is apparent at the outset.

Laitin's account of why the Somali conflict was not resolved improves on Posen's analysis in two important respects. He considers competing arguments based on greed as opposed to fear, and his argument presumes that the antagonists engage in multiple encounters. He argues that a war of attrition provides a better explanation than a security dilemma for the continued spiral of group (or clan) violence.[59] In the Somali case, a war of attrition amounts to greed: "control over the state apparatus, however emasculated it may have become[,] . . . remains relatively remunerative as compared with other routes to wealth."[60] Nevertheless, rival Somali clans also engage in security dilemmas and therefore arm themselves—"a permanent condition of life in the Somali bush," exacerbated by the former president's highly uneven distribution of weapons.[61] These security dilemmas, Laitin insists, can explain clan leaders' vigilance and acquisition, but neither the continued spiraling of clan warfare, nor the inability of combatants to negotiate peace despite the likelihood that the costs of fighting exceed the state's declining value.[62] They continued to fight because they mutually misunderstood each other's resolve, though Laitin concedes that he has "no direct information on this point."[63] Lack of evidence makes his argument unconvincing, but in suggesting that predation provides an alternative explanation to one based on a security dilemma, he broadens the possibilities for analysis of violence in failed states.

Security dilemmas and predation may also have an unanticipated and rather surprising interaction. Predation can reduce a security dilemma, or even cause it to disappear. Recent research among some of the new states that emerged from the former Soviet Union shows that the levels of violence in their internal wars after the breakup have fallen dramatically.[64] In each of four civil wars in Azerbaijan, Georgia, and Moldova, the armies of the formal state were unable to defeat the forces cobbled together in regions intent on breaking away. The secessionists managed to create the de facto states of Nagorno-Karabakh, Abkhazia, South Ossetia, and Dnestr Moldova. But instead of recognizing these secessions as new sovereign states by reaching a formal settlement, officials on both sides developed an informal equilibrium. These opponents, now only nominally hostile, cooperated with each other so that both could acquire the material benefits from controlling scarcities in travel and trade that could continue only so long as separation was maintained. The incentives for shared greed led to reduced fear.

The most important conclusion that follows from this examination of security and predation is that neither motive can be ignored in analyzing state failure. In a few cases, one or the other may not be involved, but most of the time not only will both be, but their interaction may be essential to an explanation of the causes or the consequences of state failure and expanding violence. Because control of the state, or what is left of its apparatus after state failure, is usually the crucial resource for security and predation, it is extremely difficult if not impossible *even for the actors themselves* to disentangle fear from greed. If these two motives cannot be separated, however, it is impossible to explain hostilities in failed states as the consequences of security dilemmas alone—or of violent predation by itself.

No analysis that does not at least inspect for predation can make an adequate defense of the value of the security dilemma for explaining conditions in a failed state. In addition, if state failure is analyzed solely as a security dilemma, the consequences of a potential transformation into violent predation, or the other way around, would be overlooked. Finally, motives count because they can determine whether cooperation can be built.[65] Actors locked into a security dilemma want peace, while those intent on predation do not, even though it is frequently impossible to make the distinction in practice. However, if failed states are to be restored, bargaining will be an important tool. In arranging negotiations, it would be helpful to try to find out whether groups are motivated by fear or greed.

Conclusion

Security dilemmas and violent predation provide helpful explanations for the rapid growth of violence and its baffling ferocity during and after state failure. They offer plausible accounts for the individualized brutality that former friends and neighbors mete out to each other. In the recent literature, the security dilemma has been applied to the breakup of states, mostly without considering violent predation. There are significant problems in applying both explanations that these analyses have not considered at all. First, the logic of a security dilemma requires anarchy before it can function. Many approaches to explaining failed states do not presume anarchy, largely because they are interested in problems other than security dilemmas. A strong definition of a failed state centers on anarchy—the threat of it during the process of state failure and the fact of it afterward. In other words, state failure means that public authority collapses completely and that social norms do not successfully fill the gap.[66] Anarchy is not necessary for predation, though sustained violent predation indicates that public authority has declined or lost its effectiveness. The existence of anarchy, however, enables both security dilemmas and violent predation.

Tipping focuses attention on the conditions for the chain reaction that causes public authority to break down and violence rapidly to escalate during and after state failure. The tipping model elaborates the internal mechanism of the security dilemma—the reciprocal responses among individuals and groups who fear one another. It will not necessarily work in the same way for violent predation, because the latter does not require interaction between predator and victim. When applied to security dilemmas, the tipping model can incorporate independent greedy actors by recognizing their contribution to the mass of decisions that causes other contingent fearful actors to "pile on," setting off a chain reaction. The tipping model also helps to identify cases that depend on self-negating prophecies, in which individual or group decisions support public authority and prevent tipping.

Defining anarchy as the condition of state failure that enables security dilemmas raises the question of whether domestic anarchy functions in similar fashion to international anarchy. The two kinds of anarchy are not the same, since participants in domestic anarchy believe that it can be eliminated, while states in international anarchy expect to have to live with it. But this difference does not prevent fearful people from seeking out and arming groups that provide them with protection, any less than it prevents states from doing so. Since their responses are likely to induce parallel actions by their rivals, the differences in anarchy do not cause domestic security dilemmas to vary from their international counterparts.

When a security dilemma or continuing violent predation occurs, cultural animosities among individuals in that society are no longer sufficient in themselves to explain ensuing violence or even its threat. However, security dilemmas are constructed out of units that can act upon the fears of their members. States fulfill this criterion better than most social groups. Often analysts presume that security dilemmas naturally occur in failed states without demonstrating that the social groups on which they pin their arguments are sufficiently consolidated to play their appropriate roles. The nature of state failure may produce new and less accepted groups that supplant preexisting entities, or permit new illegitimate warlords with access to arms to replace culturally sanctioned leaders. If the breakdown of public authority is followed by the sudden formation of groups that have not worked out any broadly accepted cultural or organizational procedures, these groups may not function as coherent units capable of provoking potential rivals. Confusion and violence may be rampant. Individuals may fear for their property, their families, and their lives. But there will be no security dilemma. Analysts must demonstrate and not just presume that the groups which symbolize political opposition are so coherent that frightened individuals will flock to rival groups, strengthen their military capacities, and provoke others to do the same.

The trouble with the post–Cold War literature that uses the security dilemma to explain the prospect of violence or its horrific consequences in failed states is that it does not take greed into account as an alternative, an accompanying, or an interactive variable. There is no reason to assume a priori that all groups are equally insecure. Fear cannot explain the actions of secure competitors. Despite their conceptual differences, fear and greed are usually both involved, and, under certain circumstances, they may mutate into one another. It is particularly difficult to separate fear from greed when groups are fighting for control of the state apparatus during or after state failure. The spiral character of the security dilemma, echoed in cases of predation when one initiative results in a greedy response, suggests that a dynamic frame for investigation will often be more useful than one that is static. In addition, in some civil conflicts, the greed of leaders can dampen or even overcome the security dilemma, providing some relief, though continued frustration, for their followers.

"While the world as a whole . . . was sympathetic with our agony and willing to reach across vast distances to assist us, we the Somali people were not ready to help ourselves."[67] Why not? Why instead does the violence of failed states sometimes seem an inevitable response to the anxiety of groups seeking peace, while other times it appears to issue from avarice? It is important to identify specific cultural beliefs and recent histories that cause people to kill and brutalize others in their own societies, indeed in their own villages. But the unexpected and complex interactions of two universal human emotions, fear and greed, while posing many daunting analytic problems of their own, also provide important answers in cases of state failure. The challenge is to disentangle the distinctive contributions to specific threats and ensuing spirals of violence that result from the complicated interactions among individuals seized by one or more of these motives.

Notes

Robert Rotberg's perceptive suggestions on each draft of this chapter were especially useful. I would also like to thank Mia Bloom, Kanchan Chandra, David Laitin, Ian Lustick, Donald Rothchild, and Ken Sharpe for their comments. In addition, I benefited from comments from participants in the Failed States Project, in the Department of Politics Seminar, University of Reading, in the Working Groups' Seminar in International Relations and Comparative Politics, Department of Government, Dartmouth College, and in the "Bringing the Middle East Back In" workshop, Yale University.

1. Stephen Ellis, *The Mask of Anarchy: The Destruction of Liberia and the Religious Dimension of an African Civil War* (New York, 1999), 123.

2. Scott Peterson, *Me Against My Brother: At War in Somalia, Sudan, and Rwanda* (New York, 2000), 29.

3. Peter Maass, *Love Thy Neighbor: A Story of War* (New York, 1997), 6.

4. Ellis, *The Mask of Anarchy*, 132.

5. Robert Jervis, "Cooperation under the Security Dilemma," *World Politics*, XXX (1978), 167–214.

6. The first application was made by Barry R. Posen, "The Security Dilemma and Ethnic Conflict," in Michael E. Brown (ed.), *Ethnic Conflict and International Security* (Princeton, 1993), 103–24. See also, among others, David A. Lake and Donald Rothchild, "Spreading Fear: The Genesis of Transnational Ethnic Conflict," in Lake and Rothchild (eds.), *The International Spread of Ethnic Conflict: Fear, Diffusion, and Escalation* (Princeton, 1998), 3–32; Steven R. David, "Internal War: Causes and Cures," *World Politics*, XLIX (1997), 552–576; and Chaim Kaufmann, "Possible and Impossible Solutions to Ethnic Civil Wars," *International Security*, XX (1996) 136–175.

7. Charles L. Glaser, "The Security Dilemma Revisited," *World Politics*, L (1997), at 190–191.

8. Hans J. Morgenthau, *Politics among Nations: The Struggle for Power and Peace* (New York, 1978, 5th ed. rev.), 36. Only predation that threatens or causes violence is investigated in this chapter. I exclude other kinds of domestic predation involving corruption or regulatory policies intended to benefit particular individuals or groups. These frequently studied activities could be characterized as "peaceful" predation.

9. Paul Collier and Anke Hoeffler investigate the power of greed, as opposed to preexisting grievances, for explaining the initiation of civil conflict and conclude that greed is more important. They do not consider fear. "Greed and Grievance in Civil War," Policy Research Working Paper 2355, World Bank, Washington, D.C., 2001. For discussions that focus on the independent role of greed in shaping civil conflict, see the contributions to Mats Berdal and David M. Malone (eds.), *Greed and Grievance: Economic Agendas in Civil Wars* (Boulder, 2000).

10. Jack Snyder and Robert Jervis, "Civil War and the Security Dilemma," in Barbara F. Walter and Jack Snyder (eds.), *Civil Wars, Insecurity, and Intervention* (New York, 1999) 15–37; David D. Laitin, "Somalia: Civil War and International Intervention," in Walter and Snyder, *Civil Wars*, 146–180.

11. Jeffrey Herbst, "Responding to State Failure in Africa," *International Security*, XXI (1996/1997), 123, 136; Gerald B. Helman and Steven R. Ratner, "Saving Failed States," *Foreign Policy*, LXXXIX (1992), 18.

12. Jean-Germain Gros, "Towards a Taxonomy of Failed States in the New World Order: Decaying Somalia, Liberia, Rwanda and Haiti," *Third World Quarterly*, XVII (1996), 456–461.

13. Ibid., 468.

14. Aristide R. Zolberg, "The Specter of Anarchy: African States Verging on Dissolution," *Dissent*, XXXIX (1992), 303–311.

15. I. William Zartman, "Introduction: Posing the Problem of State Collapse," in Zartman (ed.), *Collapsed States: The Disintegration and Restoration of Legitimate Authority* (Boulder, 1995), 1.

16. Ibid., 1, 6.

17. Ibid., 8.

18. Posen, "The Security Dilemma and Ethnic Conflict," 103.

19. Ibid.

20. Snyder and Jervis, "Civil War and the Security Dilemma," 16–17; David, "Internal War," 558–59.

21. Situations will differ. It is an empirical question whether any social norms that can provide the basis for negotiations among groups survive state collapse.

22. Michael Ignatieff, "The Balkan Tragedy," *New York Review of Books*, 13 May 1993, 3, quoted in Russell Hardin, *One for All: The Logic of Group Conflict* (Princeton, 1995), 161.

23. This argument does not apply so persuasively to predation, because predation can occur when government is effective as well as when it disappears. As predation becomes more violent, the parallel is closer.

24. Not all states fail through tipping. Not all security dilemmas occur in states that fail, nor in states that fail through tipping. But when states tip into failure, the situation that they create is conducive to security dilemmas.

25. The model has been applied to epidemics of all sorts: the flu, AIDS, crime, dropping out of high school, teenage pregnancy, sudden spiking in the suicide rate, and fashion crazes. See Malcolm Gladwell, *The Tipping Point: How Little Things Can Make a Big Difference* (Boston, 2000); and Jonathan Crane, "The Epidemic Theory of Ghettos and Neighborhood Effects on Dropping Out and Teenage Childbearing," *American Journal of Sociology*, XCVI (1991), 1226–1259.

26. Thomas Schelling, *Micromotives and Macrobehavior* (New York, 1978), 101–102. Schelling adds two more characteristics that do not appear to be essential to the model. He asserts that "each group may be separately tipping out or tipping in." Since all groups may also be trying to get "in," that is, to control the same resource (for example, state sovereignty), or to get "out," that is, to flee from one another, the important point for the model is whether there is change rather than the direction of the change. In addition, Schelling claims that the change behavior involves "*being* someplace rather than *doing* something." It is not clear what this distinction adds to the model, since all change behavior necessarily involves "doing something." Neighborhood migration, the most famous application of the tipping model, is an obvious case that being someplace also means doing something.

27. Mark Granovetter, "Threshold Models of Collective Behavior," *American Journal of Sociology*, LXXXIII (1978), 1420.

28. Schelling, *Micromotives*, 97–98.

29. Differences in individual motives will not necessarily parallel differences in the rival groups or organizations that individuals join as they respond to state failure.

30. Schelling, *Micromotives*, 116–118.

31. Ibid., 118; emphasis in original.

32. Ibid., 119; emphasis in original.

33. David, "Internal War," 557.

34. Ibid., 560–561.

35. Snyder and Jervis, "Civil War and the Security Dilemma," 15.

36. There is a lively argument about whether Somali cultural norms survived the debacle. I later discuss this question briefly. So far, no internationally recognized new states have emerged within Somalia.

37. David, "Internal War," 554–555.

38. Ibid., 557. David attributes this expectation to neorealism, but there is nothing inherent in its assumptions that prevents close examination of groups.

39. Posen, "The Security Dilemma and Ethnic Conflict," 103.

40. For brief summaries of the different positions, see Donald L. Horowitz, *The Deadly Ethnic Riot* (Berkeley, Calif., 2001), 43–56; and Lake and Rothchild, "Spreading Fear," 5–7.

41. Nelson Kasfir, "Explaining Ethnic Political Participation," *World Politics*, XXXI (1979), 375–376.

42. Ibid., 378–385.

43. Ellis, *The Mask of Anarchy*, 66.

44. Among those who argue that warlords have abandoned the cultural framework are Terrence Lyons and Ahmed I. Samatar, *Somalia: State Collapse, Multilateral Intervention, and Strategies for Political Reconstruction* (Washington, D.C., 1995), 7–24; Daniel Compagnon, "Somali Armed Movements: The Interplay of Political Entrepreneurship and Clan-Based Factions," in Christopher Clapham (ed.), *African Guerrillas* (Oxford, 1999), 84; Laitin, "Somalia: Civil War and International Intervention," 149–150. The view that conflict in Somalia continues to follow segmentary lineage rules is presented most forcefully by Ioan Lewis. See, for example, Ioan Lewis and James Mayall, "Somalia," in Mayall (ed.), *The New Interventionism, 1991–1994: United Nations' Experience in Cambodia, Former Yugoslavia and Somalia* (Cambridge, 1996), 105–107; and Virginia Luling, "Come Back Somalia? Questioning a Collapsed State," *Third World Quarterly*, XVIII (1997), 291–295.

45. Ellis, *The Mask of Anarchy*, 94–109.

46. Ibid., 105.

47. Ibid., 124.

48. Snyder and Jervis, "Civil War and the Security Dilemma," 19–20.

49. One might argue that to the degree the victim can signal the aggressor not to try again, they have some sort of reciprocal relationship.

50. Rui J. P. de Figeriredo Jr. and Barry R. Weingast, "The Rationality of Fear: Political Opportunism and Ethnic Conflict," in Walter and Snyder (eds.), *Civil Wars*, 263–264.

51. Snyder and Jervis, "Civil War and the Security Dilemma," 20. Their example is taken from history—Bismarck's alliances with Russia and Austria. They misstate Bismarck's commitment, however. The more precise generalization is that the third party threat would apply to threats stemming from predatory or security motives whether either or both are present or equal in importance.

52. Jervis, "Cooperation under the Security Dilemma," 186–214.

53. Jeffrey Boutwell and Michael T. Klare, "A Scourge of Small Arms," *Scientific American*, CCLXXXII (June, 2000), 48–53.

54. Snyder and Jervis, "Civil War and the Security Dilemma," 21.

55. James D. Fearon, "Commitment Problems and the Spread of Ethnic Conflict," in Lake and Rothchild (eds.), *The International Spread of Ethnic Conflict*, 107–126.

56. Ibid., 118.

57. Snyder and Jervis argue the mutation of security dilemmas into predation differently. They assert that since future changes in the capability or intention of one's opponent cannot be ruled out, it is better to defect first if the relative gains will increase one's protection in the future. In other words, what starts out as a stag hunt becomes a prisoner's dilemma. The trouble with their argument is that the meaning of "exploitation" in a prisoner's dilemma is different from what it means in predation. In their use of the games of prisoner's dilemma and deadlock, they refer only to efforts an actor makes to improve his position in a security dilemma, or to escape from it entirely. But to account for a security dilemma's metamorphosis into predation, they have to show that the actor was motivated by material gain. See their account, "Civil War and the Security Dilemma," 21–22.

Of course, a first strike may produce both, and in my argument, an actor may intend to produce both or possibly to acquire additional resources solely as a hedge against its concerns for future security.

58. Posen, "The Security Dilemma and Ethnic Conflict," 111–119. In his theoretical discussion, Posen is more careful to recognize the dynamic character of security dilemmas. His article, however, was written soon after the breakups of both Yugoslavia and the Soviet Union, before either security dilemmas or predation had time to develop fully.

59. Laitin, "Somalia: Civil War and International Intervention," 151–160. Laitin adapts the notion of a war of attrition from biology (animals that fight over prey until one gives up) and economics (duopoly competition under conditions of declining demand). A war of attrition occurs when groups continue to fight even though the losses of at least one of them exceed the value of its potential success.

60. Ibid., 153, 158.

61. Ibid., 151.

62. Ibid., 152. The value of the Somali state declined as a consequence of continued fighting and of the disappearance of foreign aid after the Cold War ended.

63. Ibid., 159. Information failure, the notion that groups have incentives to misrepresent private information about themselves to protect their interests, provides a more parsimonious explanation of misunderstood resolve than the more elaborate apparatus of a war of attrition. See Lake and Rothchild, "Spreading Fear," 11–13, relying on work by James Fearon.

64. Charles King, "The Benefits of Ethnic War: Understanding Eurasia's Unrecognized States," *World Politics*, LIII (2001), 524–552.

65. Glaser, "The Security Dilemma Revisited," 191.

66. A task that is beyond the scope of this chapter would be to determine whether security dilemmas will occur and what they would look like during and after a state failure that does not completely meet the criterion of anarchy.

67. Mariam Arif Gassem, *Hostages: The People Who Kidnapped Themselves* (Nairobi, 1994), 112, quoted in Peterson, *Me Against My Brother*, 157.

Three

The Global-Local Politics of State Decay

CHRISTOPHER CLAPHAM

STATES ARE NOT unchanging features of the global political order. Neither the international system of states as we came to know it in the second half of the twentieth century, nor most of the individual states within it have any plausible claim to permanence. States have historically derived from various specific and by no means universally realized conditions, and the global political system has until recent times comprised areas under the control of states, areas regulated by other forms of governance, and areas with no stable governance at all. The idea that the state is a universal form of governance is of very recent origin, and rests on uncertain foundations. Any analysis of state decay, failure, and collapse in the modern era—and of the prospects for state resuscitation—therefore requires an appreciation of the role of statehood in the modern global system and of the increasing pressures to which this role has been subjected.

States are organizations capable of maintaining a monopoly of violence over a defined territory, and of controlling, to a significant extent, the interactions between that territory and the world beyond it. Their creation and survival thus depend both on their ability to secure the obedience of their populations and on their ability to extract resources—financial, military, and diplomatic—from the international system, two processes that are very closely linked. Since the idea of universal statehood—the conviction that the whole inhabited surface of the globe is and should remain divided among the territories of sovereign states—is itself the result of global developments, notably in the form of imperialism, the obvious place to start understanding the problem is with statehood and its decline at the global level. State decay, however, is equally the result of the inability of many states and societies at the local level to meet the onerous demands that state maintenance makes on them. Closely linked though the two levels are, any analysis of the global politics of state decay must therefore be complemented by looking at this process from below. Africa—as the region most affected by state failure and collapse—provides the most appropriate example.

Although the export of essentially European models of statehood to the rest of the world has gained considerable success, it has not proved to be universally achievable. While some states may fail for specific and remediable reasons, there are also cases where the essential conditions for viable statehood cannot plausibly be met. The analysis of international relations therefore now needs to come to terms with the reemergence of a once familiar kind of global order, in which zones of statehood have to coexist with zones of less settled governance. We need to work out the ways in which this coexistence is likely to operate best. The alternative project of attempting to restore universal statehood is chimerical.

The Rise of Universal Statehood

Look at any map of the world prior to the twentieth century, or indeed any map of Europe prior to the nineteenth century, and striking differences from an atlas of the modern world become apparent. Much of the inhabited world, certainly, is covered by states: territories with reasonably clear boundaries, which may be supposed to come under the ultimate control of a single central authority. Much of it comes under other kinds of jurisdiction, or various forms of "native" or "tribal" authority. There is often a great deal of what may be termed optimistic coloring: large areas over which some group or another claims a jurisdiction that it is quite unable to realize. Large areas, too, are just left blank.

States occur in a variety of forms and under a variety of circumstances. Tilly has analyzed the different kinds of states that emerged in Europe from the start of the second millennium onward, and he characterized the different mixtures of coercion and capital that went into their creation and maintenance.[1] States were by no means as common outside Europe as they were within it, but in most regions of the world discernible states existed. Some, like the Sokoto Caliphate or the Khanate of the Golden Horde, covered large and often sparsely inhabited areas, and resembled Tilly's extensive or coercive states. Others, such as the emirate of Harar in what is now eastern Ethiopia, maintained intensive control over small areas and sustained themselves by extracting surpluses from international trade. Others again, like Ethiopia, Thailand, or China, rested essentially on the control and exploitation of fairly dense peasant populations, and most closely resembled the territorial nation-states that eventually attained dominance in Europe. The major difference, in very broad terms, between European states and those elsewhere was that European states were generally contiguous to one another and were therefore intensely concerned with protecting their territoriality through the definition and hardening of their frontiers; in much of the rest of the world, states were not contiguous, and islands of statehood existed within seas of sparsely inhabited and feebly administered territory. Whereas European states defined fixed frontiers (and established their internal identities) by reference to their neighbors and rivals, non-European states were generally constituted by reference to a core, beyond which the central authority was gradually diluted as it extended into peripheral areas subject to its nominal sovereignty or occasional raids.[2]

The idea that the whole world *ought* to be divided among states exercising full authority over their territories and populations dates only from the era of European colonialism and, in turn, from the creation of a global economy in which statehood was regarded as necessary to secure and regulate access to resources in hitherto inaccessible or uncontrolled areas. In a few cases, such as Thailand or Ethiopia, existing non-European states were sufficiently strong or diplomatically agile to secure their admission to the new universal state system, and generally took advantage of that status in order to extend their control over previously quasi-independent peripheries (a process that created problems of its own).

Elsewhere—in all of the Americas and Oceania, almost all of Africa, and roughly half of Asia—European states just assumed power. This resulted in the creation of a kind of state radically different from any that had existed before: a state whose territory, boundaries, and structure of government, and to a large extent economy and sometimes even population, were imposed and organized from outside. Sometimes, as in Rwanda or Burma, this process involved a superimposition of external authority on previously existing units. It also meant a hardening of the state—in terms of fixed frontiers, citizenship rules, and hierarchical structures of government—in ways that could create damaging tensions between the old form of state and the new. Sometimes, as in the Americas, the importing of a new population, and the destruction or complete suppression of the old, meant that states could effectively be transplanted into a new environment. But very often, the project of universal statehood resulted in the creation of "new states," covering areas and encompassing populations that had never previously come under the control of any single state, and that in many cases had never previously been controlled by any form of state at all. The "problem" of "failed states" is most basically about whether the "grafting" of such states (in Bayart's well-chosen phrase) onto unpromising rootstock can be made to take—even with the various kinds of fertilizer provided by the international system in the form of universalist ideologies, incorporation into the global economy, and the provision of diplomatic and military support.[3]

The Statist Ideal and Its Decline

The imposition of statehood as a global norm coincided, unsurprisingly, with the heyday of statehood within the European territories from which this new ideal derived. From its sixteenth- and seventeenth-century origins—in the experience of the Reformation, the theories of Bodin and Hobbes, and its incorporation into a set of international rules by the treaties of Westphalia—through to its apogee in the "totalitarian" states of the first half of the twentieth century, the idea developed that there was nothing that states could not do.[4] This conception of the state as an omnipotent and modern organizational technology, greatly enhanced in the nineteenth century by nationalism and industrialization, led to the development of state ideologies, state economies, and cradle-to-grave state social services. Though fascism ranks as the ultimate form of statist ideology, the state economy (in the form of command planning) and the statist organizational technology (in the form, notably, of the Leninist vanguard party) reached their peaks, ironically, under the guise of an ideology that ostensibly relegated states to temporary superstructural expressions of economic forces. In the new developmental orthodoxy, this relationship was reversed, and the creation of a modern economy became a dependent variable, conditioned on the prior existence of an effective state.

This idea of statehood readily fostered the assumptions that states provided the only legitimate and acceptable form of rule, and that all of the world's people, and all of its territory, therefore had to fall under the control of a designated state. It followed that where states did not exist already, in a form that corresponded to European conceptions of statehood, established states were entitled to incorporate the areas and peoples concerned into their own national territories, in the process destroying many previously existing states (along with numerous alternative forms of political organization), which were unable to defend themselves against European conquest. As colonialism ebbed, so the ideologies, territories and organizations that it left behind provided the basis from which new leaders of new states could promote their own statist pretensions. Anticolonial nationalism neatly combined opposition to the existing colonial rulers with adoption of the principles of governance derived from those rulers. In turn, that joint posture enabled newly independent states to gain an accepted and indeed protected place in the international order. The idea that powerful states provided the essential precondition for effective economic development was particularly welcome. With it, too, came the enthusiastic adoption of those devices through which statehood had been consolidated in its European heartland, ranging from national anthems at one end of the scale, to central planning and single-party regimes with totalitarian aspirations, at the other.

Previously dominant ideologies were adapted in order to enable postcolonial states to gain acceptability, and to encourage their leaders to believe that they, too, could achieve nation-statehood in its most developed form. One example, admirably explored by Jackson, was the alteration in the definition of statehood that was required for admission to the international system in order to enable almost any designated territory to "count" as a state for international purposes, regardless of its inability to meet hitherto established criteria for statehood.[5] Indeed, the resolutely statist biases of international relations theory can likewise be regarded as providing ideological underpinning for the international acceptability of a large number of political organizations that were able to describe themselves as states.

A related range of adaptations took place in the conception of "nationhood," which from the nineteenth century had come to be regarded as an inherent component of statehood. Whereas earlier "primordialist" ideologies of nationalism had claimed that nations derived from deep underlying cultural and linguistic identities (thus legitimizing the emergence of new states in Europe, from the "unification" of Germany and Italy in the mid-nineteenth century through to the carve-up of central and eastern Europe in 1919), new "constructivist" theories argued that "nations" could be created from almost any collection of available social materials through the purposive use of state power.[6] The Stalinist theory of nationalities, which argued that different cultural collectivities could continue to coexist, without in any way derogating from the power of the state, also found some adherents in states where unitary nationhood appeared to be beyond the range of plausibility.

The significance of decolonization continues to be intensely contested, and these debates resonate into the arena of statehood and the international system. On the one hand, what might be described as the conventional reading represents decolonization as the universalization of statehood, and with it, of nationhood: the spread of the ideology of the nation-state from its European origins throughout the world, and the establishment of statehood as the basis for global order. The rapid rise in the numbers of states in the international system, following decolonization and the end of the Cold War, may be regarded as demonstrating the continuing vitality of nation-statehood as the ultimate expression of political identity. In an alternative reading, however, decolonization and the collapse of empire (the Soviet Union included) may be regarded not as a nationalist triumph but as an imperial withdrawal. Colonial powers withdrew from empire because they were not prepared, and did not need, to pay the costs of maintaining it. This decision in turn derived from the recognition that they no longer required the raw materials that colonies provided; they did not need to maintain physical control over territory to retain access to these raw materials; and their economic development depended much more on fostering their relations with one another (through such mechanisms as the European Union) than on continuing to occupy outlying areas of no longer relevant territory. In this reading, only old-fashioned and underdeveloped imperial powers, such as Portugal and the Soviet Union, needed imperialism any longer. Where viable states could be maintained in the formal colonial territories, so much the better; but decolonization represented not the apotheosis of statehood, but its decline. Whereas the era of state supremacy was marked by a steady *diminution* in the number of states, as powerful states in true realist fashion gobbled up weak ones, so the expansion in state numbers represents a decline in the importance of the state itself.

Although many viable postcolonial states continue, the evident costs of forming states, and the declining interest of existing states in maintaining control over their previous territories, have done much to shatter the idea of statehood as a *universal* form of political organization. There are now significant areas of the world in which the existence of a state is little more than a pretense, maintained by the international system because it lacks any intellectual or legal framework other than statehood through which to understand and cope with developments on the ground. Legal fictions are of course a commonplace, in both domestic and international law, but they need to be recognized for what they are.

Simultaneously, the state and the ideologies that sustained it have declined in the developed industrial world from which they originally derived. After World War II, only the superpowers were able to assure their own security without engaging in sovereignty-sapping alliances, and even the superpowers needed such alliances to maintain a bloc of like-minded states to sustain their superpower aspirations. The idea that individual states could manage their own economies without constant deference to external factors failed to survive the upheavals of the 1970s, and gave way to global economic liberalism. The centrally planned economy proved, behind its impressive façade, to be a device of extraordinary effectiveness for promoting poverty, alienation, and environmental destruction. In the 1990s, even the social security systems of developed industrial states have turned out to be both unsustainable in the light of global competition and penetration, and incapable of achieving the welfare goals that were promised in the two or three decades after 1945. The ignominious collapse of Soviet-style communism represented an all-in-one version of the decline in state effectiveness that had taken place over a longer period and in less spectacular fashion among the capitalist states of the West.[7]

A plausible case can be made that state failure and collapse have been hastened and intensified by overambitious attempts to impose on societies a level of state control that they were ultimately unable to bear. The clearest example is the former Soviet Union, where the systematic imposition over more than seventy years of a peculiarly intense system of centralized political and economic management massively contributed to a pervasive loss of legitimacy, which resulted—at the instant that the Communist Party of the Soviet Union crumbled—in the fragmentation of the state itself into fifteen different pieces, many of which had further problems of internal management. Postcolonial states, in which colonial regimes with limited functions and ambitions were replaced by independent governments with far-reaching projects for social and economic transformation, were likewise ill-equipped for the demands made on them. In both Ghana and Uganda, for example, relatively wealthy and manageable states with highly qualified civil services were brought close to collapse as a result of the transformations attempted by Presidents Kwame Nkrumah and A. Milton Obote, and of the political instability that followed their inevitable failures.

Ideologies of state power were unsurprisingly at their most intense in states where popular participation in the political process was most rigorously controlled or suppressed. Whatever the formal commitment to democracy, these states were inhabited by subjects, not citizens, whose role was to be molded to the shape designed by their rulers. Although it could readily be argued that participatory democracy would strengthen the state, by according it a legitimacy that it had previously lacked, this argument presupposed that the existing structure of the state either met, or could be adapted without much difficulty to fit, the aspirations of its people. Where the state was structurally incapable of meeting these aspirations, the explosion in participation that followed the end of empire, and still more the end of the Cold War, could only weaken it.

In different ways around the world—in the Soviet-style communist, developing world, and even Western capitalist states—governments have had to come to terms with the discovery that the state is not an all-powerful technology through which they can mold their peoples and economies to their own wishes. Rather, it is a structure of management and control that is awkwardly and sometimes precariously posed between the people whom it tries to manage and the international setting in which it has to exist. This discovery was always likely to bear hardest on those states that were in any event least well adapted both to their own societies and to their international setting. Though many of the arguments may be expected to apply to other areas of the world in which the social basis of states is weak, the peculiarities of the African situation as well as the concentration on the continent of a high proportion of the world's failed or collapsed states make a regional focus appropriate.

Tropical Africa: Indigenous Contexts of Statehood and Decay

In comparison with any other region of the colonized world, tropical Africa was always likely to face especially difficult problems of state construction. For a start, the bases for state creation in *precolonial* tropical Africa were for the most part peculiarly feeble. Though many of the problems of African state formation derive from the distinctive nature of the continent's colonial experience, the deeper sources of state decay go back much further than colonialism. The population of the continent was sparse, and concentrated in a very limited number of locations—parts of the West African forest and savannah, the Ethiopian highlands, the Great Lakes, the southern highlands—which unsurprisingly corresponded to the major zones of statehood. Communications were poor, diseases of both humans and animals were rife, and opportunities to profit from long-distance trade (always a significant element in the development of states) were slight, save for parts of eastern Africa and the trans-Saharan caravan trade, until European contacts also opened up trading opportunities with the West African coast, largely in the form of the slave trade. As a result, state formation was discontinuous, with only the Great Lakes region and parts of West Africa providing any significant zones of contiguous statehood. The kinds of state that emerged also varied considerably, from relatively permanent political organizations based on peasant cultivation, through small trading city-states with their immediate hinterlands, to military conquest states of which the most impressive in terms of their capacity for social transformation were probably the Zulu empire and the Sokoto caliphate. In some areas, most spectacularly in the Great Lakes and highland Ethiopia, it nonetheless proved possible to sustain reasonably effective states over substantial periods of time, and in the process to build social structures and values that favored deference to authority. These structures and values were to prove enormously significant in the postcolonial period.

In much of Africa, it was necessary to maintain minimal levels of social cohesion by whatever mechanisms were available to poor and fragmented societies, in which the surpluses necessary to support states could be accumulated neither from taxing indigenous production nor from tariffs on long-distance trade. Two mechanisms that acquired considerable significance under these conditions were extended family relationships and the forms of spiritual authority and control that were readily categorized by Western observers as "witchcraft."[8] These localized and particularistic means of maintaining social order were difficult to incorporate into Westernized state structures, despite attempts to do so through the ascription of spiritual powers to autocratic leaders.[9] As a result, over very large areas of Africa, the idea of a "state" derives only from the imposition of colonial rule and is inevitably associated with the decidedly mixed blessings of European conquest and the subsequent transfer of "modernity" in its manifold forms.

The period of quasi-statehood in Jackson's account that came after independence may accordingly be seen as an attempt to build African states on the foundations provided by colonialism, in collaboration with a supportive international system. This attempt was by no means uniformly unsuccessful, and it should not be dismissed. There were certainly cases in which it worked relatively well, and may indeed have provided the basis for the long-term development of viable states. A significant element of "banal nationalism" derived from the experience of living together, and from exposure to common colonially derived experiences such as the creation of a lingua franca, an educational system, and structures of administration. The "nation-building" pretensions of early leaders were not entirely fraudulent or ineffectual. The point is not that this project worked *nowhere*, but that it could not be expected to work *everywhere*.

A familiar weakness of African state formation was the very uneven fit between such indigenous bases for statehood as the continent possessed and the imposed structures of colonial rule. The grafting process to which I have already referred was thoroughly inadequate both spatially and temporally. Spatially, the continent was divided between colonial territories that broadly corresponded to precolonial states (Rwanda, Lesotho), territories in which a "core" state or group of states was incorporated into a much larger area (Ghana, Uganda), and territories in which precolonial state traditions were either subordinated or nonexistent.[10] In historical terms, the whole process was so brief (little more than sixty years in many cases) that the level of penetration of external "governmentalities" (to adopt a term from Foucault that Bayart has usefully applied to Africa) into the domestic society was necessarily shallow.[11] Whatever the changes in institutional structures that colonialism imposed, the social attitudes that Africans brought to these structures could only be expected to reflect their own long histories rather than the matching values that (through Christianity and education) the new rulers sought to inculcate.

The central domestic problems of state formation in much of tropical Africa have thus been ones of *political culture* and notably the difficulty of adapting cultures deeply attuned to their own environments to the very different challenges involved in managing states of the kind that were imposed on the continent through colonialism. Culture is both a pervasive and an evasive feature of human societies. It comprises a complex of elements, constituted through such variables as the physical environment, language, religion, family structure, and shared experience and historical memory, which cannot be broken apart analytically into their separate sections because their impact is created precisely by the way in which they fit together. Nor are cultures fixed and static. While some elements of culture can change astonishingly quickly, others appear to be remarkably resistant to change—none more so than the complex of values concerned with the exercise and recognition of authority. Shifting, amorphous, and unpredictable though political cultures may be, they are central to the dilemmas of African states.

If we look at the process of state formation—not, as is commonly done, from the viewpoint of the colonialists and their successors who were concerned to create states, but rather from the viewpoint of the indigenous peoples on whom states were imposed—this process can readily be seen to have brought with it very significant *costs*, in social, economic, and political terms. The state-centered and state-supporting literature of political science has been so heavily concerned with emphasizing the *benefits* of statehood that the other side of the account has gone almost unnoticed. Many of these costs, moreover, were paid so long ago in most developed industrial societies that we have forgotten how heavy they often were; the very success of these societies in meeting such costs has encouraged us to assume that they can everywhere be met with the same success. But even if they can eventually be met throughout the world, there is plenty of evidence to suggest that they cannot always be met yet.

The social costs of statehood, and particularly of modern statehood, include the sacrifice of identities and structures that are inimical to the hierarchies of control that states seek to impose. While effective states do not *require* that all (or by far the greater part) of their populations should share a common sense of identity, they are unquestionably greatly strengthened if this condition is met. Ethnically diverse states have been made to work under certain conditions, as in the Habsburg and Ottoman empires, but these states (even, or perhaps especially, in Europe) eventually proved incapable of coping with the demands made on them by mass political participation. The constitutionalist mechanisms—such as federal arrangements and legally guaranteed rights—through which modern political engineers have attempted to reconcile statehood with ethnic diversity themselves depend on the shared social values that are needed to uphold the constitutionalist ideal. Often, such mechanisms are tacitly reliant on the hegemonic power of one particular ethnic group or institutional elite to keep the others in order and to preserve the façade of constitutionalism. Once the Communist Party of the Soviet Union collapsed, for instance, the elaborate apparatus of national self-government within the U.S.S.R., and indeed the U.S.S.R. itself, went with it.

But states require more than a broad measure of social homogeneity. They also require people to have the right *kind* of society—a society in which state authority is both exercised reasonably impartially by those in power and accepted by the governed. Universalist conceptions of statehood take it for granted that political authority can ultimately be created by state power imposed from the top. A very plausible argument can nonetheless be made that it depends as much on values deriving from the society, which in Africa are deeply embedded in modes of production and social relationships that long predate colonial rule. Somalia provides a classic example: despite having one of the very few ethnically homogeneous societies in Africa, it was incapable of generating forms of social power capable of holding together a society characterized both by intense individualism and by damaging clan divisions. Somali individualism—perfectly expressed in the proverb "every man his own sultan"—is ideally adapted to the need for survival in a rugged and sparsely inhabited territory, where alliances can be only temporary and those who cannot look after themselves (and their women, and their animals) do not make it. This individualism is, along with pastoralism and the manifest physical problems of ruling an area such as Somalia, particularly ill adapted to the demands of settled governance.

In short, continuities of the kind that Putnam has identified in the societies of northern and southern Italy can be replicated in Africa, and it comes as no surprise to discover that those African societies that have been best able to support effective statehood are those with a history of state formation and maintenance going back well before the era of colonial rule.[12] Somalia and Rwanda, often cited as comparable examples of state breakdown in Africa, are actually complete opposites. Whereas state breakdown did take place in Somalia from 1991 onward, Rwanda at the time of the genocide in 1994 showed an astonishing level of discipline, on the part both of the genocidal National Republican Movement for Democracy and Development (MRNDD) regime and of its Rwanda Patriotic Front (RPF) opponents; and a rapid transfer of state power from one regime to another, which, despite the traumatic circumstances of the genocide, was marked by only the briefest period of intervening anarchy. The killing in Rwanda was overwhelmingly carried out by disciplined forces under the control of the state.

The comparison between Rwanda and Somalia is an example of a much more general phenomenon. Broadly speaking, high population density and the constraints on behavior that it imposes provide the best predictor for the development of political authority, and hence the emergence of states. Specifically, those areas of Africa that maintained reasonably settled and effective state structures during the period prior to colonialism are proving best able to do so as the institutional legacies of colonialism fade. Insurgent or guerrilla movements, as the most striking mechanism for creating structures of control outside the postcolonial framework, illustrate this process with particular clarity. Whereas insurgent movements that derived from societies without a precolonial tradition of statehood—

not just in Somalia, but in northern Uganda, southern Sudan, Liberia, and Sierra Leone—have had the greatest difficulty in establishing effective political structures, those in societies with such a tradition—as in southern Uganda, northern Ethiopia, and Eritrea—have been able to set up effective structures of government, even amid the chaos resulting from the defeat of their incumbent rivals.[13] In short, some societies possess the traditional political culture required to sustain states, whereas in others such a culture is weak or almost completely lacking.

Even those parts of Africa that had well-developed precolonial traditions of statehood, however, could not always readily carry them into the modern era. Where states did exist in precolonial Africa, they had often been constructed on a highly discriminatory basis—nowhere more so than in Rwanda and Burundi. There the state was "owned" by one section of its population, at the expense of others. Demands for political participation, characteristic of the late colonial era, rapidly exposed the fractures within the social base on which they had been erected. Such states as Ethiopia and Liberia, which formed from the imposition of the power of a core political community over peripheral peoples, suffered from analogous strains.

States are likewise affected by their neighbors, as the weakening of central control within one state leads to the flight of refugees and the formation of insurgent movements, and as external intervention from across a frontier spreads the infection further. State decay in much of Africa—in the Horn, the Great Lakes, southern Africa, and Liberia/Sierra Leone—has been a regional problem. The weakening of the commitment to nonintervention in the internal affairs of other states has both followed from state failure and further undermined states in its turn. This, too, may be regarded as the modern form of a much older phenomenon—the noncontiguity of African states. Whereas in Europe, the state system was greatly strengthened (even if individual states were threatened) by the maintenance of a network of states with clear boundaries and well-controlled populations, in Africa, states were generally surrounded by more weakly governed areas, an instability that could threaten the state itself.

The relationship between statehood and economic resources, which might well have been expected to be positive, has in practice been subordinated to the impact of the *social* resources required for effective economic management. What matters, in short, is *not* states' access to a given level of wealth, which would in turn generate a higher level of legitimacy for state institutions and create among dominant classes a set of shared incentives in the maintenance of the economic system that assured their welfare, but whether governments and the societies that sustain them are capable of creating, from their own resources, the levels of authority that are needed to maintain basic structures of production. If they are to generate continuous development, states must provide the social, legal, and political institutions that are now widely regarded as essential; but these institutions require the support of underlying social practices and values. Economic performance is the dependent variable, political culture the independent one.

Africa, indeed, has many economically well-endowed states that have spectacularly failed to achieve the levels of development that their resources might have led one to expect. The diamond economies of Sierra Leone and Angola provide the most striking cases of failure, and the economic performance of Africa's principal oil-exporting countries has proved almost without exception to be dismal. Botswana, like Sierra Leone and Angola, was plentifully supplied with diamonds, but unlike them was able to use its diamond revenues as a base from which to build by far the most consistently successful economy in Africa. This dramatic contrast resulted not only from the vastly more capable initial leadership and political and governmental structures that Botswana was able to maintain, but also from the underlying social values rooted in the relatively homogeneous Tswana society that enabled those structures to operate. Economic success without the development of corresponding political institutions is likely to be short lived. Liberia was, for a period, one of the fastest growing economies in the world, until its wealth crumbled as a result of leadership failures and complete political breakdown.

The reasons for this reverse correlation between natural resources and political stability are to be found in the relationship between rentier statehood, neopatrimonialism, and bad governance. The weak social basis of African states had to be compensated for, by "buying" political allegiance through a great variety of clientelist or neopatrimonial mechanisms, which became increasingly difficult to sustain, and the failure of which further undermined support for the state. Certainly, poor economic policies and corruption exacerbated the problem, but the root causes were structural rather than merely the result of individual cupidity and policy failure. Corruption is far more plausibly analyzed as a systemic problem that arises from the societies in which it occurs than as the mere incidence of individual wrongdoing.[14] African states also depended on a revenue base that was highly reliant on a small number of primary products, often with wildly fluctuating prices, and their attempts to squeeze enough of a surplus out of the productive areas of the economy to sustain their own activities only resulted in the depression of the productive base itself. The imposition of economic reforms by international financial institutions, under the title of structural adjustment, had the short-term effect of still further depressing state revenues, while only very partially increasing the underlying level of production.

The classic patrimonial route to state collapse is illustrated by the examples of Congo/Zaire, Liberia, Sierra Leone, and Somalia. In each case, a minimal level of political loyalty could be maintained only by constructing fragile coalitions that required a delicate balance between bribery and force. As the available resources shrank—from a combination of basic economic weakness and dependence, poor management, and the consequences of patrimonialism itself—the balance became harder to maintain, and the resort to force became more compelling. The demands of leadership survival in turn involved the deliberate subversion of the institutional basis of the state and its provision of public goods, in a way that has been most clearly analyzed by Reno for Sierra Leone, but was replicated in Congo, Liberia, and Somalia.[15] This subversion led to the withdrawal of the regime's remaining external support and to the eventual formation of insurgencies that scarcely needed to destroy the state, because it had destroyed itself already. Zimbabwe—basically a very strong state—has followed the same downward spiral.

Once the spiral starts downward, the *political* costs of statehood may become unacceptably high. Though states are commonly characterized as organizations that bring benefits to their people, on occasion—not least in modern Africa—they have evidently been much more a source of suffering. And while it is likewise readily assumed that such suffering—in the form, for example, of the imposition of government on rebellious peasants—is part of the historic price that has to be paid for the creation of ultimately beneficial state institutions, in modern Africa it has often proved to be politically counterproductive. Sheer bad governance has been at the root of many of Africa's insurgencies. While a few of these (as in Uganda) resulted in the establishment of more effective regimes than those that they overthrew, in other cases (such as Liberia or Somalia, and very probably the DRC) they destroyed or at least badly undermined the basis for any kind of government at all. Political violence in Africa has rarely achieved the state-creating goals of a Henry VIII or a Louis XIV; much more often it has been state-destroying.[16]

Given the success of warfare in helping to create effective states in Europe, its failure to do so in Africa demands more than the cursory examination that can be given here.[17] The forty years or so of postindependence African experience permit no overview remotely comparable to that which Tilly was able to derive from a millennium of European history. The wars in central Africa, centered on the DRC, may, for example, turn out with hindsight to have had some state-creating rationale that is at present hard to discern. More broadly, we may be looking at the historically inevitable crumbling of a postcolonial system, the destruction of which forms a necessary prelude to the creation of new political structures on an indigenous base. Whatever may be said about the politics of warlordism as it is developing in African conflict zones, however, the kinds of political authority that it creates are very far from the models of statehood that external actors are attempting to promote in Africa.

Even the support of the international system, which has been a key element in maintaining African states, may become counterproductive. The ready assumption of the Cold War period that each superpower needed to sustain its allies, often by military means, helped to foster a level of militarization that, far from sustaining states, ultimately helped to undermine them. Weapons escaped from the control of the governments to which they were supplied—by capture from government forces by insurgents within the state concerned, or as a result of the support given by states to opposition movements across their frontiers—and were used against states, rather than for them. Governments like those of Mengistu Haile Mariam in Ethiopia, or Mobutu Sese Seko in Zaire, were encouraged by the availability of externally supplied armaments to assume that opposition could be dealt with by force, rather than by political compromise. Nor have the changed external priorities of the post–Cold War period always enabled African states to reconstitute themselves on the basis of political compromise, multiparty democracy, and respect for human rights. The experience of externally mediated state-rebuilding has been at best an extremely mixed one: for every case that has appeared to "work" (with Mozambique as the most striking example), there have been several others that have spectacularly failed.

The relationship between the identifiable causes of state collapse and its actual incidence is by no means linear. Insofar as it is possible to hypothesize about cases in which state collapse occurs and ones in which it does not, however, the most plausible guide appears to be provided by the precolonial experience of statehood. Regions such as southern Uganda, Rwanda, southern Ghana, and northern Ethiopia, which sustained effective states in the precolonial period, have proved far better able to survive the experience of bad government than regions in which political authority was constructed in different ways. Since, as already noted, regions of effective precolonial statehood in Africa occupy only a relatively small part of the continent's surface (though accounting for a much higher proportion of its people), this rough-and-ready guide leaves much of the continent at risk.

Conclusion

This chapter does not seek to suggest that state failure is exclusively determined by structural factors, nor that "fixing failed states" is necessarily a futile and fruitless quest. Just as failure has often been exacerbated, and in some cases may plausibly be reckoned to have been caused, by human agency, so mayhem can undoubtedly be reduced, if not in every case prevented, by well-crafted intervention designed not only to strengthen states, but to enable them to meet the human needs that must ultimately justify their existence. But the lesson of this chapter—and the charge that it presents to later contributions to this volume concerned with state resuscitation—is that the state is itself the product of circumstances over which individuals have at best only limited control. The demands of social engineering on which the project of universal statehood rests have been shown in recent times to have been greatly exaggerated and even counterproductive; there may well be circumstances, both in Africa and elsewhere, in which the state as we have come to conceive it may be beyond plausible hope of rescue, and in which other avenues for the pursuit of human welfare—or the avoidance of harm—must be pursued. A considerable measure of modesty is in order.

Notes

1. Charles Tilly, *Coercion, Capital and European States,* A.D. 990–1990 (Oxford, 1990).

2. This difference is illustrated, by reference to Western Europe and Africa, in Jeffrey Herbst, *States and Power in Africa* (Princeton, 2000), 40–49.

3. Jean-François Bayart, *La greffe de l'état* (Paris, 1996).

4. Jean Bodin (ed. Julian H. Franklin), *On Sovereignty* (Cambridge, 1992); Thomas Hobbes (ed. Richard Tuck), *Leviathan or the Matter, Form, and Power of a Commonwealth, Ecclesiastical and Civil* (Cambridge, 1991).

5. See Robert H. Jackson, *Quasi-states: Sovereignty, International Relations and the Third World* (Cambridge, 1990).

6. "Constructivist" theories of nationalism have been propagated especially in Benedict Anderson, *Imagined Communities: Reflections on the Origin and Spread of Nationalism* (London, 1983); Eric J. Hobsbawm, *Nations and Nationalism since 1780* (Cambridge, 1990). For a critique, see Adrian Hastings, *The Construction of Nationhood: Ethnicity, Religion and Nationalism* (Cambridge, 1997).

7. For a recent grand overview of this process, see Martin van Creveld, *The Rise and Decline of the State* (Cambridge, 1999).

8. I owe much here to John Iliffe's general history of the continent, *Africans: The History of a Continent* (Cambridge, 1995). For the significance of spiritual authority, and the forms that this has taken in postcolonial Africa, see especially Stephen Ellis, *The Mask of Anarchy: The Destruction of Liberia and the Religious Dimension of an African Civil War* (London, 1999); Stephen Ellis and Gerrie Ter Haar, "Religion and Politics in Sub-Saharan Africa," *Journal of Modern African Studies,* XXXVI (1998), 175–201.

9. The exploitation by former President Mobutu of Congo / Zaire of the leopard cult prevalent in the Congo basin rainforest provides a classic example.

10. Herbst has examined the significance of alternative geographies that were more or less favorable to state maintenance (*States and Power in Africa*, 139–172).

11. It is only fair to point out that Africanists differ markedly in their characterization of the colonial period: some ascribe to it a central significance (notably in accounting for the various ills to which Africa has been subject since independence), and others regard it as a relatively brief interlude that could do little to alter the fundamental structures and values of African societies. In opting fairly sharply for the second of these approaches, I may well have been affected by my major country of specialization, Ethiopia, in which the historical continuities are particularly striking and the impact of colonialism has been exceptionally slight.

12. See Robert D. Putnam, *Making Democracy Work: Civil Traditions in Modern Italy* (Princeton, 1992).

13. I have edited a collection of studies of African insurgencies that bring out this point very clearly. See Clapham, *African Guerrillas* (Oxford, 1998).

14. See J. P. Olivier de Sardan, "A Moral Economy of Corruption in Africa?" *Journal of Modern African Studies*, XXXVII (1999), 25–52.

15. I have examined the narratives of state failure in Sierra Leone in Clapham, "Effondrement de l'État et tentatives de reconstruction en Sierra Leone : Le jeu politique du local et du global," *Afrique Contemporaine*, (2001), 177–191.

16. This point bears on the arguments made in Edward N. Luttwak, "Give War a Chance," *Foreign Affairs*, LXXVIII (1999), 36–44. Although I share much of Luttwak's skepticism about external attempts at conflict resolution, I am far from convinced that warfare can actually produce more viable states in areas where the conditions for state formation are weak.

17. I have attempted an explanation for two of the African states in which the linkage between warfare and state formation appears to be strongest in Clapham, "Guerre et construction de l'état dans la Corne de l'Afrique," *Critique Internationale*, IX (2000), 93–111.

Four

The Economic Correlates of State Failure

TAXES, FOREIGN AID, AND POLICIES

NICOLAS VAN DE WALLE

> Every age constructs its . . . own types of war.

IN THIS CHAPTER I examine the economic factors that predispose states to fail and/or to fall prey to serious internal conflict. As was made clear by Rotberg in the first chapter of this volume, the general term of state failure covers several distinct modes of political decay. It is possible to distinguish two sets of political-economy dynamics that lead to two distinct types of state failure: a first mode in which struggles over a viable state apparatus fuels civil conflict, and a second one in which protracted state weakness leads to a progressive implosion of the state apparatus. These two modes have distinct economic explanations.

First, as Rotberg describes, a central state fails or nears failure because ethnic, racial, ideological, or regional divisions result in the breakdown of central authority and the emergence of widespread violence. Examples include Angola, Liberia, Sri Lanka, and Yugoslavia. The political community fragments as one or more identifiable groups no longer recognizes the legitimacy of the central state. A violent struggle ensues in which different groups contest either control of the central state or the right to secede from it. The state fails in the sense that insurrections prevent it from enforcing its authority and laws over a significant proportion of its territory. The central state may, however, remain strong in the regions under its control, which it may continue to administer strenuously. Indeed, in long-standing civil wars, the central state is usually relatively healthy, except for its ability to control some (large) part of the country. Thus, in countries like Sudan, Sri Lanka, Uganda, or Senegal long-standing civil wars have not had much impact on law and order in the capital. The central state's very ability to wage war for long periods of time suggests a reasonable level of extractive capacity, external support, and/or legitimacy. In fact, often combatants struggle for control of the central state, which represents a prize because of its control over significant resources.

In a second modal path toward state failure, as Rotberg indicates, the power of the state erodes without much accompanying violence. A number of low-income states, primarily in sub-Saharan Africa are often described as being in the process of "being hollowed out" despite the absence of any identifiable armed conflict or significant number of battle deaths.[1] The paradigmatic case is Ghana in the late 1970s. Such countries exhibit an almost complete inability on the part of the government to provide basic services to their population or, indeed, to collect revenues to pay their own officials. Large parts of their territories are left unadministered, laws are unobserved, and taxes go uncollected. The state is characterized by an inability to project power throughout its territory or to undertake activities that improve the welfare of the majority of its population.

What is the relationship between these two modes of state failure? Nature abhors a vacuum, and the weakness of the central state is as often the cause of civil war as its consequence. Thus, an array of factors predispose a country like Chad to civil war: arbitrary borders, a cultural and religious cleavage dividing north and south, regional economic inequalities, and so on. But, in addition, the inability of successive governments in Ndjamena effectively to govern a vast and inhospitable land has provided a constant motivation for rebellion.[2] In Sierra Leone and Liberia, similarly, the failure of the central state and the emergence of civil war among rival ethnic warlords led to the current situation; cause and effect may be impossible to disentangle.[3] Nonetheless, it is possible to distinguish civil wars that emerge as struggles for control of reasonably effective state structures, perhaps because of a contentious decolonization process (the case of Angola), or as a fight over sovereignty issues in multinational states (Yugoslavia, Ethiopia), from civil wars that emerge in the context of the demise of the central state (Sierra Leone, Somalia, Liberia, Zaire).

The Economic Causes of Civil Wars

Collier has argued that civil war in the past several decades has primarily been caused by economic factors.[4] He finds that level of income, degree of ethno-linguistic fractionalization, population, and the proportion of primary commodity exports all help to determine the outbreak and duration of civil wars. In particular, he finds that countries with a high proportion of primary commodity exports are positively correlated with the risk of a civil war, leading him to devise a utility-theory-based model in which the possibility of "loot" is an important motivating factor for the parties to the conflict.

Collier has interpreted his results as showing that countries with high levels of natural resources are more likely to engage in civil wars. He provides an attractive model, which evokes several well-known contemporary situations, such as the use of diamonds to finance insurrections in Angola and Sierra Leone, or the Angolan government's reliance on oil revenues to hold UNITA (Union for the Total Independence of Angola) at bay. He focuses attention on the fact that, first, wars have to be financed. Particularly with the end of the Cold War and the end of support from one of the superpowers or their regional proxies, there has been a premium on local sources of revenues. In Collier's research, revenues both finance the war effort and drive warlords, who are viewed as almost entirely motivated by personal gain. Second, his arguments suggest that the leaders of warring parties often have material interests in pursuing war, which may be more important than the ideological or ethnic motives they emphasize.

Collier's argument obviously appears to fit a number of contemporary cases well. Whereas many of the high-profile conflicts in the 1960s and 1970s involved guerrilla armies with a clear ideological agenda, and were financed by outsiders according to a Cold War geostrategic logic, the more recent conflicts of the 1990s have typically not had an overt ideological cause. The warlords in conflicts such as those in Sierra Leone or the Congo have no discernible programmatic agenda, and their manipulation of ethnicity often seems contrived and self-serving. Much anecdotal evidence links these civil wars with a sharp increase of commerce in various illicit goods, which often directly finance the warlords and their armies.[5]

As a practical matter, armies have to be paid. Throughout history, they have made use of available resources and tolerated looting by their soldiers. The presence of natural resources is likely to increase the length and intensity of conflicts since they can finance soldiers and weapons. Particularly since the end of the Cold War and the demise of superpower policies such as the Reagan Doctrine, whereby the U.S. provided support to any force contesting a Soviet-backed government, armies have had to turn to other mechanisms for finance. This transition was particularly clear in Angola since 1975, during which time Jonas Savimbi evolved from a Chinese-supported Maoist, to a U.S.-supported "freedom-fighter," to an international pariah—welcome only to the seedier diamond dealers of Antwerp.

It is easy to be cynical regarding Savimbi's ideological motivations. I am uncomfortable, however, with a body of research that is so completely dismissive of the force of ideology. Savimbi may well have had a largely mercenary view of the world, but the persistence of his poorly fed and ill-equipped army over the course of a long war cannot be explained by strictly mercenary motives. Deeply felt antagonisms between the Ovimbundu of Angola's south central plateau and the *assimilado*, Kimbundu, and Bakongo populations of the north and western coast are also clearly responsible for the conflict's length. Individuals may have benefited materially from the murderous ethnic conflicts in Bosnia or Rwanda, but their gratuitous savagery cannot be explained in strictly utilitarian terms.

Similarly, in the numerous civil conflicts that affected Latin America in the 1960s and 1970s, who can doubt that ideological polarization around social class structured the conflict and fed the violence?[6] Much literature attests to the salience of these ideational factors. More pertinently, a vast literature has attested to the complex interaction among individual interpretations of interest, values, ideas, and collective action in shaping civil conflict.[7] Richard's case study of the conflict in Sierra Leone, as well as Ellis's fine study of Liberia both emphasize the role of loot in those civil wars, but they also convincingly link the specific nature of the two civil conflicts to complex arrays of religious, cultural, ethnic, and environmental factors.[8] Because of its failure to incorporate noneconomic factors, Collier's model captures an undeniable component of civil conflict, but it is incompletely specified.

To be sure, Collier includes variables such as ethnic fragmentation and income inequality in his regression model, viewing these indicators as potential sources of what he calls "grievances." But these variables do not necessarily capture the kinds of grievous attitudes that are often present in civil conflicts. To cite just one example, actual income and wealth inequality may not correlate all that well with class consciousness, which is socially and politically constructed.

There are, moreover, other problems with the utility-based model of civil conflict developed in the work of Collier and others. I am skeptical, for example, that Collier and his colleagues have shown that the presence of oil and mineral wealth increases the likelihood and duration of civil wars. First, "primary commodity exports" is a poor proxy for the level of natural resources. African conflict diamonds are much in the news, but in fact their role in conflict situations may be exceptional. Diamonds are high in value and low in bulk, making them ideal sources of revenues for insurrections. A look at cases suggests that most countries with civil wars are agrarian societies, with agricultural exports. The idea that civil wars in Ethiopia, Rwanda, and Guatemala were fought over access to coffee rents is hard to accept. For a commodity like coffee, civil war is devastating and output invariably declines with a rise in violence.

Collier's results may stem from the fact that his data set includes developed countries as well as low-income countries, and that what he is finding is that low-income economies with a certain type of economic structure (i.e., small manufacturing sectors) are more prone to civil wars. By my count, there are twelve African cases in his data set, and only three are endowed with significant oil or mineral wealth.[9] Collier's other finding is that the likelihood and long duration of civil war is more likely in poorer countries. This is certainly intuitive, since his data set of ninety observations includes twenty-four OECD countries, none of which was embroiled in civil war. A much stronger test of the hypothesis would be to reestimate the equation without those rich countries.

It might be noted that the results reported by Esty and his colleagues, with a data set that favors low-income countries more than the data set reported on by Collier, appear to contradict the Collier results.[10] One of their three best explanatory variables for state failure is *the degree of trade openness*: the more open the economy, the less likely there is to be internal conflict. This more or less contradicts the Collier result that commodity exports are associated with a higher risk of civil wars, since, presumably, the kinds of low-income countries in which conflict and failure predominate tend to be highly open, exporting primary commodities. More research is needed to reconcile these two findings. For Collier and his colleagues, primary commodities serve as a proxy for the resources available to states, whereas Esty and his colleagues see degree of trade openness as a proxy for integration into the world economy and sensitivity to the pressures of the international community.[11] The use of such similar indicators to model such disparate dynamics is a problem of this quantitative research, suggesting that more conceptual work is needed to refine our understanding of civil wars and allow us better to interpret these kinds of statistical results.

Economic Structural Factors behind State Collapse

I distinguish between structural and contingent factors. Economic structural factors that predispose toward state failure are factors that put pressure on states or which impose constraints on state formation, or on "stateness" in Nettl's early formulation.[12] These structural factors make many low-income states of the developing world more or less vulnerable to state failure. But it is almost invariably contingent factors that push a country from mere weakness to failure. State failure can be conceived as a result of contingent factors *internal* to the state apparatus itself. Some states can be weak internally, but survive because they do not have to deal with specific political challenges such as coups or serious fissures within the political class. State failure can also be precipitated by unexpected factors *external* to it, which challenge political stability. Many of these contingent factors will not be specifically economic and so fall out of my area of focus. External economic challenges might include drought and famine, or major commodity price fluctuations.

I define structural factors as deep-seated economic and sociological characteristics that are fixed in the short-to-medium term. Fiscal or extractive capacity is perhaps the most important of institutional capabilities for weak states. The level of extraction largely determines the activities that states can sustain and the quality of the public infrastructure available to the state to undertake its functions. Two types of factors help to determine the level of fiscal resources available to states. A first, widely appreciated, determinant of fiscal resources has to do with economic structure. As Ardant and many others have pointed out, low levels of development lend themselves to weak extraction.[13] Agrarian economies, with their highly fragmented markets, weak market institutions, low value added, and high levels of on-farm consumption are difficult to tax. The difficulty of formulating effective fiscal instruments is heightened further when such economies are characterized by unusually low levels of population density, historically low levels of urbanization, and a difficult terrain. Thus, low population-density tends to weaken state structures, because big, empty countries are harder to administer than small dense countries, and fiscal extraction is likely to be harder from such economies.[14]

It is thus not surprising that the fiscal resources available to the states of low income countries are invariably significantly lower than those available to the economies of the OECD countries. This is revealed in table 4.1, which compares the average proportion of GDP accounted for by total government revenue across regions.

These differences in economic structure are then typically compounded by differences in governmental capacity, the second major determinant for the level of fiscal resources available to states. The level of fiscal extraction is a function of governmental capacity, which in turn is a complex function of administrative and technical know-how, political will, and state-society relations. It is generally true that fiscal instruments in low-income economies are more likely to be economically inefficient, with high collection costs and a negative effect on the productive economy, because of the structural factors just identified. There is thus something self-perpetuating about these fiscal systems. Nonetheless, capacity does vary quite a bit at a given level of economic development because of country-specific political and managerial factors, which helps to explain why economies with roughly the same structure can have such disparate fiscal extraction levels, as is also clear from table 4.1. The sharp difference between Uganda and Kenya, for instance, or between Botswana and Zambia, has far more to do with historical and political factors than it does with differences in their respective economic structures.

One factor is differences in policies, which is revealed in table 4.1 in the large differences in the proportion of taxes derived from international trade. Even so, the numbers in table 4.1 probably exaggerate sub-Saharan

TABLE 4.1
Tax Structure, by Region, 1990–96 (as a percentage of GDP)

Region	*Total revenue*	*Taxes on international trade*
OECD (n=29)	32.8	0.8
Low-income Asia (18)	20.4	4.8
Middle East (12)	21.4	2.7
Latin and Central America (22)	20.5	3.8
Africa (n=22)	21.1	6.2
Botswana	45.1	7.8
Central Africa Republic	13.0	5.7
Chad	9.1	1.8
Gabon	27.1	4.5
Kenya	24.4	3.2
Madagascar	9.4	4.4
Sudan*	12.5	6.2
Uganda*	6.5	4.0
Zambia	20.1	4.4

* indicates that numbers were taken from Parthasarathi Shome (ed.), *Tax Policy Handbook* (Washington, D.C., 1995), and that they cover 1981 to 1985.
Source: IMF, *Tax Policy Handbook, Summary Tax Structure Tables by Region, 1990–1996.* Tax Policy Division, www.imf.org.

Africa's actual fiscal performance. This is because the data cover only twenty-two of the region's forty-eight countries. Since the ability to collect statistics is not shared evenly across countries, but is probably correlated to other state capacities, it makes sense to believe that the fiscal performance of the missing countries is weaker than that of those in the table.[15]

The table also reveals another dimension of fiscal extraction, which is that the presence of a capital-intensive mining industry in a country yields higher tax revenue, since this is an easy sector to tax. So oil-producing countries like Gabon, Angola, and Congo-Brazzaville, or a diamond producer like Botswana, all have revenues well above the average for the region.

As a result of low revenues, the state apparatuses of low-income states are invariably relatively small, despite much rhetoric to the contrary in the development community.[16] On average, African government personnel totaled 2 percent of the population, compared to 7.7 percent for the OECD countries. Moreover, well over half of the OECD public sector was typically based in local government, while African public employees were three times more likely to work for the central government, thus suggesting a much greater concentration in the capital and a much sparser state presence in the countryside.[17] While public payrolls have been increased substantially over time for patronage reasons, it remains true that few low-income governments can derive the kind of political advantage out of patronage that the populist regimes of middle-income and high-income states derive from public employment. It is also true that whatever advantage is derived is limited almost entirely to the capital and one or two other major towns.

In addition, these states do not do very much. Civil service salaries usually account for an unusually high proportion of government expenditures, and not enough is left over for the provision of even basic public goods. Thus, few West African governments have ever provided education to as much as half of the school-age population, often despite spending between a quarter and a third of their budgets on education. Access to health services is similarly restricted. Road construction programs are typically quite modest, even with a substantial proportion of funding coming from the donors. As countless observers have noted over the course of the last thirty years, the ability of African and other low-income states to project power and actually enforce their de jure sovereignty over their entire territory has been weak.[18]

Let me be clear. State capacity should not be viewed as completely exogenous to the political system—something that is ineluctably the result of basic resource endowments and geographical constraints. African governments have systematically underinvested in the acquisition of capacity.[19] Various political practices that mark the region have undermined capacity building. Governments thus have weakened their civil services with patronage practices and politicization. They have prevented the emergence of greater capacity to protect corruption and rent-seeking by the political class. In turn, they have allowed these practices to weaken fiscal extraction. Politically motivated economic policy-making has resulted in economically irrational policies that have triggered an economic crisis, which has further weakened the state apparatus. In sum, these states could have become much more consequential, despite the structural constraints on state formation, had their governments been motivated to promote more effective states. The point to make is that in the short run, political leaders are bound by these weaknesses and that they make their governments vulnerable to political crises.

In sub-Saharan Africa, the weight of these structural factors is striking. But so is the cross-national variation. All the states are weak, but not equally so. First, the presence of mineral wealth has led to a different historical process of state formation. Most obviously, mineral wealth attracted British capital and immigrants to southern Africa and largely helped to finance what remains the best public infrastructure and some of the strongest public sectors on the continent. More recently, some states have used oil and mineral wealth to build states that are strong by regional standards. Thus, oil-rich Gabon or Cameroon are not impressive by world standards but have outperformed neighboring states such as Chad or the Central African Republic. A recent article posits a resource "curse" because there is some evidence that resource wealth does not result in faster economic growth.[20] Perhaps, but I would argue that natural resource wealth does increase the level of economic activity, and it provides states with easy sources of revenues. Thus, resources fuel the growth of not only public consumption (e.g., the number of civil servants) but also some public investment (e.g., schools, roads, etc.). I hypothesize that the presence of natural resource wealth may help to explain political instability and the descent into civil war, but it is much less likely to have a similarly counterintuitive effect on "stateness" and the probability of collapse. The ability to derive revenues from resources ensures that states benefit from them, even when there is considerable leakage through corruption and rent seeking.

The data presented in table 4.2 illustrate these dynamics well by comparing oil producers with non-oil states in Central Africa. The eight countries in central Africa share fairly similar colonial histories and cultural resources. Only four of them export significant amounts of oil, however; both Chad and Equatorial Guinea will soon join the ranks of significant oil exporters.

As the table suggests, oil brings with it a significantly larger national income, particularly in small states. Governments have used that oil wealth for developmental purposes only very modestly; their populations live about five years longer on average but appear no more likely to be immunized. The gross enrollment rate in primary school is also a bit higher in the oil producing states. This developmental performance is no doubt disappointing, but the data do suggest that at least some of the mineral wealth may have trickled down to health and education programs. Nonetheless, the big difference lies in the size of the state. The data indicate that oil producers in Central Africa have three times as many public employees as non-oil producers. In other words, much of the extra wealth goes into government consumption. Such spending appears to have a marginal impact on developmental performance, but in all likelihood it exerts a greater impact on patronage and presumably makes failure somewhat less likely in that regimes can more easily manipulate government consumption to promote political stability.

States that have high-value natural resources are more likely to engage the attention and assistance of the international community.[21] Oil resources attract Western banks, with promises of easy money, as well as large investments by Western oil companies. As a result, these states enjoy closer military relationships with the Western powers, which also helps them to sustain political stability. They are more likely to benefit from foreign help to resist external or internal threats. Thus, Cameroon and Gabon received timely aid from the French government, which helped

TABLE 4.2
The Impact of Oil on State Performance in Central Africa

	GNP p.c. 1995 (US $)	*Rate, measles immunization (1994)*	*Life expectancy (1997)*	*Gross school enrollments (1990)*	*Public employment as % of pop. (early 1990s)*
Non-oil producers					
CAR	350	37	45	65	0.8
Chad	210	24	49	54	0.5
Eq. Guinea	390	82	50	135	1.6
Niger	190	42	47	29	0.5
Average	285	46.3	47.8	70.7	0.8
Oil producers					
Cameroon	660	31	48	101	1.6
Congo	660	18	57	133	3.2
Gabon	3860	50	52	—	2.6
Nigeria	210	50	54	91	—
Average	1347.5	37.3	52.7	108.3	2.5
Average (Africa)	289	52	72	72	1.3

Source: The data are from the World Bank, *African Development Indicators, 2000*, except for the data on public employment, which are from Ian Lienert and Jitendra Modi, "A Decade of Civil Service Reform," IMF Working Paper WP/97/179 (Washington, D.C., 1997).

incumbent regimes resist the democratization wave that pushed through the region in the early 1990s. This external assistance was not always determinant—the Central African Republic did undergo a change of leadership through elections in the early 1990s, while French assistance did not prevent the fall of the Nguesso regime in the Congo (though France appears to have provided discreet assistance to help him regain power in 1997).

Finally, states on the coast are probably on balance richer than states in the hinterland. The economic growth literature has suggested that landlocked states grow more slowly than coastal states.[22] Access to ocean ports facilitates trade, both in commercial goods and in ideas, which appears to enhance the prospects for economic growth. In turn, commerce favors the emergence of cities and states, a point long stressed by historians.[23] In Africa, hinterland states were colonized later and were less integrated into imperial economies than coastal states.

Some might object to this argument, pointing to extremely successful states, notably in Asia, that are based in resource-poor environments. The comparison with East Asia is indeed instructive. With the exceptions of Indonesia and Malaysia, Asian states lack the natural resources of many African economies. But one can nonetheless link their much longer and complete tradition of state formation to such structural factors as much higher levels of population density, fewer landlocked states, fewer impediments to transportation and communication, and so on. Many other, nonstructural, factors help to explain the differences between states in the two regions, but the differences in performance are certainly compatible with the structural analysis factors alluded to here.[24]

Contingent Factors

Structural factors can explain only the propensity to fail, which I have situated in fiscal weakness due to structural factors compounded by low human capital. The move from weakness to failure to collapse and violence largely results from contingent factors. I define contingent factors as short-term events arising from the actions of political and economic agents. Most of these are political and thus outside of my brief; ethnic violence may be mobilized by regime change or leadership turnover. Factionalism in the army may be increased by military coups. Instability in neighboring countries may spill over through refugee flows and / or the inflow of small arms. Neighboring regimes may have a reason to seek to destabilize unfriendly governments, and so on.

Two contingent economic factors propel the movement from weakness to failure.

Bad Macroeconomic Policies

First, is the disastrous effect of bad macroeconomic policies on state capacity. Weak states that pursue reasonable macroeconomic policies and maintain sustainable fiscal policies can expect to see their states strengthen over time. In a virtuous cycle, balanced policies result in higher levels of growth. Government collects greater revenues, and public budgeting and planning is more likely to be rational. As a result, civil servants are paid on time, their purchasing power holds steady, and they are more likely to undertake their jobs more or less competently. In turn, this results in stability, which encourages investment, which fosters more growth, and so on. This virtuous cycle at work can be found for example in much of Francophone Africa in the decade after independence. These were not developmental states, by any stretch of the imagination. Their sectoral policies were no better than elsewhere in the region. But neocolonial French oversight resulted in extremely cautious macroeconomic policies, which ensured low inflation, slow but steady economic growth, and political stability.[25] Francophone West African states were usually too dependent on France to be considered as engaging in successful state formation. On the other hand, until the 1980s, these states enjoyed relative political stability, as well as significantly higher rates of growth than the rest of Africa. Nonetheless, the quality of macroeconomic policy declined slowly but surely following the Franc Zone reforms of 1972–73, which served to loosen French control and began the process of politicization and the corruption of the policy process.[26]

Contrast this result with the vicious cycle brought about by persistently bad macroeconomic policies: For a combination of ideological and political reasons, governments undertake policies that result in fiscal deficits and balance of payments crises. Public expenditures promote patronage and rent seeking, rather than public investment. A government proves incapable of disciplining the political class, which engages in a variety of corrupt practices that prove to be unsustainable. A balance of payments crisis is then precipitated by a foreign exchange shock or a natural calamity. The government responds by accumulating arrears on civil service salaries and other short-term expedients. If equilibrium is not quickly restored and discipline reasserted, the policy process becomes more uncertain to investors, who respond by withdrawing capital from the economy. Governments react to the resulting slow growth with budgetary gimmicks or deficit financing. The purchasing power of state agents shrinks and they are more likely to be tempted by rent seeking and corruption. In the grips of debt crises and the need to limit state expenditures, governments cut back on public investment.

In Anglophone Africa, the disastrous examples of economic management pursued by governments included noncredible monetary and fiscal policies that caused a great deal of uncertainty as well as high levels of inflation and increasing pressures on the official value of the currency. Large capital flight followed, and so did the end of any kind of foreign direct investment. The decline in growth and the rise of inflation led directly to a steady decline in real civil-servant salaries, which often lost over 80 to 90 percent of their real values between 1970 and 1990. As governments lurched into macroeconomic crisis, development planning and rational budgeting practices could not be sustained. Inadequate maintenance budgets further undermined government capacity. State leaders increasingly focused their attention on expedient activities that could help maintain themselves in power rather than those that increased the developmental capacity of the state or raised the prospects for economic growth. Technocrats found their positions weakened, while corruption and rent seeking increased. The "hollowed out" state is the end of this process, where state leaders continue seeking to derive the advantages of controlling the state, notably the access to international aid, but have ceased to recognize any of its responsibilities.

Bad policies can lead to the failure of the state, until the state ceases to provide virtually any public goods, and state agents become almost entirely predatory. Zaire at the end of the Mobutu Sese Seko regime is probably exemplary. By the late 1980s, the state had stopped providing official funding for any social services, though many of them continued to be provided on a fee-for-service basis, effectively privatized by state agents. On the other hand, the state had become almost entirely predatory. In a fascinating case study, Emizet reports that in the late 1980s, nearly 45 percent of refined copper exports was smuggled out of the country, more than 40 percent of coffee exports was being smuggled through Uganda, and an estimated $437 million in diamond exports were also escaping government revenue streams, albeit not necessarily the tax and customs duty officials charged with collecting them.[27] He also notes that of 425 cars surveyed in Kinshasa in 1992, only three had a tax sticker for vehicle registration on the upper corner of the windshield, suggesting the systematic nature of tax evasion and low level bribery.[28] The precise value of these unrealized government revenues may ultimately not be knowable, but the order of magnitude Emizet reports is probably correct, and his careful field work on a wide variety of goods and services makes clear the systematic complicity of Zairian state agents in illegal economic transactions that reduced state revenues. Indeed, he reports that policemen charged a set fee at the road blocks that they manned and shared the bribes with their commanding officers in a chain that went all the way up to the local colonel. Policemen who did not collect the requisite amounts were transferred to less well-remunerated desk jobs.

I am not, however, arguing that bad policies lead directly to failure or even civil war. Rather, this "hollowing out" of the state makes it harder for the political class to react to crises. State leaders lack the levers to respond to specific crises with forceful action. For example, in Sierra Leone or Zaire/Congo, state decay during the 1980s resulted in a sharp decline in tax collection efforts. In the years before these countries descended into civil war, taxes amounted to well under 10 percent of GDP.[29]

Some observers suggest that the hollowing out process is part of a purposeful strategy on the part of political elites who have chosen to "instrumentalize" the disorder that results, for various self-enrichment objectives.[30] This conclusion strikes me as only partly right. To be sure, political disorder and state collapse are to a certain extent instrumentalized by elites. The most shocking example is almost certainly the unseemly struggle by rival politicians and warlords to control the distribution of famine relief in countries like Somalia or the Sudan.[31] Nonetheless, the decline toward state failure is the mostly unintentional result of increasingly desperate leaders who have progressively sawed off the state branch on which they based their neopatrimonial rule. But it is wrong to suggest that state leaders willingly allow the state to fail because they believe that they can benefit from the resulting chaos. Instead, state elites continue to try to derive short-term advantage from every circumstance, no matter how chaotic, even as their failure to navigate the contradictions of neopatrimonial rule leads the state astray. Having too long undermined state capacity for political reasons, elites cause the bureaucracy at some point to stop performing at all, order breaks down, and leaders find it increasingly hard to manage the interelite accommodational processes that are at the core of political stability.

The Relationship with the Donors

A second factor that increases the vulnerability of states is the paradoxical effects of structural adjustment and the efforts led by the donors to improve the policy environment. The effect of the structural factors just described were long mediated by what could be called the "neocolonial peace," the period of roughly 1950 to 1995, in which the West played a largely positive role in support of states in Africa by buttressing regimes through military assistance and ever increasing amounts of foreign aid and technical assistance. In particular, the unprecedented flows of aid resources palliated the extractive weaknesses of most states in the region. As colonial powers like Britain and France withdrew, they maintained significant presences in these countries to shore up the very weak governments that they had put in place. Over time, an international regime emerged, in which virtually all the rich countries supported aid programs benefiting African governments. The donors responded to the onset of the debt crisis in Africa with a sustained increase in aid, which grew by an astounding annual average of over 5 percent in real terms between 1970 and 1995. As a result, Africa received 24 percent of total official development assistance (ODA) in 1980 but 37 percent in 1993. At their peak, Marshall Plan resources accounted for 2.5 percent of the GDP of countries like France and Germany.[32] In 1996, excluding South Africa and Nigeria, the average African country received the equivalent of 12.3 percent of its GDP in ODA, an international transfer that remains unprecedented in historical terms.

How has this international context influenced the danger of state failure? Most observers agree with the view that the backing of the international community helped support political stability in the region through the 1980s. It is usually argued, however, that the international context began to turn against existing state structures in Africa in the early 1980s with the rise of *structural adjustment*, and then that the end of the Cold War precipitated a much more hostile international context for state formation. Thus, writing in the mid-1990s, when it seemed like there was a sharp rise in the number of civil conflicts in Africa and other parts of the developing world, Stedman argued that external factors largely help to explain the rise in internal conflict, and pointed to two external factors in particular: the end of the Cold War and "the triumph of free market ideas," which he asserts "undermined the external sources of support for Africa's patrimonial regimes and left some with no legs to stand on." In sum, he adds, "economic conditionality cut at the heart of the patrimonial state."[33] Similarly Laitin's explanation for the collapse of the Somali state is that the end of the Cold War resulted in a sharp decline in international resources available to the country, leading to a "war of attrition" between rival clans over ever-decreasing revenue streams.[34] Woodward's analysis of the collapse of Yugoslavia also emphasizes the impact of structural adjustment and neoliberal economic ideas.[35] Richard's analysis identifies the changing international environment in the 1990s as a key factor destabilizing the Sierra Leone polity, speaking of "a general reduction and tightening up of overseas aid budgets" as a result of the end of the Cold War.[36]

There are two overlapping arguments. One is that the end of the Cold War resulted in a Western departure from the region, and much less attention to political stability. The other is that structural adjustment weakened states. The end of the Cold War is an important watershed for Soviet and American attitudes to the continent, and it has led to the relative withdrawal of the two superpowers from the region. Given the disastrous effects of superpower engagement in the region in the 1980s, with the

Reagan Doctrine and a Soviet-financed arms build-up, it is not at all clear that these events were not positive for political stability.

Nonetheless, exaggerating the impact of the Cold War on African politics has long been a particularly American foible and must be resisted. Other Western donors have always had different motives for providing assistance to the region, and the post–Cold War period has not seen a similar lessening of interest. On the contrary, aid to Africa underwent a dramatic increase throughout the 1980s and into the early 1990s, even as U.S. and Soviet aid declined rapidly. Although there has been some decline in the last couple years (mostly accounted for by a sharp decline in assistance to a small number of states like Zaire/Congo and Kenya), aid to the region is still considerably higher than it was at the peak of the Cold War.

A case like Somalia is instructive. The change in American attitudes to the regime may have played a role, but the story of declining economic resources told by Laitin simply does not square with the facts. The country's foreign aid held steady at $450–500 million a year from 1987 to 1990. It then declined to $186 million in 1991, but clearly as a result of the fall in stability, and it soon rebounded. Indeed, aid to the country peaked in 1993 at $890 million, albeit mostly in emergency assistance.[37] Laitin's argument is at least plausible for Somalia, long a pawn in U.S.-Soviet relations, but it does not travel well to other 1990s conflicts. Countries like Rwanda, Sierra Leone, or even close U.S.-ally Liberia, were all receiving steady and substantial flows of aid in the years before the emergence of civil conflict. The decline of aid to these countries was a result of their decline into civil war rather than a cause. To be sure, if the twenty-first century's dip in aid-resources continues, one may in years to come blame declining Western support for the rise of instability.[38] But that is not yet a reality. In sum, a fairly standard explanation for the alleged increase in African instability in the 1990s is largely false. The Cold War's end did not result in a sharp drop in aid to the region.

The second variant of the argument concerns the effect of structural adjustment policies. Here, the argument is essentially that, since 1980, the imposition of economic liberalization, austerity, and privatization has taken away significant discretionary resources and rent-seeking opportunities from governments. Without them, governments have found it more difficult to maintain political stability. This argument makes some sense for relatively developed countries transiting out of socialist systems, like Yugoslavia and the states of the ex-Soviet Union, since the adjustment really resulted in sharp reductions in resources available to state elites. The same argument is somewhat less convincing for the low-income states of sub-Saharan Africa, however.

Clearly, economic stagnation and crises undermine political stability, as politicians find it harder to distribute a shrinking pie of public resources.

But why would donor-led reform efforts also destabilize governments? Insofar as structural adjustment programs (SAPs) provide substantial financial resources to help governments overcome macroeconomic crises and restore economic growth, their net effect on stability should not be viewed automatically as negative. The logic of structural adjustment programs is to facilitate what are inevitable adjustments to new economic realities. For example, why would providing $500 million to help the government of Ruritania ease the burden of restoring fiscal balance undermine that government?

The response to this question by critics of donor-led adjustment programs is to emphasize that the donors have imposed destabilizing shifts in public expenditures. But this claim is not compelling. First, these failing states tend to be smaller and less consequential before they fell in the 1990s. Their contraction would be somewhat less problematic for political stability than in the cases of the ex-socialist states, where the state totally dominated the economy. Peasants in Sierra Leone have always had much lower expectations of the state, which they viewed as a distant, ineffective, and mostly predatory institution, than, say, farmers in Yugoslavia.

Second, one of the characteristics of aid to Africa and other low-income countries is its macroeconomic importance. In big, middle-income states, aid resources have been minor compared to the effort demanded of the state by the donors during adjustment programs. In low-income Africa, on the other hand, the flow has been massive relative to the size of the economy. Factoring in the steady rise of foreign aid during the era of adjustment, most of which is provided to the state and its agents, and which averaged 10 to 15 percent of GDP in the region from 1985 to 1995, suggests that the size of discretionary resources available to politicians may well not have declined during adjustment.

Third, and confirming this last claim, there is little evidence to suggest that the African states that failed in the 1990s were places where the size of the central state had previously suffered through a severe shock. Overall, the evidence suggests that very few states in Africa have witnessed such a contraction. Few countries have undergone a sharp reduction in the public payrolls, for example. The best available estimates from the IMF suggest that between 1986 and 1996, the number of civil servants actually increased in eleven out of the eighteen countries for which there are complete data.[39] The handful of states in which civil service retrenchment has been significant include Ghana, Uganda, the Gambia, and Mali, none of which has demonstrated increasing instability.

Similarly, the World Bank estimates that government consumption grew by an average of 2 percent a year in the 1980s and 0.3 percent a year in the 1990s, compared to private consumption growth of 1.4 and 1.6 respectively during these two periods.[40] These averages disguise large intraregional variation, but they should disabuse us of a general trend of massive state retrenchment.

There has not been a neoliberal assault on the state in low-income Africa. Does that mean that structural adjustment has had a positive impact on state strength and political stability? Hardly. The *process* of donor-assisted adjustment has in fact had a negative effect. First, the deficiencies of donor conditionality have allowed weak and incompetent regimes to remain in power thanks to donor resources; governments have received aid whether or not they undertook policy reforms. Initially, the flow of resources to the region helped to promote political stability by providing an economic boost and support to the status quo. It provided breathing room to states, within which they might have pursued reform. In time, these resources would simply comfort the status quo. Substantial increases in aid resources to the region helped the reform process along in a few cases. In most, however, it allowed governments to avoid the kind of reform that might have led to economic growth and peaceful political change. Weak conditionality strengthened the hands of rent-seeking politicians within governments and weakened the position of technocrats who might have pushed for the rationalization of decision making. Many observers have been harshly critical of conditionality, arguing that it imposed great hardship on people and governments. In fact, careful studies of conditionality show that it has been largely ineffectual and that aid allocation patterns may actually have rewarded the countries that least followed donor dictates.[41]

At the same time, donor efforts have not helped to bring about the renewal of economic growth. The persistence of fiscal and economic crises for over two decades in most countries has had a negative cumulative effect on political stability. Africa is suffering through a massive brain drain as many of its most talented men and women have given up hope. The inevitable neglect of maintenance and other key developmental expenditures means that the quality of the public infrastructure has continued to decline.

Finally, the evolution of SAPs has been characterized by increasing micromanagement by the donors and the imposition of donor-driven managerial structures, which externalize much decision making from the central state's regular administrative apparatus. Local technocrats increasingly take a back seat to the semestrial missions from the Washington institutions. Economic decision-making power is moved away from the ministries and their procedures to ad hoc donor-financed structures, often located within the presidency, which typically lack transparency and accountability. National budgeting and planning structures atrophy. One direct result is that SAPs have resulted in an increase in corruption and rent-seeking. They have comforted neopatrimonial rulers and weakened the rational-legal tendencies that exist within the state apparatus. If structural adjustment can be said to have contributed to destabilizing countries like Zaire and Sierra Leone, it is in the sense that donor programs unwittingly often undermined the very interests within the state that they sought to promote.

Adjustment programs did not destabilize countries. They made them more vulnerable to failure, however, increasing the chances that minor political incidents and disputes could cause the descent into failure and chaos. Not all states failed. Countries like CAR, Malawi, or Niger have been just as weakened by the economic forces described here as Sierra Leone or Liberia, but they have so far avoided failure.

Adjustment provided a chance for the West to strengthen what were weak and vulnerable states, given long-standing structural constraints on state formation, several decades of disastrous economic policies, and the resulting economic crises that had further weakened state structures. One of the real paradoxes of the past twenty years is that a massive foreign aid effort, in which over $200 billion in resources was transferred to the region, probably did not improve the region's prospects for political stability.

Conclusion

The failure of weak low-income states is less likely to result from the presence of large amounts of natural resources, since the latter can help build up a significant public apparatus. Instead, countries are more vulnerable to failure because of structural economic features such as low levels of economic activity, largely rural settlements, and low population densities. These characteristics then may be exacerbated when the state elite lacks a developmental concern and pursues a neopatrimonial management of the economy and political system. The result is the atrophy of state capacity and a decline in its ability to respond to various shocks. Structural adjustment programs have had a deeply ambiguous impact, promoting political stability by funneling large amounts of financial resources to tottering governments, while at the same time undermining state capacity and the emergence of development-oriented governments.

Notes

The chapter opens with a quotation from Fernand Braudel, *The Mediterranean and the Mediterranean World in the Age of Philip II* (New York, 1973), 890–891.

1. Christopher Clapham, *Africa and the International System: The Politics of State Survival* (Cambridge, 1996). See also Herbst, "Let Them Fail: State Failure in Theory and Practice," in this volume; I. William Zartman, (ed.), *Collapsed States: The Disintegration and Restoration of Legitimate Authority* (Boulder, 1995).

2. Sam Nolutshungu, *The Limits of Anarchy: Intervention and State Formation in Chad* (Charlottesville, 1996).

3. Stephen Ellis, *The Mask of Anarchy* (New York, 1999); Paul Richards, *Fighting For the Rainforest: War, Youth and Resources in Sierra Leone* (Portsmouth, 1996).

4. Paul Collier and Anke Hoeffler, "Economic Causes of Civil Conflicts and their Implications for Policy," World Bank working paper (Washington, D.C., 2000), 16, www.worldbank.org/research/conflict/papers/civilconflict.htm; Paul Collier, "Doing Well Out of War," in Mats Berdal and David M. Malone (eds.), *Greed and Grievance: Economic Agendas in Civil Wars* (Boulder, 2000), 91–111.

5. Berdal and Malone (eds.), *Greed and Grievance*; Jean-François Bayart, Stephen Ellis, and Béatrice Hibou (eds.), *La Criminilisation de l'Etat en Afrique* (Paris, 1997).

6. For a sophisticated analysis that links ideology and interests to explain the course of civil war, see Elisabeth Jean Wood, "Insurgent Collective Action and Civil War: Redrawing Boundaries of Class and Citizenship in Rural El Salvador," unpublished manuscript, New York University (2000).

7. See the excellent literature review in James B. Rule, *Theories of Civil Violence* (Berkeley, 1988).

8. Richards, *Fighting For the Rainforest*; Ellis, *The Mask of Anarchy.*

9. The twelve countries are the following: Burundi, Chad, Ethiopia, Liberia, Mauritania, Mozambique, Nigeria, Somalia, the Sudan, Uganda, Zaire, and Zimbabwe. Of these only Mauritania (iron), Nigeria (oil), and Zaire (copper, cobalt, gold) had significant oil or mineral exports during the period under study.

10. Daniel C. Esty, Jack A. Goldstone, Ted Robert Gurr, Barbara Harff, Marc Levy, Geoffrey D. Dabelko, Pamela T. Surko, and Alan N. Unger, "State Failure Task Force Report: Phase II Findings" (31 July 1998).

11. Ibid., 5.

12. J. P. Nettl, "The State as a Conceptual Variable," *World Politics*, XX (1968), 559–592.

13. Gabriel Ardant, "Financial Policy and Economic Infrastructure of Modern States and Nations," in Charles Tilly (ed.), *The Formation of National States in Western Europe* (Princeton, 1975), 164–242.

14. Ibid. See also Braudel, *The Mediterranean*, 371–75. To be sure, with rapid urbanization for the last half century in all low-income countries, this dynamic is in the process of undergoing rapid change.

15. Another study by two IMF economists reports revenue data for forty-six countries in sub-Saharan Africa for 1995. Here, the regional average is 19.5 percent of GDP, including eight countries with revenues under 10 percent. See Janet Stotsky and Asegedech Wolde Mariam, "Tax Effort in Sub Saharan Africa," International Monetary Fund Working Paper, WP/97/107 (Washington, D.C., 1997).

16. Nicolas van de Walle, *African Economies and the Politics of Permanent Crisis, 1979–1999* (New York, 2001).

17. Salvatore Schiavo-Campo, Giulio de Tommaso, and Amitabha Mukherjee, *An International Statistical Survey of Government Employment and Wages*, Public Sector Management and Information Technology Team, Technical Department

for Europe, Central Asia, Middle East and North Africa (The World Bank, Washington, D.C., 1997).

18. On the distinction between de jure and de facto sovereignty, see the seminal Robert H. Jackson and Carl G. Rosberg, "Why Africa's Weak States Persist: The Empirical and the Juridical in Statehood," *World Politics*, XXXV (1982), 1–24. See also Clapham, *Africa and the International System*; Jeffrey Herbst, *States and Power in Africa* (Princeton, 2000).

19. Van de Walle, *African Economies*, 129–137.

20. Michael L. Ross, "The Political Economy of the Resources Curse," *World Politics*, LI (1999), 297–322.

21. I thank Pierre Englebert for his comments on this point.

22. See, for example, Jeffrey Sachs and Andrew Warner, "Economic Reform and the Process of Global Integration," in *Brookings Papers on Economic Activity* (Washington, D.C., 1995), 5.

23. Charles Tilly, *Coercion, Capital, and European States,* A.D. 990–1990 (Cambridge, 1990).

24. See David Lindauer and Michael Roemer (eds.), *Asia and Africa: Legacies and Opportunities in Development* (San Francisco, 1994); Howard Stein (ed.), *Asian Industrialization and Africa: Studies in Policy Alternatives to Structural Adjustment* (New York, 1995).

25. Patrick Guillaumont and Sylviane Guillaumont (eds.), *Stratégies de Développement Comparées: Zone Franc et Hors Zone Franc* (Paris, 1988).

26. Nicolas van de Walle, "The Decline of the Franc Zone: Monetary Politics in Francophone Africa," *African Affairs*, XC (1991), 383–405.

27. Kisangani N. F. Emizet, "Confronting Leaders at the Apex of the State: The Growth of the Unofficial Economy of the Congo," *African Studies Review*, XLI (1998), 99–137. In 1988, just under 94 percent of Belgium's gold imports were from Burundi despite the fact that this country has no gold mines. Ibid., 107.

28. Ibid., 117.

29. The standard IMF data indicate that Sierra Leone's tax collection had declined to 5.4 percent of GDP in 1985–1990, Zaire's revenues had declined to under 5 percent by the early 1990s, and Rwanda's to around 7 percent. Unfortunately, the fiscal data are another casualty of state decay, and so the data available is of uncertain quality. See Stotsky and Mariam, "Tax Effort in Sub Saharan Africa."

30. William Reno, *Corruption and State Politics in Sierra Leone* (New York, 1995); Patrick Chabal and Jean Pascal Daloz, *Africa Works: Disorder as Political Instrument* (Bloomington, 1999).

31. Alex de Waal, *Famine Crimes* (Bloomington, 1997).

32. Steven O'Connell and Charles Soludo, "Aid Intensity in Africa," paper presented to the AERC/ODC conference on "Managing the Transition from Aid Dependence in Sub-Saharan Africa" (Nairobi, 21–22 May 1998).

33. Stephen John Stedman, "Conflict and Conciliation in Sub-Saharan Africa," in Michael E. Brown (ed.), *The International Dimensions of Internal Conflict* (Boston, 1996), 235–266.

34. David Laitin, "Civil War and International Intervention," in Barbara Walter and Jack Snyder (eds.), *Civil Wars, Insecurity and Intervention* (New York,

1999), 146–80. But see Nelson Kasfir, "Domestic Anarchy, Security Dilemmas, and Violent Predation: Causes of Failure," in this volume.

35. Susan Woodward, *Balkan Tragedy: Chaos and Dissolution after the Cold War* (Washington, D.C., 1995).

36. Richards, *Fighting for the Rainforest*, xvii.

37. The World Bank, *African Development Indicators, 2000* (Washington, D.C., 2000), 293.

38. Such a decline is far from a foregone conclusion. Preliminary statistics for 1998 suggest a healthy increase in aid from the West over 1997, leading to cautious optimism in the aid community. See http://www.oecd.org/dac/.

39. Ian Lienert and Jitendra Modi, "A Decade of Civil Service Reform in Sub-Saharan Africa," IMF Working Paper WP/97/179 (Washington, D.C., 1997).

40. The World Bank, *World Development Indicators, 1998* (Washington, D.C., 1998), 210.

41. Tony Killick, *Aid and the Political Economy of Policy Change* (London, 1998).

Five

The Deadly Connection

PARAMILITARY BANDS, SMALL ARMS DIFFUSION, AND STATE FAILURE

MICHAEL T. KLARE

STATE FAILURE usually results from the prolonged interaction of a number of powerful corrosive factors, including economic stagnation, political and ethnic factionalism, pervasive corruption, decaying national infrastructure, and environmental degradation. Typically, these factors operate over a long period of time, eroding civil institutions and undermining the authority of the state. At an early or intermediate stage of decay, it is still possible for an effective leader or leadership group to reverse the process and avert full state collapse; even without such leadership, an ailing state can remain in a weakened condition for many years without slipping into total disarray. But a state's capacity to resist failure can decline rapidly when armed militias emerge or the official security forces break up into semi-autonomous bands. Once established, these bands and militias tend to compete with one another for control of territory, population, and resources—thereby subjecting the country to recurring bouts of violence and disorder. Under these circumstances, the transition from failing to failed state is usually irreversible.

Greatly contributing to the emergence and destructive impact of armed bands in these situations is the widespread proliferation of small arms and light weapons. These weapons—assault rifles, submachine guns, rocket-propelled grenades, light mortars, land mines, and so on—have become the standard equipment of ethnic militias, guerrilla groups, death squads, warlord armies, and other paramilitary formations. Weapons of this type are particularly attractive to nonstate actors because they are cheap and easy to use, and are readily available from black-market sources. With tens of millions of such weapons made surplus by the end of the Cold War, it has become relatively easy for ethnic militias and other paramilitary groups to obtain sufficient arms to challenge the established forces of the state and to wreak havoc in weak and divided societies.[1]

Although the emergence of armed bands and the proliferation of small arms are not, in themselves, the causes of state decline and failure, they are significant contributing factors. At the very least, such bands generate widespread violence, thereby undermining the national economy and impairing the state's ability to deliver basic services to the populace. Once armed bands have begun fighting with one another, moreover, it is very difficult for an ailing state to restore domestic peace and stability without external military assistance. Even when such assistance is forthcoming, it is not always possible for international peacekeepers or other outside forces to effect the restoration of civil order—as shown, for example, by the tragic examples of Somalia and Sierra Leone.

The Rise of Paramilitary Bands and the Decline of State Authority

A functioning state is expected to possess many attributes, but the most significant of these is its capacity to protect the national population from external attack and internal disorder. Indeed, the very emergence of the modern nation-state is associated with the suppression of brigands, private armies, and other autonomous military formations by the central government. To protect the nation from foreign invasion and to preserve social stability, the nation-state has been endowed by law and practice with certain fundamental powers: to levy taxes, to conscript young men (and sometimes women) into the armed services, and to regulate the production and distribution of firearms. In acquiring these powers, the state also assumes an obligation to protect its constituent population from random and unauthorized violence. When a state can no longer provide such protection, its authority withers and failure is likely.

A state in decline can continue to exercise some degree of authority, however attenuated, for as long as its monopoly over the legitimate use of violence goes unchallenged. But once substate organizations of a paramilitary nature—ethnic militias, separatist forces, guerrilla groups, warlord armies, and so on—begin to form, the central government must act swiftly to disarm and dissolve these entities or its control over the nation (or the particular regions affected) will rapidly evaporate. Such formations, once established, usually seek to eliminate all vestiges of central governmental authority within their area of operations and to assume for themselves the "rights" of government: taxation, conscription, resource allocation, and so forth.[2] In a very real sense, this represents the reversal of the process of state building associated with the rise of the modern nation-state.[3] Hassner has characterized this process as a "return to the Middle Ages," in which central state authority is replaced by a welter of competing power blocs.[4]

The tug-of-war between remnants of the state and armed substate formations has been a central feature of virtually every instance of civil conflict and state failure: Algeria, Bosnia, Burundi, Cambodia, Chechnya, Colombia, the Democratic Republic of the Congo (DRC), East Timor, Georgia, Haiti, Liberia, Rwanda, Sierra Leone, Somalia, Sri Lanka, the Sudan, and Tajikistan. In some of these cases, the armed groups involved have sought to carve out an ethnic homeland in the space of a multinational state (as in Abkhazia, Bosnia, Chechnya, Kurdistan, and Sri Lanka); in others, the goal has been to seize control of the government and its tangible assets (Liberia), to impose a new system of government (Algeria, Colombia), to silence opposition to the ruling faction or elite (Haiti, Rwanda), or to control a particular region that is rich in "lootable" raw materials (the diamond zones of Angola and Sierra Leone; the gold, diamond, copper, and coltan zones of the DRC).

In all of these cases, military-type organizations have been established outside of the established armed forces and without the imprimatur of the state. Such organizations can take a variety of forms: revolutionary or insurgent guerrilla bands, such as the Revolutionary Armed Forces of Colombia (FARC) and the National Union for the Total Independence of Angola (UNITA); separatist forces, such as the Liberation Tigers of Tamil Eelam (LTTE) in Sri Lanka and the Sudan People's Liberation Army (SPLA); the paramilitary adjuncts or enforcement arms of a ruling faction or elite, such as the Interahamwe in Rwanda; warlord armies, such as the Revolutionary United Front (RUF) in Sierra Leone; criminal organizations; death squads; and various combinations of the above. Although every such organization exhibits its own distinctive characteristics, all are designed to employ violence in an ongoing, systematic fashion to achieve certain political and/or economic objectives.

Whatever their ultimate goals, these entities often inflict significant violence on civilian communities. Although seemingly random and irrational to outside observers, such violence always has a purpose: to punish a particular group for its presumed allegiance to another group or faction, to drive off members of an unwanted ethnic group, to deter opposition to the exploitation of a valuable resource, or to diminish the ability of an opponent's forces to collect taxes (or other forms of revenue) and recruit additional soldiers.[5] Indeed, the targeting of civilians by paramilitary bands in internal conflicts has become one of the most distinctive and troubling features of contemporary conflict. In a 1999 UN report on this phenomenon, Secretary-General Kofi Annan stated,

> In many of today's armed conflicts, civilian casualties and the destruction of civilian infrastructure are not simply byproducts of war, but the consequences of the deliberate targeting of non-combatants. The vio-

lence is frequently perpetrated by non-state actors, including irregular forces and privately financed militias. In many countries, belligerents target civilians in order to expel or eradicate segments of the population, or for the purpose of hastening military surrender.[6]

The deaths, injuries, and other traumas produced by such behavior further accelerate the process of state failure, because the survivors of such attacks often flee to urban centers or refugee camps, adding to the demands on the state's diminishing supplies of food, medicine, and other vital materials. Many of those killed or conscripted, moreover, are young adults, who would otherwise contribute to food production, factory labor, or child rearing—society is thus deprived of their productive labor as it faces a surge in the population of refugees and internally displaced. When combined, these pressures can stretch a society's carrying capacity to the breaking point.

This phenomenon is especially visible in the cases of Liberia and Sierra Leone. In both countries, armed paramilitary formations—the National Patriotic Front of Liberia (NPFL) in the former, the RUF in the latter—sought to maximize their control of territory and erode the power and authority of the prevailing regime by sowing fear and violence in rural areas. The resulting carnage impelled hundreds of thousands of people to flee their homes and villages, adding to the general condition of chaos and paralysis. In this environment, the security (and other) organs of the state simply disappeared into the maelstrom or morphed into autonomous paramilitary bands.[7]

The emergence of such formations is usually accompanied by several other phenomena that are closely associated with state failure. These include the outbreak of an internal arms race between competing ethnic and sectarian militias, the widespread privatization of security, and the diversion of scarce resources to arms procurement and military operations.

An internal arms race tends to occur when ethnic or political factions establish independent militias or when the security organs of the state become the enforcement arm of a particular political or ethnic group. In such situations, other groups and factions—recognizing that they cannot rely on the state for their physical protection—often form armed militias of their own. As Kasfir and Posen have suggested, this can produce a classical "security dilemma" in a domestic setting. Just as states, when operating in the international arena, tend to interpret any military buildup by their neighbors as preparation for offensive rather than defensive action (given the difficulty in distinguishing between the two, and the tendency of security organizations to engage in "worst case" analysis), so do ethnic and sectarian groups view the formation of armed militias by other such groups as a direct threat to their survival. In either case, the result is the same; each party in such a contest seeks to match the capabilities of its rivals, and, in so doing, triggers further military preparations by all concerned—producing an atmosphere of anxiety and suspicion in which even a minor incident can spark a bloody confrontation.[8]

The emergence of armed paramilitary bands and internal arms races is related to another feature of states in decline—the wholesale privatization of security.[9] As the fighting between these bands intensifies, more and more people are likely to be caught in the crossfire or to be victimized in one way or another. Because the state can no longer provide protection against such attacks, many groups and communities seek to arrange for their own defense by creating neighborhood watch groups or by hiring private security firms. It is hardly surprising, then, that private security firms are among the fastest growing economic endeavors in several parts of the world, including southern Africa, Central America, and the former Soviet Union.[10] Whatever the impact of this process on civil security—and there is no indication that the proliferation of private security forces makes a society less violent—it inevitably entails an erosion in the power and authority of the state: a state that has surrendered its domestic security function to private entities can no longer claim to exercise its overarching responsibility for the maintenance of domestic law and order.

The emergence of an internal arms race and the privatization of security lead to yet another corrosive phenomenon—the diversion of ever increasing resources from productive activities to arms procurement and the upkeep of military and paramilitary organizations. For the state, this means the diversion of funds from development projects and basic civil services to the military. Such a practice inevitably undermines the state's long-term durability and legitimacy. In Sierra Leone, for example, the percentage of central government expenditures (CGE) consumed by military spending rose from an estimated 4 percent in 1984 to 20 percent in 1994; in Haiti, the increase over this period was from 8 to 25 percent.[11] For private firms and individuals, this means the diversion of resources from productive activities to the employment of private security firms. This shift, too, contributes to state failure, as economic activity declines and more and more people are forced to rely on handouts from the government and / or foreign aid agencies.

Even more insidious, perhaps, is the tendency for armed militias and insurgent groups to morph into predatory economic organizations in order to finance the acquisition of arms and other military commodities. Whatever the original motivation for the establishment of a particular paramilitary organization, it must find some way of generating operating funds. Because such groups are usually unable to engage in legitimate businesses, they often turn to illicit commerce of one sort or another—typically, drug trafficking, diamond smuggling, kidnapping for ransom, prostitution, extortion, illegal logging, or the sale of outlawed animal products.[12] Aside from the obvious injury and damage caused by such activities, the conversion of armed bands into predatory economic organizations has important implications for state survival. As the revenues from these endeavors begin to pour in, there is a significant risk that the leaders of such bands will become contaminated by the opportunities for personal enrichment, and so will seek both to increase their illicit gains and to resist efforts by outside parties to mediate or terminate the conflict.[13]

The pursuit of personal wealth by the leaders and senior cadres of paramilitary bands appears to be a significant factor in the persistence of armed violence in many of the cases of state failure. In Sierra Leone, for example, leaders of the RUF and breakaway elements of the established armed forces—the so called "sobels," or soldier rebels—long resisted all efforts by outside forces to break their control over the lucrative diamond trade from the remote Kono region.[14] Similarly, in the Congo, military forces tied to Rwanda, Uganda, and Zimbabwe were reluctant to surrender their control over valuable sources of copper, gold, timber, diamonds, and specialty minerals such as columbium and tantalum.[15] In Angola, as in Sierra Leone, key figures have grown wealthy from diamond trafficking; in Colombia, it is the profit from illegal drug trafficking that attracts many guerrilla and paramilitary commanders.

For all of these reasons, the emergence of paramilitary bands in weak and divided societies often results in a sharp increase in civil violence and a significant decline in state authority. In many instances, it has proved impossible for the existing government to restore civic order in such situations without outside assistance. This factor has led, in some cases, to the semipermanent deployment of UN peacekeepers or other multinational forces in the countries involved; in others, it has produced conditions of persistent failure. It follows that efforts to reinvigorate and resuscitate weak and failing states must entail directed efforts to prevent the rise of paramilitary bands and to disarm and dissolve them once they are established.

Small Arms Diffusion and the Acceleration of Internal Dissolution

Closely related to the rise of paramilitary bands is another threat to the survival of weak and failing states: the widespread diffusion throughout society of military-type small arms and light weapons.[16] Small arms are not just major weapons writ small; they are a distinctive class of weapons in their own right. Small arms occupy a middle ground between nonmilitary firearms (hunting guns, sporting guns, handguns) and the major weapons used by modern military forces (tanks, artillery pieces, helicopters, combat planes, warships, etc.). Nonmilitary firearms can be used for assassinations and minor acts of violence, but are not sufficiently lethal and rugged to be employed in sustained military operations; major weapons can inflict enormous damage, but require professional military organizations to operate and maintain. Small arms and light weapons—at least from the perspective of paramilitary bands—possess none of these liabilities. They are powerful enough for use in combat against domestic security forces, but can be operated by untrained volunteers and part-time soldiers. It is not surprising, then, that such munitions have become *the* weapons of choice for irregular forces in internal conflict situations.[17]

The significant role played by small arms and light weapons in internal conflicts is plainly evident in the data (scant as it is) collected on battle casualties in war-affected areas. In an important study of this phenomenon, the International Committee of the Red Cross (ICRC) reported in 1999 that the overwhelming majority (96 percent) of people with combat-related injuries admitted in 1991–95 to a major hospital in a conflict-ridden area of Cambodia had been injured by land mines, firearms, or fragmenting munitions (grenades, mortar shells, etc.). A similar pattern was found at one of its hospitals in Afghanistan. Significantly, the ICRC found that the level of firearms violence decreased by only 33 percent after the formal cessation of hostilities in Afghanistan, suggesting that the continued presence of small arms in the area had contributed to high levels of civil violence.[18]

In reporting these results, the ICRC observed that its field workers have "witnessed the increasingly devastating effects of the proliferation of weapons, especially small arms and light weapons, for civilian populations [in areas of conflict]." These effects were magnified, the report noted, by the combination of small arms proliferation and the rise of private militias and other paramilitary formations—few of which are aware of or demonstrate any respect for the basic rules of international humanitarian law as it pertains to the protection of civilians in war-affected areas. In reflecting on this phenomenon, the ICRC concluded, "While the availability of weapons alone is not the cause of violations of humanitarian law or deterioration in the situation of civilians, the experience presented here indicates that the proliferation of arms can be a major factor in facilitating such violations and aggravating the plight of civilians during and after armed conflict."[19]

As suggested by the ICRC data and other studies, small arms possess a unique capacity to penetrate civil society at all levels. Whereas the possession of heavy weapons is almost always confined to regular military forces, small arms and light weapons are often found in the possession of civilian actors of various sorts—civil police forces, private security organizations, hunters, retired military personnel, gun collectors, criminal bands, and privileged groups of one sort or another (such as Jewish settlers in the Occupied Territories and white farmers in apartheid-era South Africa). This phenomenon can be described as the *diffusion* of small arms, so as to distinguish it from the *proliferation* of major weapons systems from one state to another.[20] The diffusion of small arms in civil society—especially in weak or failing states—poses an implicit threat to state survival because it means that antigovernment formations can readily assemble sufficient weaponry to mount a revolution or insurgency.

Small arms, as a class, possess many distinctive features that make them particularly attractive to ethnic militias, insurgent forces, criminal bands, and other paramilitary formations. They are light in weight and easy to use. *Lightness* matters because the combatants involved often move from place to place on foot, carrying all of their equipment with them. The widespread employment of child soldiers in these settings also favors the use of lightweight weapons; children of ten or twelve years of age simply cannot operate heavy weapons. Small arms are also *small*, meaning that they are relatively easy to hide from customs officials and police inspectors; for the same reason, they are easier to conceal in vehicles used for smuggling arms into areas of conflict.

Small arms and light weapons are also relatively *affordable*. While a new tank can cost $1 to $2 million and a new jet fighter costs $25 million or more, perfectly usable surplus AK-47 assault rifles can be obtained in many parts of the world for as little as $15. This means that, for the price of a single tank, an insurgent group can acquire tens of thousands of assault rifles—more than enough to destabilize a poor and vulnerable country. An all too tragic example is Liberia, where Charles Taylor's small insurgent army—equipped solely with AK-47s and similar weapons—was able to terrorize much of the countryside and mount repeated attacks on the capital, Monrovia. By the end of the conflict, an estimated 200,000 people had died and over 1 million were forced to abandon their homes.[21]

Even more significant, from the perspective of civic violence and disorder, is the widespread *availability* of small arms and light weapons. Although it is impossible to provide an exact tally of all such weapons in worldwide circulation, the numbers are staggering. According to the Small Arms Survey (a project of the Graduate Institute of International Studies in Geneva, Switzerland), there were approximately 550 million small arms in worldwide circulation in 2001, of which 305,000 were thought to be in private hands and 245,000 in the hands of government forces and insurgent bands.[22] Included in this figure are approximately 100 million military-type assault rifles—an amount that includes an estimated 50–60 million AK-47s.[23]

Greatly contributing to the easy availability of small arms around the world is the legacy of U.S.-Soviet competition during the Cold War era. As part of their policy of supporting the military and police forces of friendly developing nations, Washington and Moscow each provided such states with literally millions of rifles, carbines, and submachine guns. To gain an appreciation of the magnitude of these transfers, consider that the United

States provided South Korea with a combined total of 1.4 million M1 rifles and M1 carbines between 1950 and 1975; South Vietnam was given 1 million such weapons; Turkey, 312,000; Greece, 216,000; Taiwan, 179,000; Iran, 165,000; Pakistan, 150,000; Indonesia, 76,000; Thailand, 73,000; Venezuela, 56,000; Uruguay, 33,000; and Burma, 29,000.[24] Many of these weapons, along with those supplied by the Soviet Union to *its* allies and clients, remain in the (often poorly protected) arsenals of recipient countries or have been retransferred to other countries or to private arms dealers.

In yet another expression of their global competition, the United States and the Soviet Union provided small arms and light weapons to antigovernment insurgents in countries ruled by allies of the opposing superpower. The United States, for example, provided weapons to the *mujahadeen* in Afghanistan, the *contrarevolucionarios* ("contras") in Nicaragua, UNITA in Angola, and antigovernment insurgents in Libya and Cambodia. The Soviet Union, for its part, provided weapons to the Palestine Liberation Organization (PLO), the African National Congress, and the Farabundo Marti Front for National Liberation of El Salvador (FMLN).[25] As in the case of arms supplied to governments, many of these weapons remain in use today or have been sold or given to insurgents in other countries. Elements of the Afghan mujahadeen, for example, are believed to have provided arms to insurgents in Kashmir, while some of the former contras are reported to have sold their weapons to drug traffickers in Colombia.[26]

Equally significant, in terms of facilitating the global diffusion of small arms, is the end of the Cold War. Factories that once produced large quantities of arms for NATO and Warsaw Pact forces are now seeking customers in the developing world—in some cases, choosing to ignore the political environment in the countries involved in order to secure lucrative contracts. Factories in Bulgaria, for example, have been accused of supplying weapons to outlaw regimes and rebel forces in Africa.[27] In addition, vast quantities of arms that were once in the possession of Soviet and Warsaw Pact forces have been declared surplus and offered for sale to foreign buyers at very low prices—again with few questions asked about the nature of the intended recipient. Surplus stocks of this sort are widely believed to constitute the main source of arms for the conflicts in Bosnia, Kosovo, and Central Africa.[28]

The widespread availability of small arms and light weapons is also attributable to the global expansion of black markets and the informal economy. Just as globalization has fostered the intercontinental reach of multinational corporations (MNCs), so, too, has it fostered the reach of what Williams calls transnational criminal organizations (TCOs)—illicit enterprises that mimic the business practices of MNCs.[29] These organizations traffic in a wide variety of contraband, including illegal narcotics, diamonds and gems, ivory and products from endangered species, alcohol and tobacco products, girls and young women (for use in prostitution), and guns. Typically, these traffickers engage in two-way trade; narcotics, ivory, and diamonds are smuggled from producing areas—usually in the global South—to markets in the industrialized world, while guns and other manufactured goods are smuggled from the industrialized countries of the North to criminal and insurgent organizations in the South.[30]

For paramilitary organizations with access to cash or other readily negotiable items (such as diamonds), the global black market provides an abundant and reliable source of arms and ammunition.[31] In Angola, for example, UNITA is believed to have spent up to $700 million per year in the late 1990s on imported arms and military equipment, with income derived from the sale of illicit diamonds.[32] Similarly, in Sierra Leone, the RUF is believed to have netted as much as $200 million per year from illicit diamond sales.[33] In Colombia, the various guerrilla and paramilitary organizations have financed their extensive arms purchases by taxing the production of narcotics.

For all of these reasons—ease of operation, lightness, affordability, concealability, and global availability—small arms and light weapons constitute the principal instrument of violence in all of the internal conflicts of the post–Cold War era. Just as important, they are a conspicuous feature in many societies that are suffering from high levels of violent crime and/or political violence of a nonmilitary nature. This is particularly evident in South Africa, where criminal gangs and political factions armed with AK-47s—mostly acquired from former conflict zones in Angola, Namibia, and Mozambique—have become a significant threat to civil order.[34] As Cock suggests, "[T]he level of violent crime linked to this proliferation [of small arms] threatens the consolidation of democracy."[35] The widespread availability of small arms is also contributing to social and political instability in Kenya, Uganda, Indonesia, the Philippines, and a number of the Pacific island states, including Fiji.

The Need for International Action

Both of the factors described above—the emergence of paramilitary bands and the diffusion of small arms—represent a potent threat to the survival of weak and vulnerable states. It is the combination of the two, however, that poses the greatest threat to social and political stability. Once paramilitary groups arise in a country of this sort and acquire substantial stocks of arms and ammunition, that country is destined to face severe stress and trauma. The government involved may be able to avert total failure, but it is almost certain to lose control of significant areas of the countryside. All too often, the restoration of civil order will prove impossible without the intervention of outside forces.

It follows that efforts to prevent the disintegration of weak and vulnerable states and to resuscitate states that have already failed must address the double challenge posed by paramilitary groups and the global diffusion of small arms. The main thrust of such endeavors should be aimed, of course, at overcoming the underlying causes of decay—frozen development, political paralysis, environmental decline, and so forth. But all such efforts will come to naught unless steps are also taken to rein in and dissolve ethnic militias and other such groups and to diminish the societal availability of small arms.

Accomplishing this task will not be easy. Once formed, paramilitary groups are certain to resist any efforts by central state authorities or others to curtail their operations. It is all the more essential, therefore, that weak states be on the alert for the emergence of such organizations and move against them at the earliest possible moment. By the same token, foreign donors and other international actors should make it clear that they will withdraw support from any government that is itself implicated in the formation of political and ethnic militias. Steps should also be taken to starve such groups of operating funds by denying them access to international diamond and timber markets and by severing their ties to external financial institutions.[36]

At the same time, efforts should be undertaken at the local, regional, and global levels to curb the flow of small arms to areas of disorder and to collect and destroy arms that have been made surplus by the termination of conflict. This will require the establishment of an international regime of control mechanisms at the local, regional, and international levels.[37] Some of the components of such a regime already exist, but many others remain to be constructed.[38] Devising these mechanisms, and putting them into operation, represents a major challenge to the international community.

The objective of such a regime is not to eliminate *all* transfers of small arms between states—such a measure would never receive the support of states that lack a domestic arms industry and so depend on imported weapons for their military and police requirements. Rather, the intent should be to screen out all transfers intended for warlords, criminal bands, and other illegitimate end-users or that fail to satisfy other international standards. As well, such a regime should seek to prevent the endless recycling of arms from one conflict to another through illicit channels.

A rough blueprint for such a regime, incorporating the basic elements of a multilayered control system, was part of the "Programme of Action" adopted by delegates to the July 2001 International Conference on the Illicit Trade in Small Arms and Light Weapons in All Its Aspects, held in New York City under UN auspices. As a political document, the Programme of Action is not binding on UN member states; it does, however, assert that states have a fundamental obligation to take all necessary steps to halt the illicit trade in small arms and better to regulate the legal trade. It also calls for the convening of a review conference in 2006 to analyze progress in the implementation of the Programme and to consider further measures.[39]

It is clear, however, that much more needs to be done to construct a truly effective regime for controlling the small arms trade. In particular, such a regime must include measures for: (1) enhanced transparency, (2) supplier restraint and accountability, (3) recipient restraint and accountability, (4) the suppression of the black-market trade, and (5) the collection and destruction of surplus weapons.

Transparency

The timely release of information on global small arms flows would be extremely useful in identifying dangerous trends (such as the buildup of arms stockpiles in areas of instability) and in complicating the operations of black-market dealers. However, there is at present no international system for the publication or exchange of information on transfers of small arms and light weapons. The only existing mechanism of this sort, the United Nations Register of Conventional Arms, covers major weapons systems only. Some data on small arms deliveries are made public by individual suppliers—the United States and Canada have been particularly forthcoming in this regard—but the overall lack of information in this field is a serious impediment to further action.

Several strategies are currently being pursued to expand the pool of available information. The U.S. government is advocating the release of annual reports on small arms exports based on the report it provides each year to Congress in accordance with section 655 of the Foreign Assistance Act—a provision that is itself the result of prodding by arms control advocates and concerned members of Congress. Washington has also proposed regular exchanges of information on small arms transfers among members of the Wassenaar Arrangement, a group of industrialized nations that have agreed to coordinate policies regarding the export of arms and "dual-use" technology (i.e., technology with both military and civilian applications). The establishment of regional arms registers, modeled on the existing UN Register but extending to small arms, is also being discussed in several areas, including Africa. However, no such provisions were included in the Programme of Action adopted at the July 2001 UN conference. It is evident that more progress is needed.

Supplier Restraint and Accountability

Although the manufacture of small arms and light weapons is widely dispersed (at least in comparison to the production of tanks, aircraft, and other major weapons), a dozen or so countries are responsible for the bulk of arms sold on the international market. These include the five permanent members of the UN Security Council—the United States, Russia, China, Britain, and France—plus a number of smaller European, Asian, and Latin American countries. If these countries could agree to a common system of restraints on arms exports, it should be possible to reduce the flow of arms to areas of instability and otherwise to regulate the trade in small arms. Some weapons would still flow through clandestine channels, but most major transactions—those involving large quantities of arms and ammunition—would be subject to international scrutiny and oversight.

Not all suppliers have, as yet, agreed on the need for controls of this sort. However, important groups of countries have begun to move in this direction. Taking the leadership in this regard is the European Union (EU), which has adopted a Code of Conduct on Arms Exports and a plan for Joint Action on Small Arms and Light Weapons. The Code of Conduct requires all EU member states to bar sales of conventional weapons to states that have been cited for persistent human rights violations or that have contributed to regional instability; the action plan obliges member states to take appropriate steps aimed at "combating the destabilizing accumulation and spread of small arms."[40]

The Programme of Action adopted at the July 2001 UN conference begins with the proposition that arms-producing states have a fundamental obligation to regulate and monitor the export of small arms from their territory so as to prevent the diversion of firearms to illicit end-users. On this basis, they are enjoined to "put in place and implement adequate laws, regulations and administrative procedures to ensure the effective control over the export and transit of small arms and light weapons," and to apprehend and prosecute those who violate such measures. States are also called upon to require the marking of all firearms produced in their territory so as to facilitate the tracing of arms that fall into illegal hands (thus permitting the arrest and prosecution of those held responsible for such diversion). These steps are not legally binding, however, and so further effort will be needed to give these (and related) measures the power of an international treaty.

Recipient Restraint and Accountability

No system of supplier controls can be entirely effective if there is no effort to dampen the global *demand* for arms. It is essential, then, that any regime for controlling the small arms trade incorporate measures for recipient restraint and accountability. Similar measures are needed to help build confidence in the utility of supplier restraints. If controls at both the demand and supply sides are viewed as complementary, it should prove easier to mobilize political support for sharp cuts in weapons exports.

Recipient restraint will no doubt be harder to promote than supplier restraint. But significant progress has been made in this direction in an unlikely locale: West Africa. Under the prodding of Alpha Oumar Konaré, the visionary president of Mali, the Economic Community of West African States (ECOWAS) adopted a three-year moratorium on the importation, exportation, and manufacture of small arms and light weapons in 1998. This was the first time that a significant bloc of recipient states had adopted a measure of this sort, and so represented an important test of the viability of such initiatives. Recognizing the immense difficulties faced by the ECOWAS states—most of which are very poor—in implementing the moratorium, the EU and the United States have pledged to assist in developing the required oversight and enforcement mechanisms.[41]

If successful, the ECOWAS moratorium will pave the way for the adoption of supplier restraints in other areas. Already, member states of the Southern African Development Community (SADC) have considered such a move, and a group of East African states met in Kenya in February 2000 to discuss a similar enterprise. Other regions have been slower to address the problem of small arms, but interest in the issue is growing and several regional bodies, including the Association of Southeast Asian States (ASEAN), have agreed to consider new initiatives in this area.[42] Strong support for these measures was expressed in the Programme of Action adopted at the 2001 UN conference, and many observers believe that regional measures of this sort represent the most promising area for future progress in the small arms field.

Suppression of the Black-Market Trade

Efforts to control the *legal* trade in small arms will not prove effective if potential belligerents can obtain most of what they need from black-market sources. Accordingly, measures for curbing the *illicit* trade in arms must be incorporated into any system of comprehensive arms trade restraints. Because black-market dealers operate as transnational entrepreneurs, moreover, efforts to curb the illicit trade must involve multinational collaboration. Leadership in this area was first provided by the Organization of American States (OAS). Seeing a close link between illicit arms sales, drug trafficking, and violent crime, the members of the OAS adopted the Inter-American Convention Against the Illicit Trafficking in Firearms, Ammunition, Explosives, and Other Related Materials in 1997. The convention—which was signed by the United States but has not yet been ratified by the Senate—requires member states to criminalize the unauthorized production and transfer of small arms and to cooperate with one another in suppressing the black-market trade.[43] Many similar measures are contained in the Firearms Protocol that was incorporated in the UN Convention Against Transnational Organized Crime in 2001.[44]

Suppression of the black-market trade in small arms was, of course, the principal objective of the July 2001 UN conference. Asserting that the illicit arms trade "sustains conflicts, exacerbates violence, contributes to the displacement of civilians, undermines respect for international humanitarian law, impedes the provision of humanitarian assistance to victims of armed conflict, and fuels crime and terrorism," the states represented at the conference committed themselves to a variety of measures aimed at curbing this commerce. These included the strengthening of domestic controls on the small arms trade (so as to preclude deliveries to illicit end-users) and the vigorous pursuit and prosecution of those found in violation of national export laws. States were also enjoined to share information on illicit arms dealers and to cooperate in multilateral antitrafficking operations. In addition, the United Nations was given a role in collecting and disseminating information of interest to states.

Many delegates to the July 2001 conference hoped that the participating states would go further, adopting more stringent, binding measures. For example, several delegations proposed a treaty aimed at regulating the activities of arms brokers—the private dealers who often arrange for the sale and shipment of arms from producers in one country to buyers in another. Although brokering activities can be entirely legal when both supplier and recipient are acting in accordance with the laws of the countries involved, they can fall into the illicit realm when domestic or international law is violated at some stage in the process (as, for example, when the recipient is subject to a UN arms embargo).[45] However, while calling for further study of the brokering issue, the Programme of Action does not call for the negotiation of a binding treaty on this problem. Proposals for a treaty on the marking of firearms were also dropped in favor of voluntary efforts. It is apparent, therefore, that further political effort will be needed to persuade states to adopt legally binding measures in this area.

Collection and Destruction of Surplus Weapons

United Nations peacekeepers in Angola, Rwanda, Somalia, and elsewhere have learned a very painful lesson: unless peace agreements are accompanied by the reintegration of ex-combatants into the civilian economy, former soldiers are likely to drift into violent careers as mercenaries, insurgents, or brigands. By the same token, guns not collected and destroyed at the time of demobilization will tend to be used in these new careers or sold to combatants in other areas. Accordingly, any plan for the effective control of small arms must incorporate provisions for the reintegration of ex-combatants into civil society and for the collection and destruction of their personal weapons.

This is, perhaps, the most challenging aspect of the small arms problem, and the most difficult to solve. Nevertheless, individual states, the United Nations, and the World Bank have begun to design and implement mechanisms for this purpose. In many cases, these entail "buy-back" programs involving the provision of tools or cash to ex-combatants who turn over personal weapons. A more innovative approach has been employed by the UN in Albania, where development funds were provided to an entire community (rather than to individuals) in return for a promise by village leaders to collect and destroy all surplus arms in the area. The EU and the World Bank have also assisted in the development of job-training programs and other services for ex-combatants seeking to re-enter civil society.[46]

Seeking a Comprehensive Approach

None of these specific measures, by itself, will prove sufficient to overcome the dangers posed by the uncontrolled spread of small arms and light weapons. While each possesses certain virtues, the problem is too big and too complex to be solved by any individual initiative. Clearly, for a regime of small arms restraint to work effectively, it must incorporate elements of all five mechanisms. Such a regime must also integrate those mechanisms into a unified system of controls, akin to the systems of dams and dikes that have been built to control flood-prone rivers. Only in this manner will it be possible for the international community substantially to reduce the flow of small arms into areas of conflict and disorder.

Staunching the flow of arms to such areas will not, of course, eliminate the problem of state failure. So long as the underlying causes of decay are left unattended, weak states will continue to slide toward collapse. The priority should be to devise and implement strategies for improving the economic and political performance of failing states. But even with heroic efforts to rescue the economies and political systems of such states, the risk of failure will persist if no action is also taken to prevent the rise of paramilitary groups and the diffusion of small arms and light weapons. Such efforts must, therefore, constitute an essential component of any strategy for averting the failure of weak and vulnerable states and for managing the reconstitution of fully collapsed states.

Notes

1. For background on the proliferation of small arms and light weapons in the post–Cold War era, see Jeffrey Boutwell, Michael Klare, and Laura W. Reed (eds.) *Lethal Commerce: The Global Trade in Small Arms and Light Weapons* (Cambridge,

1995); Jeffrey Boutwell and Michael T. Klare (eds.), *Light Weapons and Civil Conflict: Controlling the Tools of Violence* (Lanham, 1999); and Jasjit Singh (ed.), *Light Weapons and International Security* (New Delhi, 1995).

2. For a vivid account of this phenomenon as manifested in the parts of Liberia controlled by Charles Taylor during the early and mid-1990s, see William Reno, "Reinvention of an African Patrimonial State: Charles Taylor's Liberia," *Third World Quarterly*, XVI (1995), 109–120.

3. For discussion, see Mary Kaldor, *New Wars and Old* (Stanford, 1999), 13–60, 69–89.

4. Pierre Hassner, "Beyond Nationalism and Internationalism: Ethnicity and World Order," in Michael E. Brown (ed.) *Ethnic Conflict and International Security* (Princeton, 1993), 125–141.

5. For discussion and numerous examples, see Bill Berkeley, *The Graves Are Not Yet Full: Race, Tribe, and Power in the Heart of Africa* (New York, 2001).

6. UN Security Council, *Report of the Secretary-General to the Security Council on the Protection of Civilians in Armed Conflict*, UN doc. S/1999/957 (8 September 1999), 2.

7. See William Reno, "Sierra Leone: Warfare in a Post-State Society," in Robert I. Rotberg (ed.) *State Failure and State Weakness in a Time of Terror* (Washington, D.C., 2003), 71–100.

8. See Barry R. Posen, "The Security Dilemma and Ethnic Conflict," in Brown, (ed.), *Ethnic Conflict and International Security*, 103–124; chapter 2 by Nelson Kasfir in this volume.

9. I first used this term in Klare, "The Global Trade in Light Weapons and the International System in the Post–Cold War Era," in Boutwell, Klare, and Reed, (eds.) *Lethal Commerce*, 40. See also Thomas K. Adams, "The New Mercenaries and the Privatization of Security," *Parameters*, XXIV (1999), 103–116.

10. See Michael Renner, *Small Arms, Big Impact: The Next Challenge of Disarmament* (Washington, D.C., 1997), 15–18; "Policing for Profit," *The Economist* (19 April 1997), 21–24. On the rise in private security firms in Russia, see Mark Galeotte, "Boom Time for the Russian 'Protectors,' " *Jane's Intelligence Review* (August 1997), 339–341.

11. U.S. Arms Control and Disarmament Agency (ACDA), *World Military Expenditures and Arms Transfers 1995* (Washington, D.C., 1996), 76, 93.

12. For background and discussion, see R. T. Naylor, "The Insurgent Economy: Black Market Operations of Guerrilla Organizations," *Crime, Law and Social Change*, XX (1993), 13–51; Naylor, "Loose Cannons: Covert Commerce and Underground Finance in the Modern Arms Black Market," *Crime, Law and Social* Change, XXII (1995), 1–57; Naylor, "Gunsmoke and Mirrors: Financing the Illegal Trade," in Lora Lumpe (ed.), *Running Guns: The Global Black Market in Small Arms* (London, 2000), 155–182.

13. For discussion of this point, see David Keen, *The Economic Functions of Violence in Civil Wars* (Oxford, 1998).

14. See Douglas Farah, "Diamonds Are a Rebel's Best Friend: Mining of Gems Stalls Peace Process in Sierra Leone," *Washington Post* (17 April 2000); Ingrid J. Tamm, *Diamonds in Peace and War: Severing the Conflict-Diamond Connection* (Cambridge, Mass., 2002).

15. See René Lemarchand, "The Democratic Republic of Congo: From Collapse to Potential Reconstruction," in Rotberg (ed.), *State Failure and State Weakness*, 29–70; United Nations, Security Council, *Report of the Panel of Experts on the Illegal Exploitation of Natural Resources and Other Forms of Wealth in the Democratic Republic of the Congo*, UN doc. S/2001/357 (12 April 2001).

16. *Small arms* are those weapons carried and used by individual soldiers; they include handguns, rifles, carbines, submachine guns, and grenade launchers. *Light weapons* are crew-served infantry weapons that can be carried by pack horses or light vehicles; they include machine guns, light mortars, and recoilless rifles. For the remainder of this paper, the term "small arms" will refer to both types of weapons.

17. For discussion of this point, see Aaron Karp, "Small Arms—The New Major Weapons," in Boutwell, Klare, and Reed (eds.), *Lethal Commerce*, 17–30.

18. International Committee of the Red Cross (ICRC), *Arms Availability and the Situation of Civilians in Armed Conflict* (Geneva, 1999), 33–41.

19. Ibid., 71.

20. I first made this distinction in Klare, "Light Weapons Diffusion and Global Violence in the Post–Cold War Era," in Singh (ed.), *Light Weapons and International Security*, 1–7.

21. For background, see "Liberia: Farewell, Guns?" *Economist* (26 July 1997), 39; Howard D. French, "As War Factions Shatter, Liberia Falls into Chaos," *New York Times* (22 October 1994); Jeffrey Goldberg, "A War without Purpose in a Country without Identity," *New York Times Magazine* (22 January 1995), 36–39.

22. Small Arms Survey (SAS), *Small Arms Survey 2001* (Oxford, 2001), 88–89.

23. Renner, *Small Arms, Big Impact*, 20.

24. John Walters, *Rifles of the World* (Northbrook, 1993), 73, 196.

25. For background and discussion, see Lucy Mathiak and Lora Lumpe, "Government Gun-Running to Insurgents," in Lumpe (ed.), *Running Guns*, 55–80.

26. On Kashmir, see Chris Smith, "Light Weapons and Ethnic Conflict in South Asia," in Boutwell, Klare, and Reed (eds.), *Lethal Commerce*, 61–80. On the contras and Colombia, see Douglas Farah, "Traffickers Said to Buy Contras' Arms," *Washington Post* (18 November 1990).

27. Bulgaria was identified by the UN Sanctions Committee on Angola as a major source of arms for UNITA. See UN Security Council, *Report of the Panel of Experts on Violations of Security Council Sanctions Against UNITA*, UN doc. S/2000/203 (10 March 2000), para. 41.

28. On arms deliveries by these countries to the military regime in Burundi and to Burundian rebel groups, see Human Rights Watch, *Stoking the Fires: Military Assistance and Arms Trafficking in Burundi* (New York, 1997), 53–56.

29. Phil Williams, "Transnational Criminal Organizations and International Security," in Michael Klare and Yogesh Chandrani (eds.), *World Security: Challenges for a New Century* (New York, 1998, 3rd ed.), 249–272.

30. For an extraordinary picture of the two-way trade involving diamonds-for-guns in Angola, see UN Security Council, *Report of the Panel of Experts on Violations of Security Council Sanctions Against UNITA*.

31. For background and discussion on the global black market in small arms, see the essays in Lumpe (ed.), *Running Guns*. See also SAS, *Small Arms Survey 2001*, 141–65.

32. See Global Witness, *A Rough Trade* (London, 1998).

33. See Farah, "Diamonds Are a Rebel's Best Friend."

34. For background and discussion, see Peter Batchelor, "Intra-State Conflict, Political Violence and Small Arms Proliferation in Africa," in Virginia Gamba (ed.), *Society Under Siege* (Halfway House, South Africa, n.d., I), 103–128; Jacklyn Cock, "A Sociological Account of Light Weapons Proliferation in Southern Africa," in Singh (ed.), *Light Weapons and International Security*, 87–126.

35. Cock, "A Sociological Account," 87.

36. A great number of recommendations to this end are contained in UN Security Council, *Report of the Panel of Experts on Violations of the Security Council Sanctions Against UNITA*. Although aimed specifically at UNITA, these recommendations would apply with equal utility to other such groups.

37. In collaboration with Jeffrey Boutwell, I first proposed the establishment of such a regime in "Light Weapons and Civil Conflict: Policy Options for the International Community," in Boutwell and Klare (eds.), *Light Weapons and Civil Conflict*, 217–230. Similar proposals can be found in Michael Klare and Robert I. Rotberg, *The Scourge of Small Arms* (Cambridge, 1999).

38. Many significant measures for the oversight or control of small arms trafficking have been adopted at the regional or subregional level. For a summary of these measures, see SAS, *Small Arms Survey 2001*, 252–276.

39. See UN General Assembly, *Draft Programme of Action to Prevent, Combat and Eradicate the Illicit Trade in Small Arms and Light Weapons in All Its Aspects*, UN doc. A/CONF.192/L.5/Rev.1 (20 July 2001).

40. For background on these measures, see SAS, *Small Arms Survey 2001*, 268–272.

41. For background on the ECOWAS moratorium, see Joseph Smaldone, "Mali and the West African Light Weapons Moratorium," in Boutwell and Klare, *Light Weapons and Civil Conflict*, 129–145. See also SAS, *Small Arms Survey 2001*, 258–261.

42. For discussion of the SADC initiative, see Hussein Solomon, "Controlling Light Weapons in Southern Africa," in Boutwell and Klare (eds.), *Light Weapons and Civil Conflict*, 147–158. For background on other such initiatives, see SAS, *Small Arms Survey 2001*, 262–268.

43. For background on the OAS Convention, see James McShane, "Light Weapons and International Law Enforcement," in Boutwell and Klare, *Light Weapons and Civil Conflict*, 173–182. See also SAS, *Small Arms Survey 2001*, 252–256.

44. For background on the Firearms Protocol, see SAS, *Small Arms Survey 2001*, 278–280.

45. For background on the brokering issue, see ibid., 95–139.

46. For discussion of the World Bank's efforts in this regard, see Nat J. Colletta, "The World Bank, Demobilization, and Social Reconstruction," in Boutwell and Klare (eds.), *Light Weapons and Civil Conflict*, 203–214.

Six

Preventing State Failure

DAVID CARMENT

POLICYMAKERS, and the research community charged with keeping them abreast of current events, too often fail to recognize the preconditions and preliminary events that culminate in situations of ethnic catastrophe and state failure. Had preliminary signals been more inquisitively monitored and the teachings of history relied upon as a dependable guide, policymakers might have been better informed. Foreign policy critics have accused foreign ministries, international organizations, and regional organizations of failing to foresee the occurrence of imminent events, failing to prevent outcomes that in hindsight were avoidable, failing to anticipate the costs of preventable occurrences, and failing to account for history.

To the uninitiated, the shortage of meaningful information capable of forecasting potentially risky situations is a source of constant dismay. However, the complexity of acquiring meaningful and informative accounts of country situations and translating them into policy recommendations presents a formidable challenge. The recent lackluster success in forecasting crises and state failure is rooted less in an underlying indifference to crises than to the inherent practical and technical limitations in translating complex international information into meaningful signals.

The challenge of remaining eternally abreast of events of consequence, significant developments, and emerging risks in the international system is onerous. Doing so effectively involves processing large volumes of information and deciphering only the most important among a myriad of signals.

Why have telltale precursors to important international events such as state failure often been realized only after the fact? An expert in a given area typically draws on a multitude of news sources, publications, and electronic databases. Forecasts and predictions of events involve more than familiarity with the splashy events that form the media universe but constitute only a small part of understanding future occurrences. Media reports tend to focus on significant events only after crises have reached relatively advanced stages, if not full-fledged war. Rather than being presented with a sequence of steps that culminate in an event like a genocide, journalists and observers may not hear of an imminent event until it actually erupts—

by then, seemingly suddenly. However, preventive policy requires focusing energies on information that can anticipate events as early as possible before they occur, if not warding off crises entirely.

In this regard, numerical data tend to provide a more steady and continual flow of information to policymakers than do media reports. Numerical data also present an ungainly body of information since important and unimportant information are mixed together with few distinctions between them. International time-series data regularly deliver country information year by year, not all of which is useful for rapid analysis. Some data merely indicate that a country is well below a crisis threshold. In trying to make sense of gathered information, an expert typically neglects information of limited significance and focuses only on a handful of recognized barometers of an escalating crisis.

Risk assessments precede and complement early warning of state failure; therefore, accurate diagnosis has implications for strategic planning. Assessments identify background and intervening conditions that establish the risk of a potential crisis and conflict and of failure. They focus monitoring and analytical attention on high-risk situations before they are fully developed and provide a framework for interpreting the results of real-time monitoring.[1]

Risk assessment has traditionally referred to the estimation of the probability that some event will occur, while "gravity" is used to describe the event's expected consequences. Combining these two notions, the risk associated with an event can be defined formally as the expected gravity of the event multiplied by the probability that it will occur. Correspondingly, the calculated risk associated with an event is weighted both by its probability of occurrence and the magnitude of its consequences. This technique produces an intuitively appealing means for policymakers to allocate risk management resources. Efforts are focused on events that are likely to occur and / or will be consequential. Conversely, decision makers can reasonably afford to overlook events with remote possibilities unless the consequences are disastrous, as well as events that are likely but the consequences of which are only moderate.

Naturally, risk assessments rely heavily on the field monitoring of specific types of behavior within countries. Somewhat less apparently, analysts should monitor related factors, proximate causes, and like-events. A recent branch of academic discussion emphasizes the importance of identifying background or structural conditions so as to establish the potential for crises and state failure. The goal is to focus monitoring and analytical attention on high-risk situations before they fully develop.[2] Ideally, with accurate diagnosis, failure could be prevented through strategic intervention once its preconditions become evident.

One of the most intuitively apparent means of predicting future international disturbances is to establish patterns. For example, analysts' regional and global observations from 1945 to the present demonstrate that ethnically based rebellions, much less genocide, do not erupt spontaneously; prior indication normally extends back over many years.[3] At least in principle, such observations provide the basis for testing predictions regarding the correlates of crisis situations; a series of situations suspected to be of high risk can be compared to the incidence of crises actually arising in such situations. Propositions established to be empirically well grounded can form the basis of predictive models.[4]

A primary goal is to undertake country risk assessments that can assist policymakers and analysts in planning for contingencies and in directing their risk management efforts. However, structural analysis alone is not meaningful enough to policymakers and regional organizations. Early warning analysis and risk-assessment information tools are made up largely of the reports provided by local analysts. Structural data analysis serves only to complement these more fundamental tools by providing access to data that is not accessible, or by divulging a "wider picture" of such structural data and their causes. At the same time, information sharing among those who do structural analyses, those who do events analysis, and local analysts creates a dynamic relationship that shapes and affects the knowledge and activities of all. This kind of linkage potentially produces a rigorous and highly credible early warning system.

From Risk Assessment to Early Warning

Most explanations of why states fail, including those that rely on comparative case studies, historical trends, leading indicators, events-based data, field monitoring, and expert opinion, are, in isolation, inadequate analytical tools for either risk assessment or early warning. This inadequacy exists because many analyses point to fundamentally different causes of state failure; others rely on the monitoring of background factors and enabling conditions that are associated with the risk of conflict but do not themselves provide accurate information on the probability of specific events leading to failure. Still others do not distinguish between causality and correlation. Others are engrossed in issue-specific problems that are symptomatic of state weakness and human insecurity—e.g., illicit gun flows, child soldiers, black-market activity, and AIDS—problems that are by themselves significant and important but are not *necessarily* associated with, or causes of, failure.

Second, these disparate and often contending analytical approaches constitute a formidable and potentially useful tool kit for risk assessment and early warning. However, there is a very large and very real analytical gap between academics and practitioners on how to develop and use early warning techniques and methodologies. This is partly because to be policy relevant, analytical tools must also be useful operationally, organizationally, and strategically. Secondarily, the accumulation and integration of research findings is vital if theoretical insights are to generate important policy relevant implications, especially at a time when academic early warning research is being criticized for its failure to provide policy-relevant diagnosis.[5] Unfortunately, theoretical insights alone are insufficient to generate effective and specific responses to state failure. Most theories by themselves lack specificity and rarely consider the "operational milieu" in which effective responses must be generated. Theoretical insights are useful as a starting point for more in-depth analysis, and then only if decision makers can be persuaded that the information is useful to finding an appropriate fit between strategy, the problem at hand, and the resources available.

These problems mean that analysts must establish a time frame appropriate to the issue at hand. In this sense, anticipating state failure is like peeling an onion; each analytical layer reveals progressively longer time lines: long-term fundamental dynamics relating to macrolevel preconditions and consequences, mid-term intermediate behavioral patterns, and immediate microlevel events such as political crises and ethnic cleansing.

For example, warning must come years in advance to respond strategically to structural problems (development, institution building, and establishing an infrastructure) but only a year or two or less when escalation is imminent and when the tasks are to engage in preventive diplomacy, dialogue, and mediation.[6]

Model development is important because it specifies the relationship between discrete levels of analysis rather than treating them as independent and isolated causal factors. A model should focus on two types of variables: configurational variables, which define state failure processes in terms of the interaction among units of analysis (e.g., state and society, warring factions, etc.), and composite variables, which characterize state failure by summarizing the attributes and performance indicators of the state over time.[7]

Thus identifying state failure is a three-step process involving the use of both composite and configurational variables. These three steps are as follows: (1) identifying the relevant configurational and composite variables; (2) postulating thresholds to identify significant transformations and shifts from states of equilibria; and (3) determining the independence of variables to isolate the causal significance of each variable. Articulating such constructs and concepts is useful in the generation of propositions or hypotheses about state change. These propositions can in turn be tested empirically to determine whether or not they have factual support. To the extent that the use of conceptualizations enables theorists to describe and explain in simple language the complex processes of state failure, the use of concepts is justified. However, the ultimate focus of the theorist should not be these constructs and models. They should be understood only as heuristic devices to explain complex phenomena to policymakers.

Models used to generate evidence for the explanation and prediction of state failure correspond to the configurational and composite approaches just described.[8] These kinds of models include forecasting as well as risk assessment models.[9] As Gupta shows, in addition to distinct levels of analyses, these approaches can also be distinguished by the following methods:[10]

1. Macrolevel *evaluation of structural indicators* (econometrically or through pattern recognition techniques), e.g., parts of the State Failure Project, Interdisciplinary Research on Root Causes of Human Rights Violations (PIOOM), Country Indicators for Foreign Policy (CIFP), Humanitarian Early Warning System (HEWS), International Crisis Behavior Data Project (ICB), Facts on International Relations and Security Trends (FIRST), Rummel's Democide database, Uppsala's Conflict database.
2. Macrolevel *time series of leading indicators*, e.g., International Organization for Migrations (IOM), Refworld, FAO's Global Information and Early Warning System (GIEWS), Reliefweb, the UN system-wide Earthwatch, HazardNet for disasters, the Global Early Warning System (GEWS).
3. Intermediate-level *conjunctural models* that track changes in prespecified events and interactions among groups (such as conflict / cooperation, genocide, nonviolent protest) using machine-coded data, pattern recognition, and neural networks, e.g., Global Event Data System (GEDS), Protocol for the Assessment of Nonviolent Direct Actions (PANDA), Kansas Events Data System (KEDS).[11]
4. Intermediate-level *structured (Delphi) and subjective* models, which utilize a team of experts who identify key actors and estimate their future position on a given issue (regime stability, turmoil likelihood, investment restrictions, and trade restrictions) with regard to their power to influence the outcome, the importance (salience) they attach to the issue, and the certainty or firmness of the actor's orientation—Decision Insights, Political Risk Services.[12] The scores that emerge from this assessment are used to provide a formal estimate of probability.
5. Microlevel *sequential models* that, using accelerators, develop risk assessments based on tracking of specific behaviors—e.g., parts of State Failure, Conflict Early Warning Systems (CEWS).
6. Microlevel *response models* that evaluate outside response to conflict and develop feasibility assessments based therein—e.g., Helen

Fein's Life Integrity Violations Approach, Peace and Conflict Assessment Initiative (PCIA).

7. Microlevel *field reporting* by NGO networks, Forum on Early Warning and Early Response (FEWER), Early Recognition of Tension and Fact Finding (FAST), International Crisis Group (ICG), Caucasian Institute for Peace, Democracy, and Development (CIPDD), using structured and/or unstructured reporting techniques.[13]

The array of choices in terms of units of analysis, deductive and inductive methodologies, qualitative and quantitative theoretical assumptions, and time frames renders politically relevant and integrated analyses of state failure difficult but not impossible. On the one hand, where conflicts are well understood in both form and content and the causes are proximate and escalation is likely, the main problem will be to identify the relevant configurational variables through an evaluation of microlevel interactions (nos. 5–7). On the other hand, where the situation is latent, where a state of equilibrium has been achieved, or where behavior is only remotely suggestive of political or economic collapse, careful monitoring of composite indicators and trends at the macro- and intermediate levels will be essential (nos. 1–4).[14]

An example of an approach integrating composite and configurational variables is Harff's sequential model for early warning of genocides and politicides. Her approach resembles a qualitative time series approach, but incorporates the role of accelerators. She identifies ten background conditions, four intervening conditions, and eight accelerators. She does not assume that state development is linear. Where processual models, without accelerators and triggers, identify stages of a conflict, these static models cannot provide adequate risk assessments that will allow for the planning of responses to "impending" situations, which is where the dynamic role of accelerators and triggers comes in, ideally those that are essential and necessary.[15]

An alternative methodology is Moore and Gurr's employment of data from the Minorities at Risk project, which compares three empirical approaches to long-term risk assessments. Their work generates risk profiles: lists of high-risk factors, or leading indicators, that are generated based on general theoretical knowledge such as group incentives, capacity, and opportunity. They apply a theoretical regression model in which an argument is expressed as a multiple equation model, and a statistical technique—three-stage least squares—is applied to the data to estimate the parameters of a predictive equation. Finally, they employ an empirical regression model; an inductive approach similar to the State Failure project, in which statistical software determines specific indicators for assessing probabilities.[16] It should be noted that each model produces slightly different results, although with a proportion of overlap.

The obvious conclusion is that barring any weaknesses in the internal validity and reliability of these methods, it is difficult to select, on the basis of findings and rigor alone, one methodology over the other. Each purports to explain and predict different facets of state failure and its causes. There remains the need to reconcile empirically valid but potentially contending claims on the causes of state failure, on the one hand, and the desire for accumulation, integration, and policy-relevance on the other.

How can multiple approaches and the accumulation of findings be simultaneously encouraged and developed? One approach would be to integrate research at the level of findings. The focus would be on those *cases, indicators, and accelerators* that appear in *multiple* assessment lists. This would entail a brief description of the method employed in policy-relevant terms and then the establishment of a "watch list." While it is true that a complex model is not necessary in order to put states on a watch list, it also true that models and theoretically generated insights can direct analysts toward causal factors that are potentially unique to a given situation and that are counterintuitive (they direct the analyst's attention to something that might otherwise be overlooked or ignored).

From Early Warning to Prevention

Understanding the root causes of state failure, identifying the point at which a conflict is likely to become violent, and deciding what to do about it is more akin to "solving mysteries" (e.g., group problem-solving) than it is to "breaking secrets" (e.g., spying). It is a truism to say that effective conflict prevention entails a substantial understanding of conflict dynamics, their structural consequences, the processes by which they become violent, and what well-meaning leaders, nongovernmental organizations (NGOs), and governments can do about them. Unfortunately, the bulk of academic research is useful for understanding why, when, and how some conflicts originate, but it is less useful in explaining or predicting when or how violent interactions will occur in a way that is directly consumable by policymakers. One response to this problem has been to ensure that policymakers are better equipped to do their own in-field analyses.[17]

In providing early warning about the risk of state failure, there is a clear need to provide country performance measures for the factors that directly and indirectly influence a country's security and level of stability. The ultimate goal is to provide risk assessments in a way that is actually useful to decision makers so they can better respond to potential, emerging, or existing risks. The salient features influencing country situations are specified in Rotberg's introductory chapter. I argue that data collected from a multitude of reputable international information sources is employable only if converted into a meaningful and understandable form and then translated into effective preventive action. In turn, the process of mainstreaming effective early warning information into the operations of states and organizations will set in motion a process of "creeping institutionalization" toward a "culture of prevention" through norm development, the enhancement of operational responses, and the implementation and evaluation of cost effective structural and operational prevention strategies.[18]

Developing a linkage between early warning information and policy response creates a distinct problem—how to render analyses of existing methodologies, instruments, techniques tools, and response strategies meaningful and practicable to practitioners and policymakers? Is conflict prevention an ad hoc action-oriented approach to emerging and potential problems or is it a medium- and long-term proactive *structuralist* strategy intended to create the enabling conditions for a stable and more predictable international environment?

One possible answer can be found in former UN Secretary-General Boutros Boutros-Ghali's *An Agenda for Peace.* To be sure, Boutros-Ghali chose to reflect only on preventive diplomacy within a range of conflict management techniques that include peace-building, peacemaking, and peacekeeping and essentially on those activities that usually, but not always, fall under the purview of the United Nations, such as confidence-building measures, arms control, and preventive deployment. Since *An Agenda for Peace* was published, preventive diplomacy has come to refer to a response generated by a state, a coalition of states, or a multilateral organization intended to address the rapid escalation of emergent crises, disputes, and interstate hostilities. Preventive diplomacy entails primarily, but not exclusively, ad hoc forms of consultation using noncompartmentalized and nonhierarchical forms of information gathering, contingency planning, and short-term response mechanisms. The risks are proximate and analysis and action are combined at once in rapid succession.[19]

Despite its post–Cold War faddishness, popular usage of the term "preventive diplomacy" can be traced back to the activities of UN Secretary-General Dag Hammarskjöld (although its underlying logic has existed at least since the emergence of the modern state system). The Westphalian Treaty at its birth was an attempt to prevent the continuation of interstate warfare of the early seventeenth century; and its rationale is deeply embedded in such fundamentals of statecraft as deterrence, reassurance, and compulsion.[20] Hammarskjöld realized that early engagement of the global organization could act to forestall the destructiveness of conflict created by external military intervention and arms transfers. Preventive action "must in the first place aim at filling the vacuum so that it will not provoke action from any of the major parties."[21] When crisis threatens, traditional diplomacy continues, but more urgent preventive efforts are required—

through unilateral and multilateral channels—to arbitrate, mediate, or lend "good offices" to encourage dialogue and facilitate peace.

Today, preventive diplomacy is considered important due in part to the evolving nature of conflict. The shift from interstate to intrastate conflict is well documented. However, this change in itself is not sufficient to generate a call for revised thinking on preventive action. It is the surrounding circumstances, the ability of such complex conflicts to spread vertically and horizontally—in essence the potential of such conflicts to do harm to others, ordinary citizens, neighboring states, refugees, and minorities—that generates efforts of preventive diplomacy.[22]

Nicolaides provides a useful conceptual framework for determining how preventive diplomacy relates to conflict prevention.[23] Preventive diplomacy is an operational response. It is premised on incentive structures provided by outside actors to change specific kinds of undesirable behavior. Preventive diplomacy is therefore targeted and short-term, and the preventive action taken relates directly to changes in conflict escalation and conflict dynamics.[24] In this regard outside actors can seek to influence the course of events and can try to alter or induce specific behavior through coercive and operational threats and deterrents or through less coercive strategies of persuasion and inducement.[25] Ultimately, outside actors can work to influence the incentives of the relevant parties engaged in conflict but cannot change the initial conditions that led to conflict in the first place.

Thus, structural approaches emphasize capacity building to provide conflict-prone societies with the means to address root causes of conflict. In this sense, structural conflict prevention strategies, such as those focusing on human security, conflict transformation, and development, cast a much broader net. They tend to be long-term and are generally applied across a range of countries, issues, and actors. The goal is to transform conflictual behavior over time. This change in behavior can be dependent on institutional inducements—such as membership in international institutions, arms control agreements, and stability pacts, or on the promotion of sustainable development, support for human security, and regional confidence building mechanisms.[26]

It is also obvious that analytical capacity alone will never be sufficient to generate effective responses.[27] There is a need for a field monitoring of indicators of specific types of behavior, of related factors, and of proximate causes through predictive models.[28] Once information is evaluated, a significant gap remains between analyzing the information and developing a strategy to deal with a problem. Analysis by itself does not generate an immediate solution. At best, monitoring of indicators helps to strengthen the flow of information to policymakers.[29]

Several problems arise in translating analysis into action. First, there is a need to know what to look for, and what should set off a warning. Ethnic warfare, regime failure, massive human rights violations, and refugee flows are the result of different combinations of factors. Hence each requires somewhat different models, explanations, strategies, and responses. Second, there is need for specificity in the combinations of risk factors and sequences of events that are likely to lead to crises and failure. Lists of variables or indicators are only a starting point. Explanations should identify which measurable conditions, in what combination or sequence, establish a potential for certain types and kinds of crises. The question of how to bring early warning into the process of policy planning also needs to be considered. There are two complementary approaches. The first is primarily an array of decentralized early warning networks for the analysis of impending humanitarian crises and complex emergencies. This option would see states and NGOs relying to some extent on global networks for their information analysis.

A second option is to pursue the integration of risk assessments into the strategic planning processes of states, regional organizations, and NGOs—beginning with developmental aid—to fashion coherent, sustainable, and long-term policies on conflict prevention. This is a five-step process. First, because risk assessment data and information must satisfy the needs of different agencies, they must be integrated more closely into routinized activities of the various departments engaged in foreign and security policy. Second, integration means that assessments are used to identify not only future risks but also to identify links between conflict processes and identifiable focal points of activity in which the end-user is engaged. Assessments should be able to identify a sequence of events that are logically consistent with operational responses. Third, the end-user should be able to use the information in a way that helps plan for contingencies. In essence, the goal is to establish a risk assessment chain that is multidepartmental, multipurpose, and multidirectional. Fourth, measurements of effectiveness need to be harmonized across states. As structured databases will continue to be an important tool despite their imperfections, the current situation of decentralized data holding will only be able to function if the information handling systems—including indicators—in the different countries are harmonized. Fifth, and finally, an essential step would be to establish conflict prevention secretariats and councils within states and organizations.

Conclusion

Anticipating state failure is a process-based approach requiring sound analysis as well as an explicit connection to policy options for preventive measures. A process-based approach means that the method and format of applied early warning is shaped directly by the operational focus of the process itself, in this case preventive action as opposed to preparedness. All of these elements point to the relevance of basic policy analysis to bridging the warning-action gap. Such methods incorporate the structuring of problems, the application of appropriate analytical tools to solve those problems, and the communication of analysis and recommendations in a format useful to decision makers. Policy planning is a type of decision-support procedure.

Such an approach requires that organizations have a better sense of their own institutional needs and capabilities. Such activities—especially those premised on long-term structural transformations—should have a built-in evaluative process or impact assessment capability that will, in effect, ensure self-monitoring and provide policy guidance. At the very minimum, activity in an economically and political fragile society should not further destabilize society. The World Bank and the IMF, for example, are leaning toward assurance that their structural adjustment programs do not contribute to the disintegration of the political and economic bases of state stability.

Equally it may, on occasion, be important to hand off many of the responsibilities for analysis and response to those who are themselves stakeholders in the process. Such approaches include local capacity building—providing the means to address root causes through blueprints and resources—for local stakeholders through such activities often associated with preventive development, support for human rights, and democratization. Any activity that advances human security, alleviates poverty, improves the environment, increases respect for human rights, or fosters good and stable governance, contributes in one way or another to long-term stabilization and the prevention of state failure and violence.

Notes

The author would like to thank Troy Joseph for his research assistance and Robert Rotberg and Debbie West for helpful comments on earlier drafts. The Social Sciences and Humanities Research Council and the Security Defence Forum of the Department of National Defence provided support for this research.

1. Will Moore and Ted R. Gurr, "Assessing Risks of Ethnopolitical Rebellion in the Year 2000: Three Empirical Approaches," in Susanne Schmeidl and Howard Adelman (eds.), *Early Warning and Early Response* (New York, 1998), 45–70; also available online at http://wwwc.cc.columbia.edu/sec/dlc/ciao/book/schmeidl/schmeidl11.html

2. Ibid.

3. Ibid.

4. Ted R. Gurr, "Early Warning Systems: From Surveillance to Assessment to Action," in Kevin M. Cahill (ed.), "Preventive Diplomacy: The Therapeutics of Mediation," conference proceedings (23–24 April 1996, New York).

5. Author's discussion with Andrew Mack, former senior advisor to United Nations Secretary General Kofi Annan at a conference on Conflict Prevention held at United Nations headquarters, New York, 14 November 2000. It should be noted that early warning is not just about facts, theory building, and model development. Early warning is also about anticipating and responding to specific events and preventing them from occurring. Early warning systems are not confined to analyzing the potential for state failure but also relate to the capacities and response strategies for dealing with them. See reports prepared by the Forum on Warning and Early Response (FEWER) at www.fewer.org.

6. Mary O. McCarthy, "Potential Humanitarian Crises: The Warning Process and Roles for Intelligence" in Suzanne Schmeidl and Howard Adelman (eds.), "Synergy in Early Warning," conference proceedings (15–18 March 1997, Toronto), 56–68.

7. See Robert I. Rotberg's "The Failure and Collapse of Nation-States: Breakdown, Prevention, and Repair," chapter 1 in this volume.

8. Of the commercial tools, the most comprehensive products are those provided by the Economist Intelligence Unit, International Crisis Group, Stratfor, Political Risk Services, and Control Risks Information Services. It is important to note that the definitions of political risk ratings vary widely among instruments. For example, the majority of the commercially available tools focus on the risk to business interests, and they define political risk very narrowly as it relates to the willingness and ability of a given state to repay its loans. Databases available through Moody's Investors Service, Standard and Poor's Rating Group, Business Environment Risk Intelligence, and Euromoney are examples of narrowly focused economic forecasting systems encompassing only limited elements of political risk. Overall, however, all of these instruments rely heavily on qualitative analysis by experienced analysts, with a surprisingly low level of methodological complexity.

9. Forecasting is about the likelihood that an event will happen. By itself it has no strategic connotation or purpose. Forecasting can either be passive (about events over which we have no control) or active (about events over which we have some control). To be policy relevant, forecasting needs to take on additional qualities. It must be diagnostic, whereby emphasis is on describing how and why things work as they do, and it must be prescriptive, offering explicit recommendations to policymakers faced with certain kinds of problems.

10. Dipak Gupta, "An Early Warning About Forecasts: Oracle to Academics" in Schmeidl and Adelman (eds.), *Synergy in Early Warning*, 375–396.

11. A leading indicator approach would use previously identified relationships or sequences of events to identify the precursors of instability or conflict. The basis for this approach holds that there are sequencing regularities that allow the forecaster to discover what variable to focus on to project a trend. The major disadvantage of a leading indicator approach is that while it can often predict the direction of change, it gives no indication of its magnitude.

12. For an example of predictions using the Decision Insights model, see Patrick James and Michael Lusztig, "Assessing the Reliability of Predictions on the Future of Quebec" in David Carment, John F. Stack Jr., and Frank Harvey (eds.), *The International Politics of Quebec Secession: State Making and State Breaking in North America* (Westport, 2001).

13. See the following websites: Interdisciplinary Research on Root Causes of Human Rights Violations (PIOOM), http://www.fsw.leidenuniv.nl/www/w3_liswo/pioom.htm; Country Indicators for Foreign Policy (CIFP), http://www.carleton.ca/cifp; Humanitarian Early Warning System (HEWS), http://www.reliefweb.int/ocha_ol/programs/pad/hews.html; International Crisis Behavior Data Project (ICB), http://web.missouri.edu/~polsjjh/ICB/;Facts on International Relations and Security Trends (FIRST), http://www.sipri.se/projects/database/index.html; Democide Research Homepage, http://www2.hawaii.edu/~rummel/; Uppsala's Conflict Database, http://www.pcr.uu.se/data.htm; International Organization for Migration (IOM), http://www.iom.int/; Refworld, http://www.unhcr.ch/refworld/country/cdr/cdrsom2.htm; Global Information and Early Warning System (GIEWS), http://www.fao.org/giews/english/giewse.htm; EarthWatch, http://www.unep.ch/earthw.html; HazardNet, http://hoshi.cic.sfu.ca/~hazard/; Global Early Warning System (GEWS), http://fugimodel.t.soka.ac.jp/FUGI/chapter6/chapter6.html; Global Event Data System (GEDS) (now defunct), http://geds.umd.edu/geds/; Protocol for the Assessment of Nonviolent Direct Action (PANDA), http://www-vdc.fas.harvard.edu/cfia/pnscs/panda.htm; Kansas Events Data System (KEDS), http://www.ukans.edu/~keds/; Political Risk Services, http://www.polrisk.com/; Conflict Early Warning Systems (CEWS), http://www.usc.edu/dept/LAS/ir/cis/cews/; Peace and Conflict Impact Assessment (PCIA), http://www.idrc.ca/peace/; Early Recognition of Tension and Fact Finding (FAST), http://www.swisspeace.ch/; International Crisis Group (ICG), http://www.intl-crisis-group.org/; Caucasian Institute for Peace, Democracy and Development (CIPDD), http://www.armazi.demon.co.uk/cipdd.html.

To establish an integrated framework for analyzing the emergence of violent conflict and conflict management, it is necessary to understand how each given type of crisis typically develops and which possible avoidance efforts can be effective. In general terms, the factors that contribute to conflict escalation are categorized as structural factors (root causes), accelerators (precipitators/facilitators), or triggers (catalyzing events). *Structural factors:* background conditions that form the preconditions of crisis situations such as systematic political exclusion, inherent economic inequities, lack of adequate and responsive institutions, the presence of ethnic minorities, resource exhaustion, and overdependence on international trade. *Accelerators:* feedback events that rapidly increase the level of significance of the most volatile of the general conditions, but may also signify system breakdown or basic changes in political causality. *Triggers:* sudden events that act as catalysts igniting a crisis or conflict, such as the assassination of a leader, election fraud, or a political scandal.

14. Portions of this part of the chapter are based on the risk assessment and conflict indicators approach developed by the Country Indicators for Foreign Policy.

15. Barbara Harff, "Early Warning of Humanitarian Crises: Sequential Models and the Role of Accelerators," in John L. Davies and Ted Gurr (eds.), *Preventive Measures: Building Risk Assessment and Crisis Early Warning Systems* (Lanham, Md., 1998), 70–78.

16. Moore and Gurr, "Assessing Risks of Ethnopolitical Rebellion in the Year 2000," 45–70. Definitional and operationalization issues are always problematic

when dealing with a class of events that are controversial, rare, and not well understood. See also Gary King and Langche Zeng "Improving Forecasts of State Failure" unpubl. ms. (Cambridge, MA, 2001). They evaluate the inherent trade-off between providing accurate forecasting and making causal inference from the same models. They suggest that a claim about accurate forecasts is also a claim about causal structure. The net result can be an overwhelming array of associations and causal relationships. Parsimony gives way to complexity.

17. Here the distinction between risk assessment and early warning is important. The policy relevance of early warning stems directly from the fact that early warning systems are not restricted to analyzing a crisis—they also assess the capacities, needs, and responses for dealing with a crisis. Second, early warning essentially consists of networks—states, intergovernmental organizations, and NGOs—conducting their analyses together to prevent likely events from occurring. According to FEWER, early warning is "the communication of information on a crisis area, analysis of that information and development of potential strategic responses to respond to the crisis in a timely manner. The central purpose of early warning is not only to identify potential problems but also to create the necessary political will for preventive action to be taken" (see www.fewer.org).

18. Michael Lund, "Creeping Institutionalisation of the Culture of Prevention?" in "Preventing Violent Conflict: The Search for Political Will, Strategies and Effective Tools," Report of the Krusenberg Seminar (19–20 June 2000), 23.

19. The form of such interventions is best seen as a continuum. Different third-party techniques are set in motion at different points within a conflict (Michael Lund, *Preventing Violent Conflict*, Washington, D.C., 1996). At one end of the intervention spectrum is pure mediation—the facilitation of a negotiated settlement through persuasion, control of information, and identification of alternatives by a party who is perceived to be impartial. Further along the spectrum of preventive strategies is "mediation with muscle," or the deliberate and strategic use of rewards and punishments to bring the belligerents to the negotiating table. Finally, where consent is absent, third parties are likely to be required to take on a multiplicity of functions, including peacekeeping, humanitarian assistance, and possibly peace enforcement (see David Carment and Frank Harvey, *Using Force to Prevent Ethnic Violence* [Westport, 2000]). At this end of the spectrum, preventive efforts involve the exercise of force either to deter or, possibly, subdue intransigent combatants. Thus, the forms of prevention range from traditional preventive diplomacy to its more forceful descendants. The specific tactics and strategies associated with these third-party efforts are examined elsewhere, for example in I. William Zartman, *Ripe for Resolution: Conflict and Intervention in Africa*, (New York, 1989, 2nd ed.); William J. Durch, *The Evolution of UN Peacekeeping: Case Studies and Comparative Analysis* (New York, 1993); John G. Ruggie, "The New US Peacekeeping Doctrine," *Washington Quarterly*, XVII (1994), 175–184; David Carment and Patrick James (eds.), *Peace in the Midst of Wars: Preventing and Managing International Ethnic Conflicts* (Columbia, SC, 1998).

Recent international developments have led to fundamental changes in the nature of conflict prevention. Before the end of the Cold War, preventive efforts were generally performed to monitor cease-fire arrangements between two warring states. The superpowers of the Cold War period could either block formal United Nations missions or deter most unilateral efforts on the part of their rival (David Carment and Dane Rowlands, "Three's Company: Evaluating Third Party Intervention into Intrastate Conflict, *Journal of Conflict Resolution*, XLII [1998] 572–99). With the reduced importance of traditional ideologically based rivalry, the ability of individual states or state coalitions to intervene in the conflicts of others has increased dramatically. Furthermore, with the loosening of ideological bonds and the erosion of strong state centers backed by foreign governments, the likelihood of intrastate conflict has risen, especially conflict over territory and identity.

20. For other definitions of conflict prevention, see Carment and Harvey, *Using Force To Prevent Ethnic Violence*; David Carment and Karen Garner, "Conflict Prevention and Early Warning: Problems, Pitfalls and Avenues for Success," *Canadian Foreign Policy Journal*, VI (1999) 103–117. For distinctions between operational and structural prevention see Bruce Jentleson (ed.), *Opportunities Missed, Opportunities Seized: Preventive Diplomacy in the Post–Cold War World* (1999); *The Carnegie Commission on Preventing Deadly Conflict: Final Report* (New York, 1998); Lund, *Preventing Violent Conflict*; Jacob Bercovitch, "Understanding Mediation's Role in Preventive Diplomacy," *Negotiation Journal*, XII (1996) 241–258; Stephen J. Stedman, "Alchemy for a New World Disorder: Overselling Preventive Diplomacy," *Foreign Affairs*, LXXIV (1995), 14–20; Diana Chigas, "Preventive Diplomacy and the Organization for Security and Cooperation in Europe: Creating Incentives for Dialogue and Cooperation," in Abram Chayes and Antonia Handler Chayes (eds.), *Preventing Conflict in the Post-Communist World*, (Washington, D.C., 1996), 25–97.

21. Dag Hammarskjöld, introduction to the 1959–1960 UN Annual Report, quoted in Raimo Vayrynen, "Challenges to Preventative Action," in Carment and Albrecht Schnabel (eds.), *Conflict Prevention: Path to Peace or Grand Illusion?* (Tokyo, 2003), 47. Hammarskjöld's approach covers only one type of conflict action—the horizontal, cross-border escalation of violence. Escalation can also be vertical when the destructiveness of violence increases within a given political unit without spilling over boundaries to other units. A critical difference between these two processes of escalation lies in their relationship with the principle of sovereignty. In the former case, national sovereignty is violated and thus the offense-defense cycle is set in motion.

22. According to the Carnegie Commission's *Report*, in declining situations, a number of steps may help manage the crisis and prevent the emergence of violence. States should resist the traditional urge to suspend diplomatic relations as a substitute for action and instead maintain open, high-fidelity lines of communication with leaders and groups in crisis. Governments and international organizations must express in a clear and compelling way the interests being affected. The crisis should immediately be put on the agenda of the UN Security Council or on that of the relevant international organization, or both, early enough to permit preventive action. At the same time, a means should be established to track developments in the crisis, to provide regular updates, and to include a mechanism to incorporate information from NGOs and other nongovernmental actors to support high-level deliberations for unfolding events. Governments should be attentive to opportu-

nities to support quiet diplomacy and dialogue with and between moderate leaders in the crisis. Special envoys and representatives of key states or regional organizations or on behalf of the UN have repeatedly demonstrated their value, particularly in the early stages of a crisis. Diplomatic and political strategies to avert a looming crisis demand creative ways of defusing tensions and facilitating mutual accommodation among potential belligerents.

23. Kalypso Nicolaides, "International Preventive Action: Developing a Strategic Framework" in Robert I. Rotberg (ed.), *Vigilance and Vengeance: NGOs Preventing Ethnic Conflict in Divided Societies* (Washington, D.C., 1996), 23–72.

24. For similar approaches linking prevention to response using an overarching framework, see David Lake and Donald Rothchild (eds.), *The International Spread of Ethnic Conflict: Fear, Diffusion and Escalation* (Princeton, 1998); Carment and James, *Peace in the Midst of* Wars; A. J. Tellis, Thomas S. Szayan, and James A. Winnefeld, *Anticipating Ethnic Conflict* (Washington, D.C., 1998); Gerald Schneider and Patricia A. Weitsman (eds.), *Enforcing Cooperation: Risky States and Intergovernmental Management of Conflict* (London, 1997).

25. In this respect, the behavior and actions of the outside actors are contingent on a specific and usually prespecified desired behavior of the internal parties. They could also support a more hands-on approach, seeking transformation or changes in the initial conditions that precipitated the conflict (Kalypso Nicolaides, "International Preventive Action," 23–72).

26. Ibid.

27. Indeed, to convince themselves that action is necessary, strategists must have knowledge about the costs of not being involved, coupled with the likelihood that a conflict will escalate. Such an approach has two implications. First, it means that the analysis of events and intelligence gathering do not fit neatly into compartmentalized and modular frameworks of responsibilities. Second, it means that to cope with events as they unfold, strategies of information-gathering and analysis become crucial. Long-term planning tends to take a back seat to more medium-term and short-term contingency planning.

28. Ted Robert Gurr, "Early Warning Systems: From Surveillance to Assessment to Action" in *Preventive Diplomacy*, 23–24.

29. Ibid., 23–24.

Part Two

POST-FAILURE RESUSCITATION OF NATION-STATES

Seven

Forming States after Failure

JENS MEIERHENRICH

THE PROBLEM OF state failure is one of the greatest political and humanitarian challenges facing the world in the twenty-first century. Failed states adversely affect the well-being of tens of millions of people the world over. They have been associated with civil war, ethnic war, and international war, but also with famine, drought, and other social and environmental disasters. Although the problem of state failure has moved to the forefront of international concerns in recent years, we know very little about what to do in situations where it has occurred.

This chapter reflects on the formation of states after failure. It asks how to form new states from scratch. The practicality of such an endeavor is not always obvious. In some instances, state reformation may exacerbate rather than cure the consequences of state failure.[1] In such situations, state formation can be dysfunctional, and alternative options may be more desirable.[2]

Conceptualizing Formation

State formation, as traditionally understood, is a macrohistorical process. Controlling and concluding such a process is an improbable task. Accordingly, I focus here only on what may be regarded as the "first stage" of state formation. States, like other institutions, house rules that constitute and constrain human behavior by affecting the payoffs for self-interested agents, be they elites or masses. In our conventional understanding, states exist not only because they are successful in generating positive payoffs for a majority of the citizens, but also because a degree of loyalty binds citizens to the state. In situations of state failure, this loyalty is frayed or entirely absent. I argue that state formation must recreate this tie by focusing on the utility of states. The rationality of the state, I submit, is purely instrumental. In the process of state formation, agents have two principal choices.

Stealing vs. Preserving

The difference, in essence, is between stealing and preserving the state.[3] Realistically, state formation after state failure will bear fruit only if powerful agents, individuals and groups, support it. The mobilization of such support involves the creation of *stakes*, by which I mean deep interests held in the state.[4] These stakes can revolve around property, rights, representation, influence, power, or other commodities deemed valuable by interacting agents bargaining over the state's future. Stakes need to engage people living in the state's shadow. The process of creating stakes should lead warring parties and other stakeholders to accept the idea that the state is an important, if not foremost, public good. In other words, agents must develop confidence in the state as a primary institutional structure. The state must be seen as an institution that creates opportunities for the acquisition of power, wealth, and security. One might raise the objection that such a constellation of opportunities brought many states down in the first place by creating incentives for aggrandizement and embezzlement. This is a valid objection. To overcome the problem, stakes must be balanced between appealing to private interests and cultivating public goods.

State formation after state failure is primarily about overcoming a history of noncompliance. Noncompliance can occur at the elite level, at the mass level, or both. Examples of noncompliance include evasion, avoidance, circumvention, abuse, and corruption.[5] Whether compliance or noncompliance emerge as responses to state formation after state failure depends on the opportunities and incentives created by the institutional structure of the state. If the institutional structure rewards opportunism, then noncompliance will become the norm. If the institutional structure of the state sanctions opportunism and rewards productive activities, then compliance will result.

When will agents preserve states? When will they steal them? Some agents have an interest in the perpetuation of failed states. Reno observed that a key reason why leaders "prefer weak formal and informal institutions, not only in the sense of straying from rule-based principles but also from the provision of public goods, lies in their fear that enterprising rivals could use control over successful institutions" to challenge their rule.[6] A similar story can be told for Russia. There, "the atmosphere of a collapsed state directly influenced elite attitudes and behavior such that they preferred to pursue short-term private interests rather than to adopt long-term goals involving the provision of public goods."[7] State formation after state failure can only succeed if underwritten by agents with a stake in its perpetuation.

Given the crucial role of stakes, the *idea* of the state appears to matter more than anything in state formation after state failure.[8] "The idea of the state," according to Dyson, "forms part of the considerations which groups have in mind when determining where their interests lie and what types of conduct will appeal to decision-makers and the public."[9] My argument is grounded in ideas about the state's utility, *not* its coercive power. As Gourevitch notes:

> Members acquire incentives to preserve institutions. The test of the power of an institution is thus its *utility*, not its coercive force. Institutions serve a purpose for their members. To withhold compliance, thus to weaken them, means losing something valuable. Members have an incentive to care about institutional preservation and, as a result, institutions have force.[10]

State formation is about the inculcation of values. It is not the state per se that matters in changing societies, but rather the state's presumed future—its potential value as a social institution, as perceived by interacting agents. New states, and the "secondary institutions" that go with them, will be held together by commitments. Examples of secondary institutions include constitutional frameworks, electoral systems, federalism, and such mechanisms as consociationalism. To achieve credible commitments among interacting adversaries, the supply of reassurance is crucial, whether it comes from internal or external sources. External reassurance is relatively easy to achieve but generally difficult to sustain. Internal reassurance is generally difficult to attain but, once achieved, relatively easy to sustain.

My argument operates chiefly at the level of perception and stresses the fundamental psychological character of stateness. "A state exists chiefly in the hearts and minds of its people," notes Strayer. "[I]f they do not believe it is there, no logical exercise will bring it to life."[11] When, and why, do agents consider an existing state "useful" and "usable," and thus worth preserving? My answer revolves around the concepts of confidence and utility. The loss of confidence in the state on the part of self-interested agents, be they elites or masses, makes its demise a self-fulfilling prophecy. Even the perception of state weakness can undermine an executive's ability to govern.[12]

Usable States

To effect state formation after state failure, the incentive structures inherent in different strategies for state formation must be understood. Strayer's "test" for the emergence of a state is helpful in this regard.[13] The test requires "the appearance of political units persisting in time and fixed in space, the development of permanent, impersonal institutions, agreement on the need for an authority which can give final judgments, and acceptance of the idea that this authority should receive the basic loyalty of its subjects."[14] Strayer's definition—broad enough to be useful, and narrow enough to be meaningful—allows for the development of straightforward, first-cut indicators. It rightly focuses on the "primary institution" of the state, its structure vis-à-vis society, and excludes considerations about regime type, government, and secondary institutions, as defined earlier, all of which clearly have an effect on state survival and are affected by stateness, but which do *not* define it. Strayer's test, in short, does not "require any particular *scale* of government, any particular *degree* of integration among the 'permanent, impersonal institutions,' or any great concentration of power in the central authority."[15] Strayer's definition avoids eurocentrism and can be operationalized easily in comparative research.

My concept of the "usable state" is a plea for minimalism that builds on Strayer. A state is usable if it offers a reasonably stable framework within which the tasks of social regulation and integration can be carried out in a changing society. The notion of the usable state is intended to convey this sense of relative utility. As in everyday language, the adjective "usable" indicates sufficiency, not perfection. Usable states are not perfect states; they are, in many respects, flawed states. They combine islands of strength and weakness. Segments of the state are likely to suffer corruption or other forms of opportunism. None of these factors, however, necessarily thwarts their utility in state formation after state failure.

The promotion and construction of legality and bureaucracy are the most important tasks in state formation after state failure. Both can "lock in" stakes for those who stand to lose from the reformation of a state. Thus, legality and bureaucracy are two necessary and sufficient conditions of state survival *after* state reformation. If they are usable, newly formed states are likely to serve any of six interrelated functions: (1) encouraging predictability; (2) creating confidence; (3) lending credibility; (4) providing security; (5) displaying resolve; and (6) controlling resources. The functions are cumulative. They can facilitate the gradual construction of trust among adversaries, thus accelerating regime formation and government formation. Legality and bureaucracy are yet again necessary and sufficient to create *usable* states.[16] The formation of usable states is key to the construction and maintenance of social order in changing societies. It is not the end of state formation, but a significant first step. This step involves "institutional" and "societal" formation processes.

Once legality and bureaucracy are established and relatively routine, secondary institutions can be introduced. The construction of secondary institutions can pose serious commitment problems. For example, a majoritarian electoral system or a presidential constitutional framework can produce zero-sum outcomes.[17] The zero-sum nature of political outcomes may cause some agents to defect from state formation and related processes altogether due to fears of victimization. However, a usable state will lengthen the shadow of the future for interacting agents, thus decreasing the chances of defection of either party. In sum, I advocate a *sequencing* of institutions because the establishment of constitutional frameworks and electoral systems entails serious commitment problems. If secondary institutions are introduced too early, interacting adversaries may operate under short-time horizons and hence may renege on commitments (despite potential for cooperation) in the absence of reassurance. Legality and bureaucracy are reassurance devices that underwrite commitments with a promise of enforcement. When legality and bureaucracy are reasonably well entrenched in a newly forming state, reaching important institutional choices that have long-term consequences will be easier for interacting adversaries, be they individuals or groups, who fear being cheated. Usable states, in short, can help make commitments credible.

LEGALITY

Law is about the stabilization of expectations of those within its reach. As such, law can constrain but also enable behavior.[18] The law has symbolic value in state formation after state failure. It signals what agents can expect from state and society and what they cannot, enabling agents to face strategic interaction with more ease. If agents have confidence in the law (in a sense of legality), they can afford to accept larger risks or uncertainty in strategic interaction.[19] Abbot and Snidal's argument in favor of "legalization" in international politics also holds for the domestic realm. It speaks of legality's pull, as conceptualized here: "Legalization entails a specific form of discourse, requiring justification and persuasion in terms of applicable rules and pertinent facts, and emphasizing factors such as text, precedents, analogies, and practice. Legal discourse largely disqualifies arguments based solely on interests and preferences."[20]

Law, lastly, stands *between* politics and morality.[21] Dyzenhaus aptly wrote that "the rationality of law, like the rationality of the economic order, is purely instrumental. Law has no inherent worth or legitimacy but it must be *taken* for legitimate by individuals, because there are no ultimate criteria to tell us what legitimacy is."[22] The instrumental value of law is exactly what makes it useful in state formation after state failure. Legality, not unlike "soft law" in the international realm, provides a basis for the construction of credible commitments among adversaries.

BUREAUCRACY

The development of administrative institutions is a minimum requirement for state formation. Weak administrative institutions are one key factor in state failure. In the absence of administrative capacity, enforcement of any kind is difficult. Interestingly, resource-rich countries are frequently associated with weak administrative institutions and, by implication, also state failure. These countries rely on external sources of revenue production, including the sale of primary commodities and labor remittances. As a consequence, institutional development is one-sided and focuses only on those institutions that are key to overseeing the export of primary goods. In modern social relations, delegation is inevitable, making the construction of administrative structures indispensable. Recent scholarship on the "criminalization of the state" in Africa suggests "that the colonial inheritance of an independent class of public servants who could detach themselves from their ethnic or religious roots and serve the nation offered Africa its best chance of developing."[23] However, forming the institutional structures of states, and by implication central authority, may produce dangerous by-products. Frequently, it is the "strengthening of central authority, rather than its weakening or collapse, that is the permissive cause of internal war."[24] Thus both weak *and* strong states can impede the crafting of social order in changing societies.[25]

State Formation from Within

States can be created from scratch. The modern state was created in Europe between 1100 and 1600 by men largely ignorant of the Greek *polis*, the Han Empire in China, and, to an extent, even the Roman Empire.

Institutional Dimensions

Bureaucracies are indispensable to modern life but prone to malfunction. There are several strategies for the construction of reliable, competent, and efficient bureaucracies, each of which can help underwrite state formation after state failure: designing contracts, screening and selection, institutional checks, creating multiple principals or multiple agents with dissonant objectives, creating competition, and decentralization.[26] The construction of bureaucracy also entails education in the identification of problems, the formulation of policy preferences, the development of policy, the implementation of policy, and the evaluation of policy effects.[27] The machinery of a bureaucratic state can improve citizen confidence and encourage commercial activity by lending enforcement power to legal institutions. State formation after state failure, while difficult and fraught with complications, may also present an unusual window of opportunity for changing societies. Goldsmith writes, "The best time to establish the basic direction for organizations . . . is at the beginning. The fledgling states in Botswana and Mauritius were fortunate to have avoided many mistakes made elsewhere in Africa (and in other developing areas, too)—mistakes that would have been hard to correct later."[28] Bureaucracies may still grow too large and they may still foster corruption. However, even slow and somewhat dysfunctional bureaucracies underwrite state formation after state failure. Slow bureaucracies are less problematic than no bureaucracies.

Societal Dimensions

For state formation to succeed after state failure, states "must be 'constructed' in the minds of least some of those who form them, including minimally those who run them."[29] Of course, states must also be constructed in the minds of those who live within their reach. In large-scale social change, contending "ideas of the state" may surface and, when they do, must be reconciled to ensure successful state formation after state failure.[30]

The promotion of the idea of the state must not be confused with the promotion of nations. As Woodward writes, states "are more than communities of political identity. In addition to legitimacy and citizens, they require strategically defensible borders, economic assets sufficient to survive against external threats, and a monopoly on the use of force over territory claimed."[31] Another important issue with regard to the restructuring of state-society relations in newly emerging states is the question of parallel institutions. Frequently, state formation after state failure has to contend with the existence of such parallel institutions, as exemplified in contemporary Somalia.[32] Unlike in early modern Europe, where the sovereign state won out over its competitors, in many parts of the developing world, the state exists alongside other, frequently "traditional" institutions.[33] Prescriptions are almost impossible to give. The decision about whether, and how, to incorporate traditional institutional fragments into a new structure of the state ultimately is empirical. Any prescription must take into account the history of cleavages and group conflict in the country in question. In sum, flexible solutions need to be devised to bridge the gap between the state and its most ardent critics if state formation after state failure is to be successful in societies with vocal constituencies.

State Formation from Without

A truly usable state can be erected only from the inside. However, international efforts at renewal may play an important role in facilitating state formation from within.

Institutional Dimensions

Three types of support from without are conceivable: (1) recognition, (2) construction, and (3) maintenance. Recognition requires the least in terms of international commitment and involvement, whereas maintenance demands the most. Recognition involves international public deliberation and agreement chiefly at the level of the United Nations General Assembly and the Security Council, but may also involve domestic public deliberation in UN member states. Construction involves more than recognition; it demands the temporary, short-term deployment of UN or other forces. It may involve a regional, international, or multinational peacekeeping operation or equivalent form of troop deployment. It should be complemented by the activities of international financial and donor institutions. Maintenance requires the temporary, longer-term presence of a regional or international force as well as international financial and donor support. Such operations may develop into international territorial administration, as currently witnessed in Kosovo and elsewhere. International maintenance operations of any kind are needed most in state formation after most serious cases of failure. Unfortunately, such missions also remain the most difficult to put together due to concerns about the sanctity of sovereignty, dynamics within the UN system, cost calculations, and the relative relevance of state failure compared with other policy considerations.

RECOGNITION

This strategy legitimizes new entities de jure as new members of the international system. Judicial statehood, of course, is an empty framework without empirical statehood.[34] However, recognition may grant some legitimacy to leaders and provide breathing space in the early stages of state formation. The strategy also has obvious risks. Recognizing new entities as "states" after state failure can have fatal consequences for national, regional, and international security. The recognition of Slovene and Croatian independence by the European Community in June 1991, and Germany's leading role in the process, illustrates the dangers inherent in the hasty international recognition of proto-states.[35] Furthermore, recognition alone is insufficient to make state formation work. Recognition can provide "temporary respite from external pressure," yet seldom more.[36] Recognition merely sustains judicial statehood and creates the space necessary to take domestic steps toward the construction of empirical statehood.

CONSTRUCTION

An important way in which the international community could aid the formation of states after failure would be through aggressive measures that aim to curtail arms trafficking. With the end of the Cold War, the international business of light and small arms has contributed greatly to the strife in weak and failed states. Consider Widner's observation that "officials in West African countries issue false import documents and permit illicit transfer of weapons to other places, fueling war well beyond [their] own borders."[37] Another related challenge that could be easily met, primarily subject to political will in advanced industrial countries, is the issue of military demobilization. Achieving demobilization is critical to the success of state formation after state failure. King and Zheng found that the "larger the fraction of the population who have weapons and are trained in military conflict, the more risk there is that internal dissent may lead to state failure."[38] Without demilitarization, the prospects for successful state formation after state failure are dim. The proliferation of small arms also has wider implications. If the flow of weapons cannot be interrupted, the causes of state failure may spread across borders. As Lemarchand writes, "[T]he risks of disintegration are significantly greater when the proximity of a collapsing state threatens to contaminate its neighbor. Just as the civil war in Liberia has decisively hastened the collapse of Sierra Leone (and vice versa), the flow of refugees generated by the continuing civil strife in Sierra Leone poses a clear and present danger to Guinea."[39] International action toward the curtailment of weapons proliferation is an important, necessary strategy to make state formation after state failure possible and sustainable. By addressing both plausible internal and external threats to state reformation, international action creates a modicum of stability that is urgently needed in any process of state formation.

State formation also involves the construction of basic infrastructure. Transportation is the backbone of any country. Developing and extending transportation is critical to reducing the distance between the core and the periphery. Achieving closeness and geographical linkage is key to sustaining fledgling states. The international community could assist recuperating states by building roads and railroads, for example.

MAINTENANCE

In the context of maintenance, three overlapping avenues for international support emerge: (1) international financial and donor support, (2) international military support, and (3) international administrative support. The first avenue refers to the activities of the World Bank and the International Monetary Fund (IMF), but it also includes the activities of NGOs.[40] International military support, next, can help to secure borders, settlements, and key transportation routes and to maintain contact between capital cities, the hinterland, and other strategically important locations. As Herbst has convincingly shown with respect to Africa, governments' inability to broadcast power into peripheral regions of state territory lies at the heart of state failure and collapse. His findings are corroborated by evidence from other world regions. It follows that international support for the maintenance of transportation routes and the institutional structure of the state in the hinterland is indispensable to state formation after state failure. Commitment to such maintenance is costly. Mechanisms for burden sharing among domestic, regional, and international actors and institutions must be devised. Without outside intervention, the formation of states after failure is likely to be in vain. Since U.S. administrations are likely to be more hesitant to commit American troops or resources to state formation in hostile environments, this type of international strategy will have to be devolved to and driven by regional organizations and regimes such as the EU (Balkans and Central Asia), ECOMOG (West Africa) and SADC (southern Africa), and ASEAN (Southeast Asia).[41]

Lastly, international administrative support is the avenue most directly related to the construction of legality and bureaucracy, the two principal pillars of the state. In situations of extreme uncertainty and institutional depletion, the idea of international conservatorship may hold some promise.[42] While the idea is very controversial, it deserves serious consideration. Despite its limitations, some form of conservatorship seems more appropriate than immediate state formation in countries that exhibit a long history of state failure and state collapse. Arguably, Somalia would have fared better had the international community abandoned its belief in the sovereign nature of the collapsed Somali state. The extreme situation in Somalia favored the imposition of international conservatorship. At this point, what I have termed strategies of construction and maintenance overlap. Conservatorship may involve international territorial administration. International territorial administration, in turn, may simultaneously involve the construction of new, and the maintenance and reequilibration of surviving, institutions of state.

Conservatorship can come in various shapes and sizes. Substantially little has been written about the properties of conservatorship as a distinct institutional form, and there is a good deal of genuine confusion in this area. However, three modes of conservatorship, ranging from the least to the most intrusive, can been distinguished: (1) governance assistance (to avert state collapse or to underwrite early state formation), (2) delegation of authority, and (3) trusteeship.[43] Cost and other practical calculations need to be weighed against the potential success of state formation by conservatorship. The UN operation in Cambodia, which was essentially state formation by conservatorship, is estimated to have cost more than 1.6 billion U.S. dollars for a two-year period. Conservatorship in the context of complex state formation, for example, in a country greater in population than Cambodia, would require significantly more external involvement and resources.[44]

International administrative support in the context of conservatorship is particularly important to combat legacies of noncompliance. Consider the examples of crime and corruption.[45] A frequent problem in the early stages of state formation after failure is not that crime and corruption go unnoticed, but rather that they remain unpunished. How can the international community assist? International actors and institutions must develop an understanding of the complex criminality in changing societies. Additionally, eradicating crime and corruption from within necessitates assistance from without. An easy and relatively inexpensive way for the international community to affect stability in state formation is through cooperation with law enforcement agencies in newly formed states. Cooperation, if administered in a professional manner, would raise the level of expertise and inculcate officials in newly forming states with norms of rule-guided behavior, norms that are often only superficially developed in these societies.[46] Members of South Africa's special law enforcement division, the "Scorpions," for example, recently underwent training by the U.S. Federal Bureau of Investigation (FBI) in Quantico, Virginia. The training reportedly cost the FBI in the range of $600,000.[47] Such relatively inexpensive training projects can go a long way in strengthening the institutional infrastructure of states in formation. The training may be necessary to expose law enforcement officials to the complexities of domestic and international organized crime—key causes of state failure today.

Societal Dimensions

A strategy that cuts across the social and institutional dimensions of state formation is the creation of international war crimes tribunals. Another strategy is the international promotion of domestic truth commissions. "Truth" is here understood in a wide sense. It could entail the revelation of human rights abuses and their perpetration, *or*, as an innovation, it could entail the revelation of patronage, corruption, and the like. Amnesty in exchange for confessions is imaginable for *both* types of crime.[48] Truth commissions dealing with human rights violations can turn law legitimate; truth commissions that deal with corruption could arguably accomplish the *same* objective, while simultaneously creating incentives for supporting state formation after state failure.[49] A third strategy is the promotion of constitutional courts.[50] Constitutional courts can be an important part of law formation, and thus of state formation after state failure. In some special cases, judicial review could be administered with the assistance of regional or international organizations such as the European Union. One important empirical case of state formation through law formation that is centered on a constitutional court is found in Bosnia and Herzegovina.

The Constitutional Court of Bosnia and Herzegovina was established according to Annex 4 of the General Framework Agreement for Peace in Bosnia and Herzegovina. This general framework, which became the constitution of Bosnia-Herzegovina, emerged from the Dayton Agreements in 1995. The current president of the Bosnian constitutional court notes that the court "has greatly contributed to the enforcement of the rule of law in Bosnia and Herzegovina."[51] What is unique about the constitutional court of Bosnia and Herzegovina is its composition: both national and international judges serve on the court. There are nine judges, six elected by the parliaments of the Muslim-Croat Federation and the Bosnian Serb-led Republika Srpska, and three appointed by the president of the European Court of Human Rights.[52] This multinational constellation of sitting judges ensures independence and, furthermore, brings European standards to the Bosnian constitutional court. Eventually, these standards are likely to trickle down to the country's changing legal system. One international justice on the court, Joseph Marko of Austria, noted that the constitutional court, particularly because of its international composition, has been crucial for state formation in Bosnia and Herzegovina. He remarked that the "reconstruction of multiethnic society is a goal of the constitutional court of Bosnia-Herzegovina, although there's no pure, positivistic legal ground for it."[53] While the formation of constitutional courts is commonly a domestic dimension of state formation, some instances of state collapse may be so grave that the formation of constitutional courts needs to be attempted from without. The constitutional court of Bosnia-Herzegovina is an example of a court that gained strength through the import of foreign justices.

Conclusions

State builders must pay attention to the crucial role of "stakes."[54] Interacting adversaries require incentives to preserve a newly formed state. New states must serve a purpose for those living within their reach. New states will have force only if and when interacting adversaries involved in their formation have an incentive to care about the preservation of these states. "Stakes in states" create incentives for interacting adversaries to care. Stakes cut to the heart of *raison d'état*. Stakes provide "reasons of state."

State formation, along the lines described in this chapter, is critical to regime formation, which, in turn, is important for government formation.[55] In theory, the three processes should be staggered: state formation should precede regime formation and regime formation should be antecedent to government formation. In practice, the three processes will often have to be tackled simultaneously. In these cases, it is imperative that state formation from within and state formation from without, as discussed, be pursued in tandem.

In sum, state formation after state failure requires the regulation of supply and demand of states. Supply and demand can be regulated through various channels. I have described the most important channels. Both supply and demand revolve around utility and its perception. If and when change agents have reason to believe that they gain more from preserving states than from stealing them, newly formed states are likely to be viable and sustainable. And inasmuch as the supply of states can be regulated from without, the demand for states can only be stimulated from within. For creating such demand, the perception of utility matters more than any other factor. As this chapter has argued, the character of stateness is inherently psychological.

Will the formation of states after failure improve the general well-being of resident populations? This question is difficult to answer in the abstract. Inasmuch as the factors identified in this chapter promise to enhance the choices available to interacting adversaries and other agents in situations of state reformation, it is impossible to predict empirical outcomes. Even the best laid plans for forming states after failure, irrespective of whether state formation proceeds from within or from without, or both, may produce unexpected outcomes. Bargaining over the future of states can stall or break down at various junctures. It is important to bear in mind that, historically, *all* processes of state formation have caused immense human suffering. Indeed this fact has prompted analysts to liken state formation to organized crime.[56]

It would be naïve to expect that state formation in the twenty-first century will occur absent human suffering. The birth of states is an inherently contentious, violent process. In this regard, the contemporary wave of state formation is likely to resemble earlier waves.[57] While the paths and tasks of state formation identified in this chapter may help defray some of the human costs involved in forming states after failure, human costs will accrue nonetheless.

Notes

1. For a discussion, see Jeffrey Herbst, "War and the State in Africa," *International Security,* XIV (1990), 117–139.

2. For this argument, see Jeffrey Herbst, "Responding to State Failure in Africa," *International Security,* XXI (1996/97), 120–144.

3. I elaborate the distinction, and the logic of the argument, more fully in Meierhenrich, "Stealing vs. Preserving: Rationality and the State," manuscript,

Harvard University (November 2000). See also Steven L. Solnick, *Stealing the State: Control and Collapse in Soviet Institutions* (Cambridge, Mass., 1998).

4. For an influential discussion of the role of stakes in politics, see Robert Axelrod, "The Rational Timing of Surprise," *World Politics*, XXXI (1979), 228–246. See also Gerald Marwell and Ruth E. Ames, "Experiments on the Provision of Public Goods: Provision Points, Stakes, Experience, and the Free-Rider Problem," *American Journal of Sociology*, LXXXV (1980), 926–937.

5. However, note that noncompliance does not always have corrosive effects. The violation of "bad rules" may in some circumstances actually yield positive consequences. See Edgar L. Feige, "Underground Activity and Institutional Change: Productive, Protective, and Predatory Behavior in Transition Economies," in Joan M. Nelson, Charles Tilly, and Lee Walker (eds.), *Transforming Post-Communist Political Economies* (Washington, D.C., 1997), 25–27.

6. William Reno, "Shadow States and the Political Economy of Civil Wars," in Mats Berdal and David M. Malone (eds.), *Greed and Grievance: Economic Agendas in Civil Wars* (Boulder, 2000), 53.

7. Pauline Jones Luong, "The 'Use and Abuse' of Russia's Energy Resources: Implications for State-Society Relations," in Valerie Sperling (ed.), *Building the Russian State: Institutional Crisis and the Quest for Democratic Governance* (Boulder, 2000), 31.

8. For comparative-historical evidence, see Meierhenrich, *The Supply and Demand of States: State Formation and State Collapse* (forthcoming).

9. Kenneth Dyson, *The State Tradition in Western Europe* (Oxford, 1980), 3.

10. Peter Alexis Gourevitch, "The Governance Problem in International Relations," in David A. Lake and Robert Powell (eds.), *Strategic Choice and International Relations* (Princeton, 1999), 138–139. Similarly, Bo Rothstein argues that "it is probably not the formal institution as such that people evaluate, but its historically established reputation in regard to fairness and efficiency." See his "Trust, Social Dilemmas and Collective Memories," *Journal of Theoretical Politics*, XII (2000), 493.

11. Joseph R. Strayer, *On the Medieval Origins of the Modern State* (Princeton, 1970), 5.

12. I develop the argument more fully in Meierhenrich, *The Supply and Demand of States.*

13. For a critique of Strayer's "soft" definition, see Charles Tilly, "Reflections on the History of European State-Making," in Tilly (ed.), *The Formation of National States in Western Europe* (Princeton, 1975), 26–27.

14. Strayer, *On the Medieval Origins of the Modern State.*

15. While Charles Tilly considers this a conceptual drawback, I see it as an advantage. Tilly, "Reflections on the History of European State-Making," 26; emphases in the original.

16. For a conceptual analysis of the "usable state" idea, and its relationship to weak and strong states, see Jens Meierhenrich, *The Supply and Demand of States.*

17. Alfred Stepan and Cindy Skach, "Constitutional Frameworks and Democratic Consolidation: Parliamentarianism versus Presidentialism," *World Politics*, XLVI (1993), 1–22.

18. Niklas Luhmann, *Das Recht der Gesellschaft* (Frankfurt, 1993), 136.

19. Ibid.; Meierhenrich, *A Theory of Law: Path Dependence and Increasing Returns* (forthcoming).

20. Kenneth W. Abbott and Duncan Snidal, "Hard Law and Soft Law in International Governance," *International Organization*, LIV (2000), 429.

21. Jürgen Habermas, *Faktizität und Geltung: Beiträge zur Diskurstheorie des Rechts und des demokratischen Rechtsstaats* (Frankfurt, 1992), 567.

22. David Dyzenhaus, *Legality and Legitimacy: Carl Schmitt, Hans Kelsen and Hermann Heller in Weimar* (Oxford, 1997), 11; emphasis added.

23. "First Bad, Now Worse," *The Economist* (7 August 1999), 73. Clapham concurs with the assessment, writing that "across the [African] continent as a whole the coexistence of artificial statehood with either French or British colonialism provided the best recipe for survival." Christopher Clapham, *Africa and the International System: The Politics of State Survival* (Cambridge, 1996), 270. The books under review were Jean-François Bayart, Stephen Ellis, and Béatrice Hibou, *The Criminalization of the State in Africa* (Bloomington, 1999); Patrick Chabal and Jean-Pascal Daloz, *Africa Works: Disorder as Political Instrument* (Bloomington, 1999). Each contains valuable insights and data regarding the problem of state failure.

24. Steven R. David, "Internal War: Causes and Cures," *World Politics*, XLIX (1997), 561.

25. Meierhenrich, *Apartheid's Endgame and the State.*

26. For a discussion of these strategies, see Adam Przeworski, "The State in a Market Economy," in Nelson, Tilly, and Walker (eds.), *Transforming Post-Communist Political Economies*, 422–423.

27. For in-depth discussions, see the contributions in Merilee S. Grindle (ed.), *Getting Good Government: Capacity Building in the Public Sectors of Developing Countries* (Cambridge, 1997).

28. Arthur A. Goldsmith, "Africa's Overgrown State Reconsidered: Bureaucracy and Economic Growth," *World Politics*, LI (1999), 544.

29. Clapham, *Africa and the International System*, 9.

30. On the notion of the "idea of the state," see Kalevi J. Holsti, *The State, War, and the State of War* (Cambridge, 1996), 82–98.

31. Susan L. Woodward, *Balkan Tragedy: Chaos and Dissolution after the Cold War* (Washington, D.C., 1995), 267.

32. See Meierhenrich, "The Sovereign State and its Competitors: State Selection in Somalia" manuscript, Harvard University (September 2001).

33. On the European development, see Hendrik Spruyt, *The Sovereign State and its Competitors: An Analysis of Systems Change* (Princeton, 1994). For perspectives on the relationship between "modernity" and "tradition" in developing societies, see Kwame Gyekye, *Tradition and Modernity: Philosophical Reflections on the African Experience* (New York, 1997); Mahmood Mamdani, *Citizen and Subject: Contemporary Africa and the Legacy of Late Colonialism* (Princeton, 1996).

34. Robert H. Jackson and Carl G. Rosberg, "Why Africa's Weak States Persist: The Empirical and the Juridical in Statehood," *World Politics*, XXXV (1982), 1–24.

35. For a discussion of the repercussions of recognition in the former Yugoslavia, see Woodward, *Balkan Tragedy*, 250–251.

36. Clapham, *Africa and the International System*, 271.

37. Jennifer Widner, "Building Effective Trust in the Aftermath of Severe Conflict," unpublished manuscript, Harvard University (2000).

38. Gary King and Langche Zeng, "Improving Forecasts of State Failure," paper prepared for the Midwest Political Science Association, Chicago, 2000, 10.

39. René Lemarchand, "The Democratic Republic of Congo: From Failed State to Statelessness," in Robert I. Rotberg (ed.), *State Failure and State Weakness in a Time of Terror* (Washington, D.C., 2003), 29–70.

40. For the argument that a "tough love" principle may be needed vis-à-vis recalcitrant agents in these situations, see Robert I. Rotberg, "Africa's Mess: Mugabe's Mayhem," *Foreign Affairs*, LXXIX (2000), 60. Clapham discusses the related principle of "political conditionality" as practiced by advanced industrialized countries after the end of the Cold War in his *Africa and the International System*, 195–200. On the possibilities for international donor support for civil society formation, see Daniel N. Posner, "Civil Society and the Reconstruction of Failed States" in this volume. For a critical evaluation of nongovernmental activities in Africa, see Clapham, *Africa and the International System*, 256–266.

41. For a useful discussion of regional security arrangements, see the contributions in David A. Lake and Patrick M. Morgan (eds.), *Regional Orders: Building Security in a New World* (University Park, 1997). See also the critical analysis in S. Neil MacFarlane and Thomas G. Weiss, "Regional Organizations and Regional Security," *Security Studies*, II (1992), 6–37.

42. For a valuable discussion, see Gerald B. Helman and Steven R. Ratner, "Saving Failed States," *Foreign Policy*, LXXXIX (1992–93), 12–20.

43. Ibid., 13–18.

44. Ibid., 19.

45. On the problem of crime more generally, see Gianluca Fiorentini and Sam Peltzman (eds.), *The Economics of Organized Crime* (Cambridge, 1995). On the problem of corruption more generally, see Susan Rose-Ackerman, *Corruption and Government: Causes, Consequences, and Reform* (New York, 1999).

46. International cooperation in crime investigations, however, may not always produce optimal results. Switzerland reportedly failed to prosecute a Russian crime boss when Russian authorities withheld assistance. In the Netherlands, the Dutch Branch of Interpol reportedly became an instrument in the hands of Russian crime leaders, caricaturing international efforts at crime control and prevention. See Louise Shelley, "Is the Russian State Coping with Organized Crime and Corruption?" in Valerie Sperling (ed.), *Building the Russian State: Institutional Crisis and the Quest for Democratic Governance* (Boulder, 2000), 106–107.

47. *Business Day* (Johannesburg, 26 October 2000). To be sure, South Africa is not, and never was, a failed state. Yet, the examples discussed here illustrate potentially useful strategies for forming states after failure.

48. For the proposal of setting up truth commissions to deal with the problem of corruption, see Meierhenrich, "The Truth about Corruption," manuscript, Harvard University (August 2000).

49. Ibid. On truth commissions as "intervening variables" that can help turn law legitimate, see Meierhenrich, *A Theory of Law*.

50. On constitutional courts in newly democratizing countries, see Cindy Skach, "Rethinking Judicial Review: Shaping the Toleration of Difference," paper

presented at the European University Institute Workshop "Rethinking the Rule of Law in Post-Communist Europe," Florence (February 2002).

51. Speech by Kasim Begic, President of the Constitutional Court of Bosnia and Herzegovina, before the presidents of European Constitutional Courts at the Preparatory Meeting in Brussels (20–21 October 2000), http://www.ustavnisud.ba/english/default.htm.

52. Skach, "Rethinking Judicial Review."

53. Joseph Marko, Comments delivered at the Annual Meeting of the Association for the Study of the Nationalities, Columbia University, New York (April 2000), as quoted in the Skach, "Rethinking Judicial Review," 22.

54. For a comprehensive analysis, see Meierhenrich, *The Supply and Demand of States.*

55. These distinctions are frequently overlooked. For the first sustained discussion of the analytical and practical relationships among government formation, regime formation, and state formation, see ibid.

56. Charles Tilly, "War Making and State Making as Organized Crime," in Peter B. Evans, Dietrich Rueschemeyer, and Theda Skocpol (eds.), *Bringing the State Back In* (Cambridge, 1985), 169–191.

57. For a comparative analysis of historical "waves" and "paths" of state formation, see Meierhenrich, *The Supply and Demand of States.*

Eight

Disarmament, Demobilization, and Reintegration

LESSONS AND LIABILITIES IN RECONSTRUCTION

NAT J. COLLETTA, MARKUS KOSTNER, AND INGO WIEDERHOFER

DEMILITARIZATION IS a precondition for reviving civil society, reducing poverty, and sustaining development in countries emerging from war. The realization of these objectives demands the demobilization of forces and the subsequent reintegration of ex-combatants into productive civilian lives. Full demilitarization often also requires landmine removal and disarmament, the reduction of arms flows, the conversion of fixed assets to civilian use, security sector reform, and civilian disarmament.

When and where violent conflict ceases, armed combatants are glaring legacies. Demobilization and Reintegration Programs (DRPs) for combatants thus constitute a vital part of demilitarization and of transitions from war to peace. The success of this step demonstrates the warring parties' commitment to the peace process and provides the security necessary for people affected by war to reinvest in their lives and their country. Furthermore, DRPs are the means by which governments can begin to downsize their militaries and reduce defense expenditures in order to shift human and material resources to reconstruction and development.[1]

The essential elements of any DRP are

1. *Demobilization*—consisting of disarmament, discharge, orientation, and relocation to a community of the ex-combatant's choice;
2. *Reinsertion*—marked by the provision of a transitional safety net of cash and/or in-kind payments calculated on the basis of a basket of basic goods / needs (food, shelter, clothing, household utensils, school fees, and medical expenses) for an average-size family in the community of return and spread out over a several month period, roughly covering a single growing season;
3. *Social and economic reintegration*—assistance in the form of access to productive assets (particularly land and capital), training and employment, and information and counseling services combined with receiving community sensitization and assistance.

The basic ingredients for the success of a DRP are (1) political will, (2) careful preparation based on rapid assessments of the opportunity structure and a profiling of ex-combatants and their families, including classifying ex-combatants according to their characteristics, needs, and desired way of earning a livelihood (mode of subsistence), (3) transparent and effective institutional arrangements, minimizing transaction costs and corruption while maximizing benefits to ex-combatants, with a simple monitoring and feedback system to ensure flexible but accountable implementation (to both donors and the community), and (4) timely and adequate financing.[2]

When a country is moving from war to peace, demobilization and reintegration issues should be addressed at the earliest stages of the peace negotiation process. Strong political will and leadership, expressed in terms of commitment, realism, and pragmatism, are critical.

In conflict environments, DRPs are often highly political, as they directly affect a party's ability to pursue its interests via coercive means and its ability to defend itself. At the Sierra Leonean peace negotiations in mid-1999, disarmament and demobilization issues were neglected until very late in the negotiation process, and then they were only treated in a cursory manner. This failure contributed to the establishment of technically unreasonable deadlines in the peace accord implementation schedule, ultimately undermining confidence in the process. The ensuing unwillingness of the Revolutionary United Front (RUF) and other national and regional parties to trust the peace process eventually undermined it.

A more positive case in point is Guatemala, where the DRP was part and parcel of the peace negotiation process, especially the agenda concerning the role of the state in security. In this instance, anchoring the DRP details in the overall peace process enhanced the implementation of the DRP.

Targeting

Ex-combatants often constitute an especially vulnerable group in need of targeted assistance. Profiles conducted in several countries illustrate common features of a poor, semiliterate underclass with primary school education, limited skills, and weak social links to job and training opportunities. Demobilizing combatants into a livelihood vacuum can lead to disgruntled warriors and increased criminal activity. The former Soviet Union, Croatia, and the Balkans are prominent examples, as former soldiers are sprinkled across criminal smuggling and protection networks in the region.

The particular challenges confronting veterans' dependents (family members), as well as female soldiers, child soldiers, and disabled ex-combatants warrant the development of especially targeted interventions. These are often referred to as special target groups. These groups, as well as their particular needs and aspirations, should be identified during the preparatory process to allow for the design of appropriate support measures.

An authentic, nontransferable, and noncorruptible identification system is of paramount importance to reduce the risk of political manipulation and resource abuse. However, defining and identifying who is and who is not a bona fide combatant, especially in civil wars where the militants range from child soldiers to all sorts of irregulars, can be extremely difficult. The process is further compounded when there are tangible benefits or entitlements awaiting entrants into a DRP.

In East Timor, the Falintil (Timorese Liberation Fighters) wanted to include "clandestines" or those who provided support to the struggle in the pool for demobilization benefits. The debate revolved around where to draw the line between a bona fide "clandestine" and someone who may have merely carried a secret message once or twice. In the end, "clandestines" were not formally included in the program.

In Cambodia, it was necessary to do a complete census of the Royal Cambodian Armed Forces (RCAF) when the numbers reported ranged from 100,000 to 140,000. In the process, some 14,000 ghost soldiers and over 100,000 ghost dependents were identified (names appeared on the payroll list of the ministry of finance, but no living soldier appeared during the census). In addition, when personal identity cards were issued, a market for counterfeit cards emerged after it was rumored that the benefits package would be sizeable.

The sheer size of the target group may require special mechanisms. In Guinea-Bissau, for instance, the government took a two-step approach. First, all ex-combatants were in principle eligible to receive reintegration assistance irrespective of their participation in the 1998/99 civil unrest. This decision avoided giving a premium to violence. Including only those who were active in the recent conflict would otherwise have provided an incentive for others to also take up arms. It also made those ex-combatants eligible for assistance retroactively who, despite earlier intermittent efforts during the 1980s which had been marred by targeting errors and favoritism), never received support.

In a second step, the Guinea-Bissau government prepared, after consultation with beneficiary representatives and other nongovernment actors, a set of vulnerability criteria. These criteria were matched with the socioeconomic profile of each ex-combatant. This approach allowed for the transparent selection of program beneficiaries and at the same time reduced cost. Simultaneously, appropriate appeals mechanisms were set up to verify the socioeconomic profile of contested cases.

Disarmament

Neutral international monitors and technical assistance can facilitate the design and implementation of DRPs, especially regarding the disarmament component. The United Nations Monitoring Mission for Ethiopia and Eritrea (UNMEE) has an integral role in the overall demilitarization process in both countries. In East Timor, the United Nations Transitional Authority for East Timor Peace Keeping Force (UNTAET-PKF) and UN military observers (UMOS) verified disarmament as well as liaising with the newly formed East Timor Defense Force. However, the effectiveness of such forces is contingent upon the quality and the nature of their mandate. Peacekeepers of the United Nations Mission to Sierra Leone (UNAMSIL) proved incapable of disarming Sierra Leonean ex-combatants in a consistent and professional manner prior to the breakdown of the Lomé peace process in May 2000. Furthermore, most weapons collected were neither securely stored nor destroyed. As a result, many were reused by the parties to the conflict following the collapse of the peace process. In addition, there was a problem created by linking (in time and space) the disarmament process too closely to the cash transitional reinsertion allowance of the demobilization and reintegration program. Ex-combatants quickly connected their surrender of a weapon (any weapon) with a $150 cash payment. The DRP was soon mistakenly perceived as an arms buy-back scheme.

Even where arms buy-back schemes are intentional parts of the DRP process, as in Chad during the earlier demobilization, collected or purchased weapons must be carefully secured and / or destroyed. In Chad, officers took weapons in the front door and sold them out the back door, thus creating a micro arms-market under the auspices of a disarmament and demobilization program.

Demobilization

Demobilization is the process whereby ex-combatants formally shift from military to civilian status. Ex-combatants should be released or discharged from military quarters or cantonment sites as soon as possible so that they do not become a serious threat to security. In Angola, nearly a third of the UNITA combatants in cantonments self-demobilized after months of awaiting formal discharge and demobilization. In Mozambique, the cantonment period went far beyond the tolerance level of the combatants. They reverted to taking UN camp personnel hostage, blocking roads, and commandeering vehicles to get out.

Prior to discharge, ex-combatants should receive information about civilian life—rights and duties, opportunities, and constraints. If feasible, post-discharge orientation, with a focus on social support and economic opportunities, should be provided in the communities where ex-combatants settle. In addition, the demobilization process provides a good opportunity to collect sufficient socioeconomic data to assess the characteristics, needs, and aspirations of the ex-combatants. These data can be used to design appropriate reintegration interventions and can help manage expectations and fears.

In Uganda, a profiling exercise revealed that about 17 percent of the combatants had symptoms related to AIDS. This led to the development of an enhanced health component within the reintegration package. In addition, a next-of-kin was identified, and doing so proved important in avoiding family battles, as over 200 former combatants died between being identified for demobilization and the actual receipt of benefits.

The concentration of ex-combatants in one location during a demobilization phase also provided a unique opportunity to provide HIV/AIDS sensitization and counseling. This is a particular concern as soldiers are a high-risk group for HIV/AIDS. In the first phase of the Ethiopia Emergency Demobilization and Reintegration Program, the government of Ethiopia provided extensive HIV/AIDS sensitization (including presentations by HIV positive soldiers), and distributed IEC materials and condoms during the demobilization phase.

Reinsertion

Reinsertion packages, which provide a safety net during the transition from war to peace, should reflect the needs of ex-combatants and their families in different socioeconomic environments. Such packages help ex-combatants and their families bridge the difficult period between demobilization and reintegration. The basic material needs of an ex-combatant family can be divided into two components: household consumption and household investment. Household consumption normally includes food, clothing, health, and education. Household investment can comprise shelter, seeds, tools, and cooking utensils.

There are three basic methods of calculating reinsertion support: (1) using in-service income (wages) and fringe benefits (nonwages, e.g., food, dependent allowances, etc.) as a reference, (2) using national household survey data as a basis (e.g., established poverty line or average household incomes), and (3) calculating a basic needs basket according to the needs identified by a socioeconomic profile of ex-combatants.

Monetizing entitlement packages has several advantages over in-kind provision: transaction costs can be reduced, leakages can be better controlled, and beneficiaries can make flexible use of their entitlements. In addition, one can avoid the negative externalities of aid, such as food, which can undercut a revitalization of the local economy. Farmers cannot compete with free food aid. In effect, cash can generate its own supply response in the local economy. However, one should assess the supply capacity (e.g., ability to produce food under prolonged drought conditions) to balance the cash and in-kind mix. In Uganda, small amounts of money, in the form of reinsertion payments, spread around the country over the course of several months, serving to stimulate local economic responses.

Using local banks or postal services for transferring cash in installments allows ex-combatants access to financial assistance throughout the reinsertion phase. The capacity of the banking system or alternate payment systems, especially in rural areas, should therefore be evaluated before transfers begin. In Uganda, an unanticipated consequence was the exposure of former combatants to the banking system, something which many of them thought was the prerogative of others in the wage economy.

Reintegration

Reinsertion and reintegration are not distinct phases after demobilization. Rather, they form part of a seamless web of transition from military to civilian life. They both commence at the moment of discharge but reintegration does not have a clear end. Rather, as the transition to civilian life proceeds, the needs of ex-combatants change and call for different, yet integrated, support measures.

Reintegration refers to the ex-combatant's long-term return to civilian life and comprises social and economic dimensions. Program interventions in support of reintegration should be geared toward helping ex-combatants and their families secure sustainable livelihoods in their communities of return. Such assistance should be based on data about the ex-combatants own characteristics, needs, and aspirations; the opportunity structure in areas of return; and communities' perceptions of the ex-combatants.[3]

Economic Dimensions

Careful market analysis of the "opportunity structure" for ex-combatants (in particular, the demand for labor and the availability of land, credit, information, and the provision of skill development) is a prerequisite not only for program design but also for targeted counseling and adequate placement.

Ex-combatants should be assigned to target groups and subgroups on the basis of their modes of subsistence and thus according to their differing needs and aspirations. This allows for the development of a differentiated, relevant, and cost-effective approach. In Ethiopia after the fall of Mengistu regime in 1991, reintegration benefits were organized around specific modes of subsistence. Those returning to uplands crop farming received coffee plants. Those who returned to lowland wheat cultivation received draft animals. And those who returned to the urban sector received skill training in various professions, access to informal sector apprenticeships, and micro credit as well as small business management training. In East Timor, there were four reintegration packages for veterans to choose from, ranging from coastal fishing and urban small and micro-enterprises to plains ranching and uplands agriculture.

Combining livelihood options with occupational counseling, information, and training is critical to the sustainability of reintegration efforts. Although short-term, labor-intensive schemes are useful for reconstructing infrastructures and for immediate employment, they are not a substitute for sustainable livelihoods, which are, in the end, the economic objective of reintegration.[4]

Access to land needs to be treated carefully. Both traditional and legal rights to the land and productive assets, as well as historically rooted inequalities, have to be assessed. In El Salvador, land for demobilized ex-combatants was part of the reintegration package stipulated in the peace accord. However, implementation was less than desirable as the land provided was late in coming, of poor quality, and without the attendant agricultural inputs needed to farm it. In the end, many demobilized soldiers sold the land that they received for a pittance. Then they turned to crime.

Reintegration in urban areas is more complex than in rural areas and requires a more diversified approach. All support measures should be based on a careful matching of opportunities and actual needs. Support measures should, to the extent possible, be demand-driven. The conversion of former military assets can help. In South Africa, the conversion of 1,100 military bases to civilian use was part of an overall security sector rationalization program. If carefully planned, such assets can readily provide infrastructure usable for the creation of needed jobs.

Ex-combatants should receive support sufficient to help them attain the standard of living of the communities into which they are being reintegrated. There is always the risk of the receiving communities resenting benefits given to demobilized soldiers. It is important in this instance to provide some form of assistance to the community and not just to the former combatants.[5] In Djibouti, a special community support component was designed to help receiving communities revitalize their social infrastructures, e.g., schools, clinics, and water systems. These were considered public goods, which provided services benefiting both the communities and the ex-combatants and their families.

Assistance to disabled ex-combatants is important for two reasons. First, as handicapped persons, their reintegration into a community is more difficult, both economically and socially. Secondly, having sacrificed their future for a united country, they expect compensation. The Ethiopian and Eritrean conflict left about 18,000 disabled veterans on the Ethiopian side alone. A special medical rehabilitation program was designed to assist them. Additionally, many of the returnees required customized economic reintegration assistance to enable them to assume productive places in their communities.

Female and child soldiers need particular attention so as to avoid their exclusion from program benefits. Economic reintegration assistance for female ex-combatants would normally not differ much from that of male ex-combatants. However, implementation may pose a particular challenge as female ex-combatants often have received proportionally less support. Critically important is the desocialization and resocialization of child soldiers, and also women, to overcome the gender barrier of many societies.

Support to child soldiers under the age of fifteen normally includes family reunification, psychosocial support, education, and income-generating opportunities. Family reunification is fundamental to successful reintegration, as experiences in Angola and El Salvador demonstrate. Where that is not possible, foster placement or support for independent living is essential. Psychosocial support is pivotal in addressing the asocial and aggressive behavior learned by child soldiers and in facilitating their recovery from highly stressful experiences. Education and economic opportunities geared to individual circumstances can offer child soldiers a positive identity through appropriate contributing roles in their family and community. In Rwanda, the *kadogo* (Kiswahali for little one) schools were set up and modeled on the Ugandan experience with child soldiers. The kadogo served as a kind of halfway house or multigrade, multiage school for child soldiers. These transitional institutions were established under the premise that a period of desocialization and resocialization had to take place prior to return to normal civilian society.[6]

Social Dimensions

Rebuilding social capital, particularly cross cutting social relationships, and the trust that could bridge social fault lines of a society is critical to the strengthening of social cohesion in the aftermath of divisive violent conflict.[7] Informal networks of ex-combatants—discussion groups, veterans' associations, and joint economic ventures—are key aids to successful economic and social reintegration. Such associations can be extremely helpful, especially when social capital has been depleted. Veterans associations in Uganda and Mozambique have proven to be particularly effective in mobilizing resources for economic development. But associations can be problematic if they are highly politicized, as in the case of Zimbabwe. Ultimately, however, it is the interplay of a community's physical and social capital and an ex-combatant's financial and human capital that determines the ease and success of social and economic reintegration.

Efforts to strengthen social capital—for example, by using existing community organizations and channels of communication—enable communities to take development into their own hands and facilitate reintegration of ex-combatants.

Reconciliation should be actively promoted through transparent policies and conflict resolution efforts at the community level. Doing so can reduce suspicion and help rebuild trust. The community development councils in East Timor provided useful connective tissue for ex-combatant reintegration assistance. In Cambodia, long-standing Buddhist village associations supplied religious as well as social support for combatants reentering civilian life. In Namibia, church-led repatriation committees rebuilt trust among former adversaries in combat, who are now neighbors in development. In Nicaragua, Contras and Sandinista ex-combatants joined forces in an NGO that trained former combatants as village conflict mediators in the former war-torn areas of the country.

In Djibouti, the DRP program supported activities that strengthened community social capital, including adult education programs, civic and peace education, music and sports groups, and the rehabilitation of religious centers. In Guinea-Bissau, the registration of ex-combatants, the definition of criteria of vulnerability (which determine access to program benefits), and the identification of beneficiaries was undertaken within a transparent and precise legal framework, unlike the opaque allocation of benefits to veterans of its war of independence.

Female ex-combatants face multiple challenges when returning to their communities. For example, the political hopes of Nicaraguan female combatants were dashed after the struggle when many male ex-combatants relegated them to former gender discriminating roles and functions. Spouses also suffer. In Uganda, the divorce rate after discharge was especially high for veterans who had married a woman from another group without the consent of the veteran's family and without following traditional customs. Appropriately trained staff are essential to help identify and address such difficulties. A legal framework determining women's rights also needs to be in place, to be known to the beneficiaries and communities, and to be applied with the help of program implementers.[8]

Coordination

Central coordination of DRPs by a single national civilian agency, balanced by decentralization of implementational authority to districts and communities through existing organizational structures, makes for a powerful institutional arrangement. The implementing agency must be perceived to be credible by ex-combatants. Furthermore, in conflict settings it is essential that the institution be perceived as neutral and fully representative.

A DRP requires considerable financial, technical, and political support from the international community. By way of technical assistance, joint missions, and regular meetings, the international community can contribute substantially to the successful implementation of the program and the strengthening of national institutions. Coordination of donor support by a credible lead donor has proved very effective. In Uganda, for instance, the World Bank acted as lead agency, coordinating efforts of individual donors and assisting the government in resource mobilization, while German Technical Assistance (GTZ) provided program management assistance to the program's executive secretariat.

The effectiveness of programmatic interventions in relation to ongoing developmental initiatives is maximized by careful coordination within government and among other project promoters. To put scarce resources to optimal use, program components should be ranked by simplicity of implementation, with the simplest components first on the list. Administrative costs need to be held down.

Once the major program objectives have been fulfilled, remaining activities should be integrated into the government's mainstream developmental efforts. In countries like Cambodia, East Timor, and Djibouti, although veterans have received initial transitional reinsertion and early targeted reintegration assistance, their economic and social reintegration has also benefited from an early mainstreaming into larger antipoverty programs. Community-driven initiatives, and basic service delivery programs are especially useful vehicles for delivering longer-term assistance.

Veterans associations from Mozambique and Uganda to Nicaragua and Guatemala have played a crucial peer support role in assisting social and psychological transitions. Furthermore, representatives of ex-combatants, as well as field-based staff, can perform crucial roles in facilitating reintegration. Such veteran counselors are the eyes and ears of program management on the ground and help identify potential problems and find locally appropriate solutions. Adequate mobility is essential for outreach staff to be effective; in Uganda, they received motorbikes, in northern Chad, camels.

Local communities should be involved directly in decision making, especially on important local matters, so that scarce public resources are allocated in a transparent and socially accountable manner. Efforts aimed at decentralization and participation in Rwanda provided a unique opportunity for community-based reintegration. In 1999 and 2001, local elections were held, establishing community development committees (CDCs). Under the overall coordination of the ministry of local government, these committees implemented reconstruction and development projects financed by donors.

The Building Blocks of Peace and Development

A peace dividend needs to be understood in social and economic terms, as well as financial terms. Such savings may be achieved over a limited number of years, as is the case with the phased demobilization in Bosnia and Herzegovina. The reinvestment of savings from military downsizing into the development of a disciplined, high-quality defense force can itself produce a peace dividend by increasing security, building confidence, and reducing public fear.

It is useful to link a country's overall macroeconomic reform program, especially as it concerns the public expenditure mix, to the planned reintegration program. In Cambodia, for instance, the World Bank's Public Expenditure Review included an analysis of defense expenditures, which was then matched with different scenarios for demobilization. The resulting assessment provided critical information to government and donors as to the potential benefits of military downsizing over time.

Rehabilitating critical infrastructure also can be linked to reintegration programs that involve training and employment schemes for both reconstructing material assets and building human and social capital. In Sierra Leone, reconstruction and the reintegration of refugees goes hand in hand with the reintegration of ex-combatants. Although they are two distinct projects, the same community-based institutional framework and implementational arrangements are being applied, thus economizing on scarce local resources.

Demobilization is also among the cornerstones of security sector reform (SSR), which aims at improving the professionalism and effectiveness of the security forces overall. In postconflict situations, a first step could entail the unification of belligerent forces leading to the establishment of new national armed forces, followed by the rationalization of the established armed forces at a later date. SSR is not only limited to the armed forces but would also include the police, gendarmerie, border guards, intelligence services, etc. In Sierra Leone and East Timor, the DRP is a vehicle for such reform, which was assisted through bilateral channels.

Revitalizing civil society entails the promotion of local associations, community participation, and peer accountability, all of which reduce individual fear, enable collective condemnation of violence, and strengthen local security. These are the minimal conditions for encouraging people to reinvest in their communities both emotionally and financially.

In the end, DRPs are important programs for addressing the pressing needs of war-affected populations and for building the confidence of nationals to invest in their own lives and foreigners to invest in the countries. Ultimately, DRPs are critical to the security and political stability of the state itself.

Notes

1. Nat J. Colletta, Markus Kostner, and Ingo Wiederhofer, *Case Studies in War-to-Peace Transition: The Demobilization and Reintegration of Ex-combatants in Ethiopia, Namibia, and Uganda* (Washington, D.C., 1996), 19–22.
2. Nat J. Colletta, Markus Kostner, and Ingo Wiederhofer. *The Transition from War to Peace in Sub-Saharan Africa* (Washington D.C., 1996), 7–22.
3. Kim M. Clark, *Fostering a Farewell to Arms: Preliminary Lessons Learned in the Demobilization and Reintegration of Combatants* (Washington, D.C., 1996), 1–30.
4. UN Department of Peace Keeping, *Disarmament, Demobilization and Reintegration of Ex-Combatants in a Peacekeeping Environment: Principles and Guidelines* (New York, 1999), 5–10; UNDP, *Harnessing Institutional Capacities in Support of the Disarmament, Demobilization and Reintegration of Former Combatants* (New York, 2000), 1–40.
5. Kees Kingma, *Demobilization in Sub-Saharan Africa: The Development and Security Impacts* (New York, 2000).
6. Beth Verhey, *Child Soldiers: Preventing, Demobilizing and Reintegrating* (New York, 2001), 11.
7. Nat J. Colletta and Michele Cullen, *Violent Conflict and the Transformation of Social Capital: Lessons from Cambodia, Rwanda, Guatemala, and Somalia* (Washington, D.C., 2000), 1–7. See Colletta, Teck Ghee Lim, and Anita Kelles-Viitanen, *Social Cohesion and Conflict Prevention in Asia: Managing Diversity Through Development* (Washington, D.C. 2001).
8. Nathalie De Watteville, *Gender Dimensions of Demobilization and Reintegration Programs* (Washington, D.C., 2001), 1–8; Coletta, Johanna M. Forman, Jan Vanheukelom, *Security, Poverty Reduction and Sustainable Development: Challenges for the New Millennium* (Washington, D.C., 1999), 12–13.

Nine

Establishing the Rule of Law

SUSAN ROSE-ACKERMAN

THE RULE OF LAW has two fundamentally different aspects. The first sets legal limits, both civil and criminal, on private interactions. The second imposes limits on the political regime. By definition, a weak state cannot engage in organized predation, but it can disrupt lives and economic activity by its very weakness and its inability to control violence and the destruction of property. This distinction between private lawlessness and public impunity raises a difficult issue for those seeking to shore up weak states. Policies that strengthen the state may simply permit those in power to act with impunity and may encourage opponents to resort to violence and threats. Yet a fragile democratic state can be undermined by its own failure to limit private lawlessness.

To understand the link between state weakness and law, one needs to trace the sources of this weakness. Two sources should be distinguished. One cause is a corrupt autocratic ruler whose iron hold on power is slipping or, as in the former Soviet Union, an authoritarian system that is not sustainable. In such cases the system operates without strong legal norms and without an independent judiciary to check the freedom of prosecutors. These systems demonstrate that the "rule of law" is not necessary for stability, but that a system without such underpinnings can unravel quickly. Initially, the state is one where private activity is heavily controlled and where people find ways to cope, including institutionalized corruption. The failure of such a state makes these entrenched methods of coping less effective. Reform is difficult because much of the state's economic activity is implicated in the corrupt system and those with vested interests may struggle to hold on to past benefits as the state deteriorates.

A second type of weak state is one with an ongoing low level of state capacity. This weakness may be the result of a long-term period of stagnation or may occur in a period of transition after the downfall of a discredited former regime. In such systems, private actors seek ways to function despite the state's weakness. Benign cooperative arrangements between neighbors or small businesses might arise to overcome the lack of legal background norms. Alternatively, criminal gangs may take over the protection function and skim off the profits of legitimate business activity at the same time as they operate illegal businesses. Outsiders, if they invest at all, work around local conditions by writing contracts governed by the law of a developed country, with disputes to be settled by international arbitration. These practices can create a group of people and business interests opposed to reform because they benefit from the status quo. Another group may be eager for the introduction of legal background norms but may not be organized well enough to articulate its demands.

The establishment of the rule of law can imply either a strengthening of state capacities or a weakening of state power. It can represent the imposition of a set of state-determined rules governing private behavior or the imposition of constraints on the personalized nature of government. Both can occur at once, but it is important to recognize the dual functions of legal regimes.

Because the control of crime is a key contributor to regime stability, I discuss efforts to establish "law and order" in that sense. Then I turn to law as an organizer of private economic activity, with property law, contracts, and liability law (torts) as basic building blocks. The next section considers law as the basis for state organization and authority. It includes the state's constitutional structure and the way in which it organizes its relations with its citizenry. I concentrate on the fundamental question of how law can be used to limit the state itself. I examine the judiciary as a key institution supporting efforts to establish a rule of law. The chapter concludes with some thoughts about priority setting in societies trying to establish a functioning legal system as they recover from state collapse. This is a daunting task that is unlikely to have a single right answer. Nevertheless, I propose a framework for approaching reform.

I use legal categories borrowed from the developed world. The premise of such borrowing is the belief that the foundations of any legal system are similar. In practice, this may not be true, and an important topic for law and development research is to discover where these standard legal categories fit awkwardly within a society's traditional way of operating. One needs to consider not just the formal rules but the impact of formal rules on society. "Law," in the sense of a set of formal written documents, will be largely irrelevant if the rules are not embedded in an institutional and organizational structure that favors compliance.[1] Societies may have developed practices and norms that serve the functions taken on by law in other countries. Even when societies share a condemnation of murder and theft, for example, their methods of assigning responsibility and imposing punishments may vary widely. Traditional practices ought not be rejected outright, but, conversely, one needs to avoid the opposite mistake of supporting practices simply because they have historical or traditional roots.[2]

Criminal Law

Criminal law operates at the boundary between the state and society. Legal systems specify which actions are crimes, which represent civil offenses, and which are legal. The placement of offenses in one or another of these categories can have profound implications for state power and private freedom. In industrialized countries, criminal prosecutions are almost always the prerogative of the state although some may need the cooperation of private individuals. Punishment can include imprisonment as well as fines or other structural remedies.

There are four interlocking issues: the substantive criminal law, the police and law enforcement, the criminal process, and the system of punishment. All four are likely to need immediate attention as a new state tries to consolidate power. The decisions that are made will have important implications for the future viability and legitimacy of the state. The goal should be to reduce criminal activity enough to permit a modest-sized police force to maintain order without unduly interfering with everyday life and personal freedom. If this goal can be accomplished, the country can spend more of its scarce funds on development-oriented activities instead of on efforts to hold on to power.[3] I do not emphasize the issue of holding prior rulers and public officials to account for past actions. This may, indeed, be a central concern of a new regime, but I argue that it should not be allowed to substitute for efforts to build a functioning criminal law system.

Substantive Criminal Law

The first concern is substantive criminal law. The line between civil and criminal offenses may need to be redrawn in a state that is rebuilding public institutions. In particular, a previous autocratic regime may have maintained power through a broad use of criminal sanctions. The criminal law may include many vague and open-ended offenses that give the state the ability to pick and choose whom to prosecute and what to charge them with. Thus it may be necessary to redraft vague statutes and to decriminalize activities related to citizen efforts to criticize and control the state.

For example, in many countries, restrictive libel laws give special protections to public officials, and violations are treated as criminal, not civil, matters. This is just the reverse of what is needed. Politicians and other public figures should be harder to libel than private citizens, not easier. They should not be immune from facing charges of corruption, and allegations of libel should be handled as civil matters.[4]

Criminal statutes may also restrict citizens from assembling to protest state policies or to support a reform agenda. The law may criminalize behavior considered deviant by the state. In both cases, decriminalization will often be the only policy consistent with accountable government.

Conversely, some formerly permissible activity may need to be criminalized, particularly white-collar crimes. Political and economic change can produce new opportunities, and the law may need to respond. For example, a country emerging from years of civil war and subsistence agriculture will likely need to establish banks, issue a new currency, and increase transportation and communication links with the rest of the world. The result can be increases in such offenses as check forgery and counterfeiting, robbery, drug trafficking, prostitution, and computer crime.[5] Laws against corruption, fraud, and self-dealing by officials may need to be strengthened or redrafted. The criminal laws inherited from the prior regime may be inadequate to deal with modern problems.

New regimes also face the problem of how to deal with the offenses of the old regime. Some new states spend considerable time and resources in purging the old regime through criminal prosecutions. Although one can understand the new rulers' desire to start with a clean slate, this effort is often misplaced. Scarce judicial and legal resources are diverted to dealing with such cases at the expense of present-day crimes, and the citizenry focuses on the past instead of on the program of state building.[6] Some of the former socialist republics in eastern Europe have carried out extensive purges of supporters of the prior regime. Many simply lost their jobs; some were criminally prosecuted. These processes were feasible because other educated people were available to replace those forced out of their jobs, but even in those countries the procedure was costly and divisive.[7] Poor and vulnerable countries have little margin for elaborate symbolic efforts. A former head of state and his close associates may need to be discredited and exiled, but a fragile new state can neither turn its back on the previous elite nor afford to divert many resources to purification through the criminal law.

Although, in general, widespread criminal prosecutions of former officials and allies of the old regime are likely to absorb resources that could be put to better use elsewhere, I make an exception for allegations of corruption. Such prosecutions can be part of an effort to locate and repatriate corrupt proceeds deposited abroad. Thus, a successful prosecution can bring a net financial gain to the state as it seizes the former officials' assets. Improvements in the willingness of some banking havens to cooperate in corruption investigations may make this type of prosecution feasible and lucrative for new governments.[8] Nevertheless, even here, judgment will need to be exercised. Too often, former rulers are accused of corruption at the same time as the new rulers are creating corrupt structures of their own that will repeat the pattern. The effort to retrieve looted funds should be combined with affirmative programs of reform.[9]

Truth commissions are one compromise adopted by some new regimes, such as South Africa. They have the advantage of avoiding most criminal prosecutions and are considerably less expensive than the widespread use of criminal trials.[10] They require commitments of money and time, but when some accounting for the past is required, a variant on the South African model may be feasible for newly established states, even in poor countries.

Nevertheless, like other reforms discussed in this chapter, truth commissions should be designed to play a role in the state-building process. In addition to providing some accounting for past wrongs, such commissions may provide information about the institutional practices and networks that maintained the old system at a low level of functioning. Unless a destructive civil war has made past structures irrelevant, a truth commission can help the present government and its citizens to understand where power lay and how it was exercised. Doing so can help inform the process of law reform and constitutional design. Otherwise, truth commissions risk becoming nothing more that a watered-down form of revenge against the former regime. However brutal that regime may have been, settling scores is not a good foundation on which to establish a stable polity.

The Police

In an enlightening study of policing in Africa, Hills argues that in most sub-Saharan states, the function of the police is to keep order and maintain the regime in power. It is essentially a political organization, and crime fighting is not its primary activity.[11] Thus the police play only a minor role in protecting citizens from the predatory behavior of other citizens. In many cases, few resources are available to the police, and they are paid very low salaries and lack uniforms and equipment. These resource constraints encourage police officers to become part-time bandits and to extort payoffs from individuals and businesses. This situation is difficult to correct because security cannot be provided without resources, but when security is low, the state finds it difficult to raise revenue.[12]

A newly established regime may seek to establish order and improve its hold on power through police crackdowns. This will not work, however, if the police, through brutal and unpredictable behavior, incite people to resist authority more fervently. The police act as an arbitrary arm of state power, not an aid to law-abiding citizens.[13] In countries emerging from violent civil war, police work will be an obvious career choice for demilitarized fighters, increasing the likelihood of excessive violence.[14] As Hills's case studies suggest, fragile new states have neither the incentives nor the resources to establish a police force that is law abiding itself and that does not use threats to extort corrupt payoffs from the public.[15]

As a result of the weakness of the police, many businesses and communities rely on private security forces—both for-profit firms and community self-help groups. Organized crime may take on the job of private protection for wealthy individuals and businesses. Mafias may ally with the police and threaten either violent confrontation or cooptation through payoffs. Even when mafia-like groups do not exist, local vigilantes may seek to keep order in the absence of a strong police presence.[16] Toleration of such groups can be a first step toward the ultimate downfall of a regime. Yet some regimes have used the lack of a professional modern police force as part of a strategy for maintaining power. Thus Mobutu Sese Seko in Zaire permitted the decentralization of police and security forces in a way that gave each group de facto permission to exploit its own local area. The economy was looted, and the people were impoverished, but Mobutu retained power by reducing the likelihood of organized internal resistance.[17] This example suggests why the creation of a police force designed to aid citizens and fight crime may not be in the interest of a nation's rulers, but it also suggests that recruiting and training a modern police force needs to be a priority in democratic countries, even in very poor ones.[18] An important issue for newly established states is whether they can use the police to fight crime in a way that builds on local networks and institutions without encouraging vigilantism. Hills provides one possible model from Somalia in which an Australian team worked with local authorities to create a trained and reasonably well-equipped force that had local credibility because the police commander was proposed by the local elders.[19] The ultimate legitimacy of the police in the eyes of the citizenry, however, will depend not only on their own professionalism and links to the local community, but also on the substantive criminal law and on the impartiality of the legal process.

Criminal Process and Punishment

Both the Anglo-American and the Continental legal systems have elaborate rules of evidence and standards of proof. A major distinction between the criminal and the civil law is the standard of proof, which is higher for criminal than for civil offenses. For example, in Anglo-American law it is "beyond a reasonable doubt" instead of "more probable than not." Furthermore, the procedures used in court provide those accused of crimes with more safeguards than those accused of civil offenses would have.

Studies of traditional societies, however, indicate that many of them make no clear distinction between civil and criminal offenses. When an offense such as a homicide or theft occurs, the emphasis in many traditional societies, at least in Africa, is on restitution for the victim and his family or tribal group. The goal is the restoration of social equilibrium.[20]

Notions of individual accountability are not well developed, so that the responsibility for paying restitution rests with the offender's family or even his village, not with himself alone. This makes the payment of restitution more feasible since individual offenders will often be unable to pay. Incarceration is seen as pointless and wasteful since the offender will be unable either to provide for his family or to pay restitution.

Traditional practices are everywhere being replaced with Western models of criminal law and punishment as traditional courts are merged with regular courts.[21] Nevertheless, many of the old views continue to resonate in the present. Imprisonment is a waste of human resources, and, especially in poor countries with weakly accountable government institutions, prisons may be places of repression and corruption. Prison officials may be able to act with impunity inside the prison—both favoring those who can pay them off and harassing ordinary inmates. Restitution is worth considering in countries with little public or private insurance.[22]

If one leaves aside other aspects of court procedures, a criminal law system based on fines and restitution would take on many of the characteristics of the civil liability system.[23] Some African countries permit compensation either out of fines paid to the state or as a payment received directly from the convicted felon. Nsereko, however, claims that, except in Tanzania, these provisions are almost never used. They have been interpreted restrictively and often require a large expenditure of time and trouble by the victim.[24] A larger problem, however, is the poverty of offenders. Assuming that no modern country is willing to permit peonage as a punishment, many offenders will be essentially judgment-proof. If we assume that the ties of family, village, and tribe are loosening over time and with them the obligations to make up for the offenses of one's kin and neighbors, a system of restitution would seem unworkable standing alone. Fines, however, could be an available punishment when offenders could raise the funds.

In short, the basic claim that very poor and fragile countries should deemphasize prison extends to the present day. However, the alternative of fines is unlikely to work, although it could be part of a broader scheme. Restitution for victims seems especially worth considering in poor countries with few social safety nets, but it would need to be an obligation of the state, not the offender. We are left with a set of unattractive options: little or no punishment, forced work in lieu of fines for those unable to pay, or cheap, shaming punishments that do not violate human rights norms.[25] Perhaps modern technology could expand the range of options to include a form of house arrest or required work with electronic monitoring. The problem is to find punishments that deter crime without imposing large costs on poor and institutionally weak countries and without setting up systems that can be cruelly exploited by those who control the system of punishment.

Economic Law

The control of crime and the creation of a credible criminal justice system are only the first step in creating a stable state. Economic conditions are unlikely to improve unless the legal building blocks for private economic activity are in place. In countries that have just become committed to democracy and the free market, laws governing the private market either do not exist or are likely to be vague and contradictory. Judges may have little experience or training in resolving the legal problems arising out of private business deals and in applying new regulatory and taxation statutes. The laws on the books may not mean much, and sometimes it may be difficult even to find out what they are. Laws need to be well drafted, relatively clear, and generally available. A first step is simply to make laws and regulations easy to locate. If the law is clear and well known, not only will the disputes that do arise be simpler to resolve, but fewer disputes will arise.

Many new democracies must do more than publicize existing rules, they need to create new law. One option is to borrow from successful market economies and established democracies. The legacy of colonialism means that some developing countries have many "borrowed" laws already in place, sometimes written in the language of the colonial power or based on obsolete and inconsistent statutes copied from other countries many years ago. For example, in those parts of Asia subject to British influence, some laws are written in English and are thus incomprehensible to much of the population.[26] In Palestine, law is a confusing mixture of Ottoman, British, Egyptian, Jordanian, and Israeli legal influences.[27] In spite of the problematic character of legal transplants, modern borrowing may, nevertheless, be a viable option especially when the goal is to integrate the country more fully into the international system.[28] Some of the Central Asian republics, for example, have foreign investment codes prepared with the help of foreign advisors that are viewed with favor by local business people.[29] Nevertheless, formal law is never sufficient. One lesson of recent reform efforts is the importance of helping "to foster the development of a favorable framework of host-country legal-institutional and government-institutional norms and practices, and broader attitudes toward law and the rule of law."[30]

Although economic law reform may seem like a technical matter far from the high politics of constitutional design, the creation of a functioning system of law governing private economic activity can help support the long-term viability of a new state. I discuss the most basic private law categories of property rights, contract law, and liability rules. Other aspects of economic law, not covered here, include the law of private organizations such as for-profit corporations, banks, and labor unions; laws governing financial markets and bankruptcy, and basic regulatory rules concerning environmental protection, working conditions, and the safety of products and workplaces.

Property

It is an article of faith in much of the law and economics literature that well-defined private property rights are a necessary condition for economic growth and political stability. Vaguely defined rights invite disputes over ownership that at best will discourage investment and at worst will produce violent and destructive clashes. Yet, it is a commonplace of legal analysis that property claims represent a bundle of rights, not a zero / one choice. Overlapping rights to land are common even in highly developed countries where easements and public rights of way are ubiquitous, and ownership of surface, subsurface, and air rights is frequently divided. The rights to use the water in flowing streams and rivers are governed by alternative sets of rules in different parts of the world. Beyond the issue of the ownership of tangible property, some modern work on business organizations argues that a salient feature of modern economic relationships is a deep ambiguity about ownership.[31] Unambiguous, unitary property claims are not a necessary condition for economic growth, and too limited a range of legal forms may stifle innovation. This reality suggests a need to rethink oversimplified arguments in favor of undivided private ownership.[32] Nevertheless, clarity concerning who has the right to do what is beneficial, and so is an acceptable, speedy forum for resolving disputes. For example, owners of forest land might be obligated to permit local people to forage in stands of timber even though the owner retained the right to harvest the trees. The meaning of "forage," however, would need to be clearly defined in a way that ordinary people can understand and accept.

The principles of property usage may have something to do with historical patterns, but a reforming state may need to recast some rules if they produce violent and contentious disputes. The reform of property relations must avoid creating complex rules that tax the state's limited ability to resolve disputes fairly.

In some new democracies, historical patterns of property use involve customary communal rights that interact with kinship systems in complex ways. Thus the new regime must decide how much of this historical legacy to preserve. There are two aspects to the problem: the underlying distribution of wealth and the legal framework that establishes property entitlements and governs their transfer.

The first distributive issue concerns the initial conditions under which economic and political development will occur and affects individuals' chances of winning and losing under the new regime. Inherited patterns of ownership can preserve some of the inequities that created civil war and state collapse in the first place. Thus new regimes may face the daunting task of taking on wealthy vested interests as part of their effort to gain legitimacy. Furthermore, democracy will be difficult to maintain if traditional ownership patterns make some people dependent on others in a way that limits their political independence. Systems of agricultural tenancy and production in Pakistan, for example, apparently make many rural families entirely dependent on large landowners with the result that they overwhelmingly support these landowners' political interests.[33] In this respect, a state emerging from civil war may be at an advantage because the war itself may have undermined the power of those who had economic influence in the past. An initial responsibility of a new regime is to determine whether to carry out a redistribution of land and other property.[34]

Second, the meaning of any redistribution depends upon the legal protections and restrictions that accompany it. Restrictions on ownership, transferability, and use obviously affect the value of ownership.[35] Spontaneous evolution in the direction of efficiency is unlikely. The state will need to establish enforceable rules. Detailed work on particular societies suggests that mixed systems sometimes can function well where elements of traditional property relations survive into the modern world.[36] There appear to be numerous examples of property rights regimes that depart from the standard economist's solution of clearing title to individual plots. The explanation for the survival of these mixed systems seems to be a blend of economic rationality and political expediency.[37]

New states will need to carry out public policies that affect the value of private property. This raises a basic question of constitutional design. Should the state promulgate a constitutional property clause that limits its ability to seize private property for public use without paying compensation? States need to balance the protection of investors against their own need for policy-making flexibility. Unfortunately, United States constitutional law concerning government taking of private property does not provide a clear-cut model. It includes many elements of ad hoc balancing that are hardly conducive to the creation of an unproblematic environment for economic growth. However, the study of American constitutional doctrine can help countries understand the importance of giving governments discretion to carry out taxation and regulatory activities that affect the returns to private investment. The United States experience illustrates that although some degree of predictability and clarity is obviously beneficial, the rule of law does not imply a rigid and unchanging set of rules.[38] Clearly, a state should not build in strong protections for the status quo distribution until it has determined that this distribution is compatible with its basic goals. A new state arising out of chaos and civil war may not want to give strong protections to previous ownership patterns.

Moreover, a fragile new state needs to avoid creating a further risk of violence by its property redistribution policies. When the state seeks to reform property relations, the risk is that it will institute dysfunctional policies that exacerbate conflict instead of reducing it. For example, a recent study argues that Brazilian land reform policies in the Amazon have contributed to violent conflict and deforestation. Landowners use violence to increase the likelihood of successful eviction of squatters, and squatters use violence to increase the likelihood that the farm will be expropriated by the government as part of the land reform program.[39] When violence by one group is used as a signal to the state to act in favor of that group, the stage is set for escalation and instability.

Laws that redistribute property more fairly and that provide for its free transferability and use can be stymied by very basic administrative failures. A prerequisite for the development of a modern property regime is a well-functioning system for land titling and property transfer. The value of nominal property rights in land is reduced if transfers are difficult to carry out because of the time and bribe payments required. For example, in Bangladesh, land ownership seems a route out of poverty. Thus it is important that small farmers be able to buy and sell land to take advantage of changing economic opportunities. In one recent household survey, 23 percent reported that they had bought or sold land. However, the present system of registering sales is riddled with corruption and delay. Furthermore, disputes that go to court are subject to long delays.[40] Such bureaucratic and judicial incapacity and venality may lead people to seek other methods of enforcing land rights. Violence and threats can prevail not only when state policies are dysfunctional but also when they are simply ineffective.

A new regime has a window of opportunity to carry out a major redistribution of property if it can establish the administrative capacity to do so and the political will to overcome vested interests. Whether or not a new state takes on such a strong policy challenge, it will inevitably face other lesser issues related to the administration of property law. The state has two very different options—either an automatic and centralized administrative system that reduces official discretion or a more community-based system centered on local institutions. The former requires clear and simple rules that can be enforced with little discretion and that provide transparency to the public. The second can be defended as an outgrowth of social practice but may systematically disadvantage some groups and individuals who have little way to respond. It may also hamper the development of a national trading and economic system. This same tension between informal structure and formal rules arises in other areas of economic law, especially in the field of contract law.

Contracts

When formal law is weak, unclear, or unenforceable, businesses will engage in various types of self-help. Newly established states must discover what coping mechanisms businesses use and decide whether they should be strengthened or replaced with formal rules enforceable in court. The most interesting recent work to shed light on these issues is a survey by Woodruff, McMillan, and Johnson on countries as different as Mexico, Vietnam, and Eastern Europe.[41] Their research raises key issues for political regimes in newly established states. When contract law is weak, business people frequently cope by limiting dealings to their families and members of their local community or ethnic group. The evidence suggests that businesses can go quite far with informal extralegal regimes—including the establishment of trade associations and other intermediaries that extend beyond the narrow bounds of people related by kinship or ethnic ties.[42] These informal arrangements permit businesses to survive and even thrive, but they almost always have social costs in the form of exclusion or collusion.[43] They exclude members of disfavored groups and make it difficult for competitive markets to develop in areas where credit is necessary and time elapses between promises and their fulfillment. Reliance on family and friends will often limit access to capital, thus constraining the scale of businesses. Ultimately, failure to reform contract law will limit the possibility for arms-length contracts and impose costly limitations on a country's growth prospects. It will also limit the number of people able to benefit from the growth that does occur. New states face difficult political choices because one group of investors and business people will be pushing for a stronger contract law regime while others, who benefit from the status quo, will oppose those changes.

A weak internal system of contract law will encourage large international investors to avoid the local system by writing contracts that use international legal norms and resolve disputes in international fora, such as the International Chamber of Commerce's Court of Arbitration. These practices permit certain deals to go through but provide a discriminatory benefit to those with access to international institutions. Their widespread use may delay internal law reform since multinationals and their allies may benefit from their privileged access to international dispute resolution institutions.

Contract law reform requires some subtlety. Reform should not simply sweep away local practices built up in response to weak formal law. Even when legal rules do need reform, existing businesses may need help in adapting to a legal system that contemplates the possibility of transactions among strangers protected by the courts. Cronies and relatives of the previous rulers are hardly candidates for sympathy, but in other cases small, local businesses face challenges in adopting to a new, more open regime.

A first requirement is a set of impartial tribunals to adjudicate disputes. In the simplest reform model, such tribunals are entirely deferential to the agreements reached between private parties. Courts base their interpretations on what the parties contracted for initially. Even here, however, some body of "contract law" would arise as drafters of contracts consider how courts have in the past interpreted various terms. The law would then develop into a set of background provisions that drafters could nullify by precise language. The courts or state arbitration tribunals would take over the enforcement function from private groups, providing a more transparent and widely available forum for resolving commercial disputes. If courts have the proper degree of professionalism and lack of corruption, they will institutionalize informal rules and permit new sorts of private deals by reducing incentives for ex post cheating. In the absence of the courts, reputational concerns are paramount. With well-functioning courts, contracting among strangers is possible.

However, such a laissez-faire approach to contract law will not address some of the most pressing problems of an informal system. In practice, even contract law in common law systems has served broader goals such as the protection of uninformed parties and the preservation of the interests of those not party to the contract. It is concerned not just with breach and the remedies for breach but also with whether the arrangement ought to be enforced as a contract at all. A contract to sell oneself into slavery or one that is the result of fraud will not be enforced. The law and economics literature has focused both on the establishment of efficient background norms and on the proper way to incorporate broader policy concerns.[44]

In addition to moving toward a contract law system consistent with international standards, the state may also need to deal directly with transitional issues in a way that recognizes both the costs and benefits of reform and that takes account of the country's level of literacy and business sophistication. If one goal is to induce people to accept more formal written ways of regularizing their relationships, the rules must be simple and easy to understand, and the method of resolving disputes must be efficient and fair. This suggests that clear statutory rules are needed, not the time-consuming and ambiguous process of judicial law-making under common law. Reforms should also acknowledge previous informal methods of doing business. Opening up the country to the international market may make existing informal methods unworkable thus imposing severe costs on local producers and leading to collapse. Woodruff, for example, provides an example from Mexico's footwear industry, where trade liberalization with the United States undermined informal methods of contract enforcement used by small manufacturers.[45] Reformers need to understand how small businesses and poorly educated producers have coped in the past and not assume that their mechanisms are dysfunctional, though they may be. If firms have been hiring thugs to threaten debtors with violence, this option is obviously not worth preserving. Furthermore, even if historical practices were functional under the old system, they may not be workable in the new regime. In that case, local businesses can legitimately demand help in making the transition to a system of more formal methods of business interaction based on written documents and legal norms.

Torts

Tort law reform presents a vexing dilemma for poor and fragile states. On the one hand, insurance markets are likely to be poorly developed, so that those who are injured or suffer economic losses will not be compensated in that way. Furthermore, the poverty of the country and the fragility of the state means that social safety nets are also weak or nonexistent. Thus harms inflicted through accidents or the careless behavior of others can have severe consequences for people in marginal circumstances. On the other hand, the very poverty that makes compensation seem necessary will mean that most of those who inflict harm are judgment-proof. Multinational firms with investments in fragile countries may be induced to pay for the harms they cause, but this will be impossible for ordinary people and small local businesses. We reviewed this dilemma earlier in discussing fines versus imprisonment under the criminal law.

In general, the tort liability system is a poor way to provide a social safety net since it singles out one class of the injured for special treatment. Nevertheless, in the imperfect world inhabited by poor and vulnerable states it may be one of the few effective ways to tap deep pockets and has the advantage of being linked to harmful behavior.

In law and economics scholarship on tort law, one of the main goals of the tort system is to create incentives for optimal accident prevention by private actors. In most cases one can imagine a regulatory substitute—for example, highway speed limits versus private lawsuits against speeders who cause accidents.[46] In a poor country where a large proportion of the population is so poor as to be judgment-proof, however, many damage judgments will not be collectable, and tort law will be of little use as a general method of deterring negligent behavior. This suggests that one might treat some behaviors as misdemeanors rather than as torts, with an accompanying state-imposed punishment. Otherwise one could face a situation where people become indentured servants to those whom they have harmed. In general, this suggests a difficulty for states that are both weak and poor. They are likely to have little state regulatory capacity, but at the same time, private tort law is unlikely to be effective.

A blurring of the distinction between torts and crimes makes a certain amount of sense in a country where most of those who cause harm cannot pay compensation. This may suggest the maintenance of local practices that blur the distinction. The problem, of course, is that such systems have costs especially if they can be used to ostracize unpopular members of the community. The distinction between bad individuals and bad practices by otherwise acceptable members of the community is not an easy distinction to maintain in a small, close-knit group.[47]

A final issue concerns the role of tort law in the context of economic development. Developed countries, especially the United States, are debating the extent of liability that business firms ought to bear for the harm caused by their products and production processes. To some extent this is a debate about the proper role of liability law versus statutory regulations as a method of controlling the social costs of business.[48] In a newly established state, this issue highlights the relative capacity of state regulatory institutions versus the judiciary. In general, in the face of state weakness, liability suits that can fill in the gaps in the statutory law and its implementation ought to be permitted. The role of liability suits against businesses could be reduced as state bureaucratic and legislative capacity increases.

In short, liability law in a fragile new state ought to look quite different from the model in stable democracies in developed countries. First, not much effort should be devoted to law suits that order judgment-proof individuals to pay compensation. Instead, other forms of deterrence are needed that concentrate on the most serious harms and treat them as misdemeanors with state-imposed punishments. Second, liability for business firms might play a greater role in such countries than in most established polities with well-functioning systems of public regulation.

Public Law: Openness and Accountability

The third part of efforts to establish "the rule of law" concerns the legal accountability of public officials.[49] The political compromise that settles a civil war or accompanies a regime change must include not only provisions for popular elections but also constraints on the behavior of elected officials and career bureaucrats.

The impunity of public officials can be limited both by internal government structures that constrain malfeasance and by external pressure from the public.[50] Limits on the power of individual politicians and political institutions and the creation of independent monitoring and enforcement organizations can both be potent strategies for establishing accountability. The public can be an important check on the arbitrary exercise of power by government. In fact, warring elites may agree to establish a democratic regime largely because they anticipate that such checks will function adequately.[51]

The citizens can act as a check, however, only if the government provides information on its actions. Citizens must also have a convenient means of lodging complaints and be protected against possible reprisals. Furthermore, government officials must find it in their interest to respond to complaints. There are two basic routes for public pressure—collective complaints by groups of citizens concerning general failures of government and objections raised by particular individuals against their own treatment at the hands of public authorities. Both collective and individual routes can help maintain accountable government structures.

The public and private institutions needed to produce public accountability are likely to be underdeveloped in weak states. Nevertheless, some combination of these options may be plausible, even in poor countries.

Information and Auditing

A precondition for citizen influence is information. It is easy to underestimate the importance of posters, fliers, and videotapes that tell people what they can expect from honest officials and how to make a complaint. In many cases such informative material represents the first time ordinary citizens have ever heard that they have rights against abusive authority.

In addition to basic information about official standards of behavior, citizen activists need more comprehensive information. Open government includes telling citizens what their government is doing by publishing consolidated budgets, data on tax collections, statutes and rules, and the proceedings of legislative bodies. Such practices are standard in developed countries, but many developing countries are seriously deficient.[52] Financial data should be audited and published by independent authorities such as the General Accounting Office (GAO) in the United States or the Audit Commission in Great Britain.[53] Both institutions are independent of the government agencies that they audit—a necessary condition for credibility. Self-monitoring is suspect because a public agency that discovers and reports wrongdoing may suffer negative consequences. Thus, it has little incentive to look closely at the behavior of its employees.

In many countries, outside review is hampered because unaudited, secret funds are available to the chief executives and top ministers. These funds are an invitation to unaccountable government throughout the world.[54] For example, before 1989, the United Kingdom simply refused to acknowledge formally that it had an intelligence service.[55] In Brazil, when President Fernando Collor's impeachment was before Congress, observers worried that his allies were seeking to use secret government funds to bribe the members to obtain a favorable verdict.[56]

The Media and Public Opinion

Even a government that keeps good records and makes them available to the public may operate with impunity if no one bothers to analyze the available information—or if analysts are afraid to raise their voices. There are three routes to accountability. If the aim is to pressure government to act in the public interest, the role of both the media and organized groups is important. If the goal is government accountability to individuals, avenues for individual complaints must be established. In all three cases—media, groups, individuals—there is the problem of fear. If government officials or their unofficial allies intimidate and harass those who speak out, formal structures of accountability will be meaningless.

The media can facilitate public discussion if it is privately owned and free to criticize the government without fear of reprisal. Nominal press freedom will be insufficient if most of the media is associated with political parties. For example, in Italy corruption only became big news when the Italian press became increasingly independent from the political system.[57] Governments can keep the press in line through advertising, printing contracts, and payments to journalists. Another subtle form of control is to overlook underpayment of taxes by editors and media companies, retaining the possibility of prosecution as a threat.[58]

In poor countries with high levels of illiteracy, the media can play only a limited role. Many people have little education and minimal understanding of governmental operations. These deficiencies have two implications for reformers. First, government or independent private organizations might provide educational programs to help people understand what they should expect of a legitimate democratic government.[59] Citizens may have no notion that public officials owe them anything and, on the contary, may view officials as hierarchical superiors who must be placated with gifts.[60]

Second, the government needs a means of identifying the concerns of poor and marginalized groups without making them subject to penalties for speaking out. A free media can help here if it can sponsor or publicize surveys of popular attitudes. Even if the media plays only a limited role in informing citizens of what the government is doing, it can still tell the government what people think and what difficulties ordinary people face when dealing with bureaucracies.

Private Associations and Nonprofit Organizations

Laws that make it easy to establish private associations and nonprofit corporations can help. Some governments, worried that nongovernmental organizations (NGOs) will be used by political opponents, limit such groups or make it very costly for them to organize. Formal legal constraints may be high, and members may be subject to surveillance and harassment. For example, Transparency International, a nonprofit focused on combating corruption, has found that setting up local chapters in developing countries can be difficult even if local people are eager to organize. In some countries, several years have passed without the chapter obtaining a formal charter. Once registered, nonprofits may face onerous formal reporting requirements and require state approval before undertaking new projects. However, in practice, such rules mean little in many countries because the state lacks enforcement capacity. Sometimes the very ineffectiveness of the state can be a source of freedom.[61]

Another problem is co-optation. Some nonprofits organize and administer development programs for the poor. Their financing may be provided by the state or by aid funds administered by the state. Thus, their very existence depends upon cooperation with public authorities. As a consequence, they may be reluctant to criticize officials openly. To avoid such tensions, an NGO that takes on a mandate to work for law reform should avoid participation in service delivery. In both South Asia and Africa, many nonprofits that deliver services to the poor are financed in whole or in part by governments. In contrast, Latin American nonprofits sometimes have a more adversarial relationship with their governments.[62] Thus, in the first two regions, anticorruption groups will need to be separate from existing organizations, and in Latin America existing groups may prove more appropriate.

Nonprofit organizations can also usefully carry out and publish surveys that reveal public attitudes toward government services. Pioneering work of this sort has been carried out by the Public Affairs Centre in Bangalore, India. One Report Card Study focused on the delivery of urban services to slum dwellers in five cities. Although the incidence of reported bribery varied across the cities, it was endemic everywhere. Across service areas, the higher the prevalence of corruption, the lower the capacity or willingness of public service agencies to solve clients' problems.[63] Such surveys are a way of isolating the impact of corruption on the poor, who may otherwise have few ways of registering complaints, especially in weak and unaccountable states.

In countries with an honest and independent judicial system, another possibility arises for the indirect control of government. Private individuals and groups can be given the right to bring suits to force compliance with tax and regulatory laws. For most weak and vulnerable states, however, this is unlikely to be a realistic option because the courts may not be independent and no lawyers may be willing to take such cases. There are exceptions: for example, in India, citizens affected by illegal or oppressive government actions can bring Public Interest Actions to vindicate the collective rights of the public. Plaintiffs need not show a direct specific injury.[64] The Indian Supreme Court has endorsed an expansive right of standing for ordinary citizens arguing that "public spirited citizens having faith in rule of law are rendering great social and legal service by espousing causes of public nature. They cannot be ignored or overlooked on technical or conservative yardsticks."[65]

Outside of the United States, the losing party in a law suit commonly pays the legal fees of both sides. The American innovation is one-sided fee shifting—private plaintiffs who bring citizen suits against the government or regulated firms are compensated for their legal fees if they win but are not required to pay their opponents' fees if they lose. This is a valuable innovation that could be applied elsewhere. Although opponents of citizen suits worry about an excess of trivial claims, one-sided fee shifting is an appropriate response. It gives public interest groups an incentive to focus on the most worthy cases. Because accusations of corruption and malfeasance can be motivated by revenge, the law might include a provision that shifts all legal fees onto the plaintiff for suits found to be harassing or vindictive—so long as the courts can be relied upon to apply such a rule sparingly.

Avenues for Individual Complaints

Limiting low-level bureaucratic malfeasance and incompetence is often in the interest of top officials, who may try to enlist ordinary citizens in the effort. This can be done without organized citizen activity if individuals can lodge complaints easily and without fear that officials who flout the law will take revenge.

To make appeals worthwhile, the processes must not only be honest but also speedy and efficient. The plaintiff must also have a right to obtain information about his case from bureaucrats. For example, one study claims that land consolidation in Uttar Pradesh in India was achieved with relatively low levels of malfeasance. The keys were an open process with real participation by those affected, time pressure, and speedy and fair appeals.[66]

Complaints are unlikely if people fear reprisals. For example, in Tanzania, ordinary people questioned in 1996 believed that if they complained to superior officers, their identity would be revealed to the suspects, who would then harass and threaten them.[67] Obviously, these concerns made most people unwilling to file complaints.

Many countries have established ombudsmen to hear complaints of all kinds against public officials. These offices can help increase the accountability of government agencies to ordinary citizens.[68] Hence, they may generate resistance from politicians and bureaucrats. In India, for example, an office similar to an ombudsman, called a Lok Pal, was recommended by an administrative reform commission as early as 1966 but has never been established.[69] Although this failure is regrettable, one should have modest expectations for ombudsmen. These officials seldom uncover large-scale systemic wrongdoing and generally lack authority to initiate lawsuits.

The power of the ombudsman depends upon the moral authority and courage of the incumbent. For example, South Africa has a Public Protector who can investigate alleged improper behavior by public officials and make reports that are usually publicized. Its mandate includes malfeasance and corruption as well as traditional human rights abuses. Like most ombudsmen, the office cannot initiate legal actions, but it can refer cases to prosecutors. At present, the office is very small and has difficulty handling the volume of complaints. A recent United Nations report not only recommends an expansion in its capacity but a redefinition in its mission so that it can initiate large-scale investigations of general problems rather than merely respond to individual complaints.[70] In contrast, an example of a strong ombudsman comes from the Pacific island country of Vanuatu.[71] Its ombudsman, operating with "almost religious zeal," investigated a fraudulent financial scheme involving top government officials working with promoters from outside the country. Although the ombudsman could not bring formal charges herself, the resulting publicity played a role in undermining public support for those involved. Unfortunately, she herself was eventually forced out of office.

Some public agencies have created routes for direct citizen complaints. In Britain, a number of local communities are experimenting with antifraud hotlines.[72] Mexico's Program for the Modernization of Public Administration created a similar system of hotlines for businesses harassed by inspectors.[73] This method will be successful, however, only if complainants can preserve their anonymity or do not fear reprisals. If telephones are not widely available to people in rural areas or in poor urban neighborhoods, other methods of collecting complaints must be found. "Hot lines" must be more than just symbolic. Public officials—ombudsmen, agency oversight units, or law enforcement agents—must follow up on complaints in a visible way. At the same time, if the complaints concern individuals, the accused must have a credible way of defending against false accusations. Otherwise, the attempt at reform can degenerate into a collection of private vendettas with people enlisting the state to settle their personal feuds.

Administrative Law

In all democracies, political actors delegate authority to the executive branch to implement statutes. General rules issued by executive agencies under enabling statutes have the force of law. The process by which rules are produced requires accountability because these processes may be honestly or corruptly influenced by narrow groups for their own benefit. One model is the American Administrative Procedures Act, under which agencies must give notice of their intent to issue a regulation, accept testimony from a broad range of individuals and groups, and issue a statement of reasons along with the final rule. The rule can be challenged in court if proper procedures are not followed or if the end result is inconsistent with the underlying statute. This process has been criticized as time consuming and cumbersome, but inconvenience is the price of limitations on the arbitrary power of an executive.[74]

By way of contrast, Germany's parliamentary system imposes fewer controls on executive branch rule making. The process is much less transparent than the American one, and has been criticized for being too open to industry influence.[75] Great Britain seems to have a less procedurally constrained administrative process than Germany. This result could imply a more rational administrative process, but there seems no logical reason why that should be the result. If interest groups want influence, they can obtain influence in a much more opaque and potentially corrupt manner under the procedurally unconstrained British system. From the point of view of limiting rent-seeking by politicians and narrow interest groups, the weak administrative law constraints produced by parliamentary governments create accountability problems.

Another set of problems can arise in political systems with weak legislative branches. Critics of Latin American governments argue that most have overly powerful executives.[76] As a consequence, incentives for rent seeking and corruption are high within the executive branch. The president frequently has extensive decree power, may control a secret financial account that can be used to reward supporters, and is little subject to popular control while in office. Furthermore, the judiciary is generally less independent in practice and, until recently, has seldom effectively constrained executives. Some Asian countries exhibit a similar pattern. For example, in Thailand the executive in the past controlled and limited legislative activity so that it could rule by decree.[77] China is an extreme case, where some courts have held that only the National People's Congress, not the courts, can decide on the legality of administrative rules.[78] The lack of executive accountability facilitates corruption and other kinds of incompetence and malfeasance by centralizing regulatory power and giving executives wide discretion.

The creation of a transparent and accountable system of administrative law ought to be a part of the design of democratic constitutions. Rule making in the executive branch should be structured to assure adequate participation and transparency. The public needs avenues for appeal to the judiciary if the government has not followed its own procedures or has acted lawlessly. The goal is to make corruption and self-dealing harder to hide by forcing review of the process and of the substantive outcome. A review process aimed at achieving good substantive policy and democratic accountability can help create a stable state.

However, countries with a judiciary that is both corrupt and unrestrained will obviously be reluctant to give it additional powers. Furthermore, if an independent judiciary enforces laws that are biased in favor of the regulated industry, reform will be difficult without a change in underlying legal standards. For example, in the Philippines, oversight of the banking industry in the 1980s was hampered by lawsuits brought by banks against both regulatory agencies and the public officials themselves. As one banker himself admitted, lawsuits were a way "of preventing officials from implementing the regulations. You intimidate the bureaucracy."[79]

Although the details of the American administrative process can surely use reform, in the United States, the basic principles express the essence of accountable bureaucratic behavior. The process of promulgating rules requires public notice, public participation, and a governmental obligation to publicize and explain its actions. These requirements not only are consistent with democratic government but also limit the scope for corrupt dealing. Even a country with a weak legislature or a unitary parliamentary system could reduce the opportunities for corruption and other types of influence by adopting more transparent administrative processes.

Anticorruption Commissions

One solution to the weakness of public institutions is the creation of an independent body that is assigned some especially sensitive task. This strategy is seldom a desirable long-term option unless it is combined with the reform of core public institutions. One alternative that is both insulated from the rest of government and designed to promote broader reform is an independent anticorruption agency, which is a popular reform proposal for developing countries. In addition to the well-known cases of Hong Kong and Singapore, a number of other jurisdictions, such as Malaysia, Botswana, Malawi, Thailand, and the Australian state of New South Wales, have created similar institutions.[80] These bodies have sometimes been effective, but even the most well-respected institutions in Hong Kong and Singapore have problematic aspects. Before its reunion with China, the Hong Kong Independent Commission Against Corruption (ICAC) reported only to the colonial governor. An anticorruption commission reporting to the chief executive could be used as an instrument of repression against political opponents, and even the ICAC has not been immune to such charges. The widespread powers of the ICAC could be abused in systems less committed to the rule of law.[81] In Hong

Kong, a series of oversight committees and an independent judiciary have checked the ICAC, but, even so, occasional scandals have surfaced.[82] As a check on its power, such an agency might report, not to the chief executive, but to the legislature—as does the General Accounting Office in the United States.

States that are otherwise weak are unlikely to be able to make impartial and effective use of independent commissions. An anticorruption agency can do little if the state leaves in place the restrictive or vague laws and the cumbersome processes that produced incentives for bribery in the first place. An anticorruption agency ought to be only one part of a larger strategy that includes more fundamental reforms that go beyond law enforcement.

The Judiciary

Judicial independence is commonly believed to be necessary for the establishment of the "rule of law." In a discussion of some African cases, Widner defines independence as "the insulation of judges and the judicial process from partisan pressure to influence the outcomes of individual cases."[83] But independence is not inherently valuable. Taken alone, it carries the risk of impunity.[84] Because judicial decisions help to determine the distribution of wealth and power, independent judges can exploit their positions for private gain. An honest government administration will be difficult to establish if the judiciary is venal. A corrupt judiciary can undermine reforms and override legal norms. When dealing with such courts, the wealthy and the corrupt operate with the confidence that a well-placed payoff will resolve any legal challenges they face. This problem extends beyond the public sector to purely private disputes over contracts, torts, and property. Business deals may be structured inefficiently to avoid encounters with the judicial system, and ordinary people may be systematically exploited because they lack access to an impartial system of dispute resolution. Furthermore, even honest judges can cause concern when they overturn or fail to enforce legislative and executive branch decisions.

Because of these worries, no country has an entirely independent judiciary. Widner's definition stresses the independence of judges to decide *individual* cases. In practice, the selection of judges in most countries is not independent of the other branches of government, and political considerations are generally relevant in the selection of justices on constitutional courts and other high courts with a role in the oversight of the government. Judicial career patterns in most civil law countries are influenced by bureaucratic review processes and affected by budgetary appropriations. In the United States, many state and local judges are elected to fixed terms of office and seek reelection in partisan contests.[85] Thus, in the United States, political factors, and in civil law countries, bureaucratic oversight, have an impact on the composition and behavior of the judiciary. The various mixtures of accountability and independence represented by the court systems in the industrialized world have produced a range of options that newly established states can consider in the light of their own needs and experiences. I highlight the fact that some form of broad-based accountability to the government and the citizens is consistent with a well-functioning judiciary and is needed as a check on corruption and other forms of self-dealing.

Weak countries trying to establish "the rule of law" frequently have poorly functioning courts and legal systems. Some courts are overly dependent on politicians, and others are swayed by the wealth of litigants. If the judicial system operates poorly, people will avoid bringing disputes before the courts unless they benefit from delay or unless they are certain to be the high bribers. For example, a survey in Bangladesh found that almost 90 percent of those questioned agreed that it was almost impossible to get quick and fair judgments from the courts without money or influence.[86] In spite of this negative judgment, there is a backlog of half a million cases with delays up to ten to fifteen years. The puzzle is why anyone bothers to bring a case. Part of the answer seems to be that some persons benefit from delay. For example, electricity customers may challenge their bills in court as a way of avoiding payment, and the delay in resolving some land disputes benefits plaintiffs. Nevertheless, such cases cannot explain the entire backlog. Instead, the demand for the services of even such a poorly working system suggests the basic role that courts play as backstops for private economic and social activity.

In many countries with weak judicial systems, people find alternatives to the courts, including hiring private arbitrators and using the protection provided by organized crime.[87] In some countries an illicit informal sector has arisen. In Peru, for example, it involves "pseudo-attorneys, false documents, forged title deeds, nonexistent identities, and virtually no legal guarantees."[88] In Indonesia, the courts are ineffective because of the widespread belief that many judges are corrupt or incompetent.[89] Alternative, private "collection agencies" are used by private creditors to extort payments. In Eastern Europe and Russia, murders of businessmen and bankers are common. Many appear to be execution-style killings that are part of a brutal private system of "dispute resolution."[90] These ways of coping are clearly inferior to an honest and efficiently run judicial system.

Given the importance of a fair judiciary both to economic development and to political legitimacy, judicial reform is a crucial part of the state-building process in newly established states. There are two questions for reformers to address. First, what motivates political actors to create courts with some degree of independence? Second, how can an institutional structure be created that is convenient and fair and that gives judges and litigants incentives to behave responsibly and not to exploit the system for private gain?

As for motivations, Landes and Posner argue that independent federal courts in the United States were created to permit Congress to bind the hands of future administrations that might not share its policy preferences. Because the American system of divided government means that laws are difficult both to pass and to repeal, an independent judiciary enforces the bargains of prior Congresses.[91] Ramseyer provides more nuance using Japanese cases. He argues that there will be no political push for an independent judiciary when a single party expects to be in power over the long term or when democracy is fragile and threatened; politicians have short time horizons. The former scenario describes Japan during the postwar period of dominance by the Liberal Democratic Party (LDP). Judicial independence would have been a threat to LDP power. The latter describes Japan in the late 1920s when the threat of military takeover seemed imminent. Politicians took a short-term perspective and saw no gains from an institution that might tie their hands.[92] Widner, however, contests Ramseyer's claim in the African context, where many states are ruled by a dominant party or have fragile multiparty democracies. In some of these states, judicial independence is on the upswing. As one example, she points to Uganda, where President Yoweri Museveni's successful rebel movement established what was essentially a one-party state and favored judicial independence as a way of establishing a political base through respect for law.[93]

Widner's counterexamples are encouraging because fragile new states often either are controlled by a single political group or face a risk of collapse (or both). A strong court system may help shore up such a state. Ramseyer argues that politicians will be wary of creating a strong judiciary in both cases, but Widner points out that new states are seeking public legitimacy and that the creation of an independent judiciary is one way to achieve it. She does, however, agree that multiparty politics will help to maintain an independent judiciary even if it is not a strictly necessary condition.[94] Furthermore, there are other reasons for politicians to support an independent and honest judiciary that are not directly related to political structure.

Courts are a key feature of the private law system that undergirds economic activity. Widner stresses this as a reason to favor an independent court system, but she points out that many African countries lack powerful domestic business lobbies that would support a competent and independent judiciary. She explains the independence of the courts in Uganda as, in part, a reflection of the new government's commitment to promoting investment and commercial activity even in the absence of strong support from organized commercial interests.[95]

Judicial reform raises a paradox. If the services of the courts improve, more people will use them, leading to the need for even more resources to maintain service quality.[96] In most markets, prices ration the quality and quantity of services, but if congestion is a problem, each service-user imposes costs on others. If the price of the service does not reflect this cost, the market will operate inefficiently. Bribery can be used as a rationing device but in a way that violates norms of judicial behavior and encourages court officials to introduce artificial delays to increase payoffs. Thus, reform strategies have to take account of the impact of reform on demand, or else corruption and favoritism are likely to reappear.

To avoid such a result, especially for commercial disputes, reformers should consider ways to impose the costs of the system on the litigants and to eliminate incentives to increase delay—such as payment schemes for lawyers that reward them on the basis of the complexity of the case.[97] One way to solve this problem is to give court personnel legal incentives to perform expeditiously. Better case-flow management systems that involve not only the courts but also the police, the prosecutors, and the legal profession can reduce delay for a given caseload.[98] Reforms could provide information on delays by type of case and provide incentive payments for judges tied to improved performance.[99]

Judicial reform should never proceed in isolation because doing so risks supporting corrupt political and bureaucratic systems. To see this point, suppose that private individuals and firms engage in secret corrupt deals with public officials. Private actors are willing to make payoffs because they are confident that the procurement contracts, concessions, and privatization deals that they obtain will be upheld by the honest, impartial judicial system. Suppose, as in the United States, that the public prosecutor is part of the executive branch of government, not a part of the judiciary. If the government, outside of the judiciary, is organized to facilitate corruption, private firms are confident that they will not be prosecuted. Even if a scandal does develop, only public officials may suffer politically. This may deter some public officials, but it does not constrain private individuals.

The best example of a corruption-friendly polity comes from the early years of the American republic. A corrupt land sale approved by the legislature of Georgia in the early 1800s was upheld by the United States Supreme Court in the case of *Fletcher v. Peck*.[100] The Court was unmoved by the fact that all but one of the legislators had been bribed. When the scandal was revealed, the entire legislature lost office in the next election, but the Court held that the contract was a legal obligation of the State of

Georgia.[101] What better way to encourage payoffs than a legal system that upholds public contracts no matter what the underlying corrupt deals?

One of the difficulties of reform may be the substantive laws themselves. The limitations of the professional judiciary in impoverished states suggest the value of simple laws that are communicated to ordinary people. Sharp differences between formal law and local practice need to be aired and resolved. Rules must be simple and clear enough so that magistrates who are not trained lawyers can resolve routine cases subject to appeal.[102]

Some reforms will be beyond the capacity of states that are struggling to avoid slipping into anarchy and civil war. Yet, as a country seeks to establish other aspects of accountable government, it needs to recognize that a corrupt judiciary can undermine these attempts because it cannot credibly either act as a watchdog of constitutional values or monitor the honesty of the other branches of government.[103] If major investment deals involve the state as purchaser, privatizer, or provider of a concession, an independent court system is a necessary guarantor of impartiality to outside investors.[104]

Priorities for Reform

Almost by definition, weak and vulnerable states have dysfunctional legal systems that provide poor protections for individual rights and property interests. When elites in such states negotiate over the shape of the state that will emerge from chaotic background conditions, they ought to take law reform seriously. Law, taken in isolation, cannot achieve much, but as a concrete manifestation of the desire to avoid anarchy, it can represent a commitment to seek solutions that limit violence and exploitation.

Western legal models provide some guidance, but in many cases alternative practices, linked to the particular society in question, may be more effective. We need much more research on the way in which indigenous practices can complement or substitute for the more familiar legal forms derived from developed societies. We also need to understand when traditional practices become dysfunctional under modern conditions and how to help reformers find ways to effect change while recognizing that changes will be resisted by the beneficiaries of the status quo.

In countries with weak courts and ineffective governments, reform efforts can be frustrating. For example, a group knows that government is working poorly, can document its failure, and speaks out in protest. The media reports the group's complaints, and they become the source of widespread public debate. But the government may not react. Even if the government does not actively intimidate its critics, it may stonewall until protest groups have exhausted their energy and resources. Serious reform may require a radical realignment of the relationship between ordinary people and the state. Citizens may rightly be afraid that complaining will only make things worse for them personally. Greater popular voice may challenge deep-seated views about the prerogatives of rulers, even in nominal democracies.

Nevertheless, whatever the difficulties of achieving reform, there are a series of obvious problems that need to be a priority for newly established states. The first is crimes against persons and property. The second is the failure of the law to provide a consistent framework for private economic and social activity. The third is the failure of legal rules and public institutions, including the judiciary, to assure a government that is accountable to its citizens. Law reform implies both a strengthening of state capacity and limits on political power that give people a way to complain about government services and actions. However, any policy that increases openness leaves government vulnerable to popular discontent. Thus many regimes, especially weak and vulnerable ones, may view such policies with suspicion.

Where should reform begin? This is a difficult question to answer in the abstract, but a few observations are possible. A state needs clear and transparent rules defining criminal and civil offenses and establishing rights to personhood and property. It needs simple and effective methods for bringing complaints against state officials. The state needs credible institutions to enforce the rules. Once these building blocks are in place, it can establish more sophisticated laws governing private economic activity and regulating society in the public interest, and it can consider how to deal with offenses committed during the period of civil war or disorganization that preceded the creation of the new state.

First come the basic rules specifying what rights people have and how property ownership is to be determined. This includes laws that define crimes against people and property, on the one hand, and civil offenses, on the other. In this regard, the state needs to determine how to restrict the private use of violence. Here the state may be able to draw on earlier laws that existed before the state collapse, but it would be well advised to ask if some of these rules contributed to the recent troubles and are obsolete legacies of a colonial or authoritarian past. In particular, both land law and criminal offenses linked to political protest are likely to need a fresh look.

The simple promulgation of legal rules, however, will be irrelevant without complementary institutions. Thus a new criminal code should be accompanied by the establishment of a new police force, prosecutorial office, and judiciary educated in the new rules. At the same time, new states frequently will need to limit the private use of violence by moving against paramilitary forces and organized crime groups that are substituting private for public protection. Otherwise the law promulgated by the state will apply only to a subset of the population. In addition to such crackdowns, the state needs to establish its claims to legitimacy by giving people ways to complain to independent officials about overreaching bureaucrats and leaders. New ways to lodge complaints are especially important with respect to the police, who may include many former soldiers.

The essence of the rule of law is not just the ability to assert power over others but also the ability to justify the exercise of power to those who feel its weight. Similarly, if land law reform or other changes in property rights are part of the new regime's agenda, it needs to make the new rules clear and easy to understand, and it needs to back up the new rules with the creation of public institutions to adjudicate disputes. The degree of property redistribution will vary widely across countries, but if it is a priority for the new regime, it should be carried out as soon as possible and should be accompanied by a set of procedures and institutions designed to administer the transfers and resolve disputes. Reform of contract and tort law, to the extent historical models are inadequate, can come afterward. The first priority in the area of private economic law is to establish the basic entitlements, including rights retained by the state to impose future restrictions in the public interest.

Enforcement of both criminal and civil laws requires a judiciary that is viewed as fair and that is not corrupt. This is a difficult task for newly emerging states in very poor environments where expertise of any kind, and legal expertise in particular, are in short supply. Under the criminal law, public prosecutors need to be viewed as competent and honest, and the system of punishment must not be too harsh. Under the civil law, access must not be unduly restricted by cost and inconvenience, and judgments must be enforceable. In both cases, the rules need to be clear enough so that people do not become unwitting criminals and so that they can negotiate private deals "in the shadow of the law" without having to bring every dispute to court.

There is no easy solution to the lack of trained professionals although some countries have had success with using local "wise men" as adjudicators, and others have created special arbitration courts for business matters to make efficient use of scarce human resources. Ombudsmen and other kinds of complaint bureaus staffed by nonlawyers may be a solution in some cases. Clear and simple rules of property, tort, and contract can help limit court cases as well.

The criminal law presents different kinds of problems. A system that does not tolerate police brutality and torture and that uses punishments other than imprisonment would help reduce the pressure on the courts to correct the problems created by other institutions. As argued earlier, prison is a costly and inefficient option for a poor country with weak institutional capacities. Other forms of punishment should be designed that do not remove productive people from society and that limit the financial burden on the state. The weakness of the court system can be offset partially by criminal laws and legal processes that are simple and clear and by fair systems of punishment.

Piecemeal approaches to law reform are likely to be meaningless. Even worse, such approaches may produce a backlash in which people express cynicism about a state that promulgates unenforceable laws with lofty goals. This difficulty suggests the value of reform packages that bundle together substantive law, credible enforcement, and public accountability. Even if the ultimate goal is a unitary legal system, reform might start with crimes against persons, followed by land law, and the law of private commercial dealings. The link between substance and process needs to be a central focus. If fair and expeditious enforcement is difficult because of a lack of trained personnel or worries about police brutality, this implies a focus on creating clear, simple, and transparent rules that will be partially self-enforcing.

Newly established states are frequently created in the aftermath of violent internal conflicts that leave a legacy of anger, violence, and resentment. Occasionally, all the contesting factions negotiate a deal that may include agreement on constitutional structures and the division of a country's wealth. These deals might not satisfy abstract ideals of social justice, but they may be a necessary precondition for the end of armed conflict. Thus the options for law reform may be limited by the very process that permits the state to exist in the first place.

In other cases, one group defeats another, and the new rulers may try to demonstrate their legitimacy by using the law to punish those who came before. This can be a risky, if understandable, reaction. Even when violations of international norms of human rights are widely accepted, a major effort designed to hold supporters of the losing group legally accountable may not be a good use of scarce resources, especially in poor states. Truth commissions or other similar efforts may be a valuable way to help people understand what happened in the past as a prelude to moving forward. However, too much focus on retribution and restitution is likely to divert energy and resources from the difficult process of building a legal system that can complement other efforts at state building and economic and social revival. More important than holding individuals legally accountable for their behavior under conditions of disorder and civil strife is the creation of a fair system of property rights and public accountability in the present. If, for example, a major land reform is needed to help distribute the benefits of economic activity broadly, a forward-looking program of that kind is a better use of scarce human and organizational resources than a massive effort at resurrecting past wrongs.

Notes

This is a revision of part of a paper prepared for the failed states project "Reinvigorating and Resuscitating Weak, Vulnerable, and Collapsing States," Kennedy School of Government, Harvard University, and the World Peace Foundation, Cambridge, Mass., 1–4 June, 2000. That paper was coauthored with Leonard Wantchekon. I am grateful to him for discussions on the topic of this paper. Amnon Lehavi provided very helpful research assistance.

1. See Jacques DeLisle, "Lex Americana? United States Legal Assistance, American Legal Models, and Legal Change in the Post-Communist World and Beyond," *University of Pennsylvania Journal of International Economic Law*, XX (1999), 179–308. On the basis of field work in Papua New Guinea, Cooter argues that law reform efforts should focus on developing institutions that can shape law so that it conforms to underlying social realities. The goal is a system of laws that people obey out of respect for its underlying principles not because they are threatened with enforcement actions See Robert Cooter, "Inventing Market Property: The Land Courts of Papua New Guinea," *Law & Society Review*, XXV (1991), 759–801; and Robert Cooter, "The Rule of State Law and the Rule-of-Law State: Economic Analysis of the Legal Foundations of Development," in Michael Bruno and Boris Pleskovic (eds.), *Annual World Bank Conference on Development Economics—1996* (Washington, D.C., 1997), 191–217. As the commentators on the 1997 article note, his is an overly optimistic and idealistic view of existing social practices in some societies. See Cheryl Gray, "Comment on 'The Rule of State Law and the Rule-of-Law State: Economic Analysis of the Legal Foundations of Development,' by Robert Cooter," in Bruno and Pleskovic (eds.), *Annual World Bank Conference on Development Economics—1996*, 218–221; Michael Trebilcock, "Comment on 'The Rule of State Law and the Rule-of-Law State: Economic Analysis of the Legal Foundations of Development,' by Robert Cooter," in ibid., 229–233. Although it is obvious that law will be more effectively implemented if it conforms with existing practices, this association will not always hold for the legal framework needed to maintain democracy and to further growth. Trebilcock's own study of property rights in Papua New Guinea demonstrates this reality and contains proposals for law reform that maintain some features of customary law while creating new legal structures that respond to modern realities. See Michael Trebilcock, "Communal Property Rights: The Papua New Guinea Experience," *University of Toronto Law Review*, XXXIV (1984), 377–420. On the transformation of property rights among the Orma in Kenya, see Jean Ensminger and Andrew Ruttan, "The Political Economy of Changing Property Rights: Dismantling a Pastoral Community," *American Ethnologist*, XVIII (1991), 683–699.

2. For a thoughtful collection of articles exploring this theme in the context of land tenure systems in Africa, see Thomas J. Bassett and Donald E. Crummey (eds.), *Land in African Agrarian Systems* (Madison, 1993).

3. Tibamanga mwene Mushanga, "Introduction" in Mushanga (ed.), *Criminology in Africa* (Rome, 1992), v.

4. In the United States it is more difficult to libel public figures than private individuals, and libel is a civil offense. Those in the public eye have assumed the risk of public scrutiny and have access to the media to rebut accusations. In a similar vein, participants in political debate in Germany relinquish some of the protections of defamation law, and the Netherlands has a public figure defense. Threats of lawsuits operate as a serious deterrent elsewhere. Great Britain has no public figure defense. Some claim that its libel law deters critical reporting of issues affecting the public interest. See Douglas W. Vick and Linda Macpherson, "An Opportunity Lost: The United Kingdom's Failed Reform of Defamation Law," *Federal Communications Law Journal*, XLIX (1997), 621–653. An especially clear example of the chilling effect of a strong libel law is Singapore, where top politicians have been active in suing both the media and political opponents. See "Singapore Leaders Awarded $5.6m in Libel Damages," *Financial Times*, 30 May 1997; "Singapore Leader Wins Libel Case," *Financial Times*, 30 September 1997, and "Throwing the Book: PAP Launches Legal Barrage Against Opposition Leaders," *Far Eastern Economic Review*, 6 March 1997.

5. Mushanga, "Introduction," v.

6. Although she is more sympathetic than I am to the use of the criminal law as part of the transition process, Teitel provides a sensitive analysis of the paradoxes and difficulties of such a policy. She writes, "While trials in these political contexts are intended to serve political purposes—relating to the extraordinary message of transitional justice to lay the foundation of the political transition, to disavow predecessor political norms, and to construct a new legal order—these very features are in tension with conventional understandings of the rule of law" (Ruti G. Teitel, *Transitional Justice* [New York, 2000], 30). She argues that criminal justice is a ritual that through known, fixed processes, liberates the past and allows society to move forward. Punishment is generally so limited that it allows return to a liberal state (67).

7. See Bruce Ackerman, *The Future of Liberal Revolution* (New Haven, 1993). Teitel (*Transitional Justice*, 163–169) summarizes the practices of several countries in Eastern Europe and also notes their questionable aspects. she writes, "[O]f what relevance is past political behavior to public decision making in the transitional regimes, when other things are changing too?" (169) Nevertheless, she ends with a conditional acceptance of measures that "bridge the individual and the collective" since "ideal expectations about the role that individual responsibility plays in the liberal state . . . are inapposite to transitional times" (188).

8. For a general discussion of money laundering see Scott Sultzer, "Money Laundering: The Scope of the Problem and Attempts to Combat It," *Tennessee Law Review*, LXIII (1995) 143–237. The main international body working on this issue is the Financial Action Task Force (FATF), set up in 1989. Originally, the emphasis was on drug trafficking, but recently efforts within the FATF and in member countries have focused on prohibiting money laundering in connection

with bribery and corruption. See Mathew Paulose, Jr., "*United States v. McDougald*: The Anathema to 18 U.S.C. § 1956 and National Efforts to Against Money Laundering," *Fordham International Law Journal*, XXI (1997), 263–280. The FATF issued a list of fifteen countries that they view as money-laundering havens. Switzerland was not on the list because it no longer shields criminal assets and generally cooperates with foreign investigators. The list prompted reform proposals in some of the countries named. See "15 Countries Named as Potential Money-Laundering Havens," *New York Times*, 23 June 2000; "All Havens in a Storm," *The Economist*, 1 July 2000; "Lichtenstein in Spotlight Over Money Laundering," *Financial Times*, 29 August 2000. For several years Nigeria has been tracking down the bank accounts of the previous ruler, General Sani Abacha, and his family and friends. President Olusegun Obasanjo claims that $1.8–2.0 billion of an estimated $3 billion has been traced. More than $1.4 billion was frozen in bank accounts in Switzerland, Luxembourg, and Lichtenstein. By mid-2000, $66 million had been transferred by a Swiss bank to the Central Bank of Nigeria, but at that time the banks claimed that they would not release the bulk of the funds unless criminal convictions were obtained in Nigerian courts. "Loot Now $3b—Obasanjo," *Africa News*, 30 June 2000; "Nigeria Recovers 66 million Dollars in Looted Funds," *Agence France Presse*, 13 July 2000. In April 2002 a settlement was reached in a three-sided deal between the Nigerian government, the foreign banks, and the Abacha family. Under the deal, over $1 billion was to be transferred to Nigeria from banks around the world, with the Abacha family keeping $100 million, and, in a side deal, Nigeria dropped criminal charges against Abacha's son Mohammed, including a murder accusation. The Swiss Federal Justice Department judged that the $100 million "demonstrably do not derive from criminal acts." The Nigerian government agreed to the deal to avoid costly and protracted litigation and to appeal to local political sentiments in the state of Kano, the home of the Abacha family. See "Loot: Switzerland Returns $535M, Mohammed to Get Pardon," *ThisDay* (Nigeria), *AAGM*, 18 April 2002; "Nigeria to Recover $1 billion from the Family of the Late Dictator," *New York Times*, 18 April 2002. One commentator pointed out that $100 million represents a return of 21 percent a year on a sum of $10,000 per year invested between 1963 and when Abacha took control in 1993. During that time he was a relatively low-paid military officer. See Floyd Norris, "Ideas and Trends: A Nigerian Miracle," *New York Times*, 21 April 2002. The dropping of murder charges against Mohammed Abacha has been criticized in the Nigerian Press as sending the wrong signal to potential law breakers and undermining the judiciary and national unity. See Bola A. Akinterinwa, "Abacha's Loot and State Pardon," *ThisDay* (Nigeria), 22 April 2002. The motivation for this action, however, presumably was the leverage held by the Abacha family over the foreign banks' decision to release funds. This leverage gave Obasanjo an incentive to settle.

9. See, for example, the policy proposals in Susan Rose-Ackerman, *Corruption and Government: Causes, Consequences, and Reform* (New York, 1999), 39–88, 127–174.

10. South Africa's Truth and Reconciliation Commission role in helping to restore society is discussed in Jennifer J. Llewellyn and Robert Howse, "Institutions for Restorative Justice: The South African Truth and Reconciliation Com-

mission," *University of Toronto Law Journal*, XLIX (1999), 355–388; Mariane Geula, "South Africa's Truth and Reconciliation Commissions as an Alternative Means of Addressing Transitional Government Conflicts in a Divided Society," *Boston University International Law Journal*, XVIII (2000), 57–84. The strengths and weaknesses of truth commissions are discussed in Robert I. Rotberg and Dennis Thompson (eds.), *Truth v. Justice: The Morality of Truth Commissions* (Princeton, 2000). A general survey of Truth Commissions is found in Priscilla Hayner, "Fifteen Truth Commissions—1974 to 1994: Comparative Study," *Human Rights Quarterly*, XVI (1994), 597–655. Teitel provides a brief analysis of truth commissions that focuses on the South African case and stresses their value as a substitute for criminal prosecutions (*Transitional Justice*, 81–88).

11. Alice Hills, *Policing Africa: Internal Security and the Limits of Liberalization* (Boulder, 2000).

12. Hills (*Policing Africa*), 146, quoting a UN consultant to Somalia.

13. "The police are not often perceived as protectors or friends of the public at large. On the contrary, they are often perceived as enemies, fault finders, and intimidators to be avoided" (Ntanda Nsereko, "Victims of Crime and Their Rights," in Mushanga (ed.), *Criminology*, 27. See also Hills, *Policing Africa*, 27–54).

14. Hills, *Policing Africa*, 10.

15. Ibid., 89–184.

16. Mushanga, "Introduction," vi–vii; Hills, *Policing Africa*, 168–71.

17. Hills, *Policing Africa*, 153–55.

18. The difficulty of police reform in a newly democratic state is revealed by the case of Nigeria where the police force is "demoralized, under-strength, under-equipped and under-paid" and is viewed by the population as "corrupt, incompetent and brutal." The president has a goal of increasing the numbers of police rapidly, but others argue that this will only encourage more corruption and brutality unless it goes along with better training programs. See "Nigeria Making a Bad Cop Good," *The Economist*, 13 May 2000.

19. Hills, *Policing Africa*, 148.

20. Leonard P. Shaidi, "Traditional, Colonial, and Present-Day Administration of Criminal Justice," in Mushanga, *Criminology*, 1–20; Nsereko, "Victims of Crime," 21–42.

21. Shaidi, "Traditional, Colonial," 13–17.

22. Nsereko, "Victims of Crime," 27.

23. Ibid., 25.

24. Ibid., 31–39.

25. In Tanzania, mandatory corporal punishment was abolished in 1972 (Shaidi, "Traditional, Colonial," 16).

26. Rance P. L. Lee, "Bureaucratic Corruption in Asia: The Problem of Incongruence between Legal Norms and Folk Norms," in Ledivina A. Cariño (ed.), *Bureaucratic Corruption in Asia: Causes, Consequences and Controls* (Quezon City, Philippines, 1986), 103.

27. Hiram E. Chodosh and Stephen A. Mayo, "The Palestinian Legal Study: Consensus and Assessment of the New Palestinian Legal System," *Harvard International Law Journal*, XXXVIII (1997), 375–441.

28. DeLisle, "Lex Americana?"

29. Philip M. Nichols, "The Viability of Transplanted Law: Kazakhstani Reception of a Transplanted Foreign Investment Code," *University of Pennsylvania Journal of International Economic Law,* XVIII (1997), 1235–1279.

30. DeLisle, "Lex Americana?" 305.

31. Mitu Gulati, William Klein, and Eric Zolt, "Connected Contracts," *UCLA Law Review,* XLVII (2000), 887–948.

32. For examples of what I have in mind see the detailed studies in Bassett and Crummey (eds.), *Land in African Agrarian Systems.*

33. For a critical discussion of General Pervez Musharraf's proposed constitution that would increase the political power of local governments, see Farhan Bokhari, "Musharraf's New Order Risks Adding to Past Failures," *Financial Times,* 21 August 2000, 5.

34. Roy L. Prosterman and Jeffrey M. Riedinger (*Land Reform and Democratic Development* [Baltimore, 1987], 87–91), show that there is a high positive correlation between countries with a high proportion of owner-cultivators and high levels of civil and political liberties. Landlessness is frequently a precursor of violent revolution followed by land reform. (7–33).

35. Susan Rose-Ackerman, "Inalienability and the Theory of Property Rights," *Columbia Law Review,* LXXXV (1985), 931–969.

36. Ensminger and Ruttan, "The Political Economy"; Trebilcock, "Community Property" and "Comment"; Bassett and Crummey (eds.), *Land in African Agrarian Systems.*

37. Thomas J. Bassett, "Introduction: The Land Question and Agricultural Transformation in Sub-Saharan Africa," in Bassett and Crummey, *Land in African Agrarian Systems,* 3–31.

38. Susan Rose-Ackerman and Jim Rossi, "Disentangling Deregulatory Takings," *Virginia Law Review,* LXXXVI (2000), 1435–1495.

39. Lee J. Alston, Gary D. Libecap, and Bernardo Mueller, "Land Reform Policies: The Sources of Violent Conflict and Implications for Deforestation in the Brazilian Amazon," working paper, University of Arizona, Tucson (1999).

40. Transparency International-Bangladesh, *Survey on Corruption in Bangladesh: Report on Phase 2 Activities: Baseline Survey, Dhaka, Bangladesh,* www.tibangladesh.org/docs/survey/phase2.htm, 3–4; World Bank, *Bangladesh: Key Challenges for the Next Millennium* (Washington D.C., April 1999), 14.

41. For an overview, see John McMillan and Christopher Woodruff, "Private Order and Dysfunctional Public Order," *Michigan Law Review,* XCVIII, (2000), 2421–2458. See also John McMillan and Christopher Woodruff, "Dispute Prevention Without Courts in Vietnam," *Journal of Law, Economics and Organization,* XV (1999), 637–658; Simon Johnson, John McMillan, and Christopher Woodruff, "Courts and Relational Contracting," *Journal of Law, Economics and Organization,* XVIII (2002), 221–277. Christopher Woodruff, "Contract Enforcement and Trade Liberalization in Mexico's Footwear Industry," *World Development,* XXVI (1998), 979–991.

42. See especially Johnson, McMillan, and Woodruff, "Contract Enforcement" on the use of trade associations in Eastern Europe.

43. McMillan and Woodruff, "Private Order."

44. The literature is vast. For a collection of leading articles, see Richard Craswell and Alan Schwartz, *Foundations of Contract Law* (New York, 1994).

45. Woodruff, "Contract Enforcement."

46. See the collection of articles in Saul Levmore (ed.), *Foundations of Tort Law* (New York, 1994).

47. For an insightful treatment of the tensions between British and African concepts of law and justice in the colonial period in Tanganika, see Sally Falk Moore, "Treating Law as Knowledge: Telling Colonial Officers What to Say to Africans about Running 'Their Own' Native Courts," *Law & Society Review*, XXVI (1992), 11–46.

48. For example, in a discussion of product liability law in the United States, I recommend a gap-filling role for such suits under a legal regime that relies primarily on statutes. Rose-Ackerman, "Tort Law in the Regulatory State," in Peter Schuck (ed.), *Tort Law and the Public Interest: Competition, Innovation, and Consumer Welfare* (New York, 1991), 80–102.

49. This section and portions of the next are derived from Rose-Ackerman, *Corruption and Government*, 143–173.

50. These dual notions of accountability are debated in Guillermo O'Donnell, "Horizontal Accountability in New Democracies," Philippe C. Schmitter, "The Limits of Horizontal Accountability," and Guillermo O'Donnell, " A Response to My Commentators" in Andreas Schedler, Larry Diamond, and Marc F. Plattner (eds.), *The Self-restraining State: Power and Accountability in New Democracies* (Boulder, 1999), 29–52, 59–62, 68–69.

51. Leonard Wantchekon and Zvika Neeman, "A Theory of Post–Civil War Democratization," *Journal of Theoretical Politics*, XIV (2002), 439–464.

52. For an overview and analysis of public expenditure management systems worldwide, see A. Premchand, *Public Expenditure Management* (Washington, D.C., 1993).

53. The GAO monitors the federal executive branch but reports directly to Congress. It resolves contracting disputes, settles the accounts of the United States government, resolves claims of or against the United States, gathers information for Congress, and makes recommendations to it. See Kevin T. Abikoff, "The Role of the Comptroller General in Light of *Bowsher v. Synar*," *Columbia Law Review*, LXXXVII (1987), 1539–62; Charles Tiefer, "The Constitutionality of Independent Officers as Checks on Abuses of Executive Power," *Boston University Law Review*, LXIII (1983), 59–103. In 1980, the GAO was granted the power to bring suit against the executive branch to assure that requests for information were honored. The British Audit Commission audits both local governments and the National Health Service and reports to the national government. United Kingdom, Audit Commission, *Protecting the Public Purse: Probity in the Public Sector: Combating Fraud and Corruption in Local Government* (London, 1993); United Kingdom, Audit Commission, *Protecting the Public Purse 2: Ensuring Probity in the NHS* (London, 1994).

54. In Venezuela, President Carlos Andrés Pérez resigned amid charges that he had misused $17 million in funds from such a secret account. See Walter Little and Antonio Herrera, "Political Corruption in Venezuela," in Walter Little and

Eduardo Posada-Carbó (eds.), *Political Corruption in Europe and Latin America* (New York, 1996), 267–86.

55. Shlomo Shpiro, "Parliamentary and Administrative Reforms in the Control of Intelligence Services in the European Union," *Columbia Journal of European Law*, IV (1998), 545–78.

56. Barbara Geddes and Artur Ribeiro Neto, "Institutional Sources of Corruption in Brazil," *Third World Quarterly*, XIII (1992), 641–61.

57. Pier Paolo Giglioli, "Political Corruption and the Media: The Tangentopoli Affair," *International Social Science Journal*, XLVIII (1996), 381–394.

58. "It Happened in Monterrey" (*The Times*, 29 November 1991) discusses the resignation of a newspaper editor after pressure was put on his paper through the cancellation of government advertising and printing contracts. "Survey of Mexico" (*Financial Times*, 10 November 1993) discusses these practices but claims that some newspapers have retained their independence. When a leading editor was arrested in Mexico City in 1996 for tax evasion, the editor claimed that the arrest occurred in response to the paper's newly asserted independence. The tax authorities claim that the editor adopted a more outspoken line only after the investigation had begun (*Mexico Business Monthly*, 1 October 1996). He was eventually acquitted of criminal wrongdoing and fined a nominal amount in 1997 (Reuters Financial Services, 26 February 1997; *Miami Herald*, 27 August 1997).

59. Jennifer Widner discusses efforts by the Chief Justice of Tanzania to increase legal literacy among the population. See Widner, "Building Judicial Independence in Common Law Africa," in Andreas Schedler, Larry Diamond, and Marc F. Plattner (eds.), *The Self-Restraining State: Power and Accountability in New Democracies* (Boulder, 1999), 184–185.

60. Pasuk Phongpaicht and Sungsidh Piriyarangsan, *Corruption and Democracy in Thailand* (Bangkok, 1994).

61. Michael Bratton, "The Politics of Government-NGO Relations in Africa," *World Development*, XVII (1989), 569–587.

62. Ibid., 578–79, 584.

63. Sam Paul, "Evaluating Public Services: A Case Study on Bangalore, India," no. 67, *New Directions for Evaluation*, American Evaluation Association (Washington, D.C., 1995); Carel Mohn, "'Speedy' Services in India," *TI Newsletter* (1997), 3.

64. B. R. Agarwala, *Our Judiciary* (India, 1996, 2nd edition), 174–84.

65. *Bangaire Medical Trust v. Mudappa*, 1991 A.I.R. 1902 (S.C.) (India).

66. Philip Oldenburg, "Middlemen in Third World Corruption: Implications for an Indian Case," *World Politics*, XXXIX (1987), 508–535.

67. Tanzania, Presidential Commission of Inquiry Against Corruption, *Report of the Commission on Corruption* (Dar es Salaam, 1996), I, 65.

68. Anthony Antoniou, "Institutional Devices in Dealing with Corruption in Government," in United Nations, Department of Technical Co-operation for Development and Centre for Social Development and Humanitarian Affairs, "Corruption in Government: Report of an Interregional Meeting," The Hague, Netherlands, 11–15 December 1989, TCD/SEM 90/2, INT-89-R56 (New York, 1990), 68–78.

69. A. G. Noorani, "Lok Pal and Lok Ayuki," in S. Guhan and Samuel Paul (eds.), *Corruption in India: An Agenda for Reform* (New Delhi, 1997), 189–217.

70. United Nations, High Commission on Human Rights, Centre for Human Rights, Programme of Technical Cooperation in the Field of Human Rights, "Report of the Needs Mission to South Africa (6–25 May 1996)" (New York, 1996).

71. Mark Findlay, "Corruption in Small States: Case Studies in Compromise," in Barry Rider, *Corruption: The Enemy Within* (The Hague, 1997), 49–61.

72. United Kingdom, *Protecting*, 1993.

73. Mexico, Federal Executive Power, *Program for the Modernization of Public Administration 1995–2000* (Mexico City, 1996).

74. Susan Rose-Ackerman, *Controlling Environmental Policy: The Limits of Public Law in Germany and the United States* (New Haven, 1995).

75. Ibid., 8–13, 57–71, 82–96, 120–140.

76. Scott Mainwaring and Matthew S. Shugart (eds.), *Presidentialism and Democracy in Latin America* (Cambridge, 1997).

77. Pasuk and Sungsidh, *Corruption and Democracy.*

78. Song Bing, "Assessing China's System of Judicial Review of Administration Actions," *China Law Review*, VIII (1994), 6–7, 17–18.

79. Quoted by Paul Hutchcroft, *Booty Capitalism: The Politics of Banking in the Philippines* (Ithaca, 1998), 202.

80. Max J. Skidmore, "Promise and Peril in Combating Corruption: Hong Kong's ICAC," *Annals of the American Academy of Political Science and Sociology*, DXLVII (1996), 118–130. On Thailand, see "Key Thai Minister Resigns in Corruption Case," *New York Times*, 30 March 2000. Thailand's National Countercorruption Commission is a new body established in 1997. A critical review of the weaknesses of earlier commissions in Thailand is found in Jon S. T. Quah, "Combating Corruption in South Korea and Thailand," in Schedler, Diamond, and Plattner (eds.), *The Self-Restraining State*, 248–254.

81. For an example of an anticorruption agency being accused of undermining rather than supporting reform, see "Arrest of Kenya Tax Officials May Hit Donor Funding," *Financial Times*, 25–26 July 1998. See also John R. Heilbrun, "Corruption, Democracy, and Reform in Benin," in Schedler, Diamond, and Plattner (eds.), *Self-Restraining State*, 227–43.

82. Skidmore, "Promise and Peril."

83. Widner, "Building Judicial," 177–78.

84. The same issue of impunity arises with respect to central banks. See, for example, the study of the Russian central bank by Juliet Johnson: "Misguided Autonomy: Central Bank Independence in the Russian Transition," in Schedler, Diamond, and Plattner (eds.), *The Self-Restraining State*, 293–312.

85. Michael H. Shapiro, "Introduction: Judicial Selection and the Design of Clumsy Institutions," *Southern California Law Review*, LXI (1988), 1555–1569. See also "States Rein In Truth-Bending in Court Races," *New York Times*, 23 August 2000.

86. TI-Bangladesh, *Survey on Corruption*, 3.

87. The Latin American judiciary is reportedly so deficient that most business people try to avoid using the courts to resolve disputes. See Edgardo Buscaglia, Jr., "Judicial Reform in Latin America: The Obstacles Ahead," *Journal of Latin

American Affairs (Fall / Winter 1995), 8–13; Maria Dakolias, *The Judicial Sector in Latin America and the Caribbean: Elements of Reform*, World Bank Technical Paper 319 (Washington, D.C., 1996).

88. Fernando Vega and Santa Gadea, "Judicial Reform in Peru," in Malcolm Rowat, Waleed H. Malik, and Maria Dakolias (eds.), *Judicial Reform in Latin America and the Caribbean: Proceedings of a World Bank Conference*, World Bank Technical Paper 280 (Washington, D.C., 1995), 185.

89. Arindam Das-Gupta and Dilip Mookherjee, *Incentives and Institutional Reform in Tax Enforcement: An Analysis of Developing Country Experience* (New Delhi, 1998), 427.

90. According to the Russian government, 269 businessmen and financiers were murdered in 1995 in execution-style slayings. See also "Mr. Tatum Checks Out," *The Economist*, 9 November 1996.

91. William M. Landes and Richard A. Posner, "The Independent Judiciary in an Interest Group Perspective," *Journal of Law and Economics*, XVIII (1975), 875–895.

92. J. Mark Ramseyer, "The Puzzling (In)dependence of Courts: A Comparative Approach," *Journal of Legal Studies*, XXIII (1994), 721–747.

93. Widner, "Building Judicial," 180, 183.

94. Ibid., 180–181, 185–186.

95. Ibid., 179–180.

96. For example, when Ecuador dramatically improved conditions for its judiciary in 1992, there was an increase in the number of cases filed. See Edgardo Buscaglia, Jr., and Maria Dakolias, *Judicial Reform in Latin American Courts: The Experience in Argentina and Ecuador*, World Bank Technical Paper 350 (Washington, D.C., 1996). Studies of a cross-section of Latin American countries found no relationship between spending on personnel and court delay. See Buscaglia and Dakolias, *Judicial Reform*, 26; Edgardo Buscaglia, Jr., and Thomas Ulen, "A Quantitative Assessment of the Efficiency of the Judicial Sector in Latin America," *International Review of Law and Economics*, XVII (1997), 282–283.

97. The lack of formal court fees creates incentives for court employees and judges to demand unauthorized fees (Buscaglia and Dakolias, *Judicial Reform*). One study of a sample of commercial cases in Argentina and Venezuela concluded that an important source of delay was the strategic behavior of lawyers at the discovery stage (Buscaglia and Ulen "A Quantitative Assessment").

98. Widner, "Building Judicial," 184.

99. Reforms designed to reduce corruption in the courts can be complemented with improvements in alternative methods of resolving disputes that keep many routine cases out of court. Gladys Stella Alvarez, "Alternative Dispute Resolution Mechanisms: Lessons of Argentine Experience," in Malcolm Rowat, Waleed H. Malik, and Maria Dakolias (eds.), *Judicial Reform in Latin America and the Caribbean: Proceedings of a World Bank Conference*, World Bank Technical Paper 280 (Washington, D.C., 1995), 78–91. Hans-Jürgen Brandt, "The Justice of the Peace as an Alternative Experience with Conciliation in Peru," in Rowat, Malik, and Dakolias (eds.), *Judicial Reform in Latin America and the Caribbean*, 92–99; Dakolias, *The Judicial Sector*, 37–43; Lawyers Committee for Human Rights and the

Venezuelan Program for Human Rights Education and Action, *Halfway to Reform: The World Bank and the Venezuelan Justice System* (New York, 1996), 67–68.

100. U.S. Supreme Court, 87–148, Feb. 1810, 3. L. Ed. 162–181.

101. Peter C. Magrath, *Yazoo: Law and Politics in the New Republic: The Case of Fletcher v. Peck* (Providence, 1966).

102. Widner, "Building Judicial," 184–185, 186–187.

103. Toshiro Fuke, "Remedies in Japanese Administrative Law," *Civil Justice Quarterly*, VIII (1989), 226; Bing, "Assessing China's System," 5–8.

104. Lawyers Committee, *Halfway to Reform*, 45–55, 104–106.

Ten

Building Effective Trust in the Aftermath of Severe Conflict

JENNIFER A. WIDNER

THERE ARE at least three broad political challenges in the aftermath of severe conflict. One is to attack the problems that have given rise to war with the aim of reducing the risk of renewed fighting. A second is to foster the attitudes and behavior essential to compromise and cooperation in the political realm and to expanded exchange and investment in economic life; cooperation and investment are vital for renewal. A third challenge is to take the idiosyncratic features of particular cases into account and to create space for experimentation and for learning. We know very little about "what works." We also know that conflict situations differ from each other.

My focus is primarily on the second of these challenges. For peace to endure in the aftermath of conflict, it is also vital to restore the trust that undergirds exchange and compromise, to give people a stake in the new government, and to encourage investment of time and energy in solving community problems and in expanding economic opportunity. Systematic comparisons can help us understand these matters. What produces the kinds of social capital important for reconstruction—specifically, trust, voluntarism, propensity to participate through legal channels, sense of well-being, and optimism? How do individual and community characteristics, security, and political leadership influence these important general orientations? What does survey evidence from nonconflict areas tell us about the priorities we should have in rebuilding polities? Governments cannot invest money in every aspect of reconstruction. Which aspects merit attention first?

If the ambition of policymakers is to create a base for peace and prosperity, policymakers first need to identify the ingredients of trust, optimism, and other attitudes essential to exchange, compromise, and investment. What do people in Africa tell us about these ingredients? What conditions foster social capital? How can we devise institutions and policies that promote rapid development of these attitudes to ensure that peace will survive beyond the short run?

I employ available survey evidence from Uganda, Botswana, and Zambia.[1] I use the survey data to test models of attitude formation using ordered probit. The models remain inadequate in many respects. Most explain only a small fraction of the variance observed. But they at least provide a way to think about the daunting task at hand.

Among other things, the findings suggest that working with local officials to improve public safety, the exercise of leadership, and enhancement of basic service delivery are especially important. Promoting local associations, an increasingly common prescription in the aid community, is less effective in strengthening most of the attitudes of interest. A strong retrospective element in some attitudes, especially optimism, places a premium on gestures that signal a sharp break with the past and highlight new successes. Because the models that I use in analyzing the survey data are rather weak, there is much room for debate and discussion, and especially for learning from other approaches.

Reconstruction and "Social Capital"

This chapter offers an anatomy of hope. It asks how and why levels of interpersonal trust, public spirit, community participation, sense of well-being, and optimism vary among people. In theory, these general orientations influence forms of behavior that entail commitment, such as investment, exchange, and compromise. The ability to make commitments is indirectly an important ingredient of economic development and a healthy polity—in other words, of peace and prosperity. Building these attitudes is an important element of successful postconflict reconstruction.

Trust is one element of the pentagon. Theoretically, people who display high levels of generalized trust are more likely to enter into political or economic exchanges with others who have different backgrounds. They enter into a wider range of contacts and are potentially able to tap the greater information and opportunity that larger circles of acquaintance and contact often bring. Because they anticipate that others will reciprocate their favors, they are more likely to compromise, tolerate improvement in others' circumstances, and enter into contracts that pay off only over time.

The second element, public spiritedness or a willingness to join others in a voluntary effort to solve community problems, helps to ensure that many small problems win attention, even though governments or markets lack the capacity to solve them. Implicit in voluntarism is the sense of honor that helps organizations, communities, and states function when calculations of individual material advantage would lead people to undersupply effort or ideas. In postconflict situations, where the central government's ability to deliver services is very limited, this attitude is especially important.

The other attitudes—predisposition to participate, a sense of being "better off," and optimism—also potentially promote the kinds of behavior that facilitate peace and prosperity. The predisposition to participate (voting, contacting officials, and attending community meetings) signals a willingness to work through legal channels to get things done. Without this sentiment, the kinds of institutions that peace agreements typically put in place cannot function as anticipated. A stronger sense of satisfaction with life is also important in the aftermath of conflict. This sense of well-being gives people a stake in preserving the peace and its associated gains. It makes it more difficult for rebel movements to secure voluntary recruits by raising the opportunity costs of defection to the rebel cause. Finally, optimism that one will be better off in the future suggests a willingness to invest in activities that generate a return over the medium- or long-term. If people think conditions will improve, they may also consider that a little sacrifice now will pay off handsomely later.

An important goal of postconflict reconstruction is to foster these five attitudes among ordinary people. What broad kinds of measures will help most?

Isolating the Ingredients of Success

This study employs survey data from three countries—Uganda, Zambia, and Botswana—to begin to think about how to generate the attitudes that are critical to success in postconflict reconstruction. All of the surveys took place in 1996. The Ugandan study (Widner) focused on people in the settled parts of a country still frayed by war. The Zambian study (Bratton), conducted as part of a study of voting in a new multiparty democracy, took place in a country without a history of extensive armed internal conflict. Nonetheless, political struggle in Zambia had produced high levels of discord and distrust. The third survey took place in Botswana (Widner), known for its comparatively long history of stability and relative prosperity. At the time of the study, a crime wave had started to sweep southern Africa, producing new levels of distrust. Because the sample size in the Botswana study was small, it is harder to derive insight from it than from the others, but some of the contrasts and similarities illuminate nonetheless.

The multi-purpose surveys provide roughly similar measurements of attitudes, the dependent variables, and of the main kinds of things that potentially shape these elements of social capital. In particular, they make it possible to evaluate the relative effects of government performance, aspects of political leadership, "rule of law" (public safety), and participation in voluntary associations, among other possible contributing factors. The details of the analysis appear in tables at the end of the chapter.

Trust

It is by now almost a truism to suggest that higher levels of generalized trust are important for cooperation and growth. Higher levels of trust help facilitate contracts, make people more likely to invest, and create a basis for compromises where one party won't realize a benefit except with a delay.

But what promotes trust? One explanation does not fit all countries, and none of the standard models is especially helpful, but it is possible to discern some regularities across African settings. The most important is that reducing crime contributes heavily to building higher levels of generalized trust, including trust among neighbors. For example, in Uganda, "rule of law," or perceived trends in crime, exercise the most important influence on levels of generalized trust. In Zambia, the measure of "safety" is not so strong as in the other two cases, but again, trust in police, likely construed as whether the police are doing a good job, influences trust in neighbors and in people from other regions. In Botswana, although small samples make the interpretation of the results more troublesome, worry about crime does not depress trust, possibly because almost everyone does worry about it, but the perceived frequency of disputes about contracts within a respondent's village causes trust to diminish. A major implication of the analysis is that building the rule of law ought to have high priority in postconflict reconstruction.

Other factors influence interpersonal trust. Government performance has an effect that is independent of public safety across all three countries. The satisfactory delivery of basic services such as primary health care, roads, and water supplies may boost interpersonal trust by removing responsibility for goods from the local community, thereby reducing grounds for dispute. Alternatively, ordinary people may take the willingness of officials to do their jobs as a bellwether—an indication that one can expect others to live up to these obligations too.

The "Putnam thesis" appears to carry some weight, although individual membership in social clubs exerts no discernible effects.[2] Being a member of a community where a high proportion of people belongs to voluntary associations heightens interpersonal trust in Uganda. With a little more uncertainty, it is possible to say the same of Zambia and Botswana. Thus, being part of a community of joiners matters. It is less important than other considerations, however.

Inequality in wealth reduces levels of interpersonal trust in Uganda and Botswana (although there is more uncertainty attached to the Botswanan case). There is no comparable measure in the Zambian study, so the degree to which this relationship holds there is unclear. Wealth measures in African settings are difficult to ascertain very accurately. My data reflect perceptions of wealth differences, not actual levels of wealth, and it could be

TABLE 10.1
What Influences Personal Trust?
(ordered probit results)

	Uganda	*Rural N=591*	*Zambia*	*Rural N=671*	*Botswana*	*Rural N=184*
Interpersonal Trust						
Wealth	–0.01232	0.816	0.048687	0.628	–0.07719	0.681
Gender (0=male; 1=female)	–0.163864	0.102	–0.073011	0.459	0.15592	0.545
Education (low to high)	–0.095179	0.197	–0.025124	0.100	0.01954	0.857
Participation in meetings of voluntary associations	0.042125	0.245	0.210561	0.000	–0.074311	0.402
Mean participation in voluntary associations, community	0.193004	0.000	0.531824	0.211	0.70112	0.290
Perceived trend in cooperation within community	0.196899	0.052			0.02846	0.820
Membership in social club	0.043238	0.685	0.138266	0.566	–0.14633	0.557
Membership in PTA			0.538475	0.500	–0.096107	0.708
Perceived safety	0.145326	0.119	0.210561	0.000	–0.027075	0.798
Perceived government performance	0.228655	0.025	0.116712	0.050	0.57777	0.016
Whether contract disputes are a problem	–0.418557	0.002			0.86414	0.000
Skew in community income distribution (low to high)	–0.11305	0.044			0.70519	0.278

that people who are less trusting are more likely to report that there is inequality in their communities. Poor though the data are, however, we can say that trust and perceptions of inequality are linked and that either preventing increases in inequality at the end of conflict, or boosting trust by other means, reduces the interaction between the two.

Feeling "Better Off": Well-Being

What makes people more satisfied with life? All three surveys asked people whether they felt that they were better off, about the same, or worse off than they were five years ago. Not surprisingly, wealth has a big effect in the contexts studied. People who earn more money or consider that their circumstances have improved financially do consider themselves better off, and that counts for a lot.

But money isn't the only thing that matters. In the Ugandan case, the country closest to the postconflict situations that are the subject of this volume, trust in government had a similarly large effect on satisfaction. The expectation that civil servants and elected officials will show no favor to friends—that one can expect to be treated like everyone else—contributes strongly to a feeling of being better off. Evenhandedness in postconflict situations is important in promoting a sense of well-being.

"Rule of law" also contributes heavily to the sense of satisfaction. Individuals who say that security is a problem in their communities feel much less well off than individuals who live in communities where security is more assured. This feeling appears to be independent of personal worry about being the victim of crime. Concern for one's own person is less important than the level of security in the community as a whole. The effect is more uncertain and smaller in Botswana than in Uganda and Zambia, but it is still present.

There are many other factors that contribute to the sense of being better off, but few matter as much as money, trust in government, and rule of law. Older people almost always feel less well off than younger people do. Women feel less well off than men.

Equally as important, the Ugandan and Zambian surveys show that well-being derives almost as heavily from satisfaction with the provision of particular local government services as from income. In Uganda, satisfaction was directly linked to the adequacy of basic infrastructure, such as roads. The Zambian study did not ask specifically about road conditions, but satisfaction with the performance of the local government overwhelmed the importance of most other considerations. Only in Botswana, a country with relatively better government performance, was the sense of well-being separate from satisfaction with service delivery.

TABLE 10.2
What Influences Personal Trust?

	Uganda	*Rural N=591*	*Zambia*	*Rural N=671*	*Botswana*	*Rural N=184*
Well-being						
Wealth	0.19252	0.001	.60752	0.018	0.53765	0.000
Age	–0.1881	0.000	–0.084175	0.017	–0.09192	0.116
Gender	–0.2147	0.043	0.047075	0.608	–0.12016	0.563
Trust in government	0.10344	0.002			0.02388	0.821
Trust in headmen			0.021036	0.654		
Safety	0.28931	0.003	0.051304	0.097	–0.106327	0.207
Infrastructure (1 if problem)	–0.1854	0.076			0.19425	0.273
Government performance			0.630948	0.000	0.13639	0.467

One possible implication of these findings is that President Yoweri Museveni's initial instincts in postconflict Uganda were probably right. His priority after peace was to build roads and to create local government units. When a postconflict government does these things well, popular senses of well-being get a big boost.

Public Spirit, or Voluntarism

Public spirit is the third attitude that is especially important in places where the reach of government is limited and people must help to carry the burdens of reconstruction. In countries, as in institutions, a willingness to contribute to voluntary problem-solving efforts can dampen conflict potential and generate some of the rudiments of growth without assistance from the center. Strong states are those that can depend in part on such activity. The surveys asked questions about whether respondents had joined with other members of their community to help solve a community problem in the previous five years.

In all three countries, participation in certain kinds of associations appears to promote voluntarism. At the individual level, people who belong to school associations (e.g., PTAs) are more likely to volunteer to help solve a community problem. Only in Uganda does membership in social clubs, the focus of the Putnam thesis, bear a similar relationship to volunteerism. In Uganda and Zambia, a sense that others are also contributing makes a difference too. Individuals are more likely to volunteer to help solve a community problem if they perceive that there is a general trend toward increasing cooperation in the community.

In Uganda, religion plays a role in civic spirit. Religiosity exercises some influence. Affiliation also matters. Although Weber (and Putnam) would be chagrined to say so, the evidence in Uganda is that being Catholic increases the probability of helping to solve a community problem—the converse of the "Protestant Ethic."

Predisposition to Participate

A fourth attitude important in this investigation is the predisposition to participate. Studies of social capital usually exclude this attitude, but because so many peace agreements seek to involve ordinary people through the exercise of the vote and through other formal institutions, this predisposition is potentially important to successful reconstruction. It signals a willingness to work through established channels, presumably as an alternative to insurrection or the kinds of gossip and foot-dragging that constitute hidden forms of resistance.

That participation is partly a function of socioeconomic status, including wealth and education, is a robust finding in most cross-national research,

TABLE 10.3
What Influences "Public Spirit" (Voluntarism)?

	Uganda	*Rural N=591*	*Zambia*	*Rural N=671*	*Botswana*	*Rural N=184*
Public Spirit						
Wealth	0.10907	0.087	0.089093	0.276	−0.007016	0.968
Gender	−0.599614	0	−0.487671	0	−0.426165	0.066
Education	0.039512	0.66	0.022378	0.161	−0.140856	0.128
Interpersonal trust	0.208801	0.018	0.208709	0.001	0.246543	0.182
Religiosity	0.175929	0.02				
Club	0.273266	0.029	−0.045413	0.859	0.032703	0.888
PTA	0.341938	0.005	0.886803	0.272	0.527639	0.025
Clan	0.055582	0.649			0.435636	0.458
Perceived trend in voluntarism in community	0.37437	0.003	0.586369	0	0.093523	0.428

and the findings here are little different. In both Uganda and Zambia, wealth and education affect the predisposition to participate. But, as in Europe and the United States, institutions also influence participation levels. Trust in government, including the perception that elected officials are concerned about ordinary people, shapes the predisposition to participate in all three countries. It is especially important in Zambia and Botswana. Local voluntary associations also appear to galvanize people to vote, contact officials, and attend community meetings, particularly in Botswana. Finally, information matters; exposure to radio news makes a difference.

In the Ugandan case, public safety also contributes to the predisposition to participate. Ugandans are more likely to play a role in community affairs and to vote in elections if they feel safe from crime and violence.

Optimism

Investment and compromise depend on having long time horizons or judgments that one is going to be better off in the future. People who are not optimistic, and therefore have shorter time horizons, may not invest and may be more likely to decline investments or exchanges and compromises that involve a payback in the future. The three surveys asked questions about optimism, to try to get at the roots of this sentiment. The Zambian study specified that the future was "next year," while the Ugandan and Botswanan studies left the timing indefinite. What makes people in rural areas think that they will be better off in the future than they are now?

The first finding is that across all three countries, optimism is partly a retrospective judgment. That is, whether one anticipates being better off in the future is heavily a function of whether one feels better off now than five years ago. If life has improved, then one expects it to continue to do so. The implication is that there may be a poverty trap after periods of conflict. If optimism depends heavily on past experience, it may be hard to "shock" people into changing the way that they think. This retrospective effect is strongest in postconflict Uganda.

A second finding is that in Uganda, but not in Zambia or Botswana, "rule of law" contributes importantly to optimism, apart from the retrospective assessment of whether one is better off. Sense of personal safety affects individual optimism about the future in societies that have recently experienced violence.

In other settings, particularly Botswana, trust in government influences optimism strongly. The belief that officials will treat all people pretty much the same way, no matter who they are, and the belief that elected officials are concerned about ordinary people, correlate strongly with optimism.

Additional analysis not presented here also implies that place of residence matters for optimism, too. In both Uganda and Zambia, living in or

TABLE 10.4
What Influences the predisposition to Participate (through Legal Channels)?

	Uganda	*Rural N=591*	*Zambia*	*Rural N=671*	*Botswana*	*Rural N=184*
Predisposition to Participate						
Wealth	0.155952	0.002	0.247171	0	0.084186	0.565
Gender	−0.76672	0	−0.381423	0	−0.143927	0.457
Age	0.1232	0	0.164002	0	0.093833	0.126
Education	0.249296	0.001	0.039119	0.009	−0.078623	0.378
Trust in government	0.098391	0.034	0.127579	0.001	0.163939	0.093
Frequency of participation in voluntary association meetings	0.118948	0			0.255689	0.000
How often listens to radio news	0.189163	0	−0.052447	0.021	0.162059	0.022
Safety	0.202576	0.018	0.059683	0.054	−0.146248	0.068
Catholic	0.14684	0.1	0.117578	0.251		

TABLE 10.5
What Influences Optimism?

	Uganda	*Rural N=591*	*Zambia*	*Rural N=671*	*Botswana*	*Rural N=184*
Optimism						
Well-being	0.54456	0	1.361449	0	0.291685	0.012
Wealth	–0.0065	0.907	0.083438	0.296	–0.004571	0.978
Age	0.080631	0.03			–0.051567	0.453
Gender	–0.169248	0.101	0.00249	0.98	–0.15079	0.475
Education	0.1172575	0.182	0.003169	0.837	–0.023045	0.810
Safety	0.135536	0.008	0.01031	0.749	0.021578	0.803
Trust in government					0.280788	0.011

near the president's home district contributes to optimism. A reasonable interpretation of the strong coefficients for district dummy variables is that personalism is still very strong in these areas, or that the perception of personalism carries a lot of weight. People from the president's home area tend to feel much more optimistic that they will be better off in the future than people from other areas.

Policy

The aim of this chapter is to identify priorities for rebuilding political institutions, not to offer specific suggestions about how best to fulfill these priorities.

Breaking Path Dependence

The analysis of the data suggests a high degree of path dependence may plague postconflict governments. In particular, it may be very difficult to generate optimism where retrospective evaluations of well-being are negative. Focusing attention on the other kinds of things that seem to influence people's sense of well-being and optimism is important while economies recover and create possibilities for wealth creation. For example, breaking the vicious cycle may be partly a matter of doing one visible thing that people want—like building roads or improving public safety in Uganda. It may extend to dramatic gestures that demonstrate that government officials will be even-handed in their work.

Rule of Law

Resource-poor postconflict governments cannot do everything. The survey evidence suggests that rule of law is an important priority. But rule of law is one of the more difficult areas in which to intervene effectively, and it has many aspects.

Courts work slowly in most developing countries. Judges cannot make decisions unless the police deliver adequate evidence and unless prosecutors are willing to handle cases. But foreign donors are justifiably skittish about training and equipping police forces, and new governments receive relatively little boost for doing so unless there is a clear and immediate improvement in levels of public safety. One possibility might be to increase the ease with which people can bring civil complaints against offenders and to allow them to invest in developing evidence themselves. A second is to develop a multinational "marshall service" that can investigate major problems effectively and reassure donors that their money is not being used to commit human rights violations. A third is to increase the ability of high court branches to travel on circuit and mediate group complaints—the kinds of disputes, for example, that can lead to ethnic violence.

Trust in Government

Evenhandedness in government is important for fostering several attitudes vital to reconstruction. Evenhandedness may entail several things. Bringing government closer to the people may help, although it is no panacea. People may be less suspicious of officials whose behavior they can more easily observe. Certainly, the Zambian data suggest that mistrust of officials varies by level and that high officials attract more mistrust than local officials do. But local governments can just "move the looting to the districts," as one Ugandan respondent observed. Working with local elected officials and civil servants to develop procedures that guarantee evenhandedness and that attend to the concerns of ordinary people should help boost participation and optimism.

Strong measures against corruption are probably in order. Criminal corruption cases are notoriously difficult to bring in courts, either because prosecutors are not independent and lack the will or because adequate evidence is hard to assemble. Permitting civil suits, instead of criminal charges with their higher evidentiary standards, is one way to reduce the difficulty of bringing politicians and officials to account. The now disbanded Heath Commission in South Africa offers one model. A second possibility is to alter laws so that private parties can bring complaints against public officials for corruption in the granting of contracts or provision of services. In both instances, statutes that grant double or treble damages would make bringing a complaint rewarding enough so that private parties might be willing to risk the dangers.

Improving Local Government Performance

The ability of governments to deliver basic services plays a larger role than anticipated in shaping social capital. Road maintenance and the extension of road networks, coupled with the provision of functional primary health care services, primary schools, and water supplies, appears to influence interpersonal trust in all countries. The exact connection is unclear, and it may be that the survey data harbor an endogenous relationship testable only with more observations, spread over time. That is, higher levels of trust produce higher levels of government performance by some mechanism, and this better performance feeds back into trust.

There is some evidence of a different kind of relationship, however. Government performance may serve as a bellwether. People may take their cues about how much they can trust others from the behavior of officials. If officials deliver on their obligations to provide services, maybe others can be trusted as well. The Ugandan survey turned up hints that the effectiveness of the courts has such an effect, and the influence of government performance on trust may have a similar interpretation.

In either case, attention to the kinds of service delivery that matter most to ordinary people is likely to bolster trust and the predisposition to participate, as well as attitudes such as voluntarism that depend partly on levels of interpersonal trust.

Creating Societies of Joiners

Finally, the analysis suggests that policies which generate a denser associational life are helpful. People take cues from trends in their communities. Where others seem to be joining together to do things, individuals become more willing to help solve community problems. They are even more inclined to do so if they are already members of a voluntary organization. The kinds of associations foreign donors have helped to inspire are not necessarily those that are important. These groups have had narrow urban bases in past years. Instead, donor effort needs to promote local Red Cross societies, the equivalents of 4-H clubs, and PTAs—something the Botswanan government has encouraged, but which are less common elsewhere. The effect of participation in associations is not as pervasive or as strong as much of the current literature implies, but careful investments in this sphere may help boost the kinds of attitudes that will sustain postconflict reconstruction.

Notes

1. The Ugandan data come from Jennifer Widner, "Social Capital and Institutional Performance Survey" (1995-1996). Conducted ten years after the cessation of conflict in southern, central, and eastern Uganda, the survey is based on a multistage area sample in which final-stage respondents were randomly selected from central village lists. The Zambian data come from Michael Bratton, "Democratic Attitudes and Participation Survey" (1996), a multistage quota sample. The Botswanan data come from Jennifer Widner, "Social Capital and Institutional Performance Survey" (1996).

2. Robert Putnam, *Making Democracy Work* (Princeton, 1988).

Eleven

Civil Society and the Reconstruction of Failed States

DANIEL N. POSNER

CIVIL SOCIETY IS said to possess almost magical qualities for improving governmental performance—from promoting good health, reducing crime, and generating economic growth to facilitating political reform and easing the reintegration of ex-combatants after civil wars.[1] Given such (alleged) beneficial powers, one might inquire whether civil society could play a useful role in a context where the state is not simply underperforming but is unable to provide even the most basic services that people reasonably expect from it. This is precisely the situation in failed states. The purpose of this chapter is to explore whether civil society might serve as an effective lever for rebuilding state capacity in such a context and, if so, how its ability to play such a role might be encouraged and strengthened.

Civil society is the reservoir of formal and informal organizations in society outside of state control. As such, it is an empty vessel. It can be filled with groups that foster social cooperation and improve peoples' lives, or with groups that sow distrust and foment violence. Warlord gangs, Mafia organizations, and paramilitary groups are as much a part of civil society as churches and women's associations. It goes without saying, however, that organizations of the former sort will have a negative impact on restoring state capacity and providing public goods. Thus, in working through the logic of how civil society might play a useful role in strengthening government institutions and improving peoples' living conditions in failed states, I focus on organizations that are not explicitly bent on destroying the state or profiting from its weakness.

The chapter begins by reviewing the received wisdom on why civil society is thought to promote good governmental performance in the first place. As this volume's opening chapter explains, governmental performance entails the provision of fundamental public goods like security, basic infrastructure, education, sanitation, and public health. Civil society employs two different mechanisms to foster these ends. The first, "advocacy," is irrelevant in a failed state context, but the second, "substitution," may be precisely what is needed in an environment where the state has ceased to play its usual order- and public goods-providing role.

The problem, however, is that state collapse tends to go hand-in-hand with the atrophy of civil society. So, if civil society is to make a positive contribution to rebuilding a failed state, it must itself first be rejuvenated. I review the literature about how the groups, organizations, and associations that make up civil society can be encouraged to develop. Then I show how the logic behind these arguments is altered when we apply them to understanding civil society formation in a context where the state has failed. Finally, I suggest what donors interested in rebuilding failed states might do to encourage the growth of civil society.

How and Why Does Civil Society Do Good Things?

Two quite different mechanisms are offered in the literature to explain the link between a robust civil society and good governmental performance. The first emphasizes how the autonomous organizations located within society articulate social interests and hold state decision-makers responsible for their actions. This "advocacy" or "watchdog" model posits an adversarial relationship between civil society and the state. Public (political) goods are provided because civil society groups monitor the behavior of state officials and confront them when they fail to provide the public goods in question. If crime becomes rampant, community groups lobby the government for more streetlights and police officers. If roads become so potholed as to be impassable, truckers' associations and market sellers' organizations demand that the government make infrastructure improvements. If bureaucrats request outrageous bribes to file simple paperwork, business groups insist that the government take measures to curb corruption. The articulation of such demands does not guarantee that they will be met, but bringing the problems to the attention of state decision-makers, and making clear the political costs that they will face if the problems are not taken seriously, almost certainly improves the likelihood that they will be. Through such pressure from civil society groups, outcomes can be achieved that would not have been possible otherwise.

This advocacy mechanism is by far the most common way in which civil society's contribution to good governance and public goods provision is conceptualized by scholars of developing societies.[2] So dominant is this understanding of civil society's effects that it even finds its way into definitions of the concept itself. Stepan's oft-cited definition of civil society as "the arena where manifold social movements . . . and civic associations . . . attempt to constitute themselves . . . *so that they can express themselves and advance their interests*" is a case in point; the advocacy mechanism is built into the definition.[3]

In the second, "substitution," model, civil society contributes to social welfare by furnishing the organizational infrastructure and human and financial resources to provide the order and public services that citizens desire. Thus, neighborhood watch groups compensate for the absence of police protection by organizing nightly security patrols. Rotating credit associations make up for the lack of state-sponsored credit by providing small business loans. Clan elders substitute for weak or corrupt courts by setting up tribunals and dispensing justice. Community organizations compensate for the lack of state-provided public services by fixing roads, staffing clinics, building schools, and providing sanitation services. Sometimes such activities operate parallel to, and serve to support, similarly directed activities of the state (as, for example, when community watch groups work with the police to reduce crime). Other times, however, the activities of civil society groups serve as *substitutes* for the state that, due to its weakness or the indifference of its leaders, fails to provide the public goods in question. Either way—as complements to or as replacements for state action—civil society groups operating through this mechanism contribute to improving the quality of life in the community.

The advocacy and substitution models describe distinct but complementary mechanisms through which civil society may generate superior social outcomes and improved governmental performance. Both causal pathways are probably at work in most functioning political systems. But what about in failed states? Are both mechanisms likely to be at work there too?

It is first useful to distinguish between three analytically distinct moments in the process of state failure and reconstruction. Figure 11.1, which traces the trajectory of the collapse and reconstruction of state capacity in a hypothetical state, identifies these moments as points labeled 1 to 3. The first corresponds roughly to what Rotberg, in the introduction to this volume, terms "weak states." Here, state capacity is still relatively high but the beginnings of its decline are evident. Many developing countries (for example, Pakistan, Kenya, Indonesia, and Colombia) find themselves in this position. At point 2, the state has fully collapsed and has ceased, or very nearly ceased, to provide basic services or to control the use of force outside of the capital city. Over the past decade, Liberia, Sierra Leone, the Sudan, Somalia, and the DRC have met this description. In the third moment, the process of reconstruction has begun and, while state capacity is still weak, the trajectory is toward increasing capacity and authority. Uganda, Ghana, and Chad passed through this phase during the past few decades.

I distinguish among these three different phases because civil society plays a somewhat different role in each. In this chapter, I draw out the logic of what it can do at point 2, when the state has completely collapsed. The contribution that civil society might make to stemming state decline

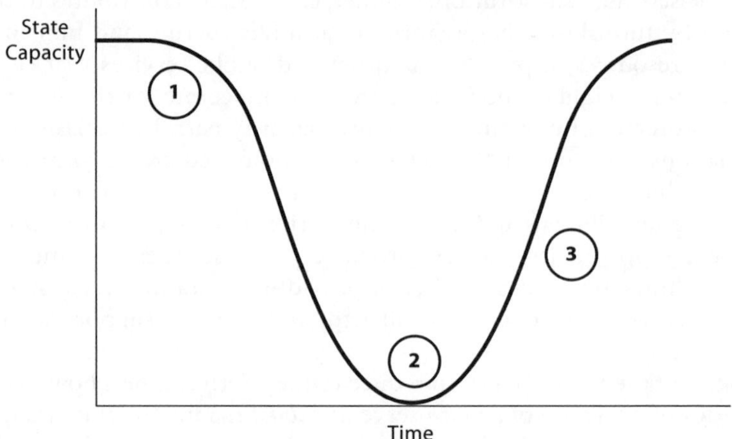

Figure 11.1 Three periods in the process of state failure and reconstruction.

in its early stages (that is, in Rotberg's terms, when the state is failing—i.e., when it is between points 1 and 2), or to facilitate the reconstitution of governmental institutions and capacities once the process of state rebuilding is already underway (in period 3), follows a different logic.

In a context of full-blown state failure, advocacy is unlikely to play more than a minor role because this mechanism depends on the existence of exactly what, by definition, has ceased to exist: a viable state to which civil society groups can direct their appeals and through which their demands can be implemented. In periods 1 or 3, civil society groups might play a useful watchdog role. But in circumstances of state collapse, their direct impact as advocates of good governance or public goods provision will be nil.[4]

In the substitution mechanism, by contrast, civil society's contribution to public goods provision does not depend on the existence of a viable state. Indeed, since, in this model, civil society *substitutes* for absent or weak institutions of central authority, its positive effects are likely to be greatest when state capacity is closest to zero. Thus, if we want to understand how civil society might contribute to improving governance and public goods provision when the state has completely collapsed, the substitution model needs to be the focus of our attention.

For civil society to play a positive role in state reconstruction, it must itself be strong. Groups must be in a position to mobilize human and financial resources for collective ends. Yet, state failure tends to coincide with the collapse of the cooperative capacity of most social groups—or, at any rate, of those groups that might contribute positively either to rebuilding the state or to substituting for it as a provider of public goods. When public order breaks down, people become more concerned with their own survival than with cooperation, and civil society groups that depend on mutual cooperation become greatly weakened. Moreover, the conflicts that emerge when the state collapses often lead to the crushing of whatever civil society may still be operating. As Reno emphasizes, political authorities in failed states cannot rely on bureaucratic institutions to control people, so they rely on violence. Civil society, where the capacity to organize against power-holders resides, is usually a principal target of this violence.[5] Thus, precisely when civil society is needed, it is likely to be too enfeebled to be of much use in rebuilding or substituting for state capacity. The central task is therefore to address how civil society can be encouraged to develop—and to do so in a context where governmental institutions have failed. The first step is to explain, in general terms, how civil society emerges and can be encouraged to grow. The next is to explore how such growth might be fostered in the particularly inhospitable environment of a collapsed state. The latter is no easy task. For, as we shall see, the same factors that lead to civil society's decay present obstacles to its resuscitation.

How Does Civil Society Emerge?

All civil society organizations face a central collective action problem.[6] Warlords and owners of private security services aside, everyone in society will benefit from the order, governmental accountability, and public service improvements that active civil society groups might bring. Such benefits are public goods, enjoyable by everyone irrespective of whether or not they contribute to the group activities that generate them. Given this fact, people should have little incentive to volunteer their time and energy to sustaining group activities, and both the benefits of such activities and the groups that generate them should be underprovided. Yet, despite this logic, we still observe functioning civil society groups that provide public goods. Why? How is the collective action problem overcome?

The literature suggests three different answers. First, people might volunteer their labor for collective endeavors if levels of trust and norms of reciprocity in society are sufficiently high as to make them confident that their cooperative efforts will be met in kind.[7] Second, public-goods-providing groups might emerge and be sustained if members enjoy sufficient selective incentives—prestige, respect, financial remuneration—for getting the organization off the ground and keeping it going despite the free-riding of the vast majority of the group's beneficiaries.[8] Finally, the collective action problem might be overcome if the state or some other powerful agent were to compel social cooperation by threat of sanction against those who shirk.

Trust and Norms of Reciprocity

High levels of trust and norms of reciprocity—together commonly referred to in the literature as "social capital"—facilitate the emergence and perpetuation of civil society groups by giving confidence to those who might otherwise be hesitant to volunteer their time and energy that the contribution they make to the group's activities will be met in kind. For example, if, having agreed upon a time and place to meet one's fellow community members to fill the potholes in the road leading to the central market, a community member suspects that she will be the only person to show up with shovel in hand, then she will not be likely to come. If others make the same calculation, then no one will show up and the potholes will go unfilled. If, on the other hand, the person in question lives in a community with high levels of trust and strong norms of reciprocity, then, having agreed to meet to fill the potholes, she will have confidence that others will make good on their promise to come, and she will not shirk. The presence of reciprocal trust thus allows the community to achieve a beneficial outcome (in this case, a smooth road) that would have been unattainable in the absence of the collective effort. Other sorts of public-goods providing organizations like neighborhood watch groups, agricultural cooperatives, and rotating credit associations also succeed or fail based on a similar logic: people will contribute their time and labor to such groups only if they trust their fellow group members to do the same.

The problem is that trust and norms of reciprocity do not simply emerge spontaneously. They are themselves the by-products of interaction within civil society groups. They are cultivated through the experience of successful cooperation with other members of the community. They are formed when people extend themselves (e.g., show up at the agreed-upon time with shovel in hand) and are not disappointed with the results (i.e., find that they are not the only ones to show up). Such experiences generate the trust that makes cooperation in the future possible, and thus the perpetuation of the public-goods-providing group itself.[9]

An aspect of this mechanism that is worth underscoring is that the purpose of the group should be irrelevant to its ability to generate trust among its members. Trust and norms of reciprocity are formed as a positive externality of collective activities undertaken for other purposes. It makes little difference whether the group itself was explicitly formed to promote effective governance or whether it was an informal organization set up to coordinate cultural activities, build membership in a particular religious group, or organize sports events. Since what generates the trust is the act of successful mutual cooperation, all of these groups should be equally beneficial. This fact has important implications for how the generation of social capital might be promoted in failed states.

But if trust is necessary for sustaining group interactions and if group interactions are, in turn, the principal means of creating trust, then we face a hen-egg problem. How can cooperation be sustained (or even initiated) if community members lack the mutual trust to cooperate in the first instance? If they do not cooperate in the first instance, how is the trust to be inculcated? The problem is that trust and norms of reciprocity constitute a social equilibrium, and this fact makes them very difficult to generate when they do not already exist. Thus, while we can easily explain why societies with lots of social trust tend to have robust networks of associational involvement, it is a far more difficult task to figure out how to develop either trust or networks when the other is lacking.

Selective Incentives

A second way in which civil society groups can be sustained—even in the absence of trust or norms of reciprocity—is if at least a critical mass of group members derive a benefit from participation that is independent of the public good that the group is designed to generate. This personal gain makes them willing to contribute their time and energy to the group (to show up at the appointed time and place with shovel in hand) irrespective of whether or not they think others will do so as well. Mancur Olson calls such benefits "selective incentives," and he explains that while they often entail direct financial compensation, they sometimes include more intangible—or, at any rate, less directly economic—rewards such as prestige, respect, standing in the community, and even the avoidance of social disapproval.[10]

In traditional kinship societies, such as are found in many developing countries, nonfinancial rewards of this sort can often be sufficiently great so as to sustain social cooperation. When membership in the community is a prerequisite for access to valuable resources like land and social insurance, the incentives for avoiding social disapproval, and thus undermining one's claim to membership, are especially strong. In such contexts, volunteering one's labor for collective activities is likely to be a smart thing to do, even when one might prefer to shirk. In such a society, the fruits of many group activities cease to be strict public goods, since they become excludable from those who did not contribute to their provision. Enjoying the public good is contingent on being a member in good standing in the community, which, in turn, is contingent on contributing to the community endeavor that generates the public good in the first place.

But because people still possess the incentive to shirk *if they can shirk without detection*, the collective action dilemma looms in such societies. The cooperation equilibrium we observe in traditional kinship communities is thus fragile—particularly in a context of uncertainty and violence such as is found in a failed state. A more reliable way to overcome the free-rider problem—and the only alternative in communities where the social rewards for volunteering and the social penalties for shirking are not large enough to enforce cooperation—is to pay individuals for their participation. Sometimes such payments are provided by a sympathetic foreign donor, sometimes by the government itself. Whatever their source, direct payments to those who bear the costs of organizing and sustaining the group lie behind the majority of the public-goods-providing organizations that we find in developing countries. Their common label as "grassroots" organization belies their top-down origins.

A 1993 study in East Africa, for example, found that thirty-six of the sixty-two civil society groups surveyed depended on foreign donations for 75 to 100 percent of their operating budgets, and another seven depended on foreign donations for between 50 and 75 percent of their budgets.[11] The problem is that because such groups are dependent on outside support, they are prone to collapse as soon as the support dries up. Paying group members for their participation may therefore be a viable short-term means of sustaining the group and putting it in a position to provide the collective benefit that it was created to produce, but it is no long-term solution.

There is, however, a way in which, at least in principle, selective incentives might facilitate the perpetuation of the group over the longer term. As we have seen, once a civil society group is up and running, the experience of successful interaction within it will generate trust among fellow group members. Thus, civic organizations, even if they are entirely products of third-party sponsorship, might, over time, generate within their own ranks the trust and norms of reciprocity that would allow them to continue functioning once the selective incentives that were responsible for getting them started are withdrawn. Unfortunately, while such an expectation is theoretically plausible, the empirical evidence suggests that civil society groups sponsored by resources from outside the community tend to be unreliable vehicles for generating trust among their members.

First, participation rates in donor-sponsored groups tend to be low. Dicklich reports that, within the civil society groups that she studied in Uganda, "participation by the targeted beneficiaries in decision-making and programme implementation appears to be much less than expected."[12] She points out that this result dramatically undermines the groups' trust-building potential. Even more importantly, she notes, the dependence on external sources of funding detaches civil society groups from the societies that they are supposed to be serving, and this further undermines their ability to generate mutual trust among their members.[13] Summarizing a survey of grassroots organizations, also in Uganda, Gariyo reported that only ten of twenty-nine groups could claim more than ten paid-up members. He concluded that "with such a limited membership, it is difficult to move accountability from being donor driven to being membership driven."[14] Drawing on his experience in Rwanda, Uvin argues similarly that a vibrant civil society cannot be created by outside funding. "Social capital accumulation," he writes, is "a slow, long-term, internal process of gradual accumulation of the capacity and the willingness to negotiate, compromise, and shape the political arena. . . . Any attempt to rapidly create a civil society through development aid (and with the tools of the typical development project) will lead to fake, superficial results."[15] If the idea of underwriting the start-up costs of civil society groups is to promote participation that will, in turn, build trust within the community, then the evidence suggests that this may be false hope.

The State as a Third-Party Enforcer

A third means of solving the collective action dilemma also involves the intervention of a third party. This time, the role of the outside actor is not to provide selective incentives but to enforce participation among those who would prefer to free-ride. The stick, in short, replaces the carrot. The most logical party to wield this stick is the state. The problem, however, is that unless the state is extremely strong it is unlikely to be interested in taking actions that will strengthen the social forces that, once energized, will be in a position to challenge and even undermine its authority. It would prefer to keep civil society weak.

Indeed, the governments of many developing countries employ the resources they have at their disposal not to support civil society but to stifle it. They co-opt labor unions, agricultural cooperatives, and professional associations. They muzzle the press. They set up nongovernmental organization (NGO) registration boards to regulate and control civil society groups.[16] And they try to undermine civic organizations by branding their leaders as foreign agents. While such attempts to restrict civil society groups' activities are often ineffective, this failure stems more from these states' lack of resources and incompetence than from their lack of desire to control civil society's activities.

The hostility that state leaders display to civil society organizations makes sense if we think about such organizations solely in their advocacy mode. But in addition to serving as watchdogs, many civil society groups also provide valuable public goods—often goods that governments themselves are not able to provide. Why would governments not welcome this assistance? Why would they not view civil society groups as valuable allies? The answer is that sometimes they do, but only if state leaders think that they, rather than the civil society groups, will get credit for having provided the services in question. Governments, particularly in developing countries, know that their legitimacy derives from their ability to provide resources for their citizens, and they jealously guard their reputation as the key providers of public goods in their societies. Groups whose actions threaten this reputation are viewed as dangerous.

But governments compete with development-oriented civil society groups not just for the favor of their citizens, but also for the favor of international donors. On the one hand, this provides donors with leverage to demand that governments give civil society groups the "breathing room" that they need to operate. But on the other hand, it provides a disincentive for governments to let civil society groups demonstrate their abilities as alternative public goods providers. For even if the government can gain credit among its citizens for having furnished the security, roads, or other services that the civil society groups provide, it may fear that such groups might start competing with the state for outside donor funds if they demonstrate too much proficiency as public goods providers. For these reasons, Gariyo notes, "most African governments remain suspicious of any independent initiative that attempts to mobilize and provide services to disadvantaged communities without the direct involvement of the state."[17] Thus, while the "state as third-party enforcer" mechanism is theoretically possible, the competition between civil society groups and the state in most developing countries make it empirically unlikely.

Can Civil Society Be Built in Failed States?

Civil society is difficult to build even in the best of circumstances, and the anarchic and violent conditions of a failed state makes it even harder. In such a context, trust and norms of reciprocity are extremely low, or even absent, and so the social capital mechanism is not likely to be of much help in building civil society. The "state as third-party enforcer" mechanism is also likely to be ineffective since, even if it were inclined to help, a collapsed state would be in no position to enforce social cooperation. The selective incentives mechanism, on the other hand, does offer a potentially viable means of developing civil society under conditions of state failure. Subject to the caveats previously outlined, if civil society is to be invigorated in a failed state, then the selective incentives mechanism will be the means by which it will be advanced.

Time inconsistency presents an additional obstacle. Time inconsistency refers to the fact that investments made in civic associations today may not pay dividends until some time in the future. Organization costs must be borne up-front, but the fruits of the collective endeavor cannot be enjoyed until later. While this is always an issue for would-be group builders, it becomes particularly acute when environmental factors like political instability, civil war, and arbitrary or predatory rule make the future unpredictable. Unpredictability leads people to discount the value of the benefits that contributing to group building might eventually bring them. This fact reduces their incentives for investing in groups in the first place, and the result is that people will stop investing in social cooperation.

Indeed, getting people to commit time and resources to associational life should be extremely difficult in a context of state collapse. When states fail, anarchy reigns. The police no longer provide security. Infrastructure crumbles. Formal markets fail. Public services cease to be provided. Courts stop functioning and contracts become unenforceable. The basic order and public goods that states ordinarily furnish go unprovided. In such a situation, individuals' discount rates will soar, and they will be far more likely to retreat into the household than to seek out opportunities for organized collaboration in civil society.

The literature reflects this position. Again and again, authors stress that a functioning state that provides basic public order and security is a prerequisite for the existence of civil society. As Bratton argues, associational life "cannot flourish amid political disorder, lawlessness, an inadequate physical infrastructure or intermittent essential services. *Civic organizations depend upon the state for the creation of certain basic conditions of existence.*"[18] Lowenkopf makes a similar point when, reflecting on the possibilities for the reconstruction of Liberian society in the early 1990s, he asks "how is [a reinvigorated civil society] to come to pass unless the prerequisites of a civil order—effective laws and their enforcement, security of self, property and one's labor, to begin with—are established?"[19] This is not to suggest that civil society groups can never emerge in a context of state collapse. But they will have the cards stacked against them.

A more serious problem with civil society building in failed states is that those organizations that *are* able to emerge are not likely to be particularly civic. The disintegration of centralized authority and the collapse of law and order that state failure brings provide an opening for Mafia organizations and militia groups to thrive. Neither the goals nor modus operandi of such groups are likely to be supportive of state reconstruction or the provision of public goods.[20] Indeed, given that their highly profitable activities depend on instability and disorder, one can count on such groups to resist any attempt to reassert centralized authority and rebuild a functioning state. These groups also encounter collective action problems of their own. But their coercive powers, combined with the profits that they can generate if they are able to organize successfully, are usually enough to permit their development. Lootable resources and the rents extracted through protection rackets constitute powerful selective incentives for bearing the costs of organization.

As plausible and well-accepted as this story of the doom that state failure brings upon civil society may be—or at any rate the "civil" component of it—there is reason to believe (and evidence to suggest) that in some cases the collapse of the state may actually have the opposite effect: energizing associational activity by providing the necessary breathing room and freedom from repression for civil society groups to emerge and flourish. As long as the state is functioning and strong, civil society groups in developing nations typically "face a choice—insist on autonomy and suffer repression, or allow themselves to be co-opted by and subordinated to the state in order to secure inclusion and enjoy patronage."[21] If the state were to disappear, it is easy to see how this might be liberating for civil society. Indeed, in Somalia, the collapse of the state in 1991 proved to be a boon to the development of civil society groups. Reflecting on the flowering of small-scale economic activity in the rubble of the Somali state, Mubarak observes that the "absence of government has proven to be better than the repressive institutions and improper policies of Barre's government." In some areas, in fact, the vibrancy of the local economy was so great as to "rais[e] the question of whether absence of government [might be] a blessing in itself."[22]

How can these contradictory assessments about the impact of state collapse on civil society be reconciled? How can state failure both condemn civil society to weakness and endow it with strength?[23] Part of the problem may be that different authors have in mind different stages of state decline and different kinds of associational activity. It may be that the total collapse of the state (i.e., period 2 in figure 11.1) provides such a powerful need for public goods and such high returns to cooperation that at least some social actors will be able to overcome the collective action problems that once beset them and collaborate for mutual benefit. A declining but still predatory state (period 1 in figure 11.1), on the other hand, may possess just enough leverage over markets to discourage economic activity and just enough coercive power to foil attempts at social organization. Associational activity might reemerge when the state has totally collapsed, but not beforehand. It is also possible that different authors simply have different kinds of states in mind. Predatory states can probably best help civil society grow by getting out of the way, while developmental states can help it by providing the order and basic public goods that facilitate group cooperation. In this regard, the degree of state power is almost certainly less important than the uses to which it is put.

It may also be that the effect of state collapse on civil society is conditional on other factors, like the presence of civil war or lootable resources, both of which vary not only across failed states but also within them.[24] In areas where state failure goes hand-in-hand with civil war and warlordism, civil society—or, at any rate, the kinds of civil society groups that are likely to contribute to state building and public goods provision—will not thrive. But in places where the collapse of government does not trigger widespread violence and disorder, local grassroots organizations may emerge to fill the void. Mubarak's discussion of state failure in Somalia suggests that this may be the case. While he finds many local activities springing up following the collapse of the Siad Barre regime, he points out that almost all of these activities were located in places where "war, political violence and fragmentation of territory into hostile or unstable political alliances" had been more or less brought under control.[25] The implication would seem to be that for meaningful associational activity to emerge, order within the local community must come first.

What Donors Can Do to Support Civil Society Formation

For civil society to emerge as a meaningful social and political actor in a failed state, it will need to be helped along by outside forces. As we have seen, the trust that might lead to its spontaneous emergence is absent. And the state is likely to be both unwilling and unable to facilitate its growth. This brings us naturally to the question of what outside actors like donors might do to support the emergence of civil society under such circumstances. The logic of the preceding discussion suggests two possibilities.

Direct Support for Civil Society

Donors can support individual civil society groups directly by providing financial support (selective incentives) to leaders who have shown a willingness to bear the cost of organizing them. But which kinds of groups should donors support? Those that claim to be explicitly dedicated to promoting good governance would seem to be the most obvious target of funding. But if promoting good governance—or, as is the case in failed states, just plain governance—is the goal, then supporting groups of this sort may not be such a good idea, for two reasons.

First, governance-oriented groups tend to be advocacy groups. As explained, groups devoted to advocacy and interest articulation can play little role in promoting state reconstruction in a context where the state is too weak to respond to pressure. Such groups might—and in fact often do—play extremely useful roles in situations where the state is strong enough to do good if pushed in the right direction or ill if its leaders are left to their own devices. But this is not the situation in failed states. What is needed in failed states are groups that can furnish the services and public goods that the state is incapable of providing.

To be sure, the social interaction that advocacy groups foster among their members might generate the trust and social capital that would facilitate the emergence of groups that *could* act as public-goods-providing substitutes for the enfeebled state. But advocacy-oriented civil society organizations would have no advantage over nonadvocacy groups in this regard, since all associational groups should generate trust as an externality of their activities.

For another reason, however, nonadvocacy groups *would* have an advantage over advocacy groups. Political entrepreneurs in developing countries know that democracy and good governance issues are high on the donor agenda. This awareness gives them incentives to set up civic organizations that appear to be geared toward those ends, even when the groups that they have formed are nothing more than vehicles for "shaking the donor funding tree" to secure salaries and perks for themselves and their close associates. So by focusing on civil society groups that are not explicitly set up to promote democracy and good governance, donors can avoid funding groups that are just "telling them what they want to hear."

An article in *The Monitor*, a Zambian human-rights-oriented weekly newspaper, titled "How to Identify a Fake NGO" summarizes the problem well. Commenting on the "mushrooming of so many NGOs that it is increasingly difficult to keep track of them," the author writes,

> Once registered, [the NGOs] adopt the word "advocacy" as their clarion call and then proceed to write convincing proposals for funding to Western donors. . . . Soon the leaders of these NGOs dump their erstwhile two-roomed shack in Chibolya [a poor residential area in Lusaka] and move to a five-bedroomed mansion in Sunningdale [a comparatively well-to-do residential area]. Next you see them driving the very latest 4x4 Japanese vehicles while their children are enrolled at the Lusaka International School. . .The problem, however, is that the majority of these NGOs are not there to serve the people they claim to serve. They are there to benefit their leaders and their sidekicks.[26]

Gariyo's data bears out this description. In the civil society organizations that he surveyed, he found that administrative expenses—salaries, perks, travel expenses—often constituted as much as 60 percent of operating budgets. In one proposal that he analyzed, submitted by the umbrella organization for NGOs in Tanzania, "salaries and consultants' fees were allocated 14.2 percent and 29.2 percent, respectively; equipment and travel 19.6 percent; rent 3.0 percent; and other miscellaneous charges 15.5 percent." In all, less than 20 percent was directly budgeted for the training program that the proposal was allegedly submitted to make possible.[27]

This is not to say that there are not genuine human-rights- or civic-education-oriented groups in Africa and elsewhere that are richly deserving of donor assistance. It is only to point out that donors interested in supporting such groups will have no way of distinguishing them from those whose leaders are simply telling them what they want to hear. Of course, so long as groups of the latter sort are actually mobilizing their members to provide public goods and promote good governance—even if highly inefficiently—the true motivations of their leaders may be immaterial. But nongovernance-oriented groups offer a second advantage over explicitly governance-oriented ones: they are more likely to sustain themselves after the donor funding dries up.

Since non-governance-oriented organizations were originally set up to promote interests independent of the donor agenda, they should be immune from many of the weaknesses of the groups that were established explicitly to capture donor funding. These groups are still liable to be affected by the shock of the inevitable withdrawal of donor support. But the fact that they *do* have what Kasfir terms "effective social roots" means that the likelihood of their survival will almost certainly be greater than that of groups set up explicitly to promote agendas furnished by outsiders.[28] Rebuilding a failed state is a long-term process, and resources would best be spent on supporting groups that have some likelihood of outliving the donors' financial contributions. We are thus led to a counterintuitive conclusion; donors should support church groups, rotating credit associations, cultural societies, and professional organizations, not civil society groups that are set up for explicit governance-strengthening purposes.

Creating an Enabling Environment

Apart from supporting groups directly, a second strategy that donors can pursue is to promote an environment that facilitates the emergence of civil society groups on their own. From a theoretical perspective, the goal of such interventions should be twofold. The first objective should be to reduce the costs of social interaction. One way of doing so is by reducing the costs of communication. A well-developed communications infrastructure not only makes it easier to organize meetings and coordinate activities once a group is up and running, but also facilitates the free flow of information about reputations that can make investments in group activity more likely in the first place. Collier's finding of a strong and significant positive relationship between the density of telephone networks and the degree of social capital in a sample of twenty-three countries provides suggestive empirical support for this assertion.[29] Donor support for communications infrastructure like telephones, newspapers, local radio stations, and even transportation infrastructure may thus be a second lever for promoting civil society in failed states.[30]

The second goal should be to try to incapacitate the forces that seek to undermine civil society groups supportive of state reconstruction. Part of this may involve applying pressure on governments to allow community groups the freedom that they require to operate. But the most severe threats to civil society groups in failed states are less likely to come from the government than from nonstate actors like warlords and militia organizations. The key to keeping such groups in check is to provide the state with the means of providing law and order. Thus, to strengthen civil society, donors might do well (paradoxically) by investing in strengthening the military and police forces of the state. So long as warlords are preying on civilians and Mafia organizations are in a position to outbid donor-sponsored civil society groups for the loyalties of citizens, the reinvigoration of civil society is likely to prove an unachievable goal.

In the end, however, these strategies are likely only to have an impact on the margin. The "cure all" reputation of civil society, and the hope that it inspires that civil society groups might play useful roles as tools for rebuilding failed states, confuses correlation with causation. A vibrant civil society must be viewed as an indicator of a well-functioning state and society, not as a source. This chapter has shown why this is particularly so when the starting point is state failure.

Notes

1. On health and crime, see Robert Putnam, *Bowling Alone: The Collapse and Revival of American Community* (New York, 2000). On economic prosperity, see Deepa Narayan and Lant Pritchett, "Social Capital: Evidence and Implications," in Partha Dasgupta and Ismail Serageldin (eds.), *Social Capital: A Multifaceted Perspective* (Washington, D.C., 2000), 269–295. On civil society and political reform, see John W. Harbeson, Donald Rothchild, and Naomi Chazan, *Civil Society and the State in Africa* (Boulder, 1994). On the reintegration of ex-combatants after civil wars, see Nat Colletta, "Disarmament, Demobilization, and the Social and Economic Integration of Ex-combatants: Lessons from the World Bank Africa Experience," paper for the conference "Reinvigorating and Resuscitating Weak, Vulnerable and Collapsing States," Harvard University, January 19–21, 2001. On "making democracy work" more generally, see Robert Putnam, *Making Democracy Work: Civic Traditions in Modern Italy* (Princeton, 1993).

2. A World Bank study is a case in point. The authors write, "A vibrant and diverse civil society is . . . needed to hold governments accountable. . . . Civil society organizations have an important role to play in articulating popular interests, monitoring government performance, and facilitating participation in governance." World Bank, *Can Africa Claim the 21st Century?* (Washington, D.C., 2000). Note the emphasis on *articulating* interests, *monitoring* performance, and *holding the government accountable.* For similar advocacy-oriented conceptualizations of civil society, see Emmanuel Gyimah-Boadi, "Civil Society in Africa," in Larry Diamond (ed.), *Consolidating the Third Wave Democracies: Themes and Perspectives* (Baltimore, 1997), 278–292; Harbeson et al., *Civil Society and the State*

in Africa; Dwayne Woods, "Civil Society in Europe and Africa: Limiting State Power Through a Public Sphere," *African Studies Review*, XXXV (1992), 77–100; and Larry Diamond, "Developing Democracy in Africa: African and International Imperatives," *Cambridge Review of International Affairs*, XIV (2000), 191–213.

3. Alfred Stepan, *Rethinking Military Politics: Brazil and the Southern Cone* (Princeton, 1988), 3–4; emphasis added.

4. This is not to say that civil society groups may not play an important role in articulating demands to sympathetic actors outside the state—like donors—who *do* possess the ability to respond. My point is simply that demands by civil society groups directed at their own governments are unlikely to yield positive ends in such circumstances.

5. William Reno, "Clandestine Economies, Violence and States in Africa," *Journal of International Affairs*, LIII (2000), 433–59.

6. In principle, a distinction can be made between civil society groups that generate public goods (and that face collective action) dilemmas, and civil society groups that generate private goods, the benefits of which are restricted to those who participate and which are thus not subject to free-riding. Unions and neighborhood crime watch organizations are examples of the first kind of group. Sports clubs and singing groups are examples of the second. The civil society literature, particularly that part of it which embraces the advocacy model, tends to emphasize the former. For an elaboration of this point, see Carles Boix and Daniel N. Posner, "Social Capital: Its Origins and Effects on Governmental Performance," *British Journal of Political Science*, XXVIII (1998), 686–693.

7. This "answer" is most closely associated with the work of Coleman and Putnam. See James S. Coleman, *Foundations of Social Theory* (Cambridge, Mass., 1990); Putnam, *Making Democracy Work*.

8. Mancur Olson, *The Logic of Collective Action: Public Goods and the Theory of Groups* (Cambridge, Mass., 1965).

9. Widner's finding, based on survey work in Uganda and Botswana, that people who belonged to civil society groups like social clubs or parent-teacher associations were more likely to volunteer to help solve a community problem, underscores the circular relationship between participation in community groups and civic spiritedness. See Jennifer A. Widner, "Reconstructing Political Institutions in the Aftermath of Severe Conflict," paper for the conference "Reinvigorating and Resuscitating Weak, Vulnerable and Collapsing States," Harvard University, 19–21 January 2001, and in this volume.

10. Olson, *The Logic of Collective Action*. Also see Jan Elster, *The Cement of Society: A Study of Social Order* (Cambridge, 1989).

11. Zie Gariyo, "NGOs and Development in East Africa: A View from Below," in Michael Edwards and David Hulme (eds.), *Beyond the Magic Bullet: NGO Performance and Accountability in the Post–Cold War World* (West Hartford, 1996), 156–165.

12. Susan Dicklich, "Indigenous NGOs and Political Participation," in Holger Bernt Hansen and Michael Twaddle (eds.), *Developing Uganda* (Oxford, 1998), 153.

13. Ibid.

14. Gariyo, "NGOs and Development in East Africa," 161.

15. Peter Uvin, *Aiding Violence: The Development Enterprise in Rwanda* (West Hartford, 1998), 171.

16. Tellingly, such boards are usually overseen by the ministry of internal affairs rather than the ministry of economic development or some other development-oriented department. Dicklich interprets this tendency as suggesting "that the state is more concerned about security issues pertaining to NGOs than development issues" ("Indigenous NGOs and Political Participation," 149).

17. Gariyo, "NGOs and Development in East Africa," 161.

18. Michael Bratton, "Beyond the State: Civil Society and Associational Life in Africa," *World Politics*, XLI (1989), 427–428; emphasis added. For a similar argument, see Nelson Kasfir, "Civil Society, the State and Democracy in Africa," *Journal of Commonwealth and Comparative Politics*, XXXVI (1998), 123–149.

19. Martin Lowenkopf, "Liberia: Putting the State Back Together," in I. William Zartman (ed.), *Collapsed States: The Disintegration and Restoration of Legitimate Authority* (Boulder, 1995), 104.

20. On this point, see also Hussein M. Adam, "Somalia: A Terrible Beauty Being Born?" in Zartman (ed.), *Collapsed States*, 69–89; William Reno, *Warlord Politics and African States* (Boulder, 1998).

21. Gyimah-Boadi, "Civil Society in Africa," 285–86.

22. Jamil A. Mubarak, "The 'Hidden Hand' Behind the Resilience of the Stateless Economy of Somalia," *World Development*, XXV (1997), 2027–2028. Young and Turner make a similar observation about the liberating effect of the failure of the state in the Congo. They argue that "the decay of the state has opened up new economic and social space. . . . The vitality of these mechanisms demonstrates not only the creative energies of civil society but also the possibility of survival." See Crawford Young and Thomas Turner, *The Rise and Decline of the Zairian State* (Madison, 1995), 405.

23. Indeed, some authors make both arguments in the same essays. Bratton, for example, argues both that "civic organizations depend upon the state for the creation of certain basic conditions of existence" and that "the retreat of the state will create. . .an enlarged political space within which associational life can occur" ("Beyond the State," 428, 412).

24. Civil war and lootable resources are not unrelated. Collier and Hoeffler find that dependence on primary commodity exports (which they take to be a proxy for lootable resources) significantly increases the likelihood of civil war. I distinguish between the two factors here simply because each sometimes occurs in the absence of the other, and each may have an independent effect on the relationship between state collapse and the viability of civil society. See Paul Collier and Anke Hoeffler, "On the Economic Causes of Civil War," *Oxford Economic Papers*, LIV (1998), 563–573.

25. Mubarak, "Resilience of the Stateless Economy of Somalia," 2030.

26. *The Monitor* (30 June–6 July 2000). Dicklich concurs: "Many NGOs are composed of elite persons, often bureaucrats or professionals who have discovered NGOs as an alternative, lucrative source of income. Most civil servants are unable to make even a 'living wage' in government jobs. Consequently, with the influx of donor money, many civil servants have turned to the NGO sector for personal profit. Because the private sector is still very weak, and because the state has lost

its former attractiveness, many have switched to NGOs instead to further their ambitions. . . . [The] promise of foreign travel (to seminars, etc.), upcountry travel, networking, subsistence allowances and other perquisites associated with being a member of an NGO, often tend to overshadow any strictly 'voluntary' motivation for involvement" ("Indigenous NGOs and Political Participation," 148).

27. Gariyo, "NGOs and Development in East Africa," 159.

28. Kasfir, "Civil Society, the State and Democracy in Africa," 133–134.

29. Paul Collier, "Social Capital and Poverty," World Bank Social Capital Initiative Working Paper Series (1998).

30. On the central contribution of radio to civil society development in poor nations, see Diamond, "Developing Democracy in Africa," 202.

Twelve

Restoring Economic Functioning in Failed States

DONALD R. SNODGRASS

When nation-states fail, their aggregate production and per capita income decline absolutely, and sustained economic growth becomes impossible until state functioning is restored. This is what happened in Afghanistan, Angola, Burundi, the Congo, Liberia, Sierra Leone, and Somalia. Their economic performance sank. In Angola, GDP per capita (expressed in constant U.S. dollars) fell by 40 percent from 1980 to 1994.[1] Between 1988 and 1995, Burundi suffered a 22 percent drop in GDP per capita. The Congo experienced a long and severe economic decline even before the nation's ills boiled up into a crisis. GDP per capita fell almost continuously from 1974 on, reaching a mere 30 percent of the 1974 level in 1998. After that, the World Bank's statistics give out. In Sierra Leone, a long period of stagnant GDP per capita was followed by a decline of 48 percent in 1990–2000. Only in the Sudan (out of the nations that form the focus of this book) was there some economic growth during the period of political decay. Sudan's GDP per capita reportedly rose by 52 percent between 1984 and 2000. In Afghanistan, Liberia, and Somalia, conditions were so chaotic that economic statistics could not be collected, but GDP per head undoubtedly fell from already abysmal levels in all three countries.

Intrastate war is the great destroyer. Sri Lanka, although an exception, essentially proves the paradigm. There, the localization of the war in the northern and eastern regions of the country made it possible to maintain a semblance of normal economic activity and keep the economy growing during a very long civil war. Economic activity was concentrated in the densely populated southern and western regions, which were less affected by the war.[2] The Sri Lankan experience shows that a weak state can avoid becoming a failed state if the territory controlled by the rebels is of marginal economic importance. In most cases, this condition could not be satisfied.

Even though national economic growth continued in Sri Lanka, the human and economic cost of the civil war was staggering. More than 62,000 people died. The Sri Lankans are far worse off materially than they would have been in the absence of civil war and will continue to suffer well into the future.[3] The major direct costs of the war were cutbacks in nonmilitary government spending and damage to infrastructure. Important indirect costs include lost income from foregone investment, reduced tourism, loss of human capital through death and injury, displacement of people, and output foregone in the war zone. The cumulative sum of all these costs through 1996 is estimated to have been $20.6 billion, or 1.7 years of GDP at the 1996 level.[4]

Production and per capita income decline in wartime for several reasons. First, physical capital (directly productive and infrastructural) is destroyed. Second, capacity utilization drops because it becomes difficult to obtain inputs and labor, or to market output. Third, trained and skilled workers are displaced or killed. Fourth, investment in both physical and human capital declines. Net investment (gross investment minus depreciation) may turn negative. In other words, capital stock may fall as owners of capital assets fail to invest locally and transfer financial assets abroad (capital flight). If population keeps growing, per capita income declines by a larger percentage than GDP.

Life becomes less predictable.[5] People's time horizons shorten as they discount the highly uncertain future more deeply. This shortening encourages them to engage in opportunistic behavior because they become less concerned about long-term harm to their reputations than they would be in a more stable and predictable environment. Criminality increases, abetted by reductions in government expenditures on policing and by rising military spending needs.[6]

Population is displaced. War always creates refugees, often in huge numbers (e.g., one-third of the population in Mozambique and Liberia). Serious losses of professionals and entrepreneurs may occur, as in Nicaragua (through emigration), Cambodia (through slaughter), and Uganda (through both). The populations of major cities swell as people flee insecure towns and rural areas.

Security remains a problem, even after the main fighting stops. Wars tend to peter out and it may take a long time to disarm rebels and divert their energies to peaceful activities.

Infrastructure decays. Roads, railroads, ports, airports, electric facilities, water supply, sewers, and phones may all be targeted in the fighting, or at least are subject to collateral damage. Even if the facilities themselves are not destroyed or damaged, the quality of the services that they provide declines because maintenance is neglected and necessary reinvestment is deferred.

Human capital is depleted. Professionals such as doctors, lawyers, teachers, and government officials may be particularly targeted during civil wars. Even if this is not the case, such persons have the greatest opportunities for international mobility and frequently flee war-torn countries in large numbers. Replacing lost professionals is even more difficult than in peaceful times because educational opportunities decline as schools close and teachers and students take up arms.[7]

Money supply balloons and inflation occurs. High inflation (more than 20 percent) is universal because governments want to spend more on war needs and find it harder to raise tax revenues, so they print money. This process, known as seigniorage, is a major source of peacetime government revenue in some poor countries and becomes more important in wartime. Hyperinflation (more than 100 percent) is unusual but did occur in Cambodia, Nicaragua, Zaire, Zimbabwe, and Uganda. Uncertainty about the future prompts people to liquidate holdings of local currency; doing so makes inflation worse. Dollarization often takes place as people flee the local currency. The exchange rate is usually overvalued and exchange controls are used to allocate foreign exchange to military needs.

The fiscal system is distorted. The government often raises tax rates in an attempt to obtain more revenue, but such an effort is frequently thwarted by the shrinkage of tax bases. Military spending balloons while budget allocations to other sectors are reduced, at least in real if not in nominal terms.

The structure of the economy is also distorted. Production often falls sharply in the industrial and construction sectors while subsistence agriculture may be little affected, except in war zones. Outputs of cash crops and other export items are also likely to fall because of marketing difficulties. Incentives are distorted as people learn that more money can be made from the war, often corruptly, than through legal and conventional activities.

Markets are disrupted. The level of competition declines, particular trades are monopolized, and marketing margins rise.

Rent-seeking and criminality increase. Rebels often prey on producers and traders. Sometimes government officials and soldiers join them, removing their uniforms and posing as rebels by night.[8] "Various identifiable groups will 'do well out of the war,' " writes Collier. "They are opportunistic businessmen, criminals, traders, and the rebel organizations themselves."[9]

The quality of life declines, or at least stagnates or improves less rapidly. The main social indicators (life expectancy, infant mortality, school enrollment rates, and numbers of doctors and nurses per thousand persons) may worsen as markets and government services are disrupted.[10] This contrasts with the situation in poor societies at peace. In the latter circumstances, social indicators typically improve over time, even if GDP per capita stagnates or declines.

Population continues to grow. War-related deaths often come to represent a significant percentage of the population. Numerically, however, the population that was lost can usually be replaced by one or two years of natural increase. If population growth pauses at all, it usually resumes within a year or two. Population losses equivalent to two years of population growth or less occurred in Bangladesh, El Salvador, Ethiopia/Eritrea, Guatemala, Liberia, Nicaragua, Sierra Leone, Tajikistan, and Uganda. In most other cases, population losses were only a bit greater. Afghanistan, Angola, Lebanon, Rwanda, Somalia, and the Sudan all lost two to three years of population growth. In only two instances were population losses more severe than that. The worst losses occurred in Cambodia, where more than 12 percent of the population died. This was equivalent to six years of population growth. In Bosnia, losses were smaller as a percentage of population, but a very low rate of population growth resulted in an estimate of 11.5 years of lost population growth. Because lost population is replaced relatively rapidly in most cases, national consumption needs continue to grow. The capacity to meet these needs, however, is likely to be curtailed. The heavy population losses mentioned earlier may be concentrated among the most productive adult members of the population. While the replacement of lost population may proceed rapidly in numerical terms, restoring the economic quality (productivity) of the population is likely to take much longer. War can also result in disproportionate numbers of male deaths. In postcrisis Cambodia and Rwanda, women accounted for two-thirds or more of the adult population, and there were unusually high numbers of female-headed households.[11]

Institutions are weakened. Many institutions of all kinds are seriously damaged by neglect, underfunding, and direct war losses. Social capital is destroyed as people come to distrust each other. Property rights are often weakened by the threat of physical destruction or the appropriation of property by the military.

There are, however, a few offsetting advantages. Once the conflict is definitely over, donors are typically interested in supporting rehabilitation and reconstruction. Second, emigrés who have amassed wealth and acquired skills overseas may begin to send remittances, invest, and even return home. Third, wartime entrepreneurs who have accumulated liquid assets and learned how to operate in difficult circumstances may seek new opportunities in the postwar environment. Finally, resistance to policy reform is typically low because entrenched interest groups have been destroyed or disrupted. This may make it much easier than it normally would be to enact reforms that promote economic growth.

Restoring Economic Functioning

The transition from war to peace and from economic crisis to revitalization is a fragile process characterized by intense political, economic, and ethnic rivalries.[12]

Goals

The magnitude and range of economic costs imposed by civil wars and other forms of state failure make the restoration of normal economic functioning a challenging task. A basic objective for the postcrisis government and its friends and allies is to adopt economic policies that will promote a restoration of precrisis levels and patterns of economic activity. This is difficult enough, but the task must also be accomplished in a way that does not exacerbate—indeed, if possible ameliorates—the politicoeconomic problems that contributed to state failure in the first place, as well as any new ones that may have arisen in the course of the conflict. Economic policy, in other words, must be formulated and implemented in a politically sensitive way.[13]

Economic goals in a postconflict situation typically include bringing about a revival of economic growth and restoring the quality of life and per capita consumption to preconflict levels as soon as possible. To achieve these objectives, investment in physical and human capital must resume and damaged institutions must be restored or reformed. Before that process can begin, however, several short-term problems must be dealt with. After a brief period of rapid catch-up growth, sustained GDP growth at 5 percent or better should be achieved over a number of years. This growth must be based on investment in physical and human capital and not merely on cutting down the forests or providing services to aid donors. The prospect of further civil war should become remote and there should be a reasonable level of personal freedom.

Sequencing of Actions

The sequencing of reforms in postconflict situations has been debated as part of the broader issue of the sequencing of policy reforms in general. Movement away from a more controlled economic system toward a more market-oriented one can be especially attractive in a postconflict situation because the government may have been weakened significantly in the conflict and its ability to intervene constructively in the economy (e.g., to administer promotional schemes, regulate business, and collect tax and tariff revenues) may have been compromised. It may be faster and easier to reduce the economic role of a weak and corrupt government than to improve its functioning.

The three-stage process followed by Indonesian economic reformers in the late 1960s and early 1970s is instructive: financial stabilization, rehabilitation and reconstruction, and only then development.[14] Stabilization is not very time-consuming, and reconstruction needs to follow very closely on its heels.

Financial Stabilization

At the start, the government must install a capable and credible policy team in its ministry of finance. Then, very early on (in year one), it must establish a macroeconomic environment conducive to revival of the private economy. The aim should be to cut inflation below 20 percent, preferably to 10 percent per annum or less, since higher inflation has been shown to retard economic growth. This reduction can be made quickly, provided that the government deficit can be lowered, monetary funding of the deficit eliminated, and lending to private and state-owned enterprises curbed.[15] If the deficit can be reduced, the exchange rate is most easily handled by allowing it to float. If, however, bringing domestic fiscal and monetary policy under control is considered an impossible task, it may be necessary to achieve credibility by such extreme measures as establishing a currency board or officially substituting an international currency, such as the United States dollar, for the local currency. Such measures deprive the government of potentially useful policy levers, but they may help to achieve financial stabilization in desperate circumstances.

Steps should be taken to liberalize trade during the financial stabilization phase, since trade reform has often proven easier to carry out in the immediate postconflict period than in more normal times. The cooperation of foreign creditors should be sought to suspend debt payments. Foreign aid should be sought for general budget support.

Rehabilitation and Reconstruction

A country emerging from war has other urgent priorities for the first two years after the cessation of hostilities:

Resettlement of refugees. A large-scale return of refugees from abroad or from other parts of the country to their normal abodes must be expected and supported.

Restoration of security. To prevent any resumption of hostilities, ex-combatants need to be released from detention as soon as possible and assisted with their reintegration into civilian life.[16] The military and police need to be demobilized, reorganized, and professionalized. In an increasing number of cases, the removal of landmines is critical to returning land to agriculture and other peaceful uses.

Reopening of infrastructure facilities. It is important to secure and reopen the main ports, roads, rail lines, and airports whenever possible (i.e., when major reconstruction is not needed).

Provision of emergency food and agricultural aid. It may be necessary to provide temporary food aid in hard-hit areas and to supply seeds and tools for one season to farmers in severely affected regions as well as to returning migrants.

In the somewhat longer run, roughly years two to five, the work of reconstruction should be completed. Four massive tasks are involved:

1. restoring and rebuilding infrastructure,
2. reopening and revitalizing service networks for education and health,
3. rebuilding public institutions, and
4. training people in key development skills: project appraisal, economic and financial policymaking and management, and education and health planning and management.

Development

The agenda of development is very broad and can only be hinted at here. The nature and degree of state intervention in the economy are obviously key issues. Although weakened state capacity further strengthens the already strong case for relying on market forces and private business initiative, the state must still provide a framework that will induce the private sector to make a socially constructive contribution. Whatever the framework selected, reasonable provision must be made for the orderly development of the nation's capital, human, and natural resources. These resources form the basis for bringing the level of human welfare back from its crisis-induced decline and raising it to previously unknown heights. Infant, child, and maternal mortality should be reduced, life expectancy lengthened, and illiteracy abolished. The government's economic performance will be judged in large part by its success in lessening the suffering of the many who are poor, especially those who live in politically sensitive regions and belong to politically sensitive social groups. Extensive public welfare systems are beyond the financial means of low-income countries, and so large-scale employment creation and improved access to land and other natural resources as well as financial services become critical ways to help the poor earn higher incomes on their own. Government activities must be supported by an adequate fiscal system, including moderate tax rates and high collection rates. Business should be relatively free, yet adequately supported by laws, regulations, the financial system, and mechanisms for dispute resolution.

Role of National Governments

Encouraging private investment involves defining and implementing suitable tax systems, simple and transparent investment promotion schemes, and clarified systems of commercial law.[17] Relatively swift and appropriate action along these lines will help prime the investment pump. In a particularly unattractive investment environment (for example, where property has been seized and / or nationalized in the past), exceptionally generous investment terms may have to be offered to the first one or two large pioneer investors to help jumpstart the economy. Indonesia did so in the early 1970s with considerable success.

The legal framework bears a close relationship to economic policy.[18] The establishment of clear and transferable property rights and fair, effective, and speedy mechanisms for resolving disputes are important goals in much of the developing world.

Other structural reforms that may be undertaken in particular circumstances include land reform, asset restitution, privatization, and tax reform. For development to succeed, important national assets must be controlled by parties who will use them productively. In many countries, an important part of this is the privatization of assets formerly under state or oligarchic control. Allowing legitimate entrepreneurs to run the mines, plantations, and firms involved can make a critical contribution to national development.

Role of Donors

In the early postconflict stage, most economies need budget support and assistance, plus relief for refugees and other severely impacted groups. Bilateral donors and international bodies are good at budget support while private voluntary organizations and the United Nations can handle relief. In the longer run, important donor roles include lending and training projects. A coordination mechanism is needed to increase the effectiveness of the separate donor contributions. Donors should also listen carefully to expressions of local needs and plan their activities accordingly, rather than imposing the standard aid package used in large numbers of countries. Patience and persistence are required, as many of the problems require years of effort before solutions are achieved.

The Political Economy of Stabilization and Reconstruction

The political aspect of stabilization and reconstruction involves efforts to reduce the risk of resumed conflict. According to Collier, this means that economic policy-making must address the risk factors that were present before the conflict and that presumably helped to bring it on.[19] At the same time, policymakers should also address the grievances that were created during the crisis itself.

The three major policy-related preconflict factors identified in the Collier-Hoeffler research are the presence of natural resource rents, the lack of alternative economic opportunities, and a pattern of ethnic group dominance. While these risk factors are likely to have been present prior to the conflict, they will probably be even more marked in the postconflict situation. Dependence on natural resources may have increased, economic opportunities are likely to have contracted, and the percentage of the population constituting the dominant ethnic group may have risen because members of ethnic minorities have emigrated or become refugees.[20] In any particular case, one or another of these risk factors might be judged to pose the most dangerous threat to efforts to restore political stability and economic growth. However, although the same risk factors may be present postconflict as well as preconflict, they may impose different influences on the new environment. A test of this hypothesis indicates that two of the risk factors—natural resource dependence and lack of alternative economic activities—are indeed somewhat more likely to bring about a resumption of conflict in postconflict situations than they were to cause conflict in the first place.

What are the main policy implications? The danger of heavy dependence on natural resources suggests that, rather than merely trying to return the preconflict economic structure to good working order, it would be better to promote economic diversification. That strategy meshes well both with the economic need to promote new investment and with the other major politicoeconomic need, which is to create large numbers of alternative economic activities. If an economy that had relied mainly on the production and export of a few mineral or agricultural products can be converted into one in which large numbers of workers have jobs in export-oriented factories, both economic growth and political stability should benefit.

Another policy option with politicoeconomic significance is expanding secondary education. Besides improving the income-earning potential of the young people who extend their schooling, it may also have a "jail effect," in that students in secondary schools are harder to recruit for rebel activities than their out-of-school contemporaries.[21]

Yet another policy that might have political as well as economic benefits is the widening of access to natural resources through land reform and other redistributive measures. Doing so would not only spread the wealth more evenly, but also reduce the number of large targets attractive to predators. Land reform poses all but insuperable political challenges in normal times, but it may be feasible in a postcrisis situation in which normally strong interest groups have temporarily lost much of their power.

Still another important issue is prioritizing regions for reconstruction activities. It is usually impossible to rehabilitate all regions simultaneously, or at least at the same pace, and for political economy reasons it may be desirable to select certain regions for emphasis. Collier suggests four reasons why particular regions might pose risks of renewed rebellion and thus merit special attention in the reconstruction process.[22] The first is poverty:

it is a cause of conflict and poorer districts are more likely to rebel. The second reason arose in the Ugandan case: if rebels use neighboring states as safe havens and / or draw logistical support from them, then border regions can be particularly sensitive. Third, regions with the largest numbers of ex-combatants might be given special attention. Finally, regions that are least well represented in the government might be more likely to revolt because their needs may not be met through the political process.

Societies marked by ethnic dominance also need to craft constitutional solutions that grant either equal protection to all or specific protections to minorities.[23] The Malaysian experience shows that preferences for the poor majority combined with specific protections for minorities can be made consistent with rapid economic development in a situation of ethnic dominance.[24] The Sri Lankan experience is far more sobering, in that efforts to craft a political solution repeatedly failed. A critical problem is credibility. Malaysia's New Economic Policy of 1971, which called for a major redistribution of wealth and power to take place over two decades, gained credibility from the predictability of succession within the Malaysian political system. Later, Prime Minister Mahathir Mohamad's "Vision 2020," enunciated in 1991, became an effective focal point for official developmental efforts and helped the regime to gain considerable support from its Chinese and Indian ethnic minorities. Vision 2020 inspired "visioning" exercises in many other developing countries, generally with less impressive effects. Sri Lanka's two-party democracy lacks the predictability that benefited the Malaysian regime, and few, if any, African governments can even begin to approach the Malaysian level of predictability.[25]

Prospects of Rejuvenated Economies

These policies to stabilize and rehabilitate war-damaged economies can help bring about economic resuscitation under difficult circumstances. They have their limits, however, and can be expected to yield only gradual progress toward economic goals. Commenting on Mozambique's experience in the late 1980s, Kyle observes that "[t]he most important lesson from the Mozambique experience is that progress will take time—more time than is commonly allowed in planning reform programs. Even without Mozambique's problems of incessant and widespread warfare, the building of physical and institutional infrastructure will constrain the pace of any reform program. As it is, it is clear that a resolution to the armed conflict is a prerequisite for substantial progress."[26]

The statistical evidence suggests that while it is possible to bring about a resumption of economic growth in postcrisis societies, the pace of growth is frequently so slow that war losses are not made up for a long while and the precrisis peak income level may not be restored for many years to come, if ever. The World Bank's *World Development Indicators 2002* database permits comparison of GDP per capita between the first postcrisis year and 2000 (the latest available year) for eighteen previously war-torn countries.[27] After varying periods of time since their crises ended, all but one of these countries (Eritrea) had been able to bring about some increase in GDP per capita. In four cases, however (Kuwait, Mali, Nicaragua, Togo), only marginal improvement had been achieved.

It is much harder to restore the precrisis level of production and income. The World Bank's database permits comparison of GDP per capita in 2000 with the precrisis peak year for eleven countries. Out of this group, only four countries (Bangladesh, Bhutan, Indonesia, and Mozambique) had been able to regain their precrisis income level by 2000. In Croatia, El Salvador, Iran, Kuwait, Mali, Nicaragua, and Togo that level of income had still not been recovered by 2000. Although the magnitude and timing of each national crisis affects these statistics, the message conveyed is accurate: postwar economic recovery is difficult and time-consuming.

Notes

For comments on earlier drafts, I am grateful to Robert I. Rotberg and participants in the Failed States Project meetings held at Harvard University, 19–21 January and 29 June–1 July 2001.

1. Unless otherwise noted, the source for all statistics quoted in this chapter is the World Bank's *World Development Indicators 2002*, available online at http://publications.worldbank.org/WDI.

2. They were not unaffected. There were periodic bombings and assassination attempts, resources were diverted from peaceful uses to war, and many thousands of young men reluctantly consented to being drafted into the armed forces.

3. See Lisa Morris Grobar and Shiranthi Gnanaselvam, "The Economic Effects of the Sri Lankan Civil War," *Economic Development and Cultural Change*, XLI (1993), 395–405; Saman Kelegama, "Economic Costs of Conflict in Sri Lanka," in Robert I. Rotberg (ed.), *Creating Peace in Sri Lanka: Civil War and Reconciliation* (Washington, D.C., 1999), 71–87; Nisha Arunatilake, Sisira Jayasuriya, and Saman Kelegama, "The Economic Cost of War in Sri Lanka," *World Development*, XXIX (2001), 1483–1499.

4. Arunatilake, Jayasuriya, and Kelagama, "The Economic Cost," 1495.

5. See Paul Collier, "On the Economic Consequences of Civil War," *Oxford Economic Papers*, LI (1998), 168–183; Paul Collier, "Doing Well Out of War," in Mats Berdal and David M. Malone (eds.), *Greed and Grievance: Economic Agendas in Civil Wars* (Boulder, 2000), 91–111.

6. Collier says that livestock herds often decline drastically during civil wars. Because thieves lack clear title, they often move stolen cattle out of the country ("Economic Consequences," 170).

7. Nicole Ball with Tammy Halevy, *Making Peace Work: The Role of the International Development Community* (Washington, D.C., 1996), 21.

8. Collier, "Economic Consequences," 176.

9. Collier, "Doing Well Out of War," 103–104.

10. In fact, however, available statistics seldom indicate a worsening situation. These statistics probably give an unrealistically positive picture in many cases. While the extent of decline in social indicators is uncertain, it is clear that war-torn countries improve their social indicators less rapidly than do other countries. The UNDP's Human Development Index (an amalgam of income, health, and education variables) has been compiled for each year from 1987 to 2001, although the formula for calculating it has changed. See United Nations Development Programme, *Human Development Report 1990* and *Human Development Report 2000* (New York, 1990 and 2000).

11. Ball, *Making Peace Work*, 22.

12. Nat Colletta, Markus Kostner, and Ingo Wiederhofer, *The Transition from War to Peace in Sub-Saharan Africa* (Washington, D.C., 1996), v.

13. See Gilles Carbonnier, "Conflict, Postwar Rebuilding and the Economy: A Critical Review of the Literature," ILO Report (Geneva, March 1998). Carbonnier emphasizes the primacy of political stability over economic efficiency in postconflict situations and vilifies all economists for the insensitivity and compartmentalized thinking of some.

14. This discussion assumes that a functioning government exists. If that is not the case, as in East Timor after Indonesia withdrew, formation of a functioning government becomes a top priority. Since the creation of a new government is an exquisitely complex and time-consuming task, however, economic resuscitation cannot simply be put on the shelf until the political job is completed. Instead, whatever authority is acting in place of the government must move ahead with the actions described in the text.

15. However, it may not be politically advisable right at the start to impose budget cuts that release people from the civil service, police, or army. The timing of such actions needs to be carefully considered. Delay for security reasons may put off the achievement of financial stabilization. A further complication is that the operations of peace and humanitarian organizations exacerbate the inflationary problem if their contributions to money demand exceed the real resources that they bring into the country.

16. The World Bank has drawn up a blueprint for demobilization and reintegration programs for ex-combatants in sub-Saharan Africa. See Colletta, Kostner, and Wiederhofer, *The Transition from War to Peace in Sub-Saharan Africa*.

17. Again, this assumes that a functioning government exists and can take the recommended steps. If that is not the case, the road to resumed economic development is bound to be much longer.

18. See Susan Rose-Ackerman, "Establishing the Rule of Law," in this volume.

19. Paul Collier and Anke Hoeffler, "Economic Causes of Civil Conflicts and their Implications for Policy," World Bank working paper (Washington, D.C., 2000), 16; also available online: www.worldbank.org/research/conflict/papers/civilconflict.htm

20. A larger population share for the dominant ethnic group may have been deliberately sought through "ethnic cleansing." According to the Collier-Hoeffler calculations, however, a rise in this share increases the probability of resumed conflict only within the 45–80 percent range. Beyond 80 percent or so, the probability of further conflict declines, basically because there is no one left to fight with.

21. Collier, "Economic Causes of Civil Conflicts," 7.

22. Paul Collier, "The Challenge of Ugandan Reconstruction, 1986–98," World Bank working paper (Washington, D.C., 1999), 7–8.

23. See the discussion in Donald L. Horowitz, *Ethnic Groups in Conflict* (Berkeley, 1985).

24. Malaysia's New Economic Policy, initiated in 1971 after brief race riots in 1969, promised to redistribute jobs, educational opportunity, and corporate wealth from the relatively prosperous ethnic Chinese minority to the much poorer but politically dominant Malays. It also promised to eradicate poverty among all ethnic groups. The NEP set ambitious quantitative goals but allowed a period of twenty years for the goals to be realized and pledged to reach them in a context of rapid economic growth, without depriving anyone of a job or business that he or she already possessed. Broadly speaking, the outcome was that the rate of economic growth accelerated (rather than declining as many had predicted) and the redistributive goals were substantially achieved. In the late 1990s, however, Malaysia was severely affected by the Asian economic crisis, the impact of which was aggravated by the subsequent inability of an entrenched regime and its "cronies" to respond pragmatically to the economic crisis (as they had in the 1980s), and to enact the necessary policy reforms.

25. Even in Malaysia, predictability and credibility appear to be eroding in the early years of this century as a result of the Islamic Party's challenge to the longtime domination of the United Malays National Organization as the dominant political vehicle of the Malay community. Ironically, Chinese and Indian support for Mahathir has come to seem more dependable than Malay support.

26. Steven Kyle, "Economic Reform and Armed Conflict in Mozambique," *World Development*, XIX (1991), 637–649.

27. Bangladesh, Bhutan, Bosnia, Cambodia, Croatia, El Salvador, Eritrea, Ethiopia, Indonesia, Iran, Kuwait, Lebanon, Mali, Mozambique, Nicaragua, Togo, Uganda, and Vietnam.

Thirteen

Transforming the Institutions of War

POSTCONFLICT ELECTIONS AND THE RECONSTRUCTION OF FAILED STATES

TERRENCE LYONS

FAILED STATES often are analyzed as periods of chaos as the social, political, and economic institutions that support order disappear and violence fills the ensuing void. This chapter takes a different view. Rather than existing in an anarchic vacuum, actors engaged in conflict following state-collapse create alternative institutions that allow them to accumulate power and sustain the conflict. These social, political, and economic institutions are based on violence, fear, and predation. Institutions of war, such as militia organizations, black-market networks, and chauvinistic identity groups, develop and even thrive in the context of state failure. The challenge of reconstructing failed states is therefore to develop mechanisms that will transform the institutions that developed in response to conflict into structures that can sustain peace. A comparative examination of recent cases suggests that elections may serve to encourage such institutional development only if they are embedded in a broader process to demilitarize politics.

In the context of a failed or collapsed state, where no overarching authority can promise security, many of those caught up in the conflict will mobilize on the basis of exclusive identity groups that provide safety and the means to survive. Those subject to pervasive fear and insecurity often perceive militia leaders, characterized as brutal warlords by outside observers, as protectors. Productive economic activity and markets are replaced by the predatory institutions of the black market and by the looting and criminal activity that develop in the absence of law as alternative means to accumulate assets. For new institutions capable of supporting peace to develop and take root, the most important challenge is to create an environment where fear is diminished and confidence established in a peace process that will reconstitute a state capable of delivering security.

In nearly all recent cases following state failure and civil war, reconstruction of political order has involved elections. Such elections have become the principal means to legitimate the new leadership and the institutional structures that emerge from a peace process. Western policymakers as well as parties to conflicts often regard elections as "the only alternative on the table."[1] Such postconflict elections, however, carry tremendous burdens. They are called upon to settle the contentious issues of internal and external legitimacy and must be organized under difficult circumstances of insecurity. Often none of the conditions that generally favor transitions to democracy is present. Yet there seem to be few options other than elections to organize the transition from war to peace and to certify the process of reconstructing failed states.

The challenge of reconstructing political authority following state failure requires the development of mechanisms to bestow internal and international legitimacy on a new set of political institutions and a leadership capable of maintaining order. In many cases, the question of who should govern and on the basis of what legitimacy is solved when one party wins the war, as in Uganda (1986), Ethiopia-Eritrea (1991), and Rwanda (1994).[2] In other cases, no side could win the war, and the parties negotiated a settlement with elections as the implementing mechanism to bring to power a new government and a return to constitutional rule. This was the case in Angola (1992), Cambodia (1993), El Salvador (1994), Mozambique (1994), Bosnia-Herzegovina (1996), Liberia (1997), and Tajikistan (1999 / 2000).[3] Even in the cases where one side won the war, over the long term, elections have been used or will be used to legitimize the new government. Elections are one of the very few mechanisms available to provide internal and external legitimacy to a new government.

In the context of a failed state, elections serve as important opportunities for institution (re)building as well as competition for political power. New institutions must replace the institutions that characterized the period of state collapse if peace and democracy are to be sustained. The reconstruction of a failed state begins on the new foundation of transitional institutions created during the critical interim period between the end of the war and the inauguration of the new government following elections. The patterns, norms, and precedents established during the transitional period therefore create the context for political competition. To the extent that such new institutions supportive of peaceful, democratic politics (such as political parties and electoral commissions) develop during the interim period, opportunities to reconstruct the state on a sustainable basis will be created.

The literature on democratization and transitions from authoritarian rule argues that such transformations are strongly influenced by the institutional legacies of the old order.[4] A number of scholars on regime transition have developed ideas relating to "path dependency" and "structured contingency" to examine how institutional legacies shape the course of a transition.[5] Thelen and Steinmo, for example, argue that "institutions shape the goals that political actors pursue and . . . structure power relations among them."[6] Linz and Stepan similarly base their analysis of transition paths on the characteristics of a previous regime.[7] Institutional change is an incremental process in which opportunities seized in the short run accumulate to create long-term outcomes.[8]

Following a period of state failure and protracted civil war, a critical characteristic of the transition will be the distortion or collapse of peacetime political institutions and social structures and the legacy of institutions that developed during the war. Recent studies of the political economy of civil war point out how alternative structures based on the use of violence to accumulate assets and sustain political power arise and demonstrate how institutions and leaders based on the economics and politics of violence, rather than anarchy and chaos, characterize internal conflict.[9] The nature of the interim regime that manages the peace implementation is critical because it will create the institutional setting that bridges the structures of wartime and creates the structures needed to support peace, state building, and democracy.

Any transition to democracy is a long-term process, and no single set of elections can represent more than a first, tentative step. The initial paths chosen during the peace implementation phase, however, are important because they establish critical precedents, norms, and organizational frameworks that structure the postconflict political order and channel the transition in a specific direction. Interim periods therefore contain particular opportunities and risks as local leaders assess the relative benefits of working to sustain peace and build democratic institutions in societies still polarized and distorted by war, societies where demagogues can capitalize on people's fears.

Democracy is more than elections. For a new political order to be sustainable, state reconstruction must be premised on a movement toward politics based on peaceful competition and accountability. There is a growing literature on the timing and sequencing of democratization and the impact of different electoral systems following conflict, but few options exist other than to move toward political pluralism in the long run.[10] As will be discussed, transitional regimes of national unity based on political pacts may be useful to help manage some transitions. Once security has been established and the institutions of wartime transformed, however, pressures for political liberalization and democratization will build and threaten stability unless a process moving toward greater participation and competition is put in place.

An examination of recent cases indicates that postconflict elections sometimes have provided a mechanism for selecting new political leadership and building institutions capable of preserving the peace and serving as the first step in a process of democratization, thereby promoting peace building and state reconstruction over time. This was the result in El Salvador, Mozambique, and (partially and more tentatively) in Cambodia. In other cases, elections precipitated renewed and even more violent conflict, as in Angola, thereby furthering the collapse of the state. In a third set of cases, including Bosnia-Herzegovina, Liberia, and Tajikistan, elections served more as a mechanism of war termination with only a limited (and perhaps negative) relationship to democratization.

The record is mixed in part because postconflict elections serve multiple, often contradictory, goals. They are designated in peace agreements as a primary instrument of implementation and hence play critical goals with regard to war termination. At the same time, they are designed to promote a process of democratization and to serve as "breakthrough" elections that initiate a new set of rules and institutions for competitive, multiparty politics.[11] Postconflict elections are important to the broader international community for a separate set of reasons. International peacekeeping missions generally need clear "exit strategies" to win the support of important states. The United States, for example, insisted on a clear end-point before agreeing to participate in the peacekeeping force that implemented the Dayton agreement in Bosnia-Herzegovina; the United Nations pressed for elections in Tajikistan in order to withdraw; and the West African ECOMOG peacekeeping force in Liberia demanded quick elections as part of its exit strategy. International support for economic reconstruction often requires elections. International financial institutions such as the World Bank and International Monetary Fund and important bilateral donors need a recognized government in order to begin dispersing money for critical development programs.[12] "Success" with relation to one goal, say war termination, does not necessarily mark "success" relative to another, such as democratization. Similarly, success with relation to international peacekeeping strategy may not coincide with success in relation to local political dynamics.[13]

Postconflict elections sometimes have succeeded in providing a mechanism for selecting new political leadership and institutions capable of preserving the peace, and in serving as the first step in a process of democratization, thereby promoting peace building and state reconstruction over time. This chapter suggests that a concept of "demilitarizing politics" best captures the dynamics of these successful transitions. To demilitarize politics entails building norms and institutions that bridge the structures of wartime based on violence, insecurity, and fear (such as militias, black markets, and chauvinistic identity groups) to structures based on security and trust that can sustain peace and democracy (like political parties, open economies, and civil society). The powerful actors that developed and were sustained during a protracted civil war following state failure cannot be wished away. Neither can the enabling environment for peaceful political competition be proclaimed into existence. To the extent that politics is demilitarized during the transitional period, postconflict elections are more likely to result in a new political order that can sustain peace and democracy.

Interim institutions during the implementation phase will be critical arenas in which ex-combatants and civilian leaders make assessments regarding whether the postconflict environment will protect their interests and whether such leaders will support democratization. The creation of political parties and the administration of the electoral process are tasks at the heart of the preparations for postconflict elections and provide important opportunities for interim regimes to establish the norms, precedents, and institutions needed to start the demilitarization of politics. In some cases, interim regimes have been built around joint decision-making bodies that foster confidence building and a new institutional context that can structure competition toward a path of democracy and peace. As I will later explain, this type of transition took place in El Salvador, Mozambique, and Cambodia. In other cases, interim regimes have failed to promote the demilitarization of politics, leading either to renewed conflict, as in Angola, or to the electoral ratification of wartime institutions and leaders, as in Bosnia-Herzegovina, Liberia, Tajikistan, and, to an extent, in Cambodia.

Elections represent a critical mechanism to legitimize new leaders and institutions following state failure and civil war. Such elections can serve as important opportunities for institution building and therefore contribute to state reconstruction by advancing conflict resolution and democratization. Processes to demilitarize politics are key variables in determining whether postconflict elections serve to promote sustainable peace and democracy; the more politics is demilitarized prior to elections, the greater the chance for a successful transition toward peace and democracy. Demilitarization of politics, as I will soon show, entails an effective interim administration constructed around broad consultation and joint decision making, the transformation of military organizations into political parties, and the construction of electoral authorities that are credible to all parties.

The Legacy of Fear and Voting for Peace

Fear, distorted social structures, and (mal)distribution of power created by the war will shape the political context of voting in postconflict elections unless politics is demilitarized during the transitional period prior to the election. This institutional legacy of war strongly influences the path of postconflict transitions and creates the context for postconflict elections. Unless an effective interim regime and processes to demilitarize politics are in place during the period between cease-fire and elections, the powerful organizations of war are likely to dominate the campaign and win the election. In a context where the legacy of fear remains powerful, postconflict elections are dominated by concerns for peace and security and are therefore unlikely to provide the range of choice necessary to promote democracy.

Voters in postconflict elections often choose to use the limited power of their franchise either to appease the most powerful faction in the hope that this will prevent a return to war, or to select the most nationalistic and chauvinistic candidate who credibly pledges to protect the voter's community. Outside observers often regard these leaders as warlords or war criminals, but to vulnerable voters they are seen either as powerful protectors capable of defending the voter from rival military or ethnic forces or as intimidators to be appeased in order to preclude a return to the violence that they threaten to unleash if they lose. Civilian candidates, and those who do not have a convincing answer to the issue of postelection security, are unlikely to prevail.

In Liberia, for example, memories of the brutal conflict clearly shaped how many voters viewed the July 1997 election and the choices available to them.[14] As one observer put it, the voters "were intimidated not by thugs at the polling stations but by the trauma of the last seven years of war."[15] Many Liberians believed—with good reason—that if the powerful factional leader Charles Taylor lost the election, then the country would return to war. Taylor's rivals pointed to his violent past during the campaign but could not propose credible actions to contain him if he refused to accept the results.[16] Many Liberians made a calculated choice that they hoped would more likely promote peace and stability and used their vote to appease the powerful ex-militia leader. Samuel Kofi Woods, a leading Liberian human rights advocate, explained that "the only thing Liberians wanted was an end to the war."[17] During the campaign, young Taylor supporters frightened voters by chanting "He killed my Pa, he killed my Ma, I'll vote for him."[18] In the end, the elections ratified and institutionalized the political topography and imbalance of power created by seven years of war. The nature and ending of the war and the lack of a successful process to demilitarize politics—not the election itself—created this result. An organization and leader that amassed great power during the conflict through violence and intimidation converted that influence into positions of constitutional authority through elections. This result, understandable in the fearful context of Liberia in 1997, did little to advance democratization and raises considerable concerns regarding long-term stability and peace building and the ability of the electorate to constrain their ruler.

Similar patterns of voters in postconflict elections supporting the party that offered security in a context distorted by fear are evident elsewhere. Nationalist parties in Bosnia-Herzegovina campaigned in 1996 on the basis of chauvinistic pledges and threats. The Croat Democratic Party (HDZ) issued advertisements warning that the "survival of their nation" depended on the vote, while Republika Srpska television warned that a vote against the Serb Democratic Party (SDS) would constitute a vote "against the Serb people."[19] Bosnian Muslim's made the same sort of appeals: "A vote for the SDA (Party of Democratic Action) is a vote for the survival of the Muslim nation" went the slogan in 1996.[20] Fear of other nationalist factions still powerful under the Dayton peace agreement led voters to rally to the nationalist faction that could most credibly promise security for their group. Small, multiethnic parties, such as Joint List '97, that could not promise security, won few votes.[21] In Ethiopia, fear and memories of the authoritarian rule of the old regime of Mengistu Haile Mariam led many voters to acquiesce to the ruling Ethiopian People's Revolutionary Democratic Front's power. As one Oromo farmer explained his 1995 vote for the ruling party, "I was afraid. The government said I should vote so I voted. What could I do?"[22]

In Angola, many observers expected the late Jonas Savimbi's Union for the Total Independence of Angola (UNITA) party to do well in the 1992 elections. UNITA had successfully used force to compel the ruling Movement for the Popular Liberation of Angola (MPLA) party to hold elections, had a strong ethnic base among the Ovimbundu people, and was led by the charismatic (if demagogic) Savimbi. The period of the MPLA's rule under President Jose Eduardo dos Santos had seen unrelenting conflict, economic hardship, and corruption. During the 1992 campaign, however, Savimbi used threatening language that heightened fears and persuaded many that continuing to live with the MPLA was better than the uncertain and potentially violent future promised by UNITA. Unlike in Liberia, Savimbi's threats backfired and lost him support. The election results were close, with the MPLA winning a thin majority in the parliament and dos Santos being held just below 50 percent in the presidential race. In a context in which both parties had fought to a stalemate prior to the peace agreement, Angolan voters differently perceived which party could best deliver peace and security to their communities.[23]

In Tajikistan, a prolonged conflict ended in a settlement between the government and the United Tajik Opposition in 1997. The agreement created a cease-fire and allowed the government to develop its administrative presence in some parts of the country. The agreement, however, failed to settle the contentious issue relating to the place of Islamic parties in the secular state. Its power-sharing provisions were not implemented. Elections were held for the presidency (November 1999) and parliament

(February and March 2000), but international observers regarded the exercise as flawed. State-controlled media and candidate registration favored the ruling People's Democratic Party and observers questioned the vote-counting procedures.[24] Incumbent President Imomali Rahmanov ran unopposed and was reelected with 97 percent of the votes.[25] Regardless of this questionable outcome, the United Nations ended its observer mission in 2000. The process of elections did little to increase the popular mandate of the regime, and power in Tajikistan remained divided among rival warlords. As one report concluded, "[T]he formal structures of the country have proven almost irrelevant to the daily political processes."[26]

While the issue of peace will dominate the agenda in postconflict elections, voters do not always choose the most militant parties. In Cambodia, the royalist National Union Front for an Independent, Neutral, Peaceful, and Cooperative Cambodia (FUNCINPEC) coalition won the 1993 election over both the ruling Cambodian People's Party (CPP), which controlled the state's security forces, and the Khmer Rouge, which retained a significant military capacity. Many voters regarded FUNCINPEC as the party best positioned to settle with the Khmer Rouge and rejected the brutal and violent behavior of the ruling CPP during the election campaign. The CPP campaign suggested that FUNCINPEC was in league with the Khmer Rouge, and since many Cambodians believed that a deal with the Khmer Rouge was necessary for peace, they voted for FUNCINPEC.[27] In Cambodia many voters believed that a vote for FUNCINPEC would lead to an accommodation with the Khmer Rouge and an end to the armed conflict, thereby making a vote for FUNCINPEC a vote for peace.

In El Salvador and Mozambique, more successful processes to demilitarize politics reduced the legacy of fear and put in place institutions that could better sustain peace and democracy. Relatively strong interim regimes, consultative processes to manage the challenges of implementation and electoral administration, and successful programs to transform militias into political parties established a new institutional context that served to bridge the conditions of war to those of peace and democratization. In Mozambique, some voters engaged in tactical voting to balance the two powerful parties by selecting the ruling Frelimo candidate as president while choosing the opposition Renamo candidates for the parliament.[28] Salvadoran voters made their selection on the basis of policy preferences, with less concern that the outcome would reignite conflict, although some voters reportedly voted against the Farabundo Marti National Liberation Front (FMLN) due to their involvement in the war.[29] In both cases, the ruling party won the elections, but the opposition won significant representation and completed the transition from insurgency to loyal opposition, operating within a rough but reasonably effective democratic system.

The results in these recent cases suggest that unless politics have been demilitarized, postconflict elections may best be characterized as referendums on peace in contexts where legacies of fear and violence dominate voters' concerns. For elections to be fully meaningful, however, they must give voters a significant choice. In many of these cases, voters understood their choice to be war or peace in the hands of a nationalistic military leader, an unenviable range of options. To the extent that the transitional period of peace implementation prior to the elections can demilitarize politics and build confidence that a return to war is unlikely (as in El Salvador and Mozambique), then a greater range of choice and elections that can better promote democracy is possible.

Interim Institutions and Demilitarizing Politics

The implementation period leading to elections following extended civil war and state collapse can develop opportunities to build new institutions to sustain peace. To the extent that the structures of war can be weakened and a new institutional framework can be created during the peace implementation phase, the prospects for postconflict elections that promote the reconstitution of the state and democratization are increased. While demilitarizing politics takes time, initial steps and precedents may be built into the transition in the shortterm and thereby channel the transition along a path toward sustainable peace and democratization. Three aspects of demilitarizing politics are particularly important for successful postconflict elections—the construction of effective interim administrations, the transformation of military organizations into effective political parties, and the creation of credible electoral authorities.

Interim Administration

Interim governments derive their authority from the extent to which they prepare the country for meaningful elections and turn power over to the winners.[30] In the meantime, however, the country needs to be governed. Critical and contentious policy decisions relating to peace implementation in general and the electoral framework and demilitarization in particular must be made and implemented. The process through which such policies are made will shape the expectations of the major actors and may either inspire confidence or ignite fears.

An agreement to end a protracted internal conflict following state collapse must include mechanisms to help sustain the agreement by managing disputes during the implementational process. The processes by which these conflicts are managed and by which policies are determined and executed will create the norms and institutional setting for elections. As argued by Holsti, peace agreements succeed or fail by their ability to "anticipate and devise means to cope with the issues of the future."[31] What makes peace implementation and state reconstruction so difficult is that it is a process of managing the transformation of multiple institutions simultaneously. A balance of power or some mechanism to maintain security must be preserved while each actor undergoes profound change at differing rates. New institutions that favor some organizations (such as political parties) more than others (such as militias) need to be created and protected from those who are likely to lose power. A peace settlement should not freeze a moment in history, particularly a moment distorted by the fears and insecurities of war. An agreement should provide structures and institutions that can evolve as increased security and confidence in the peace process allow power to shift away from militarized organizations and toward organizations capable of sustaining peace. As Doyle writes, "[S]uccessful contemporary peace building changes not merely behavior but, more important, it transforms identities and institutional context."[32]

Disputes are inevitable during the transition, as the broad (and often vague if not contradictory) principles listed in the peace agreement must be made operational in a difficult atmosphere characterized by fear and distrust. As suggested by analysts of security dilemmas in civil war termination, a key to a successful interim administration is to build institutional frameworks that bind the parties in self-restraint and mutual cooperation without increasing the risk of exploitation from a spoiler who does not comply.[33] Institutions based on joint decision making and consultations provide a framework for continuing cooperation and building a constituency that supports such cooperation. Parties engaged in such problem-solving institutions may develop a sense of partnership (even if only tentatively and tactically) and perceive a joint interest in managing risk and marginalizing extremists and spoilers within their own parties who desire to derail the peace process. A process of self-interested mutual adjustment of behavior may initiate a process of increased cooperation. In a number of cases, provisions for ongoing negotiations, bargaining, and collaborative problem solving during the implementation period have helped to build norms of nonviolent governance that foster confidence, legitimize decisions, and thereby reinforce the momentum for successful democratization.[34]

The period between the signing of an agreement and an election provides the context for testing and assessing the risks and benefits of cooperation and the intentions and commitments of each party. In many cases, parties to a conflict adopt the extreme rhetoric of total war during the conflict but shift their language and tactics (if not their goals) during the peace implementation process. During the period between the cease-fire and elections, each party will look for evidence to confirm its fears that its rival is cheating. Noncompliance, however, may be the result of fear or of a poorly designed or implemented demobilization or electoral process rather than a lack of commitment to the new rules of the game.[35] Many analysts doubted that Renamo in Mozambique could make the transition from a fighting organization (some characterized it as a bandit or terrorist organization) into a viable political party able to play a constructive role in a multiparty democracy. At the same time, many anticipated that UNITA in Angola had a solid base of support and could function successfully as a political party. Yet Renamo made this transformation while UNITA remained a military organization. It was only through the process of implementation that the capacity of each to contribute to peace and democratization became clear. Many observers expected Taylor to receive few votes in Liberia in 1997, given his record of human rights abuses, and wrongly predicted an opposition victory. It is worth recalling some of the pessimism of well-informed observers in advance of the South African transition. Horowitz described the "long-shot character of the democratic gamble in South Africa."[36] Ottaway spoke of "the gulf that separated the two sides" and concluded that in 1992 "the first phase of the transition process was over; it ended with no progress toward narrowing the gap between the two positions."[37]

The transitions in El Salvador and Mozambique illustrate how effective interim institutions based on joint decision making encourage transitions that advance both conflict resolution and democratization and may serve to promote the reconstruction of failed states. In El Salvador, the peace accords led to the creation of a National Commission for the Consolidation of Peace (COPAZ), a body with representation evenly split between the government and its allies and the opposition including the FMLN insurgents, with observer status for the United Nations and the Catholic Church. COPAZ debated and passed implementing legislation under the peace agreement, ranging from a new electoral law to constitutional amendments that redefined the role of the armed forces. Because the commission was evenly split between the government and the opposition, "hammering out compromises became a political necessity—and a newly acquired skill for many politicians."[38] When problems arose over the electoral system, over delays in reforming the police, or when an FMLN arms cache was uncovered after the deadline for disarmament, COPAZ was able to keep the parties talking and to keep the process moving toward elections. The parties came to recognize that while the transition was uncertain, at least the interim institutions in which they had an effective voice were managing their fears of losing everything.

In Mozambique, the "the construction of a lasting peace . . . required still more negotiation and planning," following the Rome Accord.[39] Joint decision-making bodies such as the Supervisory and Monitoring Commission (CSC) and the Cease-Fire Commission (CCF) brought together the major political actors with the major donors in a consultative process chaired by Aldo Ajello, a resourceful special representative of the UN secretary-general. Other specialized joint commissions dealt with reintegration of ex-combatants, reform of the Mozambican defense forces, and preparations for an election.[40] These interim institutions created the context for overcoming some of the legacies of the civil war and thereby promoted the demilitarization of politics. In both El Salvador and Mozambique, the international community supported these transitional arrangements through effective United Nations operations. The contribution, however, was not in the form of international guarantees but rather in support of joint decision-making institutions that encouraged transparency, confidence building, and a sense of security.

For Cambodia, the Paris Agreement established a complicated set of overlapping institutions to administer the country during the peace implementation period. The four Cambodian parties formed a Supreme National Council (SNC) that was designed to work with both an expansive United Nations Transitional Authority in Cambodia (UNTAC) and the incumbent bureaucracy. When the SNC could not reach an agreement by consensus, Prince Sihanouk had the authority to give advice to UNTAC and UNTAC had the authority to act. In addition, the United Nations special representative acted as the final arbiter regarding whether SNC decisions adhered to the Paris Agreement. Representatives of the permanent members of the UN Security Council and a number of other interested states and donors also had resources and authority. Some of the most important consultations were undertaken by Prince Sihanouk, who had the charisma and traditional authority to call the Cambodian parties together and mediate disputes. This set of institutions therefore contained a number of checks and balances, incentives for collaboration, and opportunities for a wide range of opinions to be heard. Doyle describes this arrangement as an "ad hoc, semi-sovereign artificial body." Decision making was cumbersome and slow but regular consultations among this "circle of authority" helped to manage unilateral actions that may have threatened any party.[41]

Angola, Liberia, Bosnia-Herzegovina, and Tajikistan, in contrast, demonstrate how weak and ineffective transitional institutions failed to build the confidence or norms to establish a new path toward democracy. Under the 1991 Bicesse Accords in Angola, pro forma meetings among the parties within the Joint Political-Military Commission (CCPM) did not act to change behavior and may have created a false sense of confidence in the parties' commitment to the agreement.[42] In December 1991, nine months before the elections, President dos Santos stated that the CCPM was not capable "of resolving the problems the country is facing today within the framework of pacification and national democratization."[43] Demobilization failed, the military structures remained in place at the time of the elections, and war resumed immediately after the vote.

Under the Yamoussoukro, Cotonou, and Abuja agreements for Liberia, interim administrative responsibilities were parceled out to each of the factions with only a weak and generally stalemated Council of State, which was assigned the impossible job of coordination. The dysfunctional interim government and a failed demobilization process created a context in which most voters feared a return to war unless the most powerful military faction won. Under the Dayton Accords in Bosnia-Herzegovina, a Joint Interim Commission that included the prime ministers of Bosnia-Herzegovina, the Bosnian-Croatian Federation, and the Serbian Republika Srpska met regularly, with the UN High Representative as the chair. The commission discussed a broad range of issues, but each entity responded to an autonomous and contradictory set of political dynamics based on the institutions of the three entities, making cooperation difficult. Each party continued to pursue unilateral advantage, thereby preventing effective forms of joint decision making and forcing the United Nations to act unilaterally on a number of contentious decisions. The Tajikistan transition was managed by the Commission on National Reconciliation (CNR), which included both the government and the United Tajik Opposition umbrella group. Tajik parties had experience in bargaining and dialogue, derived in part from their experience in monitoring the 1994 Tehran cease-fire and from their involvement in the Track 2 Tajikistan Dialogue. But the CNR struggled to contain forces outside the framework of the agreement and failed to settle the question of the secular nature of the regime.[44]

Interim institutions responsible for administration during the period between a cease-fire agreement and elections therefore have an opportunity to begin the process of demilitarizing politics. In El Salvador, Mozambique, and Cambodia, interim administrations helped to create the context for successful elections, while in Liberia, Bosnia-Herzegovina, Angola, and Tajikistan, weak interim governments left the structures of war in place and failed to alleviate the legacies of fear prior to elections. To the extent that transitional regimes operate on the basis of joint decision making and collaborative problem solving, and create norms that protect the interests of key constituencies, they can build confidence in the peace process and provide an institutional context that encourages successful elections. Effective interim regimes will be better positioned to promote demilitarization of politics, particularly with regard to the development of democratic institutions such as political parties and electoral administrations.

Electoral Commissions

One of the key tasks of an interim administration is to conduct the postconflict elections. Electoral commissions therefore assume particular prominence and are often a key arena for the development of trust. Commissions to organize and manage postconflict elections combine functions relating both to conflict resolution and democratization. The primary purpose of any electoral administrative body is to deliver credible election services to the candidates and voters.[45] Issues relating to impartiality and independence, efficiency, professionalism, and transparency are particularly important in the context of suspicion and mistrust that characterize postconflict elections. The inherent tensions among administrative efficiency, political neutrality, and public accountability make electoral governance contentious. An electoral commission must create procedural certainty and reliability in order to create substantive uncertainty of outcomes and hence legitimacy.[46] Furthermore, the precedents established in a postconflict election—as in any "breakthrough" or "founding" election in a process of democratization—are likely to shape popular perceptions for years to come. Yet another challenge to postconflict electoral authorities are the memories of earlier electoral fraud, as in El Salvador and Liberia. In cases where a stolen election was a cause of a conflict, the character of the postconflict election will be watched closely.

There is no single best model for electoral commissions, and international practice is diverse.[47] In a number of postconflict cases, an international organization has played an important role in electoral administration as a means to increase public confidence in the process. The United Nations played a major role in Cambodia and Mozambique, a smaller but critical role in El Salvador, and a lesser role in Angola and Tajikistan. The Organization for Security and Cooperation in Europe supervised elections in Bosnia-Herzegovina and the Economic Community of West African States had oversight along with the UN in Liberia. All of these postconflict elections had international observers, from international organizations and nongovernmental organizations, as well as domestic observers.[48]

Mozambique provides an example that demonstrates that the manner by which disputes relating to electoral administration are managed can provide the context for building new institutions and developing norms that promote the demilitarization of politics. The Rome Accords left many issues relating to the elections vague and subject to decisions made by the parties through the Commission for Supervision and Control. A series of controversies between Renamo and Frelimo over the composition of the National Elections Commission (CNE) threatened to derail the peace process and forced the postponement of the election. Both parties used the issue of the CNE to test each other's commitment and intentions and to see if the interim institutions could protect their most important interests.

After a series of discussions and with the active involvement of the UN special representative, the parties reached an agreement on the composition of the CNE. Frelimo received ten seats, Renamo seven, and other political parties three. The partisan balance made decision making difficult but increased the confidence of each party in the process. Over time and under the leadership of the Brazão Mazula, its independent chair, the CNE developed a reputation for nonpartisan decision making.[49] Unlike the Cease-Fire Commission and other commissions that included international actors along with representatives of the parties, the CNE was an independent and wholly Mozambican organization. The presence of UN technical advisers working within the Technical Secretariat, however, provided the parties with additional confidence in the process.[50]

El Salvador demonstrates that a consultative interim administration and other components that demilitarize politics can counterbalance the distrust created by a weak electoral administration. The peace agreement in El Salvador created a new electoral commission, the Supreme Electoral Tribunal (TSE) composed of representatives from five political parties, including the leftist Democratic Convergence (CD), but partisanship, "institutionalized distrust," and incompetence created gridlock, a crisis over voter registration, and chaos on election day.[51] A multiparty Board of Vigilance that had oversight over the tribunal alleviated some of the suspicion toward the TSE.[52] Despite these concerns, the presence of COPAZ and greater success on demobilization and creation of political parties resulted in a successful process of demilitarization of politics.

Political Parties

It is extremely difficult for militias and other militarized institutions that derived their power from the conflict to play the role of competing political parties in a democratic system if they remain organized and are led as they were during the period of armed conflict.[53] In the more successful cases of transition, processes to demilitarize politics encouraged military organizations to transform themselves into political parties able to operate effectively in a multiparty context. In the less successful or failed cases, militias retained the ability to operate as military forces, weakening the capacity of post-conflict elections to mark a transition to civilian rule.

In El Salvador, one of the keys to the success of the postconflict elections was the insurgent FMLN's ability to convert itself successfully into a legal political party capable of winning significant votes.[54] As the election neared, the interim institutions provided the context and incentives for the FMLN to focus its resources on creating a national network of party workers and building alliances with other parties on the left. The United Nations called the FMLN's transformation "the very core of the Peace Accords."[55] At the same time as the FMLN was moving away from its origins as a militarized insurgent movement, the incumbent Alianza Republicana Nacionalieta (ARENA) party shifted its base of support. Initially founded by individuals closely associated with the repression of the left, it evolved into an effective political party that represented a broad range of landowners, bankers, merchants, and industrialists. Leadership of ARENA shifted from Roberto D'Aubuisson, who had ties to right-wing death squads, to the more moderate, pro-business, Alfredo Cristiani.[56] Postconflict elections in El Salvador therefore provided the context for two key organizations involved in the civil war to make the transformation from warring factions into political organizations able to compete effectively in elections.

In Mozambique, the international community recognized that building Renamo into a viable partner in the peace process was a condition for successful peace implementation.[57] UN Special Representative Ajello stated that "it was necessary to help Renamo to achieve a minimum level that could allow the functioning of the whole mechanism" of the peace agreement.[58] Renamo insisted that there could be "no democracy without money," and Ajello agreed: "Democracy has a cost and we must pay that cost."[59] After initial concerns from donors reluctant to fund a party that had a particularly brutal reputation, a $19 million fund was established to help Renamo transform itself into a political party. In addition to financial inducements, the international community worked to "socialize Renamo into the rules of democratic competition, and to make its legitimacy contingent on fulfilling its commitment to peace."[60]

In Cambodia, the Royalist FUNCINPEC developed during the transition into a relatively effective political party with a grassroots base, while the incumbent CPP continued to behave as it had when it was the sole legal party and the Khmer Rouge continued to operate as a guerrilla movement.[61] In Angola, before 2002, neither the ruling MPLA nor the insurgent UNITA made the transformation from a military organization to a competitive political party. In Liberia, the skill and ease by which the National Patriotic Front for Liberia transformed itself from an insurgent military organization into the populist National Patriotic Party suggests that some skills and structures developed during an armed struggle can occasionally be used to create an effective political organization.[62] The other main Liberian military factions, however, failed to demonstrate an ability to remain viable actors in electoral competition.

The creation of political parties able to represent key constituencies and compete effectively in an electoral process is an important component of any democratic transition. In a transition following state collapse and civil war, the viability of political parties plays an additional role with relation to war termination. To the extent that powerful military leaders and their followers perceive that they have the option to operate as a political party rather than as a militia or military government, the chances of a successful transition are increased. Demilitarizing politics through the transformation of militias into political parties therefore promotes both war termination and democratization.

The period between the signing of a cease-fire agreement and the implementation of the settlement through elections therefore provides a number of opportunities to demilitarize politics and increases the chances that the voting process will serve to advance the goals of peace building and democratization. Strong interim institutions that establish patterns and norms of bargaining and collaboration, the precedents and habits put in place in the establishment of electoral administrations, and the opportunity to encourage the transformation of militias and militarized organizations into political parties, can begin to demilitarize politics and increase the opportunity for postconflict elections to advance both peace building and democratization.

Initial Conditions and Opportunities

A number of scholars of comparative peace processes have focused on how a variety of conditions shape the opportunities for successful implementation. Stedman, for example, argues that multiple parties to the conflict, the potential for a party to act as a spoiler, and the availability of "lootable" resources, such as diamonds, are the variables that most often are present in cases of failed implementation.[63] Berdal and Malone, among others, have developed a set of arguments relating to how certain types of resources (such as diamonds and remittances from diasporas) provide the resource stream necessary for parties to sustain their conflicts.[64] Others have noted the effect of neighbors and the importance of a supportive regional environment for successful peace implementation.[65] Walter argues that international "guarantees" and the presence of an appropriate international peace implementation force are the most important variables differentiating successful from unsuccessful cases. She argues that "if an outside state or international organization is not willing or able to provide such guarantees, the warring factions will reject a negotiated settlement and continue their war."[66]

Focusing on the conditions that shape the prospects for successful implementation provides insights into the often difficult context following state failure and civil war. The availability of resources to sustain the conflict in Angola, the multiple parties in Bosnia-Herzegovina, the absence of an appropriate international implementation force in Liberia, and the destabilizing region around Tajikistan undoubtedly made postconflict political reconstruction more challenging. At the same time, the lack of resources to sustain conflict after the Cold War, supportive regional environments, and relatively strong UN peace operations all promoted successful implementation in El Salvador and Mozambique. This chapter, however, explores a related but separate question of how variations within the transitional process itself provide additional opportunities for successful peace building. Regardless of the structures in place at the time of the cease-fire, a transition from war to peace is inherently fraught with uncertainty and risk. How a given peace implementation process is managed can shape how opportunities are constructed and whether they are seized or missed. The transition from war to peace, like a transition from authoritarian to democratic rule, is inherently a process of "institutionalizing uncertainty."[67]

An indication of the high levels of uncertainty is the difficulty in making a priori assessments regarding outcomes. It is generally difficult to judge in advance whether a given peace process is a strong candidate to end in a successful transition or doomed to fail. Some may suggest that the parties' character, commitment, or "political will" will determine whether the agreement is implemented. Ascertaining commitment in advance, however, is difficult. Furthermore, any party to a protracted civil conflict will weigh the dangers and opportunities in a peace process continuously and not surrender the option to return to war if necessary to protect its survival. The question then is not a given party's inherent nature or the honesty of its leadership but the manner by which the implementation process can build confidence in the peace process and increase momentum toward a sustainable settlement.[68]

Some argue that a flawed agreement explains the failure of implementation and they urge greater attention to the challenges of postconflict peace building during negotiations. Negotiated agreements to end internal wars, however, are by their nature imperfect documents. The settlements, signed under pressure to reach a cease-fire and end humanitarian suffering, generally include what they can, leave out what cannot be settled, and gloss over differences in an effort to stop the killing. Many peace agreements represent "the maximum compromise that could be achieved when they were being negotiated" and are at best the imperfect first steps in a process of peace building.[69] Mediators may emphasize best-case scenarios (or even engage in wishful thinking) to convince nervous parties to accept the risks of laying down their arms and pursuing their objectives nonviolently.

It is important to understand how developments during the period between the signing of the peace agreement and elections leading to a new government shape outcomes, and not to restrict our focus to the conditions in place at the time of the signing. A weak peace agreement may still provide new opportunities and alter the political calculations of parties previously engaged in conflict. As Rothstein explains, peace agreements often do not create peace but, rather, create "a new set of opportunities that can [either] be grasped or thrown away."[70] Hampson speaks of "nurturing" peace agreements and encouraging them to strengthen and grow from their initial, imperfect state.[71] El Salvador, Mozambique, and, to an extent, Cambodia had more auspicious initial conditions but still required skillful implementation to demilitarize politics successfully and create the supportive institutions and norms for an effective postconflict election.

Rather than relying on guarantees in the form of provisions to the peace agreement or international promises, actors in a postconflict transition will examine and draw their conclusions from the patterns, precedents, and institutions developed during the interim period. The ability of these transitional arrangements to build confidence and shape expectations will play a more important part in overcoming the security dilemmas and commitment problems than formal guarantees. The period between the signing of a peace agreement and the culmination of the transition in elections is therefore a critical time of testing during which each party's expectations of the behavior of the others and the viability of institutions and norms created during the transition will be shaped. It is on these expectations that decisions relating to compliance with the electoral process will be made.

Timing, Power-Sharing Pacts, and Electoral Systems

Given the many ways in which fear and insecurity distort electoral processes in the context of postconflict elections, a number of analysts have urged longer transitional periods, power-sharing pacts, and special electoral rules to help manage these challenges. Focusing on elections in the extremely difficult cases following state failure and civil war, however, suggests that these policy tools are not likely to play a decisive role in determining success or failure of the initial postconflict election. Pacts, power-sharing, and electoral rules require a degree of confidence in the process that often is lacking in these cases. If politics have not been demilitarized—thereby providing no opportunity for confidence building and the construction of an effective set of institutions—additional time, pacts, or electoral systems are unlikely to be sufficient to overcome the legacies of fear.

Timing

The timing of postconflict elections shapes their capacity to promote the dual goals of war termination and democratization. In some cases, the pace of implementation may be different for the two distinct challenges. Democratization requires time and will be encouraged by a slower pace that places elections at the end of a sequence of events such as demilitarization, repatriation of refugees and displaced persons, and rebuilding the basis of a functioning state. Many have suggested that postconflict elections in a context where demilitarization is incomplete, and other supporting conditions are not present, are "an exceptionally risky venture."[72]

War termination, however, may require a more rapid tempo to obtain the consent of the warring parties, to build momentum from a cease-fire, and to assure sufficient participation by international peacekeepers and funders. Rothstein notes this tension and states that "measures such as phased implementation, close supervision of terms (or high initial standards), starting with small pilot projects, and clear and powerful sanctions for violations are perfectly sensible and may succeed in diminishing the risk of catastrophic, worst-case outcomes; but they may also delay the achievement of the kind of rapid, substantive benefits that are necessary to build support for an agreement and to avoid a rapid descent into disillusionment and bitterness."[73]

Waiting too long may lead to the collapse of the peace process and a return to war. Policies relating to demilitarization, repatriation, human rights, and reconstruction—and indeed, democratization—may need to be delayed until after the peace agreement has been implemented and the fighting ended.

In a number of cases, postponing elections and extending the transition was impossible because of the nature of the conflict, the continuing belief of one or more parties that they could win militarily, the ineffectiveness of the interim regime, and the lack of political will and resources from the international community to support a more drawn out transition. Such circumstances compel quick elections. Delaying an election may risk the breakdown of the cease-fire or the withdrawal of peacekeeping forces. To insist that postconflict elections should not be held until the enabling environment of democratization is in place may risk missing an opportunity to assist war termination and thereby lead the country back into conflict. In such cases, the postconflict elections may advance the war termination goal but are unlikely to contribute in a significant way to the goal of democratization.

In several cases it seems likely that additional time would have threatened to derail the peace process rather than improve the prospects for a more democratic outcome. In Angola, a longer transition that did not change the fundamental flaws of the peace implementation or construct a strategy to contain Savimbi's threat as a spoiler most likely would not have changed the outcome.[74] The shortcomings in the Bosnian election were tied fundamentally to the Dayton Accords and international policy and also would not have changed substantially by delay.[75] In Liberia, the dysfunctional nature of the interim institutions and the unwillingness of the regional peacekeepers or the broader international community to support a longer transition made holding elections quickly after the cease-fire imperative. While some analysts suggested that the quick elections favored Taylor, his superior resources gave him the ability to hold his political organization together over a longer period of time than his rivals, suggesting that he would have won a postponed election, as well. In any event, it is at least highly uncertain that later elections in these difficult postconflict cases would have made a democratic outcome more likely unless politics had been demilitarized during the additional time.

Power-Sharing Pacts

Some of the literature on political transitions suggests that the best way to manage conflicts in the context of breakthrough elections is to negotiate power-sharing arrangements or political "pacts" to construct broad coalitions. Political pacts are a set of negotiated compromises among competing elites prior to elections that distribute power and thereby reduce uncertainty.[76] A number of transitions in Latin America, the Round Table talks in Poland, and the Convention for a Democratic South Africa process were organized around implicit or explicit agreements designed to provide powerful actors with sufficient guarantees so that they would accept the coming change.

Pacts, however, ultimately rely upon other mechanisms for enforcement and do not by themselves end uncertainty or resolve the difficulty in making credible commitments.[77] The strategic problems in reaching the initial cease-fire (information failures, inability to make credible commitments, spoiler problems, and security dilemmas) will recur in the pact-making negotiations. Pacts are more likely among elites with relatively clear and loyal constituencies, such as traditional political parties, labor unions, or other institutions in a corporatist setting. In the aftermath of a civil war and state failure, such political and social organizations generally are absent and the ability of militia leaders to deliver the compliance even of their own fighters is often a question. In addition, the polarization and extreme distrust arising from the conflict will make such pacts more difficult, if not impossible, to negotiate. Finally, the ability to assess the political strength of a military faction is difficult, and the identity of the critical constituencies to include in a pact is unclear immediately following a conflict. Even if the military balance among factions is relatively clear (as indicated by a stalemate on the battlefield), the relative political power of these factions and the extent to which they are capable of representing significant civilian constituencies in peacetime may be unknown.[78]

In Liberia, for example, the principle behind the negotiating process that culminated in the Abuja Accord was that each faction had an equal number of representatives in the transitional government. Without any mechanism to assess relative strengths, it was difficult to construct any alternative power-sharing arrangement. Following the 1997 elections, however, it became clear that only Taylor's National Patriotic Party represented significant political power and that the other factions were marginal political players.[79] The ability to assess the relative strengths of parties and thereby create a formula for a power-sharing pact prior to elections is inherently difficult. Many observers expected UNITA to win the Angolan elections in 1992 and many others were surprised by the ability of Renamo in Mozambique, FUNCINPEC in Cambodia, and the FMLN in El Salvador to win significant numbers of votes. It is notable that the best examples of power-sharing pacts took place *after* postconflict elections, when the relative political power of the parties was clearer. In Nicaragua, the Sandinistas negotiated control over the military and in Cambodia the CPP forced a power-sharing arrangement following the elections—when relative political power was more apparent.

In addition, putting pressure on parties to negotiate a power-sharing pact prior to elections may put the peace agreement and cease-fire at risk. Parties often accept a cease-fire and agree to hold elections in the expectation that they will win the vote and gain power. Such parties will resist additional constraints, preferring to compete in a winner-take-all election. The Carter Center tried to engage Taylor in discussions of postelection power-sharing in Liberia, but Taylor (correctly) believed that such an agreement would limit his power after he won the elections. To have insisted that Taylor accept a power-sharing pact would have placed the cease-fire and the rest of the peace process at risk. Furthermore, most Liberian citizens also opposed power-sharing pacts. The continuing violence that occurred under the twelve previous peace agreements, which had established interim governments based on power-sharing, left many Liberians convinced that a return to "normal" government with a single president was better than another set of weak and divided interim institutions.

In Angola and Mozambique as well, the international community, inspired by the success in South Africa, pressed the parties to agree to a government of national unity. The parties to the conflict, however, refused to accept such limits, anticipating that they would achieve more power through winner-take-all elections. Dennis Jett, the U.S. ambassador to Mozambique, urged the parties to accept a postelection power-sharing pact. But "the government-owned press, and even the independent media, vehemently condemned any such notion."[80] Even when a powerful international implementational force compelled power-sharing in Bosnia-Herzegovina, parties to that conflict simply refused to cooperate in the establishment of the new multiethnic and inter-entity institutions.[81] In the difficult circumstances following state collapse, negotiating a power-sharing pact, while desirable, is likely to be impossible without placing the entire peace process at risk.

Electoral Systems

There is a substantial body of literature that analyzes the influence of electoral system choice on the potential for conflict.[82] A recent study by Sisk and Reynolds concludes that "electoral systems—the rules and procedures under which votes are translated into seats in parliament or the selection of executives—are a critical variable in determining whether elections can simultaneously serve the purposes of democratization and conflict management."[83] The electoral rules of the game will shape the strategic decision making of key leaders, convincing some that accepting democratic competition is the best way to assure at least a voice in policy-making. Proportional representation systems are generally regarded as more suitable for societies that are divided because they more often create broad, inclusive governments. Other schemes designed to overcome social cleavages involve various types of vote pooling and federalism.[84] Some advocate consociational systems that emphasize accommodation by ethnic group leaders at the political center combined with guarantees for group autonomy and minority rights (as in Lebanon and Bosnia).[85] Others promote integrative power-sharing arrangements that are designed to encourage cross-ethnic alliances (as in South Africa).[86]

As with power-sharing pacts, however, electoral systems generally fail to overcome the security dilemmas and fears that drive transitions following state failure and civil war. The same inability to make credible commitments that trouble the demobilization process and other security dimensions of the transition will make agreements to limit power through electoral rules unpersuasive to parties who fear elimination by their rivals. Decisions regarding the choice of electoral system are not trivial but are unlikely to provide sufficient leverage to convince parties to cooperate in peace building unless politics has been demilitarized. Recently warring factions are more likely to concentrate on short-term issues relating to their survival in the first postconflict election rather than on a longer-term agenda of political participation. Processes relating to the security dimensions and the construction of new norms and institutions that foster mutual restraint are more likely to shape the strategic decisions of ex-combatants. As Reilly and Reynolds state, "while electoral systems can be powerful levers for shaping the content and practice of politics in divided societies, their design is highly sensitive to context."[87] The context following state failure and civil war will lead parties to emphasize short-term security issues rather than the long-term advantages of different electoral systems.

It is difficult to imagine what type of electoral system or separation of powers would increase the attractiveness of a postconflict election to some competing parties in the immediate aftermath of civil war. Stedman has argued that "Savimbi and UNITA received more from the Angolan settlement than any of the losing parties in El Salvador, Mozambique, Nicaragua, and Zimbabwe received in theirs."[88] Yet Savimbi defected from the agreement after losing the election. The political and economic structures of many postconflict states are such that even an offer of local or regional leadership positions is unlikely to be sufficient to a party that lost the election for national leadership. Most resources, and international aid in particular, flow through the capital and are under the control of the executive, making the position of regional governor or mayor a weak power base. Renamo decided not to compete in the 1998 local elections in Mozambique in part because it perceived that such posts were unimportant and subject to budget allocations under the control of their rivals in Maputo.[89] Seats in a parliament, or even cabinet positions, meant little to the opposition in Liberia, given the strong presidential system enshrined in the Liberian constitution.

While electoral system choice is likely to have less of an impact on postconflict elections following state collapse than the degree to which institutions have been created to manage the legacies of fear and create a more secure context, initial decisions on electoral system design will have a lasting impact. As with any other set of institutions, the early decisions regarding electoral system and constitutional design will channel subsequent political developments along a given path. While many analysts conclude that proportional representation systems (PR) are more likely to create a broad-based, coalition government, and will therefore decrease the chances of later conflict, others argue that other considerations, such as representativeness and the linkage between a given legislator and a specific constituency, argue for single-member districts.[90] PR systems generally support democratic transition by favoring inclusiveness and transparency, but may not be as effective in encouraging democratic consolidation where single-member districts reinforce accountability and responsiveness.[91]

Conclusion

Postconflict elections can serve as a mechanism to demilitarize politics and transform the institutions of war that characterized the period of state failure into new political and social structures capable of sustaining peace and beginning the process of state reconstitution. In El Salvador, Mozambique, and, to a more limited extent, in Cambodia, relatively effective interim regimes based upon broad consultation and joint decision making created precedents and new institutions that set the stage for the rehabilitation of the state. Effective transitional authorities require resources and capacity, but what is particularly important in a postconflict context are the processes by which decisions are made and the degree to which these processes overcome the security dilemmas, build confidence, and manage fears. In the aforementioned countries, the transformation of militias into political parties and the creation of credible electoral commissions helped diminish the pervasive distrust among the ex-combatants and put in place the fledgling institutions of a democratic political order. In other cases, however, including Angola, Liberia, Bosnia-Herzegovina, and Tajikistan, the transitional period contributed little to the demilitarization of politics. Weak interim regimes failed to institutionalize consultation and joint decision making, thereby leaving in place the legacies of fear. These transitions lacked effective processes to dismantle militias and create political parties, thereby leaving the structures of war in place at the time of the vote.

For the international community, the peace implementation process following state failure and internal war presents a number of opportunities to encourage peace and state reconstruction. First, leaders in major powers and international organizations should be clear on the multiple agendas postconflict elections are designed to advance. When goals relating to democratization and war termination clash, priority should be given to ending the conflict, since stability is a prerequisite for sustainable peace building and democratization. In the long run, democracy is a necessary ingredient in a process to reconstruct a failed state and to resolve internal conflict, but democratization is a process that needs peace to succeed. War termination precedes democratization both in sequence and in priority.

Second, greater emphasis should be placed on the processes that shape how the parties in the conflict relate to each other during the transition rather than to elements in the peace agreement or international policy. By emphasizing the internal dynamics among parties and institutions during the interim phase rather than power-sharing arrangements in the peace agreement or international guarantees, we shift our attention to incentives that support successful implementation. Rather than asking for additional provisions in the peace accord (a difficult challenge given the imperatives to negotiate a cease-fire), it is more useful to ask how the implementation process can overcome insecurity and strengthen patterns of cooperation and trust. Rather than placing responsibility on the international community to "guarantee" compliance, successful peace processes have developed institutions that create expectations among the parties to encourage them to abide by their agreement. The peace agreement becomes the starting point for another series of negotiations, bargaining, and institution building rather than a blue print to be enacted. The interim period will represent a fluid period during which parties and leadership change, expectations are formed, and the fears and interests that motivated the initial cease-fire agreement are transformed. The outcome of this period of continued bargaining and maneuvering for advantage provides the context for postconflict elections more than the initial agreement or the international community.

Third, to the extent that a process to demilitarize politics can be initiated, the precedents and institutional basis for sustained democratization can be supported. Donor support for strong and effective interim administrations, particularly those based on consultation and collaborative problem solving, can help to create a new institutional context that bridges the chasm from war to sustainable peace and democracy. In particular, donors and international organizations should examine electoral commissions and recognize them not only as opportunities to create organizations that can administer good elections but also as potential models for new forms of cooperation and peaceful competition. Finally, the transformation of militias into political parties has enormous potential to bolster both the war termination and democratization agendas of postconflict elections. The process of implementing peace and promoting democracy following state failure is difficult, but recent experience suggests that institutional transformation can—and must—begin during the transitional period.

Notes

The author would like to thank the United States Institute of Peace for its support. The author also thanks Robert I. Rotberg and the participants in the Failed States conferences along with Stephen Stedman, Donald Rothchild, I. William Zartman, Gilbert Khadiagala, and Agnieszka Paczynska for their comments.

1. Larry Garber, Senior Policy Adviser for Democracy and Human Rights, United States Agency for International Development, cited in Timothy D. Sisk, "Elections and Conflict Management in Africa: Conclusions and Recommendations," in Timothy D. Sisk and Andrew Reynolds (eds.), *Elections and Conflict Management in Africa* (Washington, D.C., 1998), 146. See also Christopher Clapham, "Rwanda: The Perils of Peacemaking," *Journal of Peace Research*, XXXV (1998), 195. In Ethiopia, U.S. officials warned the transitional government that Washington's policy toward the rebuilding state would be "no democracy, no co-

operation." See Terrence Lyons, "Closing the Transition: The May 1995 Elections in Ethiopia," *Journal of Modern African* Studies, XXXIV (1996), 121–142.

2. The literature on conflict resolution suggests that mediated settlements to end internal conflicts are rare and that most civil wars end in victory by one side and the surrender, if not destruction, of the other. Stephen John Stedman, *Peacemaking in Civil War: International Mediation in Zimbabwe, 1974–1980* (Boulder, 1991), 9; Roy Licklider, "The Consequences of Negotiated Settlements in Civil Wars, 1945–1993," *American Political Science Review*, LXXXIX (1995), 685–687.

3. These seven provide the primary cases analyzed in this essay. Each had a peace agreement that used elections as an instrument of implementation following a period of state collapse and civil war. In other cases, the peace process failed prior to elections, as in Rwanda and earlier efforts in Liberia, or elections were held in the context of civil war but without a peace agreement, as in Nicaragua and Sierra Leone (1996). In South Africa and Haiti the conflict did not reach the level of state collapse. In Namibia, East Timor, and Eritrea the conflict ended in national liberation and withdrawal. In Ethiopia, Uganda, and Rwanda elections were held to consolidate the power of the winning party to a conflict.

4. For a classic study, see Guillermo O'Donnell and Philippe C. Schmitter, *Transitions from Authoritarian Rule: Tentative Conclusions about Uncertain Democracies* (Baltimore, 1986).

5. Douglass North, *Institutions, Institutional Change, and Economic Performance* (Cambridge, 1990); Terry Lynn Karl, "Dilemmas of Democratization in Latin America," *Comparative Politics*, XXII (1990), 1–21.

6. Kathleen Thelen and Sven Steinmo, "Historical Institutionalism in Comparative Politics," in Thelen, Steinmo, and Frank Longstreth (eds.), *Structuring Politics: Historical Institutionalism in Comparative Analysis* (Cambridge, 1992), 1–32.

7. Juan J. Linz and Alfred Stepan, *Problems of Democratic Transition and Consolidation: Southern Europe, South America, and Post-Communist Europe* (Baltimore, 1996), 55.

8. Douglass C. North, "Privatization, Incentives, and Economic Performance," in Terry L. Anderson and Peter J. Hill (eds.), *The Privatization Process: A Worldwide Perspective* (Lanham, Md., 1996), 29.

9. Mats Berdal and David Malone (eds.), *Greed and Grievance: Economic Agendas in Civil Wars* (Boulder, 2000).

10. Krishna Kumar and Marina Ottaway, "General Conclusions and Priorities for Policy Research," in Krishna Kumar (ed.), *Post-conflict Elections, Democratization, and International Assistance* (Boulder, 1998), 231–237; Timothy D. Sisk and Andrew Reynolds, "Democratization, Elections, and Conflict Management in Africa: Exploring the Nexus," in Sisk and Reynolds (eds.), *Elections and Conflict Management in Africa*; Ben Reilly and Andrew Reynolds, *Electoral Systems and Conflict in Divided Societies* (Washington, D.C., 1999); Peter Harris and Ben Reilly (eds.), *Democracy and Deep-Rooted Conflict: Options for Negotiators* (Stockholm, 1998).

11. O'Donnell and Schmitter, *Transitions from Authoritarian Rule*, 57.

12. See James K. Boyce and Manuel Pastor, Jr., "Aid for Peace: Can International Financial Institutions Help Prevent Conflict?" *World Policy Journal*, XV (1998), 42–50.

13. For more on the multiple goals of postconflict elections see Terrence Lyons, "The Role of Postsettlement Elections," in Stephen John Stedman, Donald Rothchild, and Elizabeth M. Cousens (eds.), *Ending Civil Wars: The Implementation of Peace Agreements* (Boulder, 2002).

14. Terrence Lyons, *Voting for Peace: Post-conflict Elections in Liberia* (Washington, D.C., 1999).

15. Victor Tanner, "Liberia: Railroading Peace," *Review of African Political Economy*, XXV (1998), 140.

16. For example, anti-Taylor posters with pictures of the brutalities of the war and the caption "Chucky [Charles Taylor] did it" served to increase the levels of fear and raise anew concerns that the civilian candidates would not be able to prevent him from doing it again.

17. "Interview with Samuel Kofi Woods of Liberia," *African Affairs*, XCIX (2000), 107.

18. Stephen Ellis, *The Mask of Anarchy: The Destruction of Liberia and the Religious Dimensions of an African Civil War* (New York, 1999), 109. Such characterizations were featured in a number of press reports on the election. A Liberian was quoted as saying "He [Taylor] killed my father but I'll vote for him. He started all this and he's going to fix it." John Chiahemen, "Liberians Vote in Peace Against War," Reuters (19 July 1997). Another voter is quoted as saying, "Charles Taylor spoiled this country, so he's the best man to fix it." Donald G. McNeil, Jr., "Under Scrutiny, Postwar Liberia Goes to Polls," *New York Times* (20 July 1997).

19. International Crisis Group, *Elections in Bosnia and Herzegovina*, 22 September 1996.

20. Cited in Susan L. Woodward, "Bosnia and Herzegovina: How Not to End Civil War," in Barbara F. Walter and Jack Snyder (eds.), *Civil Wars, Insecurity, and Intervention* (New York, 1999), 96.

21. Joint List '97 did better in the local elections of September 1997. In Tuzla, Bosnia's second largest city, where multiethnic institutions protected minorities during the war, Mayor Selim Beslagic of the Joint List '97 defeated the SDA. See Bill Egbert, "A Noble Act of Harmony in the Balkans," *Christian Science Monitor* (9 October 1997).

22. Quoted in Stephen Buckley, "Ethiopia Takes New Ethnic Tack: Deliberately Divisive," *The Washington Post* (18 June 1995), A21.

23. Marina Ottaway, "Angola's Failed Elections," in Kumar, *Post-conflict Elections*. For an insider's view, see the account by the United Nations Special Representative Margaret Joan Anstee, *Orphan of the Cold War: The Inside Story of the Collapse of the Angolan Peace Process, 1992–3* (New York, 1996), 133–151.

24. Organization for Security and Cooperation in Europe, Office for Democratic Institutions and Human Rights, *The Republic of Tajikistan Elections to the Parliament, 27 February 2000: Final Report* (Warsaw, 17 May 2000).

25. Nasrin Dadmehr, "Tajikistan: Regionalism and Weakness," in Robert I. Rotberg (ed.), *State Failure and State Weakness in a Time of Terror* (Washington, D.C., 2003), 245–264.

26. International Crisis Group, *Central Asia: Crisis Conditions in Three States* (ICG Asia Report, 7 August 2000).

27. Judy Ledgerwood, "Patterns of CPP Political Repression and Violence During the UNTAC Period," in Steve Heder and Judy Ledgerwood (eds.), *Propaganda, Politics, and Violence in Cambodia: Democratic Transition under United Nations Peace-keeping* (Armonk, N.Y., 1996), 117, 130.

28. Alex Vines, *Renamo: From Terrorism to Democracy in Mozambique?* (London, 1996), 159.

29. Tommie Sue Montgomery, *Revolution in El Salvador: From Civil Strife to Civil Peace* (Boulder, 1995), 266.

30. Yossi Shain and Juan J. Linz, *Between States: Interim Governments and Democratic Transitions* (Cambridge, 1995), 3–21.

31. Kalevi Holsti, *Peace and War: Armed Conflict and International Order* (Cambridge, 1991), 353. See also Louis Kriesberg, *Constructive Conflicts: From Escalation to Resolution* (Lanham, Md., 1998), 322–323; Hampson, *Nurturing Peace*, 3.

32. Michael W. Doyle, "War and Peace in Cambodia," in Walter and Snyder (eds.), *Civil Wars, Insecurity, and Intervention*, 206.

33. On the security dilemma and applications to civil war settlement, see Robert Jervis, "Cooperation under the Security Dilemma," *World Politics*, XXX (1978), 167–213; Barry R. Posen, "The Security Dilemma and Ethnic Conflict," in Michael E. Brown (ed.), *Ethnic Conflict and International Security* (Princeton, 1993), 103–124; Stedman, "Negotiation and Mediation in Internal Conflict," 341–376; Stedman, "Spoiler Problems," 5–54; Barbara F. Walter, "The Critical Barrier to Civil War Settlement," *International Organization*, LI (1997), 335–364; Jack Snyder and Robert Jervis, "Civil War and the Security Dilemma," in Walter and Snyder (eds.), *Civil Wars, Insecurity, and Intervention*; Lake and Rothchild, "Containing Fear."

34. Donald Rothchild, "Bargaining and State Breakdown in Africa," *Nationalism and Ethnic Politics* I (1995), 54–72. See also Timothy D. Sisk, *Power-sharing and International Mediation in Ethnic Conflict* (Washington, D.C., 1996), 115, 85.

35. Stedman, "UN Intervention in Civil Wars," 57. See also Rui J. P. de Figueiredo, Jr., and Barry R. Weingast, "The Rationality of Fear: Political Opportunism and Ethnic Conflict," in Walter and Snyder, (eds.) *Civil Wars, Insecurity, and Intervention*, 261–302.

36. Donald Horowitz, *A Democratic South Africa? Constitutional Engineering in a Divided Society* (Berkeley, 1991), 263.

37. Marina Ottaway, *South Africa: The Struggle for a New Order* (Washington, D.C., 1993), 2.

38. Montgomery, *Revolution in El Salvador*, 233–234. Holiday and Stanley criticize COPAZ for its slow and cumbersome decision making, which compelled endless rounds of negotiations among parties. From the perspective of building new norms to demilitarize politics, such continuous discussion is a strong asset. See David Holiday and William Stanley, "Building the Peace: Preliminary Lessons from El Salvador," *Journal of International Affairs*, XLVI (1993), 427–429.

39. Richard Synge, *Mozambique: UN Peacekeeping in Action, 1992–1994* (Washington, D.C., 1997), 52.

40. J. Michael Turner, Sue Nelson, and Kimberly Mahling-Clark, "Mozambique's Vote for Democratic Governance," in Kumar (ed.), *Post-conflict Elections* 153–175.

41. Michael W. Doyle, "War and Peace in Cambodia," in Walter and Snyder (eds.), *Civil Wars, Insecurity, and Intervention*, 203, 205.

42. Anstee, *Orphan of the Cold War.*

43. Radio Nacional de Angola, 10 December 1991, cited in Keith Somerville, "The Failure of Democratic Reform in Angola and Zaire," *Survival*, XXXV (1993), 62.

44. Abdullaev and Barnes, *Politics of Compromise*; Dadmehr, "Tajikistan."

45. Peter Harris, "Building an Electoral Administration," in Harris and Reilly (eds.), *Democracy and Deep-Rooted Conflict*, 310; Robert A. Pastor, "The Role of Electoral Administration in Democratic Transitions: Implications for Policy and Research," *Democratization*, VI (1999 / 2000), 1–27. Yonhyok Choe and Staffan Darnolf, "Evaluating the Structure and Functional Role of Electoral Administration in Contemporary Democracies: Building 'Free and Fair Election Index (FEEI)' and 'Effective Election Index (EEI),' " paper presented at the ninety-fifth annual meeting of the American Political Science Association, Atlanta, Georgia, (2–5 September 1999); Jørgen Elklit and Andrew Reynolds, "The Impact of Election Administration on the Legitimacy of Emerging Democracies: A New Research Agenda," paper presented at the ninety-sixth annual meeting of the American Political Science Association, Washington, D.C., (31 August–3 September 2000).

46. Shaheen Mozaffar and Andreas Schedler, "The Comparative Study of Electoral Governance," *International Political Science Review*, XXIII (2002).

47. Guy S. Goodwin-Gill, *Free and Fair Elections in International Law* (Geneva, 1994).

48. Thomas Carothers, *Aiding Democracy Abroad: The Learning Curve* (Washington, D.C., 1999), 281–302.

49. When Renamo leader Afonso Dhlakama charged fraud and announced a boycott of the election, the Renamo representatives on the CNE joined their colleagues in rejecting it unanimously.

50. Turner, Nelson, and Mahling-Clark, "Mozambique's Vote for Democratic Governance."

51. Montgomery, Revolution in El Salvador, 248–259; *Report of the Secretary-General on the United Nations Observer Mission in El Salvador* S/26606 (New York, 20 October 1993).

52. Enrique A. Baloyra, "El Salvador: From Reactionary Despotism to Partidocracia," in Kumar, *Post-conflict Elections*, 21.

53. Ottaway makes a similar point with relation to national liberation movements. See Marina Ottaway, "Liberation Movements and Transition to Democracy: The Case of the A.N.C.," *Journal of Modern African Studies*, XXIX (1991), 61–82.

54. Gerardo L. Munck, "Beyond Electoralism in El Salvador: Conflict Resolution Through Negotiated Compromise," *Third World Quarterly*, XIV (1993), 87. Nongovernmental organizations allied with the FMLN went through a similar transformation. See Nicole Ball and Tammy Halevy, *Making Peace Work: The Role of the International Development Community* (Washington, D.C., 1996).

55. United Nations, *Further Report of the Secretary-General on the United Nations Observer Mission in El Salvador (ONUSAL)* S/26005 (New York, 29 June 1993), para. 11.

56. William Stanley, *The Protection Racket State: Elite Politics, Military Extortion, and Civil War in El Salvador* (Philadelphia, 1996), 220, 254–255. See also Sara Miles and Bob Ostertag, "D'Aubuisson's New ARENA," *NACLA Report on the Americas*, XXIII (1989), 14–38.

57. See the excellent study by Carrie Manning, "Constructing Opposition in Mozambique: Renamo as Political Party," *Journal of Southern African Studies*, XXIV (1998), 161–190. See also Donald Rothchild, *Managing Ethnic Conflict in Africa: Pressures and Incentives for Cooperation* (Washington, D.C., 1997).

58. Aldo Ajello, "O Papel da ONUMOZ no Processo de Democratização," in B. Mazula (ed.), *Moçambique: Eleições, Democracia e Desenvolvimento* (Maputo, Mozambique, 1995), 127; cited in Martinho Chachiua and Mark Malan, "Anomalies and Acquiescence: The Mozambican Peace Process Revisited," *African Security Review*, VII (1998), 22. See also *Report of the Secretary-General on ONUMOZ*, S/25518, 2 April 1993, para. 58.

59. Vines, *Renamo*, 146; "Mozambique: Funding for Peace," *Africa Confidential*, XXXIV (14 May 1993), 4.

60. Stedman, "Spoiler Problems in Peace Processes," 41.

61. Frieson, "The Politics of Getting the Vote in Cambodia."

62. In Lebanon a number of political parties, such as Kamal Junblat's Druze-based Progressive Socialist Party, proved adept at making the transformation from partisan politics to militia politics, suggesting that change in the other direction is also possible. Nazih Richani, *Dilemmas of Democracy and Political Parties in Sectarian Societies: The Case of the Progressive Socialist Party of Lebanon, 1949–1996* (New York, 1998), 91–94. See also Oren Barak, "Lebanon: Failure, Collapse, and Resuscitation," in Rotberg, *State Failure and State Weakness*, 305–340.

63. George Dawns and Stephen John Stedman, "Evaluation Issues in Peace Implementation," in Stedman, Cousens, and Rothchild (eds.), *Implementing Peace Agreements.*

64. Berdal and Malone, (eds.), *Greed and Grievance.*

65. Francis M. Deng, Sadikiel Kimaro, Terrence Lyons, Donald Rothchild, and I. William Zartman, *Sovereignty as Responsibility: Conflict Management in Africa* (Washington, D.C., 1996), 131–167; Peter Wallenstein and Margareta Sollenberg, "Armed Conflicts, Conflict Termination, and Peace Agreements, 1989–96," *Journal of Peace Research*, XXXIV (1997), 339–358.

66. Barbara F. Walter, "Designing Transitions from Civil War: Demobilization, Democratization, and Commitments to Peace," *International Security*, XXIV (1999), 139. See also Hampson, *Nurturing Peace.*

67. Adam Przeworski, "Some Problems in the Study of the Transition to Democracy," in Guillermo O'Donnell, Philippe C. Schmitter, and Laurence Whitehead (eds.), *Transitions from Authoritarian Rule: Comparative Perspectives* (Baltimore, 1986), 57, 58. See also Adam Przeworski, "Democracy as a Contingent Outcome of Conflicts," in Jon Elster and Rune Slagstad (eds.), *Constitutionalism and Democracy* (Cambridge, 1988), 62; O'Donnell and Schmitter, *Transitions from Authoritarian Rule*, 23.

68. Stephen John Stedman, "UN Intervention in Civil Wars: Imperatives of Choice and Strategy," in Donald C. F. Daniel and Bradd C. Hayes (eds.), *Beyond Traditional Peacekeeping* (New York, 1995), 40–63.

69. Vladimir Goryayev, "Architecture of International Involvement in the Tajik Peace Process," in Kamoludin Abdullaev and Catherine Barnes (eds.), *Politics of Compromise: The Tajikistan Peace Process* (London, 2001); online at www.c-r.org/accord/accord10/architecture.htm.

70. Robert L. Rothstein, "Fragile Peace and Its Aftermath," in Robert L. Rothstein (ed.), *After the Peace: Resistance and Reconciliation* (Boulder, 1999), 224.

71. Hampson, *Nurturing Peace*, 3.

72. Timothy D. Sisk and Andrew Reynolds, "Democratization, Elections, and Conflict Management in Africa" in Sisk and Reynolds (eds.), *Elections and Conflict Management in Africa*, 14; Krishna Kumar and Marina Ottaway, "General Conclusions and Priorities for Policy Research," in Kumar (ed.), *Post-conflict Elections*, 229–237.

73. Robert L. Rothstein, "Fragile Peace and Its Aftermath," in Robert L. Rothstein (ed.), *After the Peace: Resistance and Reconciliation* (Boulder, 1999), 225.

74. On the role of spoilers see Stephen John Stedman, "Spoiler Problems in Peace Processes," *International Security*, XXII (1997), 5.

75. Susan L. Woodward, "Statement to the Senate Foreign Relations Committee," Hearings on the Midterm Assessment of the Dayton Accords in Bosnia and Herzegovina (10 September 1996).

76. Karl, "Dilemmas of Democratization in Latin America," 1–21; O'Donnell and Schmitter, *Transitions from Authoritarian Rule*, 37–47; Frances Hagopian, "Democracy by Undemocratic Means? Elites, Political Pacts, and Regime Transition in Brazil," *Comparative Political Studies*, XXIII (1990), 147–170; Giuseppe Di Palma, *To Craft Democracies: An Essay on Democratic Transitions* (Berkeley, 1990), 86–90. See also Ottaway, "Democratization in Collapsed States," 235–249.

77. David A. Lake and Donald Rothchild, "Containing Fear: The Origins and Management of Ethnic Conflict," *International Security*, XXI (1996), 41–75; Adam Przeworski et al., *Sustainable Democracy* (Cambridge, 1995), 24–30.

78. J. 'Bayo Adekanye, "Power-Sharing in Multi-Ethnic Political Systems," *Security Dialogue*, XXIX (1998), 33.

79. Taylor received 75.3 percent of the total vote and a majority in every county while Kromah and Boley, his rival factional leaders, received only 4.0 percent and 1.3 percent of the vote, respectively, both concentrated in their ethnic heartlands. Militia leaders treated as equals in the negotiations leading to the peace agreement clearly were not equal when measured by their ability to win votes in an election. See Lyons, *Voting for Peace*, 76.

80. Dennis Coleman Jett, "Cementing Democracy: Institution-Building in Mozambique," *Harvard International Review*, XVII (1995), 24. Synge notes that "concerted efforts by members of the international community to force the government into forming a postelection pact with Renamo were unsuccessful." Synge, *Mozambique*, 116.

81. Susan L. Woodward, "Bosnia and Herzegovina: How Not to End Civil War," in Walter and Snyder (eds.), *Civil Wars, Insecurity, and Intervention*, 94.

82. Kenneth D. McRae, "Theories of Power-sharing and Conflict Management," in Joseph Montville (ed.), *Conflict and Peacemaking in Multiethnic Societies* (Lanham, Md., 1990). Classic studies include Arend Lijphart, "Consociational Democracy," *World Politics*, IV (1969), 207–225; Arend Lijphart, *Democracy in Plural Societies* (New Haven, 1977).

83. Sisk and Reynolds, "Democratization, Elections, and Conflict Management in Africa," 3–4. Reilly and Reynolds, *Electoral Systems and Conflict in Divided Societies*, similarly argue that "electoral systems can be powerful levers for shaping the content and practice of politics in divided societies" if the design is sensitive to context. See also Harris and Reilly, *Democracy and Deep-Rooted Conflict* (Stockholm, 1998); Arend Lijphart, "The Power-Sharing Approach," in Montville (ed.), *Conflict and Peacemaking in Multiethnic Societies*; Arend Lijphart, "Constitutional Choices for New Democracies," in Larry Diamond and Marc F. Plattner (eds.), *The Global Resurgence of Democracy* (Baltimore, 1993).

84. Donald Horowitz, *Ethnic Groups in Conflict* (Berkeley, 1985).

85. On consociationalism, see Arend Lijphart, *Democracy in Plural Societies* (New Haven, 1977).

86. Donald Horowitz, *Ethnic Groups in Conflict* (Berkeley, 1985); Timothy Sisk, *Power-sharing and International Mediation in Ethnic Conflicts* (Washington, D.C., 1995); Timothy Sisk, "Electoral System Choice in South Africa: Implications for Intergroup Moderation," *Nationalism and Ethnic Politics*, I (July 1995), 178–204.

87. Reilly and Reynolds, *Electoral Systems and Conflict in Divided Societies*, 1.

88. Stephen John Stedman, "Negotiations and Mediation in Internal Conflict," in Michael E. Brown (ed.), *The International Dimensions of Internal Conflict* (Cambridge, 1996), 370.

89. John Blacken and Terrence Lyons, *Mozambique: From Post-Conflict to Municipal Elections* (Washington, D.C., 1999).

90. Joel D. Barkan, "Rethinking the Applicability of Proportional Representation for Africa," in Sisk and Reynolds (eds.), *Elections and Conflict Management in Africa*.

91. Reilly and Reynolds, *Electoral Systems and Conflict in Divided Societies*, 29, 55.

Fourteen

Let Them Fail: State Failure in Theory and Practice

IMPLICATIONS FOR POLICY

JEFFREY HERBST

THE PHENOMENON of state failure is now, as this volume readily attests, a significant problem in several parts of Africa, and also a threat to some countries in central and southeast Asia. However, the international community—as demonstrated by the reverses in Liberia, Sierra Leone, and Somalia—has had a difficult time conceptualizing and implementing responses to profound state decline. Part of the analytical problem is that the post–World War II state system was extremely stable until the early 1990s, due to the adoption of only one unit (the nation-state) as the organizing principle, and to the extraordinary stability of most states. Indeed, between the end of the World War II and 1989, the only forcible boundary changes that were unrelated to the end of colonialism were the creation of Bangladesh, the annexation of the Golan Heights, and the absorption of South Vietnam.[1] However, the world is now beginning to return to the status quo ante, where a certain amount of state failure was normal and, to some degree, predictable.

This chapter reviews historical and current patterns of state failure in order to understand the magnitude of the problem. It concludes with a set of options about how the international community might react to current patterns of state failure. The chapter concentrates largely, but not exclusively, on Africa because that continent contains the most failed political organizations and it is where the international community has had the most trouble conceptualizing a different order.

The international community has had such difficulty coping with failed states in part because its legal blinders prevent it from recognizing the phenomenon. The standard international legal practice almost always equates sovereign power with control of the capital city. For instance, Mobutu Sese Seko was recognized as the ruler of Zaire even though he controlled little more than Kinshasa and its environs for the last years of his rule; he continued to be recognized as the leader while the forces of Laurent Kabila marched through the country in late 1996 and early 1997.

Kabila was only recognized as the legitimate ruler when he captured Kinshasa on 17 May 1997. International legal practice is inadequate for understanding the actual forces on the ground because it is almost always the case (Somalia is the major exception) that some force can claim control of the capital. However, control of outlying territory is often a very different matter. Indeed, as argued later, the current practice of equating control of the capital with control of the state is part of the failed state pathology.

State Failure in History

There is nothing novel about the phenomenon of state failure. For instance, Tilly estimates that the "enormous majority" of states in Europe after 1500 failed. Further, he notes, "The substantial majority of the units which got so far as to acquire a recognizable existence as states during those centuries [after 1500] still disappeared. And of the handful which survived or emerged into the nineteenth century as autonomous states, only a few operated effectively—regardless of what criterion we employ."[2] Tilly concludes by noting that this record of profound failure is not fully appreciated: "The disproportionate distribution of success and failure puts us in the unpleasant situation of dealing with an experience in which most of the cases are negative, while only the positive cases are well-documented."[3]

There were innumerable reasons why states in Europe failed after 1500: problems in the collection of taxation, the primitive nature of basic transport, shifting military balances, and the inability to overcome religious, ethnic, and national divisions. More generally, establishing a national political order over even relatively small distances is, as the chapter by Meierhenrich in this volume makes clear, a distinctly difficult task (a lesson largely forgotten today). The constant in the saga of European states was an extremely difficult external environment where neighbors were always a threat. Tilly notes that one of the central reasons for the creation of relatively centralized state apparatuses in Europe was the "continuous aggressive competition for trade and territory among changing states of unequal size, which made war a driving force in European history."[4] Even those states that survived frequently changed their makeup given the hostility of their environments. For instance, it took between 300 and 500 years for the modern French frontier to be established.[5] As a result, during the critical period of state formation (and disintegration) in Europe, there were both centrifugal and centripetal forces at work in terms of state design: states would fail and sometimes the subsequent unit would be larger (if a neighbor could take over) and sometimes a unit (e.g., the Austro-Hungarian empire) would implode and its constituent parts would attempt to rule themselves.

State failure continued throughout most of the twentieth century but with one critical departure from the historic European pattern: political units only became smaller.[6] Indeed, the history of the twentieth century was largely driven by the universal failure of a particular type of state organization: empire. Since 1900, the Austro-Hungarian, Belgian, British, Danish, Dutch, Ethiopian, French, German, Italian, Japanese, Ottoman, Portuguese, Russian, Soviet, and Spanish empires have all failed, leaving in their wake a large number of smaller states. As a result, the number of sovereign states has increased from roughly fifty-five at the start of the past century to 192 today.

Further, the failure of some of the states that were created out of the colonial empires is again largely an internal phenomenon. That is to say, political units in Africa, and some other parts of the world, are collapsing because of internal strains and not because their neighbors want formally to annex parts of their territories. While neighbors almost certainly do play a role in all failing states, the pattern of failure is overwhelmingly toward the devolution of power to actors controlling smaller pieces of territory. For instance, even though Nigeria was the most significant military force in Liberia for most of the 1990s, it did not want to annex Liberia, but to restore power to Monrovia. Similarly, South Africa under white rule was not interested in expanding its territory but only in destabilizing its neighbors to keep them from posing a potential threat. Indeed, the Iraqi invasion of Kuwait in 1990 was surprising not because a big country invaded a small, defenseless country (that would merely have been a repetition of a continual theme in world history) but because this sort of action occurs so seldom in a world where there are many small states that cannot defend their boundaries.

The Diminishing Value of Size

The direction of state failure in favor of ever-smaller units is a response to one of the fundamental developments of the past one-hundred years: the ever-diminishing relative value of land and what is underneath it. Countries do not become rich today by mining a vast hinterland or by dint of large labor forces. Rather, they become rich by possessing advanced manufacturing sectors that produce semiconductors and supertankers and have service sectors that write software and sell insurance to the world market. The most successful economies outside of Europe since World War II—Japan, Korea, and Taiwan—succeeded despite (or because) they had very little land and the territory that they possessed was notably bereft of natural resources. Their peculiarly poor resource endowment may actually have propelled these countries to success because their leaders knew (unlike Argentina or Australia) that they could not rely on their wealth in the ground but had to develop skilled labor forces and efficient manufacturing sectors.

The dominant economic strategy today furthermore centers on export-led growth, implying that the size of the domestic market is not nearly as important as previously thought. An export orientation is particularly attractive because the world economy is growing quickly, and developing countries have been successful in capturing an increasing share of manufactured exports. Put simply, if a country is producing for the world market, does the size of its domestic market matter?

Nowhere can the new attraction to smallness be seen than by the international rush to become "the next Hong Kong." Not surprisingly, given its success, Tallinn, Estonia, has repeatedly declared itself the "Hong Kong of the Baltics."[7] Similarly, Poland hopes to become the "Hong Kong of Central Europe"; El Salvador's ambition is to be the "Hong Kong of Central America"; Ciudad del Este, Paraguay, is often called the "Hong Kong of South America"; Ghana wants to become the "Hong Kong of Africa"; Jamaica's goal is to be the "Hong Kong of the Caribbean"; Crimea, in the Ukraine, thinks that it will be the next Hong Kong; while Vladivostok aims to be the "Hong Kong of Siberia."[8] Perhaps inevitably, the title of "Hong Kong of the Middle East" is contested: Dubai, Gaza, and Tel Aviv all hope to duplicate the performance of Britain's former colony.[9]

As a result, states are no longer compelled to expand their territorial reach to get rich. Indeed, expansion of the amount of formal territory under control for the leader who seeks to enrich himself, his colleagues, or his country appears to be a waste of time. Instead, for arguably the first time in world history, there is considerable attractiveness to being small; countries now produce for the world economy rather than for domestic markets. As a result, even states that can be easily conquered are no longer in danger because what they have is not worth fighting over. The threat to Sierra Leone comes from within, no outsider could be bothered to take it over. While much international commentary is devoted to the growing gap between rich and poor, significant developments in the international economy have made the world a safer place for the weak.

At the same time, what could be called the dark side of globalization further encourages subnational rulers who seek to rule something less than a national state. With the global liberalization of finance have come sophisticated systems that allow African warlords, corrupt leaders, and others to access capital. As Chabal and Daloz note, "African entrepreneurs are closely connected to an informal world economy which serves their purposes well. The instrumentalization of violence and crime at the local level readily finds international channels which make possible the trade on which wealth is built."[10] Reno has also demonstrated how, in certain cases, states can use their weakness as a commercial advantage: "For weak-state rulers, foreign firm partnerships are flexible, which gives rulers capabilities and access to resources they would otherwise find difficult to obtain. New foreign firm partners . . . permitted rulers to jettison threatening clients and bureaucracies and to rework relations with others on new terms."[11]

The reliance of leaders at the national or local level on the drug trade or on smuggling or the overexploitation of natural resources (e.g., timber, diamonds) are hardly developmental strategies. Trading narcotics to Ukrainian arms merchants for weapons is not a long-term substitute for a national army. Providing a safe haven for another dictator's stolen funds is not a substitute for building a banking system. However, the vast informal international economy provides new opportunities for leaders, who may in the past have had to foster development in their own country, to advance their interests and the interests of their constituency. Now, leaders at the national level or challengers at the subnational level may not be particularly interested in increasing the amount of territory that they formally control, because they can survive and enrich themselves on an individual basis through informal networks of commerce and finance. Again, the incentives facing leaders are no longer in favor of territorial aggrandizement. Even some national leaders may no longer feel compelled to control the territory defined by their boundaries because they can enrich themselves by pursuing informal or illegal trade. Indeed, formal control over territory may be an obstacle to the enrichment of leaders. Unlike the past, leaders who feed off the state or parts of it do not face any external challenge that might have compelled them to create viable states.

The International Protection of Weak States

The diminishing value of land was both ratified and accentuated by the post–World War II political system, which essentially froze the boundaries of most states. The Cold War had the effect of providing African countries and other weak states with patrons when their boundaries were challenged internally or externally. The superpowers were concerned with cultivating clients in all parts of the world and therefore were willing to help African nations crush ethnic rebellions or threats from neighbors. A secret 1963 U.S. document argued that an important U.S. interest, right after keeping Africa free of communists, was "to restrain violence in general and preserve the present territorial order as the most feasible alternative to chaos."[12] Thus, Zaire won crucial aid from the United States in turning back the Shaba rebellions; Chad relied on France to retain its territorial integrity in the face of Libyan aggression; and Ethiopia was given critical military support by the Soviet Union to resist Somalia's irredentist claims.

During the Cold War, the superpowers were actually exceptionally attentive to African sensibilities concerning boundary maintenance. Despite continual meddling throughout the continent, not once did either superpower, or any other outside power, offer significant support to an African effort to overturn an existing boundary. This deference continued after 1989. For instance, when President Laurent Kabila was threatened by a rebellion in eastern Democratic Republic of the Congo (as Zaire had become known) in 1998, the United States immediately said that it wanted, "the Government in Kinshasa to be in a position to control its territory" and "believe[d] strongly in the territorial integrity of the Democratic Republic of the Congo," despite compelling evidence that such integrity did not exist.[13]

In particular, the international community embraced the goal of boundary stability established by the Organization of African Unity effectively to prevent the application of the norm of self-determination to a group of people once their country had become independent.[14] More generally, the world community has allowed any country, no matter how underdeveloped its political and economic institutions, to enjoy the full privileges of sovereignty. Thus, a late Eisenhower administration document on Africa recognized that while many West African countries were "sorely lacking in both human and economic resources, this fact does not and will not slow the drive toward self-government and independence." The document noted with approval the desire for African countries to be "accepted as equals and be treated with dignity and respect," sentiments that were to be operationalized partially by membership in the United Nations.[15]

Therefore, African boundaries have remained almost unchanged since independence; the only significant deviation was the secession of Eritrea from Ethiopia. However, even this development was, especially from the perspective of the Eritreans, to a significant degree a question of decolonization rather than of secession. Most of the interstate conflicts in Africa that have occurred were not, as in Europe, wars of conquest that threatened the existence of other states, but conflicts over lesser issues that were resolved without threatening the existence of another state. For instance, Tanzania invaded Uganda in 1979 to overthrow Idi Amin, not to annex Uganda. In the few conflicts that did have the potential fundamentally to threaten the existence of states—Somalia's attempt to invade Ethiopia in the 1970s and Libya's war against Chad in the 1970s and 1980s—the aggressor did not succeed in large part because the international community came to the aid of the victim.

The growth and structure of African militaries are indicative of the relative peace that they have experienced on their external borders for most of the postindependence period. African armies expanded rapidly after independence and took roughly fifteen years to reach maturity. In 1963, at the dawn of independence, the average African army had 0.73 soldiers for every thousand people. By 1979, that figure had more than quadrupled to 3.10 soldiers per thousand citizens. The size of African armies then began to decrease, so that by the mid-1990s, there were only two soldiers per thousand citizens across the continent. African armies are, by comparative standards, small. In 1997, African countries (including the relatively well-armed countries of North Africa), had on average only 69 percent as many soldiers per thousand citizens as the average developing country worldwide (2.2 versus 3.2).[16]

The Challenge to Theory

The fundamental change in the twentieth century was that the political existence of states was no longer necessarily threatened by obvious failure. Political organization on a large scale was still difficult, but there were no longer threatening neighbors that were motivated to take over an adjoining territory if problems arose. In the vast majority of instances, annexing a neighbor was not worth it, either in terms of the price that would have to be paid in men and materiel or the international opprobrium that would surely follow.

As a result, a significant component of international relations theory has little to say about inward state failure. For instance, the security dilemma—the notion that each state's effort to become more secure threatens another state—is rooted in a world where armies had to be massed on frontiers to protect territory. Waltz notes that "contact generates conflict and at times issues in violence."[17] More generally, African and failed-states politics has been the opposite of traditional political science models of domestic and international politics: the politics among countries was extremely well ordered (as opposed to the Hobbesian model of international relations) while domestic politics did not evidence many signs of stability.[18] Indeed, what is remarkable about Africa and failed states today is that the failure of domestic orders—rather than the international system of states—has caused such transnational turmoil.

At the same time, there is strikingly little innovation among diplomats to try to revise current international legal practice to take account of the failed state phenomenon. The boundaries received at independence are still assumed to be the boundaries that a state should have even if those borders do not accurately describe how power is exercised. The nation-state is still assumed to be the only possible unit of political organization despite significant evidence that it sometimes does not work. Indeed, it is amazing to review the enormously innovative work that has been done on peace operations in the past ten years. It has fundamentally changed the way armies work on the ground, interact with civilians, and pursue their objectives in conjunction with others. Yet, there has been little change in the vision of what peacekeepers are working toward: resurrecting the old, failed state is still the disappointing objective of a tremendous amount of work by talented, innovative peacekeepers. Thus, a large number of soldiers and enormous resources were devoted to peace operations in Sierra Leone with the limited ambition of restoring a state that had a track record of several decades of failing.

It is interesting to compare the lack of innovation in thinking about political organization to the record of change in the corporate sector. The notion of what a company is, how it is organized, and how it has relations and alliances with other companies has evolved continuously since 1900, and the rate of change is arguably at its highest point today. Yet, the nation-state as currently theorized today is not significantly different than what was in place one hundred years ago.

There are many reasons for this comparative development. Clearly, the nature of competition in business has forced companies continually to evolve while states for the past fifty years have had a much greater margin of safety. There is now a much greater threat to at least some nation-states than in the past, but diplomats and practitioners are still locked into thinking about a world where there is no alternative to the sovereign nation-state. At least some attention should be given to the possibility of states losing their sovereignty if the government on the ground cannot control the agents of violence. What comes after is a fascinating question that should at least be discussed openly.

The Challenge to Practice

In order to construct an array or appropriate policy responses to today's crisis, the general patterns of state decline must be understood. While each unhappy state is unique, it is possible to make some overall observations that can guide the construction of policy.

First, states fail within their existing boundaries. Unlike the practice throughout most of European history, even failed states are today safe from formal takeover by their neighbors. These neighbors may intervene to affect the balance of power (as in the DRC) or to take advantage of economic opportunities presented by failure (as in Liberia), but the formal boundaries of the state will continue to be recognized by all concerned. At the same time, the international community has no way of withdrawing recognition from a state once it has received independence from its colonial power. For instance, the entire international community recognizes the political entity called the Democratic Republic of the Congo, although it is nothing more than a geographic expression. Indeed, the international community is extremely reluctant to recognize new political units emerging out of the ruins of old units, even when the facts on the ground are clear. For instance, the World Bank and the International Monetary Fund offered no assistance to Somaliland because it did not have a recognized status, despite the fact that the government in Hargeisa was at least providing some services to its citizens.[19]

The tendency to fail within the straitjacket of existing boundaries poses extraordinary problems for a world still concerned with the sovereign rights of states. In particular, the ghostly presence of the old, failed state has reinforced a tendency to try to put the old political arrangement back together again despite seemingly decisive evidence that the national order cannot work. For instance, even though it was obvious to all concerned that Somalia had collapsed by December 1992 when the U.S./UN intervention force was being planned, no one seriously considered trusteeship or other legal concepts other than continuing the fiction that Somalia was still a sovereign nation-state.

Second, there may be few incentives for local actors to help reestablish the old order. As noted earlier, there are now a set of powerful economic processes at work that allow the enrichment of leaders and followers and do not require them to reestablish a national political order. The resurrection of an even nominally capable national political order may interfere with the patronage opportunities of some actors. Rather, given the international community's attachment to the current map of states, outsiders are more interested in reestablishing the old national order. Not surprisingly, due to this asymmetry of interests, many outside interventions to correct state failure appear perverse, and eventually fail.

Third, there are strong pressures for power to continue to fracture in failed states. Precisely because the world has become safe for those who hold sway over smaller units and because the international system does not seem to be willing to adjust boundaries according to how power is actually expressed, failed states have a tendency to fracture into smaller factions of rebel groups. If a time and motion study had been done of Mohamed Farah Aideed when he was confronting the U.S./UN forces in Somalia, it probably would have revealed that he spent far more time trying to keep his own coalition together than fighting outsiders. The devolution of power to ever smaller units is also a well-observed phenomenon in Liberia and the DRC.

Potential intervenors usually understand the fractious nature of politics in failed states but respond in different ways. The instinct of some intervenors is to try to build up the major protagonists so that there is someone with whom they can do business. Thus, rival claimants may be ignored, as was the case in the American response to Laurent Kabila after he took power. However, if the leader does not consolidate power according to a schedule imagined by the intervenor, powerful spoilers may emerge.

Alternatively, some intervenors, notably the Nigerians in Liberia, have tried to deter potential spoilers by actually encouraging further fractionalization of power. This strategy has the advantage of weakening those who contributed to the failure of the state, but the disadvantage of making postconflict negotiations much more complicated. How the trade-offs balance out will vary depending on the circumstances of a particular case, but the very real compromises still must be understood.

Fourth, state failure is likely to spread beyond the territorial boundaries of a particular state. One of the factors that promotes state failure is that powerful political agents can establish transnational political and economic networks that lessen the need to strengthen the national political apparatus. At the same time, failed states are a convenient stage for neighbors to enter because there are economic assets to be taken or because there is the opportunity to resolve pressing security issues. The clearest example of how state failure crosses a territorial boundary is the DRC, where almost a dozen neighbors have been involved in the conflict in one way or another. Similarly, the war in Liberia slowly spread to Sierra Leone and Guinea, and ebbed back and forth.

The possible spread of the failed state contagion is of interest to intervenors for several different reasons. Obviously, understanding the role of outsiders in the state failure drama is critical to any eventual resolution. Perhaps as important, one of the critical tasks of the international community may be to halt state failure from spreading, even if there is little that can be done for the failed state itself. Further development of the strategies and tactics that can be deployed to prevent drugs, guns, smuggled goods, and disease—some of the most common exports of failed states—from contaminating their regions would be particularly useful.

Responses to State Failure

Given the likelihood that state failure is again a "normal" aspect of global society, developing responses to failure is critical.[20] The overarching goal of developing alternatives to failed states should be to increase the congruence between the way that power is actually exercised and the design of units. Many of the reasons for state failure can, as noted earlier, be traced to a fundamental gap between how states govern territory and what the boundaries and state system suggest that they should control. Alternatives must therefore work to reduce, in a variety of ways and depending on the situation, the salience of some current boundaries.

Some still suggest that alternatives to the nation-state will not develop because the international system has been so conservative in recognizing the viability of alternatives. Rotberg, in his introduction, makes clear the powerful forces in favor of inertia. However, as Spruyt has argued, it is not the case that change in the nature of the constitutive units of the international system has always taken place in a slow, incremental manner. Rather, there are long periods of stability followed by periods of sudden, chaotic institutional innovation. In such a manner did the sovereign state become the dominant institution in Europe.[21] Similarly, decolonization—the greatest transfer of power in world history—came as a surprise to even most of the participants in the middle of the twentieth century. Thus, it is possible that there may be sudden change in the international order once it is clear that the old-fashioned precepts surrounding international practice are bankrupt.

Breaking the Intellectual Logjam

Thus, the first step toward developing new alternatives would be to provide the intellectual space necessary for persons living in failed states to present alternatives by declaring that the international community is not blindly wedded to the current state system. This revolutionary act might help to break the intellectual logjam that devotion to the status quo has caused. Given the quality of universities in failed states, the international community might have to go further and provide resources for individuals and think tanks to analyze alternatives to the nation-state. However, once it is clear that there is at least some fluidity in the state system, alternatives, be they ideas for new states, formulations for new divisions within states, or innovative ideas on how subnational units can relate to the capital, will not be long in coming.

Decertifying Old States

A further step that the United States, and other countries can take would be to recognize officially that some states are simply not exercising formal control over parts of their country and should no longer be considered sovereign. It is critical that the international community, at least tentatively move away from the notion that once a state achieves membership in the General Assembly, it is sovereign forever, no matter what happens within its boundaries. For instance, the U.S. government decertifies countries (effectively reducing their eligibility for U.S. aid) that are not attempting to stop the production and transshipments of narcotics. Indeed, U.S. legislation goes further and demands that countries prevent and punish both the laundering of drug-related profits and "bribery and other forms of public corruption which facilitate the production, processing or shipment" of drugs. Thus, Nigeria was decertified in part because it did not investigate any senior officials alleged to be involved in drug trafficking.[22] The United States effectively argued that such countries are not executing their sovereign responsibilities in regard to the enforcement of their own laws. It would seem reasonable that a similar decision could be reached if a state is not exercising other aspects of sovereign control, including the failure or inability to project authority and to provide basic services in large parts of its territory. During the Mobutu era, the United States should have recognized Zaire for what it was, or was not, and decertified it as a sovereign nation. It would certainly be no more difficult to ascertain that a state is not governing parts of its own country than to determine that senior officials are involved in drug trafficking but are not being prosecuted.

Decertification would be a strong signal that something fundamental has gone wrong in a country, and that parts of the international community are no longer willing to continue the myth that every state is always exercising sovereign authority. Concretely, decertification might trigger the initiation of new efforts at finding other leaders who are exercising control in parts of the country. Decertification would also be a signal that a country should not be accorded the usual privileges of sovereignty including such prestigious appointments as a rotating position on the Security Council. It is puzzling that the United States strongly opposed Libya's attempt to gain a seat on the Security Council (because of its support for international terrorism) but seemingly had no problems with the DRC's being on the United Nations' most powerful body, despite that country's obvious dysfunctional nature.

Whatever the concrete measures taken, decertification would provide an avenue out of the current impasse, where there is no status to accord a country other than sovereignty, irrespective of domestic realities. Decertification should be a rare step that would be used only as a last resort. Making decertification relatively difficult would also make its signal that much more powerful when it was used. Decertification would also have the advantage of stating that the United States, or other important actors, understand that some countries are not sovereign, even if it is not clear what they are. Decertification could thus be a halfway house for countries that are at some later point able to reconstitute their sovereign authority. Alternatively, decertification could be the first step in recognizing that a state has died (if it ever lived), and that something else has to take its place.

It is an irony that the states that the United States does not recognize (including Cuba, Iraq, Libya, and North Korea) are, by any measure, states. The problem with those countries, according to United States, is that their regimes have far too much control over the citizens of those societies. Yet states that have little control over weak societies continue to be recognized as states despite their own limited control. Decertification would provide a way out of this ridiculous situation while not immediately equating weak states with pariah countries like Libya or North Korea.

Recognizing New Nation-States

After forty years of assuming that the boundaries of even the most dysfunctional states are inviolable, another important initiative, and the logical next step after decertification, would be to consider the possibility of allowing for the creation of new sovereign states. The primary objection to recognizing new states has been the basis for selection. Given that there are very few "natural" boundaries that would allow for the rational demarcation of land on the basis of ethnic, geographic, or economic criteria, the worry is that recognizing new states will lead to a splintering process that would promote the creation of ever-smaller units while entailing seemingly endless political chaos. Gottlieb argues against the creation of new states because he fears "anarchy and disorder on a planetary scale."[23] The very real costs of new nation-state construction, especially the almost inevitable mass movement of people with all the suffering that such movements usually entail, is another important consideration for those who argue that the boundaries of failed states must be preserved at any cost.

However, at some point, the reality of disintegrating, dysfunctional states stands in such contrast to the legal fiction of sovereign states that experimentation with regard to new states is in order. The argument that once new states are recognized, descent down the slippery slope of micro-state creation is inevitable, gives the international community and, especially, local leaders, no credit to discern the specifics of situations on a case-by-case basis. To say that new states should be recognized does not mean that criteria for state recognition cannot exist. It simply suggests that the criteria have to be created and that the dogmatic devotion to the current boundaries be discarded. The inevitable disruption caused by state creation will also have to be balanced against the profound harm that existing states (knowing that they cannot go out of business) do to their populations every day.

The new type of state disintegration that countries are undergoing opens the way to a better and more constructive appreciation of the right to secession. While there may be full-fledged civil wars in the future, the more likely path for secessionists to take is simply to exit a disintegrating state. The case of Somaliland (the part of Somalia that was ruled by the British before independence and that declared itself independent after Mogadishu was left without a government when Siad Barre fell in 1991) is more the future than that of Eritrea: the province that simply goes its own way because the central government, if there is one, lacks the ability even to contest the secession. Similarly, while eastern Democratic Republic of the Congo will not secede, it is clear that Rwanda and Uganda will require that it exercise a certain amount of control as Kinshasa's writ has attenuated and Kigali and Kampala face real security threats across their western borders.

This type of secession is different from what occurred in former Yugoslavia. In Yugoslavia, there were, arguably, at least some federal institutions that could still have mediated conflict, but the Slovene and Croatian decisions to secede (and the international recognition of those declarations) destroyed whatever hope there might have been of the crisis being managed from Belgrade.[24] Correspondingly, the Yugoslav breakup has also been extremely bloody because the old order's army was still functioning and could be appropriated by the warring parties. However, in many cases where states are collapsing, the central institutions that might have mediated the conflict atrophied long ago. Similarly, many armies of failed states suffer from the same institutional weaknesses as the rest of the government and are not viable fighting forces.

An innovative criteria for recognition that is relevant to the particular circumstances of failing states would be an answer to the following: does the break-away area provide more political order on its own than is provided by the central government? The international community would thus be asking an extremely relevant question that goes to the core of the problems of state consolidation because the test would center on whether the broadcasting of power and boundaries could be made more coincidental. Such a hurdle would necessarily rule out many attempts at secession that were not of the utmost seriousness. The long-term aim would be to provide international recognition to the governmental units that are actually providing order to their citizens as opposed to relying on the fictions of the past. The development of such a realistic, nuanced perspective would acknowledge what is happening on the ground while avoiding the anarchy that Gottlieb and others fear. Such a criteria would also be more relevant to granting sovereignty that actually mattered than a putative nation's commitment to human rights, a market economy, or the Nuclear Non-Proliferation Treaty—three of the many criteria Halperin and Scheffer suggested that new states should have to meet in order to be recognized by the international community.[25] These qualifications, while highly desirable, reflect the assumption that physical control of the hinterland is not an issue. In fact, control of outlying areas *is* the critical problem.

This is not to say that granting the right to secession to at least some groups that are able to establish order within their own areas would be without its dangers. Clearly, any signal from the international community that its commitment to the territorial integrity of states is being reduced could result in considerable instability and uncertainty, and would be met by voracious opposition on the part of the many states that have grown dependent on the post–World War II understanding of sovereignty. However, the reality on the ground in some countries is that sovereign control is not being exercised by central states in outlying areas; subnational groups are already exerting authority in certain regions.

By recognizing and legitimating those groups, the international community has the opportunity to ask that they respect international norms regarding human rights and also has a chance to bring them into the international economy. A less dogmatic approach to sovereignty would allow the international community to adjust to reality and to begin helping substantial numbers of people. If the new subnational arrangements are ignored, they will continue to be more like institutionalized protection rackets than states that guard the rights of their citizens. At the same time, local rulers who are actually exercising elements of sovereign control will continue to survive on informal trade, often involving drugs, guns, and poached animals, rather than beginning initiatives to promote more routine economic development capable of aiding all of the people in their special region. The international community thus can ignore potential secessionist movements and force them to remain semicriminal affairs or can try to help create new state institutions. The fact that some states will dissolve will be a reality, no matter which policy stance is adopted.

Conclusion

Since forming national units is difficult, states tend to fail. The rigidities imposed by the Cold War, the euphoria of decolonization, and the rules of sovereignty developed by the United Nations caused analysts to ignore this simple truth for fifty years. Now, not surprisingly, historical processes have resumed and a limited number of states are failing. Yet, in the face of clear evidence of a resumption of the cycle of state creation and destruction, the international community seems determined to do no more than resurrect what has not worked, although the lesson of history is that political orders evolve by changing form and scale. Whether this failure is due to a lack of imagination and will, or whether it reflects the simple reality that state failure is not important enough to justify changing standard operating procedures, is unclear.

Notes

1. Given the strange geography of postindependence Pakistan, one could arguably trace even the creation of Bangladesh to decolonization.

2. Charles Tilly, "Reflections on the History of European State-Making," in Charles Tilly (ed.), *The Formation of National States in Western Europe* (Princeton, 1975), 38.

3. Ibid., 38–39.

4. Charles Tilly, *Coercion, Capital, and European States,* A.D. 990–1992 (Cambridge, Mass., 1990), 54.

5. Malcolm Anderson, *Frontiers: Territory and State Formation in the Modern World* (Cambridge, 1996), 23.

6. In this discussion, I ignore the European Union because it is not clear yet exactly what it is (especially if it will take sovereign power from the states that have formed it) and because it was formed by states that were not in danger of collapse.

7. "The Baltics' Would-Be Hong Kong," *The Economist* (6 November 1993), 95.

8. See, respectively, "An Emerging Market," *The Warsaw Voice* (27 March 1994); Daniel Alder, "El Salvador Emerging as Business Center," *UPI Press Report* (15 August 1992); James Brooke, "Free Trade Fatefully Near for Paraguay's 'Hong Kong,' " *New York Times* (25 March 1991); Moyiga Nduru, "Ghana: Aiming to Become the Hong Kong of Africa," *Inter Press Service* (9 October 1991); "Jamaica Sells Textile Mill to Hong Kong Interests," *Agence France Presse* (8 November 1993); Celestine Bohlen, "Russia vs. Ukraine," *New York Times* (23 March 1994); Gerald Nadler, "A Parley to Create the Hong Kong of Siberia?" *United Press International* (30 September 1988).

9. Marcia Scott Harrison, "Dubai," *Los Angeles Times* (13 February 1994); Sam Aboudi, "Gaza Sees Construction Boom with Self Rule," *The Reuter European Business Report* (12 May 1994); Charles W. Holmes, "With Middle East Peace Comes Hope for Profits," *The Times-Picayune* (31 July 1994).

10. Patrick Chabal and Jean-Pascal Daloz, *Africa Works: Disorder as Political Instrument* (Bloomington, 1999), 90. See also Jean-François Bayart, Stephen Ellis, and Béatrice Hibou, *The Criminalization of the State in Africa* (Bloomington, 1999), 26–31.

11. William Reno, *Warlord Politics and African States* (Boulder, 1999), 225.

12. "The Strategic Importance of Africa," 25 May 1963, reprinted in Nina Davis Howland (ed.), *Foreign Relations of the United States: Africa, 1961–1963* (Washington, D.C., 1995), 331.

13. Steven Erlanger, "U.S. Sees Rwandan Role in Congo Revolt," *New York Times* (5 August 1998).

14. Gino J. Naldi, "The Case Concerning the Frontier Dispute (Burkina Faso/Republic of Mali): *Uti Possisdetis* in an African Perspective," *International and Comparative Law Quarterly,* XXXVI (October 1987), 901–902.

15. National Security Council, "Statement of U.S. Policy toward West Africa," NSC 6005/1, 9 April 1960, reprinted in Harriet Dashiell Schwar and Stanley Shaloff (eds.), *Foreign Relations of the United States: Africa, 1958–1960* (Washington, D.C., 1992), 117.

16. Calculated from Donald George Morrison, Robert Cameron Mitchell, and John Naber, *Black Africa: A Comparative Handbook* (New York, 1989, 2nd ed.), 167–168; U.S. Arms Control and Disarmament Agency, *World Military Expenditures and Arms Transfers 1985* (Washington, D.C., 1985), 47; ACDA, *World Military Expenditures and Arms Transfers 1999* (Washington, D.C., 1999), table 1.

17. Kenneth Waltz, *Theory of International Politics* (Reading, Mass., 1979), 103. See also, Robert Jervis, "Cooperation under the Security Dilemma," *World Politics,* XXX (1977), 168–169.

18. See Robert H. Jackson and Carl G. Rosberg, "Why Africa's Weak States Persist," XXXV, *World Politics* (1982), 23–24.

19. John Drysdale, *Whatever Happened to Somalia?* (London, 1994), 147.

20. This discussion is borrowed from Jeffrey Herbst, *States and Power in Africa* (Princeton, 2000), 137–198.

21. Hendrick Spruyt, *The Sovereign State and its Competitors* (Princeton, 1994), 186–187.

22. The relevant U.S. laws are cited in Committee on Foreign Affairs, U.S. House of Representatives, *International Narcotics Control and United States Foreign Policy: A Compilation of Laws, Treaties, Executive Documents and Relevant Materials* (December 1994), 31. The presidential message decertifying Nigeria can be found on 543.

23. Gideon Gottlieb, *Nation Against State* (New York, 1993), 26.

24. Susan L. Woodward, *Balkan Tragedy: Chaos and Dissolution after the Cold War* (Washington, D.C., 1995), 144.

25. Morton H. Halperin and David J. Scheffer, *Self-Determination in the New World Order* (Washington, D.C., 1992), 84–93.

Contributors

David Carment is Associate Professor of International Affairs at the Norman Paterson School of International Affairs, Carleton University, Ottawa. His most recent book is *Using Force to Prevent Ethnic Violence: An Evaluation of Theory and Evidence* (Westport, 2000). In addition, Carment serves as the principal investigator for the Country Indicators for Foreign Policy project and is a member of the Board of Directors for The Forum on Early Warning and Early Response.

Christopher Clapham is an Associate of the Centre for African Studies at Cambridge University. He specializes in African politics and international relations. He edits the *Journal of Modern African Studies*, and is past President of the African Studies Association of the United Kingdom. His most recent books include *African Guerrillas* (Bloomington, 1998) and *Africa and the International System* (Cambridge, 1996).

Nat J. Colletta is an international expert in post conflict management. He was founding manager of the World Bank Post Conflict Unit, where he played a key role in developing the bank's policy toward peaceful transitions. He is currently Research Professor and Co-Director of the Institute for Peace-building and Development, George Washington University. Among his publications are *Privatizing Peace: From Conflict to Security* (Brussels, 2002) and *Social Cohesion and Conflict Prevention in Asia: Managing Diversity Through Development* (Washington, D.C., 2001).

Jeffrey Herbst is Professor of Politics and International Affairs at Princeton University and chair of the Department of Politics. His interests include the politics of political and economic liberalization, peacekeeping in Africa, and the politics of state failure and consolidation. His most recent book is *States and Power in Africa* (Princeton, 2000).

Nelson Kasfir is Professor of Government at Dartmouth College. He is currently working on a book on guerrilla governance—how guerrillas choose to organize civilians politically, administratively and economically. He also writes on African democratization, civil society, no-party rule, and rural political economy. He edited *Civil Society and Democracy in Africa* (London, 1998) and is the author of "Movement, Democracy, Legitmacy and Power in Uganda," in Mugaju and Oloka-Onyango (eds.) *No-Party Democracy in Uganda: Myths and Realities* (Kampala, 2000), 60–78.

Michael T. Klare is the Five College Professor of Peace and World Security Studies and director of the Five College Program in Peace and World Security Studies. He is the author or coauthor of several books, including *Resource Wars: The New Landscape of Global Conflict* (New York, 2001), *Light Weapons and Civil Conflict* (Lanham, Md., 1999), and *Rogue States and Nuclear Outlaws* (New York, 1995).

Markus Kostner is with the World Bank's Africa Region. He has worked on numerous demobilization and reintegration programs in Africa, Europe, Latin America, and Southeast Asia.

Terrence Lyons is Assistant Professor at George Mason University's Institute for Conflict Analysis and Resolution. From 1990 through 1998 he was a Fellow at the Brookings Institution in Washington. Among his publications are *Voting for Peace: Postconflict Elections in Liberia* (Washington, D.C., 1999), and *Sovereignty as Responsibility: Conflict Management in Africa* (cowritten with Francis M. Deng, Sadikiel Kimaro, Donald Rothchild, and I. William Zartman), (Washington, D.C., 1996).

Jens Meierhenrich teaches in the Department of Government and at the Committee on Degrees in Social Studies at Harvard University. He is the author of "A Theory of Law: Path Dependence and Increasing Returns" (forthcoming) and "The Supply and Demand of States" (forthcoming). He served as the Carlo Schmid Fellow in Trial Chamber II of the international Criminal Tribunal for the Former Yugoslavia at The Hague.

Daniel N. Posner is Assistant Professor of Political Science at UCLA. He has been an Academy Scholar at the Harvard Academy for International and Area Studies and a National Fellow at the Hoover Institution at Stanford. He is the author of "Social Capital: Explaining Its Origins and Effects on Government Performance," *British Journal of Political Science, XXVIII* (1998), 686–693.

Susan Rose-Ackerman is the Henry R. Luce Professor of Jurisprudence and Co-Director of the Center for Studies in Law, Economics, and Public Policy at Yale University. Her most recent book is *Corruption and Government: Causes, Consequences, and Reform* (New York, 1999). She was a visiting research fellow at the World Bank in 1995–96.

Robert I. Rotberg is President of the World Peace Foundation, and Director of the Program on Intrastate Conflict and Adjunct Professor at Harvard's Kennedy School of Government. He is the author and editor of numerous books and articles on U.S. foreign policy, Africa, and Haiti, most recently *State Failure and State Weakness in a Time of Terror* (Washington, D.C., 2003) *Ending Autocracy: Enabling Democracy: The Tribulations of Southern Africa 1960–2000* (Washington, D.C., 2002), *Peacekeep-*

ing and Peace Enforcement in Africa (Washington, D.C., 2000), and *Truth v. Justice: The Morality of Truth Commissions* (Princeton, 2000).

Donald R. Snodgrass is Institute Fellow Emeritus at Harvard University. A specialist on human resource development and Southeast Asia, Snodgrass has written or coauthored numerous articles and six books, including *Economics of Development* (New York, 2001, 5th ed.), a widely used textbook.

Nicolas van de Walle is Professor of Political Science at Michigan State University. His recent books include *African Economies and the Politics of Permanent Crisis, 1979–1999* (Cambridge, 2001), and *Democratic Experiments in Africa: Regime Transitions in Comparative Perspective* (with Michael Bratton) (Cambridge, 1997).

Jennifer A. Widner is Professor of Political Science at the University of Michigan. She is the author of several books and articles on political liberalization, law, and development in Africa. Her most recent book is *Building the Rule of Law* (New York, 2001), a study of judicial independence in Africa.

Ingo Wiederhofer is a consultant working on postconflict projects for the World Bank's Africa Region. He has worked on demobilization and reintegration programs in Ethiopia, Guinea-Bissau, Rwanda, and Sierra Leone.

Index

Page references followed by *fig* indicate a figured illustration; references followed by a *t* indicate a table.